THE
GREAT WALL
AT SEA

THE GREAT WALL AT SEA

China's Navy Enters the Twenty-First Century

Bernard D. Cole

NAVAL INSTITUTE PRESS
Annapolis, Maryland

Naval Institute Press
291 Wood Road
Annapolis, MD 21402

Library of Congress Cataloging-in-Publication Data
Cole, Bernard D., 1943–
The great wall at sea : China's Navy enters the
21st century / Bernard D. Cole.
p. cm.
Includes bibliographical references and index.
ISBN 1-55750-239-0 (alk. paper)
1. China. Zhongguo ren min jie fang jun. Hai jun.
2. China—Military policy. I. Title.
VA633.C65 2001
359'.00951—dc21
2001018009

Printed in the United States of America on
acid-free paper ∞

08 07 06 05 04 03 02 01   9 8 7 6 5 4 3 2
First printing

This manuscript does not necessarily represent the
views of the National War College or any other
organization of the U.S. government.

CONTENTS

Preface vii

List of Abbreviations ix

Introduction 1

1 The PLAN's Heritage 16

2 China's Maritime Territorial Interests 30

3 China's Maritime Economic Interests 54

4 PLAN Establishment 67

5 Ships and Aircraft of the PLAN 92

6 Personnel, Education, and Training 113

7 Doctrine and Operations in the PLAN 138

8 China's Maritime Strategy 159

Conclusion 179

Notes 191

Bibliography 263

Index 281

PREFACE

⌒

My research for this book concentrated on translated Chinese documents and media reports, as well as on interviews with Chinese and other serving officers and observers of the Chinese military. A note about names and transliteration: I have used the Pinyin system throughout, retaining Wade-Giles for only a few well-known names, such as Kuomintang vice Guomindang, and Chiang Kai-shek vice Jiang Jieshi.

The National Defense University Foundation provided much-appreciated financial support for my research. The librarians at the National Defense University Library in Washington, D.C., were unfailingly helpful, cheerful, and a wonderful resource. The staffs and faculties of the Asia-Pacific Center for Strategic Studies and the East-West Center in Honolulu were very welcoming and helpful. The Virtual Information Center, also in Honolulu, has become a valuable source of current information about Asia under the leadership of Carl Schuster and his tireless staff.

A version of the material in chapter 8 was presented as a paper at the September 1999 PLA Conference held under the auspices of the American Enterprise Institute and Ambassador James Lilley, and the Army War College; a version of that in chapter 4 was presented as a paper at the August 2000 CAPS-RAND Conference on the PLA, under the leadership of Richard Yang, Andrew Yang, and Michael Swaine. These gentlemen and their organizations are leading the way in PLA studies.

My interest in China and maritime strategy was sparked by my thirty years in the Navy and by my graduate studies; I owe a special debt to the faculties of the University of Washington's Far East and

Russian Institute, and Auburn University's History Department, especially Frank L. Owsley Jr. I must also offer my thanks to many colleagues. At the risk of omitting some of these, I am particularly grateful to Dr. Cynthia Watson, my colleague at the National War College, who turned her unerring editorial eye to many iterations of this manuscript. I also owe a debt to my fellow "PLA watchers," especially Kenneth Allen, Dennis Blasko, John Corbett, David Finkelstein, Bates Gill, Alexander Huang, Ellis Joffe, Tai Ming Cheung, Nan Li, Michael McDevitt, Eric McVadon, Ellis Melvin, Vance Morrison, James Mulvenon, William Pendley, David Shambaugh, Alfred Wilhelm, Allen Whiting, and Larry Wortzel, who so patiently answered my questions and many of whom read part or all of this manuscript. Peter Swartz also read the entire manuscript and offered several valuable suggestions. Many serving officers in various militaries were very helpful, but must go nameless. Ronald Montaperto of the National Defense University originally suggested that I undertake this work and has been a special friend and reviewer. Most important has been the friendship, encouragement, and the sharp editorial eye of Paul H. B. Godwin, who has taught me so much about China and its military. Of course, all errors of omission and commission are solely my responsibility.

Finally, I owe an incalculable debt to my family.

ABBREVIATIONS

AAW	Antiair warfare
AIP	Air independent propulsion
AOR	Area of responsibility
ARF	Asia Regional Forum
ASEAN	Association of Southeast Asian Nations
ASW	Antisubmarine warfare
ASUW	Antisurface warfare
BP	British Petroleum
CCP	Chinese Communist Party
CMC	Central Military Commission
CNNC	China National Nuclear Corporation
CNOOC	China National Offshore Oil Corporation
CNPC	China National Petroleum Company
COC	Code of Conduct
CS	Continental shelf
CSC	China Shipbuilding Corporation
CV	Aircraft carrier
CVBG	Aircraft carrier battle group
DDG	Guided-missile destroyer
DEPT	Department
EEZ	Exclusive economic zone
FBM	Fleet ballistic missile
FFG	Guided-missile frigate
GPCR	Great Proletarian Cultural Revolution
GSD	General Staff Department
IORC	Indian Ocean Rim Association for Regional Cooperation
IRBM	Intermediate-range ballistic missile

JMSDF	Japan Maritime Self-Defense Force
KMT	Kuomintang
LNG	Liquid natural gas
LSM	Landing ship, mechanized
LST	Landing ship, tank
MIW	Mine warfare
MR	Military region
MSA	Maritime Safety Administration
NCO	Noncommissioned officer
PAP	People's Armed Police
PLA	People's Liberation Army
PLAAF	People's Liberation Army–Air Force
PLAN	People's Liberation Army–Navy
PLANAF	People's Liberation Army–Navy Air Force
RAS	Replenishment at sea
RMA	Revolution in military affairs
ROKN	Republic of Korea Navy
ROTC	Reserve Officers Training Corps
SAR	Search and rescue
SEATO	Southeast Asia Treaty Organization
SINOPEC	China National Petroleum Corporation
SLOC	Sea line of communication
SOE	State-owned enterprise
SRBOC	Super rapid blooming off-board chaff
SS	Diesel/electric-powered attack submarine
SSB	Diesel/electric-powered ballistic missile submarine
SSBN	Nuclear-powered ballistic missile submarine
SSM	Surface-to-surface missile
SSN	Nuclear-powered attack submarine
UN	United Nations
TMD	Theater missile defense
UNCLOS	United Nations Convention on the Law of the Sea
WTO	World Trade Organization

THE
GREAT WALL
AT SEA

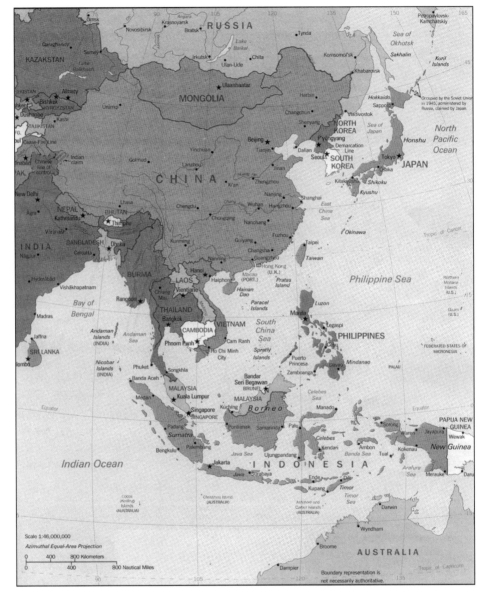

East Asia

CENTRAL INTELLIGENCE AGENCY

Introduction

Despite its nine thousand miles of coastline and six thousand islands, China historically has been a continental rather than a maritime power. It has more often viewed the sea as a potential invasion route for foreign aggressors rather than as a medium for achieving national goals, a view that has contributed to a weak Chinese maritime tradition.

This attitude may have changed as China's view of post–cold war Asia has focused on offshore sovereignty, economic, and resource issues. A key question in evaluating the People's Liberation Army-Navy (PLAN) is whether China's leadership understands the maritime element of national strategy, including the part maritime interests and naval policy have played in China's history.

China has always depended primarily on ground forces to guard its national security interests—for the simple reason that threats to those interests have consistently arisen in the northern and northwestern Asian vastness. China's historic focus on continental security concerns, however, has not ignored its maritime boundaries.

Imperial China

The PLAN can trace its lineage back through the dynasties; the earliest recorded naval battle in China occurred in 549 B.C., during the Spring and Autumn Period, when rival rulers used ships to attack each other's coasts.[1] Large-scale naval operations continued to play a role in Chinese warfare through the Han Dynasty (206 B.C.–A.D. 220). The sea also probably provided the earliest trading routes with southern and western Asia.[2] Chinese seagoers were the first to control their ships with sails and rudders. They also greatly increased their vessels' seaworthiness through compartmentation and by painting vessel bottoms to inhibit wood rot. China's shipwrights were among the first to build dry docks and a shore-based infrastructure to support the fleet. They developed the art of navigation to a high degree, including use of the portable compass as early as 1044.[3] Regular commercial sea routes as far as southwestern Asia and western Africa were established by the end of the Tang Dynasty (A.D. 907).[4]

The high point of naval developments in imperial China was probably during the Song Dynasty (A.D. 960–1279), part of a five-hundred-year period during which China deployed "the world's most powerful and technologically sophisticated navy."[5] The Army at this time organized fleets composed of several hundred warships and supply vessels in times of emergency. One Song fleet in A.D. 1274 reportedly totaled 13,500 ships.[6] Chinese maritime technology also matured during this age, and the maritime sector was an important part of the national economy. Perhaps most significant, the Song regime was the first in China to establish a permanent national navy, functioning as an independent service administered by a central government agency. The Imperial Commissioner's Office for the Control and Organization of the Coastal Areas was established in 1132 to supervise a navy of fifty-two thousand men.[7]

The Song maritime experience was based on a rapidly expanding national economy with a particularly strong maritime sector encompassing commerce, fisheries, and transportation. As the navy expanded, so did port facilities, supply centers, and dockyards; soldiers were trained specifically as marines, and coast guard squadrons were established.[8] Song navies used both sail and paddle-wheel-driven craft, the latter powered by laborers on treadmills. Doctrine, including the development of formation maneuvering, long-range projectile launchers, and complex tactics, was formalized at this time.[9]

China remained a sea power during the two succeeding dynasties. In fact, the overthrow of the Song regime by the Yuan (Mongol) Dynasty resulted in significant part from the latter rapidly mastering naval warfare. The Yuan later used large fleets to undertake invasions of Vietnam, Java, and Japan: the 1274 expedition against Japan numbered 900 ships and 250,000 soldiers; that of 1281 included 4,400 ships.[10] Maritime commerce continued to expand, and cannon made their appearance aboard ship.[11]

China reached the pinnacle of its overseas naval deployments during the Ming Dynasty (1368–1644) but also saw its naval power collapse. The crux of the successful Ming struggle to succeed the Yuan was a series of battles on the lakes of the Yangtze River valley that are best described as "inland naval warfare."[12] The waterborne forces employed by the Ming and their opponents were not independent navies but Army units assigned to ships on the local lakes and rivers. Their original mission had been to transport men and supplies, but the armies quickly recognized the advantages of using these craft as warships, against both land forces and each other. The Ming ships were manned by about twelve thousand troops and armed with archers, cannon, and "flame weapons." The "lake campaign" was an effective use of ships and men to take advantage of the battlefield topography but did not result in the establishment of a regular Ming navy.

Also during the Ming Dynasty, the early-fifteenth-century voyages of Zheng He to the Middle East and Africa represented a standard of Chinese shipbuilding, voyage management, and navigation ability well beyond European capabilities. Zheng He led large fleets of ships, some displacing more than four hundred tons, on four voyages halfway around the world at a time when Portuguese explorers were still feeling their way down the western coast of Africa in fifty-ton caravels.

The Ming rulers deliberately ended these voyages for domestic financial, political, and ideological reasons, just when European nations were beginning to use the high seas to achieve economic wealth and to proselytize.[13] Why were such epochal maritime expeditions ended? First, the voyages were expensive and the Ming pursued a rigid economic policy. Second, the court was concerned about the growing power of the eunuchs, who were the voyages' chief sponsors. Third, "Confucian-trained scholar-officials opposed trade and foreign contact on principle."[14]

Perhaps most important, the threat from Mongols and other Asian aggressors grew stronger, which increasingly focused government concerns inland and absorbed a growing portion of the national budget. By 1500, "anticommercialism and xenophobia [had] won out," and the government was attempting to deal with maritime problems by ignoring them. The Navy was allowed to deteriorate; by the end of the sixteenth century, the Ming government was unable even to defend Chinese maritime traders against pirates.

During this long period of brilliant maritime scientific progress and dominating power, however, the focus of China's national security concerns still lay to the north and west—with good reason, since that was where the threat to the regime lay. Imperial naval missions were defense of the coast, control of maritime trade, defending the regime, and ensuring economic benefit to the state. No dynasty fell as a direct result of maritime invasion or pressure: usurpers emerged from the Asian interior, and the crucial battles were land battles. The Navy was at various times capable and even powerful, but never was it vital to a dynasty's survival, even in the face of the centuries-long threat from Japanese "pirates," as the Chinese habitually referred to their neighbors.

Typical of the process of dynastic progression, the Qing (Manchu) Dynasty replaced the Ming Dynasty after a long period of land warfare in which naval power played a very small role. The Qing made no concerted effort to rebuild the Navy or expand the maritime sector of China's economy following its 1644 assumption of power. This was not the result of neglect: the Qing faced no significant threat from the sea during its first century and a half in power, and there seemed little justification for a large naval investment.[15] This was especially true after the most notable Qing maritime campaign, when the new dynasty conquered Taiwan in 1683. The island was described as inhospitable: "flat, malarial plains along the west, backed by inhospitable mountain ranges. . . . [An] unfriendly aboriginal population further discouraged exploration or settlement."[16]

Overseas trade grew, despite Qing indifference, however, due in part to the extensive settlement of "overseas Chinese" throughout Southeast and South Asia that had begun during earlier dynasties. The Qing Navy remained powerful enough to prevent coastal piracy from getting out of hand, to maintain order on the canals and rivers, and to perform other coast guard–type functions. China had fallen so far behind the global norm in naval power, however, that it was unable to defeat the late-eighteenth- and early-nineteenth-century imperialists—who came by sea.

As the Qing reeled from the imperialist onslaught, major "restoration" movements occurred in China following the end of the Taiping Rebellion in 1864. These "self-strengthening" efforts, bearing the slogan "Chinese learning as the fundamental structure, Western learning for practical use," included building and training a modern navy. This facet of modernization probably resulted from admiration of the technology embodied in a modern warship, and the fact that China's humiliating defeat by the imperialist powers had been made possible by their navies.

An arsenal was established in Shanghai to build steam-powered gunboats, but efforts to modernize China's Navy too often fell victim to Confucian traditionalists who were the rigid ideologues of the day: it was in part a case of ideology defeating professionalism, a problem that has continued to this day.

Nonetheless, by 1884, China had deployed a modern navy, led by the efforts of Li Hongzhang, one of the most prominent of the scholar-bureaucrats who appreciated how far behind the foreign powers China had lagged. Li used three approaches to build the new Navy, which he thought should be oriented toward coastal defense: indigenous production, purchases abroad, and the reverse engineering of foreign systems.

Unfortunately, the Navy suffered from high-level governmental corruption and weak administration.[17] It was organized into four fleets that were essentially independent navies. The Beiyang Fleet, organized by Li Hong-zhang, was the most modern and powerful; by 1884 it included two seventy-five-hundred-ton-displacement, German-built battleships. The Fujian Fleet was home ported in Fuzhou; the other two fleets were the Nanyang and Guangdong.

The new Chinese force soon became embroiled in war with two foreign navies. Disputes with France over its colonization of Vietnam led to the outbreak of hostilities in August 1884, and the local French fleet attacked the outgunned Chinese Fujian Fleet in Fuzhou Harbor, sinking every ship.[18] China's other fleets were not sent to fight the French; Li wanted to conserve and strengthen remaining naval strength. His efforts, which included establishment of a national Navy Office, a more organized training regimen and shore establishment, and in 1888 standardized naval regulations, were successful—at least on paper.[19]

Despite these achievements, China's fleets failed to become a coherent national Navy, and the most powerful fleet, the Beiyang, came to grief in the effort to halt Japanese incursions into Korea in the 1890s. The Beiyang Fleet—two battleships, ten cruisers, and two torpedo boats—lost a sea battle to the Japanese in September 1894. The fleet then withdrew to Weihaiwei, a strongly fortified harbor on the northern Shandong coast. In January 1895, however, the Japanese landed troops, who seized the forts guarding the harbor and turned their guns on the Chinese ships.[20] The Chinese ship losses, in conjunction with the suicides of the fleet commander and other senior officers, eviscerated the Beiyang Fleet.[21] Again, the other Chinese fleets failed to join the fight.

These naval conflicts with the French and the Japanese demonstrated that while Beijing had successfully acquired the ships and weapons of a modern navy, it had failed to institute effective central administration, training, logistical and maintenance support, or command and control. Furthermore, operational doctrine was almost completely lacking; naval leaders failed to establish interfleet coordination, exercises, or mutual support. Finally, China failed to provide its new navy with a coherent strategy tied to national security objectives. As a result of these factors, China's attempt to deploy a modern navy in the late nineteenth century failed miserably.[22]

Republican China

Chinese naval forces during the republican period (1911–48) relied almost entirely on ships leftover from the Qing or obtained from foreign nations. No significant efforts were made to rebuild the navy; in any case they probably could not have been justified amid China's general political and economic disarray. Individual warlords occasionally made effective use of naval forces, but their ships were employed to augment ground forces, which was how navies were traditionally employed by Chinese leaders. The low point was probably reached during the height of the warlord period, in the mid- to late 1920s, when a Western observer dismissed the Chinese Navy: "There has been a steady deterioration in the discipline of the Chinese Navy since the establishment of the Republic, and it has now ceased to exist as a national force, the different units being under the control of various militarists, who treat the vessels as their own private property. . . . It is impossible today to obtain a complete list of Chinese warships, showing to which party or militarist faction they belong.

Vessels have been changing their allegiance . . . with bewildering frequency."[23]

The government did not develop a maritime strategy, since the primary threats to the new regime were ground threats from the Chinese Communist Party (CCP), Russia, and warlords. Naval actions that did occur took place chiefly on the rivers, especially the Yangtze and the waterways of the Canton Delta. Many of the warlords who struggled to gain control of various provinces and districts during the revolutionary period, from 1916 to 1928, used China's inland waterways for transportation, as military barriers, or as sources of revenue— taxing the dense river and canal traffic. These efforts led to frequent "fire fights" between provincial forces and the imperialist gunboats that patrolled China's rivers and lakes but were of no significance insofar as coherent maritime thought or navy-building by China was concerned.

There were two notable exceptions. First was a battle at the upper Yangtze River port city of Wanhsien in September 1926. The local warlord, Gen. Yang Sen, first commandeered British-owned steamers to transport his troops; when a British gunboat, HMS *Cockchafer,* attempted to free the steamers, it ran into an ambush very capably managed by Yang and suffered severe casualties. There was also an October 1929 naval and land engagement on the Heilong (Amur) River between Chinese and Soviet forces that foreshadowed the 1969 incident over disputed boundaries.[24]

Foreign sea power was an effective "force multiplier": foreign powers were able to use sea and river transport to move troops rapidly from crisis area to crisis area.[25] Great Britain, the United States, and Japan were thus able to influence the course of events in revolutionary China with relatively small military forces. Japan introduced a new element of maritime warfare in 1932, when it used bombers from an aircraft carrier stationed off Shanghai to bombard Chinese forces threatening Japanese interests in the city. Republican China was unable to contest such maritime strength.

China's record as a naval power during the long period of empire and republic shows an understandable focus on the continental rather than the maritime arena. Navies were built and employed almost entirely for defensive purposes. Maritime strength was regarded as only a secondary element of national power.

Nevertheless, China influences and is influenced by the Asia-Pacific region's maritime nature. The Sea of Japan and the Yellow, East

China, and South China Seas define the region. These seas in turn are marked by several straits. La Perouse (Soya) Strait between Russia and Japan divides the Seas of Okhostk and Japan; the Tsugaru and Tsushima (Korea) Straits mark the northern and southern ends of the Sea of Japan. The Osumi Passage connects the Yellow Sea to the Pacific Ocean, while the Taiwan Strait's importance requires no emphasis; it is potentially one of the most dangerous bodies of water in the world.

The South China Sea is marked by the Taiwan and Luzon Straits in the north, through which passes almost all seaborne traffic from the Indian Ocean to Northeast Asia and the Americas. This sea contains several other strategically vital seaways. None is more important than the Malacca Strait between the Malay Peninsula and Indonesia. This strait is the primary corridor between the Indian and Pacific Oceans and is about 600 nautical miles long.[26] It also has a bottleneck just 1.5 nautical miles wide at its eastern end and is generally shallow, able to accommodate ships with drafts of 19.8 meters or less.

To the east, the Lombok and Sunda Straits traverse the Indonesian archipelago. They are less frequently used than Malacca, but the Lombok, although longer at 750 nautical miles, is much deeper, and hence used by extremely deep draft vessels not able to transit the Malacca Strait. The Sunda Strait is only about fifty nautical miles long, but relatively shallow.

The Asia-Pacific region is a major factor in global trade. Half of the world's twenty largest container lines are owned and based in Asia; eighteen of the world's largest container ports are located in the region. About one-third of the world's shipping is owned by Asian nations.

Despite this maritime environment, except for the Taiwan crises of 1954–55 and 1958, China's national security concerns during the past century have focused almost entirely on internal security and continental threats, primarily from the Soviet Union but also from the United States during the Korean War. China fought Japan, the Soviet Union, Vietnam, India, and the United States during that period, and none of those wars involved significant Chinese naval participation, although the sea provided Japan and the United States with a haven from which China could be attacked.

It has only been in the past two decades that modern China has become navy-minded, and then apparently by a small number of national security policy makers. Beijing's Navy today is the third largest in the world, trailing only the United States and Russia, and is acquiring modern ships and weapons systems. The PLAN relies on U.S. and other Western systems, in recognition both of the limited capabilities of China's military industrial complex and foreign naval expertise.

Jiang Zemin, China's president, chairman of the Central Military Commission (CMC), and general secretary of the CCP's Central Committee, recently wrote that China must "strive to establish a modern navy with a strong, comprehensive combat capacity."[27] These remarks indicate the realization that China's offshore national security concerns—Taiwan, the South China Sea, and the sea lines of communication (SLOCs)—are problems whose resolution will require the ability to prevail in a maritime environment.

An appreciation of the Asia-Pacific as an overwhelmingly maritime region has been described by one author as the "territorialization of the seas" as China strives to control ocean areas under the "idea that a state's jurisdiction over the land is simply pushed seaward in terms of rights and duties concerning good order, the exploitation of resources and the exercise of limited sovereignty." This concept includes "environmental concerns, nationalism and above all, economic exploitation. . . . 'Sovereignty protection' is now a high priority naval mission."[28]

Chinese maritime strategists discuss the need for a strong navy in geopolitical terms, including the demand for increased *lebensraum* for a nation that supports almost a quarter of the world's population on approximately 7 percent of its arable land.[29] Defending its sovereignty is another major Chinese concern. Beijing's focus on its maritime borders was summed up in a 1996 statement by a PLAN strategist who claimed that "in the last 109 years, imperialists have repeatedly invaded China from the sea. . . . 470 times, . . . 84 of these being serious invasions. The ocean has become an avenue for the aggressors to bring in their troops and haul away our wealth. . . . The ocean is not only the basic space for human survival, but also an important theater for international political struggle. . . . The better people can control the sea, the greater they have the sea territorial rights [that have] become inseparable from a country's sovereignty."

China was urged to draw lessons from this experience: "(1) a strong naval force is a protection of the land, (2) a nation not understanding the importance of the ocean is a nation without a future, and (3) a major sea power incapable of defending its sea territorial rights will not be a major sea power for very long."[30]

The PLAN was hailed during the fiftieth anniversary of the People's Republic of China (PRC) in October 1999 in the following words: "The Chinese navy has traversed a 50-year journey of struggle. . . . It started from scratch [and has] equipped itself with missile fast attack craft, missile destroyers, missile frigates, naval missiles, naval fighter-bombers, strafers, antisubmarine patrol planes . . . and has accomplished important scientific studies and experiments. [It has steamed from the Arctic to] the Antarctic, . . . successfully conducted an experiment on the underwater launch of a carrier rocket from a nuclear submarine."[31]

There was no PLA Navy when the PRC was proclaimed in 1949. The CCP believed, however, that China's nineteenth- and twentieth-century humiliation had been greatly facilitated by the imperialists' ability to invade from the sea. The new government in Beijing saw the need to defend its coastline and island territories against two would-be aggressors: the truncated Kuomintang (KMT) regime that had fled to Taiwan, and the United States. The PLAN was officially established in May 1950.[32]

Does the PRC have a strategy to take advantage of its maritime environment? Does it aspire to take advantage of the "ubiquitous striking force of sea power?"[33] China is undoubtedly modernizing its Navy; does this program aim to change the PLAN from a coastal, "brown-water" force to an open ocean "blue-water" service able to secure Beijing's vast maritime territorial claims?[34]

"Blue water" is part of a maritime strategy paradigm with "brown" and "green" water. For our purposes, brown water refers to littoral ocean areas, within about one hundred nautical miles of the coastline; green water is less definite, referring to ocean areas from about one hundred nautical miles to the next significant land formation. For China, for instance, green water extends from brown water to Okinawa or from brown water throughout the South China Sea. "Blue water" is represented by Gen. Liu Huaqing's "second island chain," delineated by a line from Japan through the Bonin Islands, the Mariana Islands, and the Caroline Islands. A "blue-water" PLAN, then, will have to be capable of projecting power to a distance of at least fifteen hundred nautical miles from China's coast and beyond, including the Yellow, East China, and South China Seas.

In 1953, Mao Zedong wrote, "We must build a strong navy for the purpose of fighting against imperialist aggression." In 1979, Deng Xiaoping called for "a strong navy with modern combat capability," and in 1997, Jiang Zemin urged the Navy to "build up the nation's maritime Great Wall."[35] China is clearly determined to expand and modernize its Navy, having celebrated its fiftieth year, by focusing both on the hardware and strategy required for a modern fleet. Beijing is learning, however, that modern navies are technology-dependent and resource-intensive; they cannot be acquired quickly.[36]

Beijing currently views the international security situation as peaceful but dangerous. President Jiang Zemin has stated that the world "is moving deeper towards . . . the relaxation of international situation and world peace," but that "the Cold War mentality still lingers on as hegemonism and power politics manifest themselves. . . . New forms of 'gunboat policy' are rampant."[37] While describing the current international situation as "relaxing," Jiang also noted that "the world is not peaceful."[38]

From Beijing's point of view, U.S. naval dominance in East Asia in the near-term seems assured. In the longer-term, however, U.S. presence is unclear and Japan is a military threat. The maritime environment also directly impacts China's most serious resource problems: energy and food, the import of which depends on the sea.

Since the NATO air operations against Serbia, the Chinese press has been marked by strong condemnation of the "new gunboat policy"; the United States is accused of pursuing "under the cover of . . . so-called security globalization" a plan "to dominate the world."[39] In the Asia-Pacific region, the United States is charged with using the new defense agreement with Japan and theater missile defense (TMD) "to prepare the ground for future military intervention," and with a "Eurasian strategy" to position the United States for a "one superpower-dominated 'U.S. century.'"

Theater missile defense (to include coverage of Taiwan) is described as another U.S. instrument for "actively pushing its 'neo-interventionism' to dominate the world," through a "two-flank encirclement of Russia and China." The United States is accused of wanting to control Taiwan because it is China's "most direct door . . . to the Pacific," and the Spratlys, since they offer China "a strategic base closest to the Strait of Malacca." A variation on this theme is the idea that the United States is "hatching six major conspiracies against China" by "creating trouble and stirring up unrest in China"; using Japan "to create disturbances in Asia [and] to intervene in events occurring in areas surrounding China" and "attempting to drag China into the mire of the arms race" through pursuing TMD;

"preparing to intervene in the war in the Taiwan Strait"; and "trying to undermine China's national policy of reform and opening up." The thread of continuity throughout these views is the United States using TMD and a militaristic Japan to help enforce the Asian part of a policy of global hegemony, in part by containing China. [40]

China insists it is a developing country still facing injustice and unfair treatment on the international scene.[41] Gen. Zhang Wannian, vice chairman of the CMC, has claimed that China is "threatened by hegemonism and power politics, by militarism, and by foreign military intervention in Taiwan. . . . [We] must absolutely not lower our guard." He accuses the United States of seeking the collapse of the Beijing regime during a "full-fledged civil war," as a result of which China "will disintegrate."[42]

This is a strategic picture of China besieged by a hostile world in which the United States is using Europe and Japan to contain China and prevent it from attaining its rightful global status. The analysis offered by two senior naval officers at the PLAN's leading research institute is worth quoting at length:

> The seas have become the new high ground of strategic competition [including] rivalry over ocean islands, rivalry over sea space jurisdiction, rivalry over marine resources, rivalry over the maritime strategic advantage, [and] rivalry over strategic sea lanes. . . . The seas are a key national security defense [and] remain of crucial strategic value, . . . not only a protective screen, [but also] providing invaders with a marine invasion route. . . . We have to first establish a solid coastal defense. . . . The coastal wing of the land battlefield is directly exposed and threatened. So expanding the defensive depth of the naval battlefield is of crucial importance. . . . Controlling our sea space in more defensive depth enables us to more effectively stand off enemy invasions from the sea. . . . The naval battlefield is no longer limited to the traditional sea battle alone, rather gradually developing in the direction of sea-control-of-the-land with the seas as the base. . . . Military operations on the naval battlefield are often more suited to local wars on modern technological, particularly high-tech, terms. . . . Sea space is no longer limited to the surface, rather being 'four-dimensional' space covering sea air, sea surface, the water itself, and the seabed. . . . Militarily, the naval battlefield is both a springboard for attack and a natural screen for defense. The seas are of crucial importance to a country's prosperity [and] honor [because]:
> (1) The new world maritime order is not yet established;
> (2) the UN [United Nations] will become the main arena of maritime contention [in a new multipolar world];

(3) maritime development will become the major means by which certain countries achieve their political aims;

(4) instability in local sea areas will tend to escalate [as] reinforcing naval quality and contending for the technical advantage in naval operating equipment has become one of the key features of world arms development;

(5) the Asia-Pacific region will become one of the priority regions of maritime strategic competition [as] 'one of the regions controlling the world economy.' . . . Certain countries are acting to illegally seize maritime rights and interests, even to the extent of doing all possible to internationalize maritime disputes between countries.[43] [The] Chinese nation was one of the first in the world to develop [and] utilize marine resources [in the eighth century B.C.]. . . . Establishing a Chinese maritime strategy has become a task of top importance [as we look] to the seas for our future survival space.[44]

In the chapters to follow we will examine the current state of maritime thought and navy-building in China, and attempt to clarify Beijing's ambitions for the PLAN.

Chapter 1 will briefly examine the history of China's modern attempts to become a maritime power. China has an extensive history of maritime power, characterized throughout its long history by an inconsistent development and application of naval power as an instrument of national security strategy.

Chapters 2 and 3 examine China's maritime territorial and economic interests, especially those in the South and East China Seas. China's development of a modern Navy results directly from its need to secure offshore interests, which is what these two chapters will discuss. The importance of these issues illustrates Beijing's emphasis on sovereignty as a national security concern. Chapter 2 reviews Beijing's territorial claims in the East and South China Seas and describes the current actions of the competing claimants.

In Chapter 3 we will survey the nation's offshore mineral and other resources, a classic rationale for building a powerful Navy capable of protecting vital national resources. Exploiting these resources, particularly mineral deposits, has been a relatively recent development in China's history. The rapid economic modernization that has occurred since 1978 has been to a significant extent possible because of the availability of affordable energy-producing resources. Coal and petroleum deposits continue to furnish the overwhelming majority of China's energy needs; the relative paucity of the latter in China is forcing the country increasingly to seek offshore sources, both from foreign nations and from its own continental shelf. Both of these sources are maritime-dependent.

Chapter 4 examines the current organization of the PLAN. Again, there are many questions for which we lack clear answers in this mundane but crucial area of inquiry. PLAN organization is both cause and effect, reflecting the service's history, but also connoting its intentions and capabilities.

Chapter 5 addresses the ships, submarines, aircraft, and weapons systems with which the Chinese Navy is equipped. The Navy's effectiveness is tied directly to the capabilities of its component parts, and reviewing the open literature on these "parts," the ships and aircraft operated by China's sailors, should yield an idea of how well that Navy will perform.

In Chapter 6, we will investigate how the PLAN is manned and trained, with particular attention to the interplay between concerns for professional expertise and political reliability. No area of inquiry into China's Navy is less clear than how that force manages and trains its personnel. The normal demands of recruiting, educating, training, and managing the personnel force of a modern navy are complicated by Beijing's insistence on political reliability as well as professional expertise, the need for its personnel to be both "Red" and "expert." Understanding these already complex issues is difficult, owing to the Chinese obsession with secrecy.

In chapter 7, we will trace the development of maritime strategy in China, focusing on Beijing's current intentions in this crucial but often overlooked topic. The level of sophistication of maritime strategy as it is currently understood in Beijing is not clear. Beijing appears to be trying to draw on both classic Chinese concepts of strategy and the role of the military on the one hand, and on Western concepts of "sea power" and reliance on military technology, on the other hand.

Chapter 8 looks at the way doctrine is developed and applied in the PLAN. This discussion includes a review of the naval environment in East Asia and reviews specific scenarios in which China might choose to employ naval power. The concluding chapter will sum up what we have learned about Beijing's policies and intentions regarding the deployment of a powerful, modern navy, focusing on the Asia-Pacific maritime theater.

This work attempts a description and analysis of China's Navy: the background, organization, force composition, insular claims, maritime economic interests, doctrine, and strategy that drive Beijing to aspire to a maritime force capable of defending national interests on the high seas. A strong Chinese Navy is being developed and deployed. How is that being accomplished? And does it serve as an indicator of Beijing's national security posture and international power in the twenty-first century?

1

The PLAN's Heritage

The Communist victory in 1949 was an Army victory; the People's Liberation Army was unable to project power across even the narrow Taiwan Strait. The Kuomintang Navy continued raiding coastal installations, landing agents, attacking merchant craft and fishing vessels, and threatening invasion of the mainland on a larger scale.

The Early Years: 1949–1954

The new government in Beijing sought to defend its coastline and island territories against both the United States and the KMT regime on Taiwan. Coastal defense was emphasized in January 1950 with the creation of the East China Military Command, headquartered in Shanghai and deploying more than 450,000 personnel. Beijing ordered these troops to defend China's coast against "imperialist aggression from the sea," to continue the fight against Chiang's forces, and to help with economic reconstruction.[1] The East China People's Navy was established on 1 May 1949 as part of this command. This first PRC Navy was formed mostly by the defection of the former KMT Second Coastal Defense Fleet.[2] The new Navy's commander said it was needed "to safeguard China's independence, territorial integrity and sovereignty against imperialist aggression[,] . . . to destroy the sea blockade of liberated China, to support the land and air forces of the People's Liberation Army in defense of Chinese soil and to wipe out all remnants of the reactionary forces."[3]

The new Navy was also required to establish law and order on coastal and riverine waters, to help the Army capture offshore islands still occupied by the KMT, and to prepare for the capture of Taiwan. The CCP Politburo further charged the Navy with "defending both [eastern and southeastern] China coasts and the Yangtze River."[4] The first commander (and political commissar) of the East China Navy was Gen. Zhang Aiping. Among his first acts were the establishment of a naval staff college at Nanjing in August 1949, organization of a rudimentary maintenance and logistical infrastructure, and in September 1949 a visit to Moscow to discuss Soviet naval assistance. The PLAN was officially established in May 1950 under the command of Gen. Xiao Jingguang. The Chinese wanted a defensive force that would be inexpensive to build and could be quickly manned and trained.[5]

Zhang and Xiao were typical of early PLAN leadership: revolutionary officers who had spent their entire career as ground commanders and were transferred to the Navy for reasons of political reliability and proven combat record rather than for any particular naval experience. This trend, in fact, continued until 1988; Liu Huaqing was an Army officer before he was appointed to head the PLAN in 1982. After six distinguished years in that position, Liu again became a general and vice chairman of the CMC.[6]

The new PLAN was established with Soviet assistance obtained by Mao Zedong during his 1949–50 visit to Moscow; he planned to use half of the initial Soviet loan of $300 million to purchase naval equipment. The new PLAN also ordered two new cruisers from Great Britain and attempted to obtain surplus foreign warships through Hong Kong, efforts that were nullified by the outbreak of the Korean War.[7] China acquired mostly small vessels suitable to combat the coastal threat from Taiwan.

China initially obtained four old Soviet submarines, two destroyers, and a large number of patrol boats. The new force also included

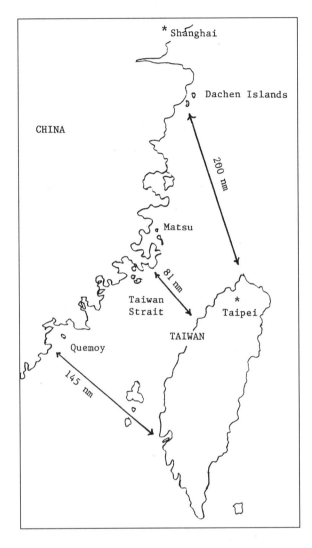

Distances between Taiwan and mainland China
CENTRAL INTELLIGENCE AGENCY

about ten corvettes, forty ex-U.S. landing craft, and several dozen miscellaneous river gunboats, minesweepers, and yard craft, all seized from the Nationalists.[8] The Soviets also helped establish a large shore-based infrastructure, including shipyards, naval colleges, and extensive coastal fortifications.[9]

Beijing's goal was seizure of the offshore islands still occupied by the KMT, with the invasion of Taiwan scheduled initially for the spring of 1950 but soon postponed to the summer of 1951. Mao Zedong considered the capture of Taiwan "an inseparable part of his great cause of unifying China."[10] He lacked experience in naval warfare but quickly learned that a successful campaign against Taiwan would require adequate amphibious training, naval transportation, "guaranteed air coverage," and the cooperation of a "fifth-column" on the island—requirements that still apply.[11]

China achieved a major victory in April 1950, when the PLA occupied Hainan, after Taiwan the second-largest island held by the Nationalists. The campaign cost Beijing heavy personnel losses but included the capture of more than ninety thousand Nationalist troops. This victory resulted from careful PLA planning, its ability to neutralize superior Nationalist naval and air forces by use of shore-based artillery to gain effective control of the sea and airspace between Hainan and the mainland, and a typically poor performance by Taiwan's senior commanders.

China's fear of American aggression was heightened in June 1950, when President Harry Truman ordered the U.S. Seventh Fleet into the Taiwan Strait at the outset of the Korean War. Although he explained America's reentry into the Chinese civil war as a means of preventing either side from attacking the other, Beijing understood that Truman was committing the United States to the defense of Taiwan—after having refused to do so for many months.[12] Premier Zhou Enlai called Truman's move "violent, predatory action by the U.S. Government [that] constituted armed aggression against the territory of China and total violation of the UN charter."[13] Beijing also understood, as it does today, that the United States possessed complete air and sea superiority in the western Pacific Ocean.

Beijing's concern was reinforced in February 1953, when President Dwight Eisenhower withdrew the U.S. fleet from the Taiwan Strait, thus in theory "unleashing" Nationalist forces on Taiwan to attack China.[14] In December 1953, Mao Zedong assigned the PLAN three priority missions: eliminate KMT naval interference and ensure safe navigation for China's maritime commerce, prepare to recover Taiwan, and oppose aggression from the sea.[15]

The PRC's young Navy faced many problems, including the lack of trained personnel and amphibious ships, as demonstrated in the very spotty record of assaults on KMT-held coastal islands. Furthermore, in February 1952, Mao diverted the Navy's ship-acquisition funds to the purchase of aircraft needed to fight in Korea.[16] Acquisition of equipment from foreign sources was constrained by western reluctance and budgetary limitations.

In addition, despite several visits to Moscow by senior PLA leaders, the Soviets continued to insist on payment for their ships, although most of them were obsolete.[17] The PLAN also lacked air power and was just beginning to establish a modern maintenance and logistical infrastructure. None of these problems should have been unexpected, but they have remained characteristic of the PLAN during its first half-century of existence.

1955–1959

The Korean War presented mixed naval lessons to China. The amphibious landing at Inchon in September 1950 was a major turning point of the war, while allied command of the sea allowed free employment of aircraft carriers and battleships to bombard Chinese and North Korean forces. The UN forces suffered at least one significant maritime defeat, however, when a planned amphibious assault on the east coast port of Hungnam in October 1950 had to be canceled because North Korea mined the harbor. Overall, however, Korea was not a maritime conflict, and the PLA's success in land and air battles in Korea contributed to continued reliance on a defensive, coastal Navy.

This conclusion was not unanimous; after witnessing the effects of modern weaponry firsthand in Korea, including the threat of nuclear warfare, some PLA leaders wanted to modify Mao's theory of "People's War" to one of "People's War under Modern Conditions." The most prominent proponent was Peng Dehuai, who had commanded the Chinese forces in Korea. Peng reportedly stated that "People's War and such stuff are outdated [at sea because] in battle the Navy relied upon the tonnage of its vessels, the caliber of its guns and the slide rule." Peng's attempts at "regularization and modernization" of the Army brought the accusation that he was trying to "negate the principle of people's war" by placing "military technique in the first place and [denying] that political and ideological work is the primary factor in building up" the PLA's "combat strength." Peng's attempt to modify Mao's military theories was one of the reasons he was dismissed from office in disgrace in 1959.[18] The necessity to continue conforming to Maoist ideology meant a continued concentration on large ground formations, with the Navy remaining in a subsidiary role.

Beijing initially relied on Soviet nuclear forces to counter the American nuclear threat during the 1950s. The stresses in the alliance with Moscow became more divisive as the decade progressed, however, in part because Mao Zedong was determined that China develop its own nuclear forces, proclaiming that "even if it takes 10,000 years, we must make a nuclear submarine."[19] The budgetary emphasis on nuclear weapons, the economic disruptions resulting from the disastrous "Great Leap Forward," and the continuing belief in Maoist orthodoxy all contributed to the lack of resources for developing a strong Chinese Navy during the late 1950s and 1960s.

PLAN operations in the mid-1950s continued to focus on KMT attacks against the mainland and on capturing islands still held by Taiwan. The 1954–55 Taiwan Strait crisis included the PLA capture of the Dachen Islands, an effort that took advantage of superior PLA air power and a well-coordinated amphibious assault against an outlying island.[20]

In neither of the decade's crises did Beijing intend capturing Quemoy or Matsu, but the incidents drew the United States more firmly into the conflict between China and Taiwan and emphasized the PLAN's weakness. Furthermore, Chiang Kai-shek used the 1954–55 shelling to pressure U.S. Secretary of State John Foster Dulles into signing the mutual security treaty with the "Republic of China." The incident did not redound to Beijing's benefit.[21]

The decade ended with Chinese possession of all the disputed islands except Quemoy, Matsu, and of course Taiwan. The PLA also stopped most of the KMT raids on the mainland, as well as attacks on merchant and fishing vessels.[22]

The Navy's First Aviation School was founded at Qingdao in October 1950; the Navy's air force, the People's Liberation Army–Navy Air Force (PLANAF), was formally established in 1952. Its mission was support of anti–surface ship and antisubmarine defensive operations.[23] Initial inventory was eighty aircraft, including MiG-15 jet fighters, Il-28 jet bombers, and propeller-driven Tu-2 strike aircraft. The PLANAF had grown to about 470 aircraft by 1958.[24]

PLAN operating forces were organized into three fleets. The North Sea Fleet included the majority of the PLAN's submarine force, perhaps because it was the fleet nearest the U.S. naval forces based in Japan.[25] The East Sea Fleet, headquartered in Ningbo, was the busiest and most important in the PLAN, since it faced the American-supported KMT forces across the Taiwan Strait. The South Sea Fleet, once the Vietnamese-French war ended in 1954, faced a hostile Southeast Asia Treaty Organization (SEATO) but a relatively quiet maritime situation. The PLAN had been organized, sent to sea, and proven effective as a coastal defense force within ten years of its founding.

A New Situation: 1960–1976

The 1960s were marked by major foreign and domestic events that further constrained development of a seagoing navy. Most important was the split with the Soviet Union, signaled during Nikita Khrushchev's October 1959 meeting with Mao Zedong in Beijing and dramatically executed in mid-1960, when Soviet advisors (and their plans) were withdrawn from China. The Navy suffered with the rest of the PLA, as military development projects were left in turmoil.

Other significant events in the early 1960s included war with India, the reemerging Vietnam conflict, turmoil in the new African states, and revolutionary movements throughout Southeast Asia. None of these major international events directly involved the Navy; they did not provide justification for improving the PLAN, but served to limit naval modernization. Maoist orthodoxy continued to dominate strategic thinking.

Minister of Defense Lin Biao apparently wanted to change the situation by instituting a policy of technological development with "politics in command." He did not succeed, and the decade ended with Lin coming down solidly on the side of "politics," writing "long live the victory of people's war."[26] This may have simply resulted from Lin's belief that the CCP had to remain firmly in control of the PLA for China to survive; hence, ideological reliability was more important than modern hardware.

Taiwan was too weak to act on its invasion rhetoric; America's involvement in Vietnam and resolve not to repeat its 1950 provocation to Beijing meant that China faced no overseas threat during the 1960s.[27] By the end of the decade, however, relations with the Soviet Union had deteriorated to the point of armed conflict along the Amur River. The former ally was now the enemy; soon the United States would be China's ally.

Beijing viewed the Soviet Navy at this time as a major amphibious invasion threat. This estimate probably owed more to the history of threats and invasions from the north, and to the Soviet Union's proximity to Beijing and the economic resources of northeastern China, than it did to the weak Soviet amphibious forces in the Pacific.[28] The

Great Proletarian Cultural Revolution (GPCR), lasting from about 1966 to 1976, precluded significant naval developments.[29] The PLAN continued to serve as an extension of the Army; modernization was limited, since People's War portrayed technology and weaponry as insignificant compared to revolutionary soldiers imbued with Mao's ideology.

The GPCR seriously hampered technological development in general; even the relatively sacrosanct missile, submarine, and nuclear weapons programs were affected.[30] A review of global naval developments indicates that PLAN modernization was retarded by perhaps two decades as a result of the program restrictions and personnel losses that occurred during this political maelstrom.[31] Except for the evolution of maritime nuclear power, the PLAN missed or was very late joining common developments in most warfare areas, including guided missiles in antiair (AAW), antisurface (ASUW), and antisubmarine warfare (ASW); automation and computerization of command and control (C3); the expanded use of ship-borne helicopters; automation of gunnery and sensor systems; and even the advent of automation and gas turbine technology in ship propulsion.

PLAN modernization was still hamstrung at the end of the GPCR by the "Gang of Four." Mao's widow, Jiang Qing, led the attack on naval missile development. Another member of the clique, Zhang Chunqiao, expressed the Gang's anti-Navy position and support for the "continentalist view."[32] Despite this attitude and a lack of resources for major conventional force development, the PLAN had moved into the missile age by 1970, deploying a Soviet-designed ballistic missile submarine and ten Soviet-built patrol boats armed with cruise missiles.[33]

Furthermore, Mao was determined that China join the nuclear club. Despite the ideological turmoil of the late 1950s and the 1960s, Beijing invested heavily in developing nuclear-armed missiles and the nuclear-powered submarines to launch them. These were national rather than PLAN projects, however, and did not significantly increase the Navy's ability to obtain the military resources necessary for modernization.

After the GPCR

Mao Zedong reportedly directed the development of a modern Navy in May 1975 at a meeting of the CMC.[34] He was probably reacting both to the Soviet threat and to the development of a powerful Navy by China's ancient protagonist, Japan. The PLAN's first priority in the 1970s was defending against possible Soviet amphibious assault from the northeast. Other missions included combating criminal activities such as smuggling, piracy, and illegal immigration; sea and air rescue (SAR); and safety of navigation.

Perception of an increased Soviet maritime threat resulted from the naval revolution of the 1970s in that nation, even though that event was defensive in motivation and aimed primarily at the United States. China, however, was a significant national security concern of Moscow's as well, which Beijing understood. China's concern about Soviet maritime power was strengthened when Moscow demonstrated its new global Navy in the 1975 Okean exercises.

Chinese interests threatened by the Soviet Navy in the late 1970s and 1980s included SLOCs vital to Beijing's rapidly increasing merchant marine, as Moscow's maritime forces maintained continual naval presence in the Indian Ocean and North Arabian Sea. The Soviet Pacific fleet almost doubled in size during the 1970s and was upgraded by the assignment of Moscow's latest combatants, including nuclear-powered and nuclear-armed surface ships and submarines. Soviet merchant and fisheries ships were also omnipresent in Pacific waters historically vital to China's economic interests.

Several factors continued to impede development of a large, modern Chinese Navy. The political aftershocks of the GPCR, as Hua Guofeng and Deng Xiaoping contested for leadership of post-Mao China, limited the resources devoted to military modernization. This struggle was not resolved until 1980, with Deng emerging on top.

After the Gang of Four were arrested in October 1976, Premier Hua Guofeng seemed to move away from a strictly continentalist position, at least so far as to reemphasize the PLAN's nuclear deterrent mission. In 1980, however, Deng Xiaoping reemphasized the Navy's role as a coastal defense force, a view retained throughout the first half of the decade. "Our navy," Deng asserted, "should conduct coastal operations. It is a defensive force. Everything in the construction of the navy must accord with this guiding principle."[35]

Naval growth was also limited by the disorder in China's economic and social structures that lasted beyond the end of the GPCR. In particular, this turmoil affected China's military-industrial complex, hindering modernization efforts in the PLA. Furthermore, the lessons of the 1979 "punishment" of Vietnam must have been sobering to the PLA, but this conflict did not involve significant naval efforts. Hence, the PLAN probably benefited only marginally from corrective budgetary measures.

Finally, the triangular play among China, the Soviet Union, and the United States meant that by 1980 Beijing could rely on the world's largest and most modern Navy to counter the Soviet maritime threat. This argued against China developing a similar force. Furthermore, given the U.S.-Japan security treaty, Beijing could subsume concern about future Japanese aggression within its strategic relationship with Washington.[36]

Major changes in China's domestic and international situation in the 1980s soon altered Beijing's view of the PLAN, and maritime power became a more important instrument of national security strategy by the end of the decade. Beijing's second maritime priority, after the Soviet threat, was securing offshore territorial claims. Taiwan was the most important of these, but the South China Sea was also significant. Although successful action against South Vietnamese naval forces in 1974 resulted in Chinese possession of the disputed Paracel Islands, this fight indicated that other claimants to the islands and reefs of the South China Sea would not accede meekly to Beijing's territorial claims. Furthermore, the Soviet naval base at Cam Ranh Bay was flourishing as the 1970s ended.

These factors contributed to a significant change in the South Sea Fleet's organization: the Marine Corps, first formed in 1953 but disbanded in 1957, was reestablished in December 1979 as an amphibious assault force and assigned to the southern fleet. The PLAN's slender amphibious assets were concentrated in the south, as that fleet's training regimen included "island seizing" exercises. In 1980, for instance, a major fleet exercise in the South China Sea focused on the seizure and defense of islands in the Paracels.[37]

The South Sea Fleet's organization benefited from the PLAN's force structure changes, which for the first time centered on Chinese-built warships. Although still heavily reliant on Soviet designs, the *Luda*-class guided-missile destroyers, *Jianghu*-class frigates, and *Houjian* fast-attack missile boats marked a significant increase in China's maritime capability.[38] The submarine force included the first Chinese-built nuclear-powered attack submarines, as well as about sixty conventionally powered boats. A seaborne nuclear deterrent force continued under development, following Mao's earlier declaration that the Navy had to be built up "to make it dreadful to the enemy."[39]

Deng Xiaoping's Navy

Naval expansion and modernization were spurred during the 1980s by the coastal concentration of China's burgeoning economy and military facilities. Furthermore, the resources necessary for a modernized PLAN became available as a result of China's dramatic economic development and increasing wealth. Recovery from the GPCR, well underway by 1985, included a reinvigorated if more decentralized military-industrial complex.

Three events contributed prominently to the development of China's Navy in this decade. The first was Deng's evaluation of the military at an expanded CMC meeting in 1975 as "overstaffed, lazy, arrogant, ill-equipped, and ill-prepared to conduct modern warfare," an opinion strengthened by the PLA's poor performance during the 1979 conflict with Vietnam.[40] This conflict did not directly involve the PLAN; the Soviet naval presence in the South China Sea probably inhibited the employment of Chinese naval forces, and the Navy could contribute little to the overland invasion of Vietnam.[41]

Second was Beijing's 1985 strategic decision that the Soviet Union no longer posed a major threat to China in terms of global nuclear war, and that in the future the PLA would have to be prepared instead for "small wars on the periphery" of the nation.[42] The emphasis on a "peripheral" (to a significant extent maritime) rather than continental strategic view improved the PLAN's position in obtaining resources within the PLA.

Third was the rise to prominence of Gen. Liu Huaqing. Liu had been schooled in the Soviet Union, had served most of his career in the science and technology arms of the PLA, and was close to Deng Xiaoping.[43] His appointment to head the Navy was unusual, as Liu held substantive (general/admiral) rank senior to that (lieutenant general/vice admiral) normally held by the PLAN commander, and represented Beijing's determination to improve its maritime power.

Liu exerted a strong force on naval developments as Navy commander from 1982 to 1987, and then vice chairman of the CMC until 1997. He is best known for promulgating a three-stage maritime strategy for China that provided justification on which PLAN officers and other navalists could base their plans for a larger, more modern Navy. More important were his accomplishments in reorganizing the Navy, redeveloping the Marine Corps, upgrading bases and research and development facilities, and restructuring the school and training systems.[44]

China's widening maritime concerns and increased budget resources in the 1980s raised interest in a strong modern Navy. PLAN modernization proceeded along three paths—indigenous construction, foreign purchase, and reverse engineering—much as had Li Hongzhang's "self-strengthening" Navy of a hundred years earlier. The 1980s program proceeded at a measured pace, however; Beijing did not embark on a major naval building program.

Construction included guided-missile destroyers and frigates, replenishment-at-sea ships, conventionally and nuclear-powered attack-submarines, and support craft including missile-tracking ships and officer-training vessels. Foreign purchases were concentrated in the west, with the United States selling China a small number of modern ship engines and torpedoes and western European nations selling weapons and sensor systems, including Italian torpedoes, French cruise missiles, and British radars.

Protecting offshore petroleum assets, other seabed minerals, and fisheries also received increased attention.[45] The PLAN acquired its only *Xia*-class fleet ballistic missile submarine. The successful submerged launch in 1988 of the Ju Lang-1 (JL-1) intermediate-range ballistic missile (IRBM) from this submarine meant that China for the first time could deploy nuclear strategic weapons at sea.[46]

During the 1980s, the PLAN also demonstrated its increasing capability in other maritime missions. China invested in four large space-surveillance ships to support its growing military and commercial space program, with these ships conducting the first long-range PLAN deployments, in support of space launches, in 1980. Task forces supported scientific expeditions to the Arctic and Antarctic. The PLAN's first foreign port visit was conducted in 1985, when two East Sea Fleet ships visited Bangladesh, Sri Lanka, and Pakistan; the officer-training ship *Zheng He* became the first PLAN vessel to visit the United States when it made a 1989 port call to Hawaii.

During the 1990s, Beijing continued to expand and modernize the Navy it had begun building in the 1970s, but at a measured pace. The PLAN also engaged in a series of long-range deployments throughout East and South Asia, as well as deploying a three-ship task group to the Western Hemisphere, where it visited the United States, Mexico, Peru, and Chile in 1998. Foreign purchases of improved ships, submarines, and aircraft earn the PLAN headlines as China acquires *Sovremenny*-class guided-missile destroyers (DDG), *Kilo*-class submarines, and Su-27 fighters from Russia, but these constitute only incremental improvements to a large but very limited Navy.

The Communist regime recognized the need early on to deal with maritime issues, but only after forty years and a dramatically altered international situation has Beijing apparently recognized the need for a modernized Navy. Beijing currently may view "the ocean as its chief strategic defensive direction," as "China's political and economic focus lies on the coastal areas [and] for the present and a fairly long period to come, [its] strategic focus will be in the direction of the sea."[47] The Chinese Navy being built for the twenty-first century owes a good deal to its history, which has been marked by some notable consistencies. First has been recognition of the maritime element in China's national security. Second, Chinese naval efforts have been closely linked to the nation's economic development.[48] Hence, naval modernization should be expected, in view of China's economic boom of the past twenty years.

Third, Chinese naval development since the eighteenth century has been marked by significant interaction with foreign navies. Qing Dynasty modernization efforts drew on Japanese, German, British, and American naval professionals as advisors, administrators, and engineers. This trend continued under the People's Republic of China, with a sporadic but pervasive reliance on Soviet/Russian advisors, strategy, equipment, technology, and engineers. Russia has been an important influence on the development of naval thought in the PRC.[49]

Fourth, the Chinese government has not hesitated to employ naval force in pursuit of national security goals. These efforts have not always been successful—witness 1884 against France and 1894–95 against Japan—but oftentimes they have, as in 1950, 1954–55, and 1958 in the Taiwan Strait, and in 1974, 1988, and 1998 in the South China Sea. Beijing's willingness to resort to naval force even when significantly outgunned bears a cautionary message for foreign strategists viewing China's possible reactions to Taiwan's efforts to resist reunification.

Finally, China has historically employed naval force over issues of sovereignty—about national control of specific islands or provinces. Hence, recent employment of naval forces has almost always been discussed in terms of sovereignty issues involving Taiwan, the Diaoyutai (Senkaku), and South China Sea claims, especially the Paracel [Xisha] and Spratly [Nansha] Islands. Although naval forces have been present throughout China's history, their employment as coherent fleets, operating under a nationally determined, coherent maritime strategy has been lacking.

China today aims to deploy a modern navy capable of operating on, above, and below the sea's surface to "become a Great Wall at Sea."[50] Is the PLAN approaching this goal, or is it still "best suited to fight a People's War . . . with weapons designed in the 1950s and 1960s"?[51] Answering that question requires a closer look at the maritime interests that demand a modern, capable Chinese Navy.

2

China's Maritime Territorial Interests

Territorial sovereignty is certainly important to any nation-state, but it holds a special place in Beijing's national security calculus. This is in part the result of the "hundred years of humiliation," the period from approximately 1842 to 1949 during which China was torn by foreign aggression and, in Mao Zedong's words, was "a semi-colonial country."[1] Senior Chinese civilian and military officials remain extremely sensitive to sovereignty claims, no matter how contested or tenuous under international law.

Beijing is party to six of East Asia's more than two dozen maritime territorial disputes: the Diaoyutai/Senkaku Islands with Japan; Taiwan; the Paracel Islands, with Vietnam; the Spratly Islands in the South China Sea, with Vietnam, the Philippines, Brunei, and Malaysia; water areas of the South China Sea, with the above nations and Indonesia; and the maritime border with Vietnam.[2]

United Nations Convention
on the Law of the Sea

East Asia's maritime claims must be considered within the UNCLOS, which Beijing signed and ratified in 1996. This convention was promulgated in 1982, following nearly a decade of international negotiations, and embodies important changes from previous maritime and international law. UNCLOS changes the concept and limit of "territorial seas," defined as the offshore area subject to a state's sovereignty, including the air space above the sea, as well as seabed and subsoil.[3] The previous definition of territorial seas as extending twelve nautical miles from a state's coastline was retained, but three additional sovereignty areas were defined.

A state's territorial waters continue to be sovereign: the state may, for instance, require submarines to transit those waters on the surface, and may require ships of any sort to obtain approval before transiting the area. It may also impose sea lanes and traffic-separation schemes, requiring transiting ships to follow specific, limited routes through the area.

As the first new area, UNCLOS establishes a contiguous zone (CZ), extending an additional twelve nautical miles, or twenty-four miles from a state's coastline. A state does not possess full sovereignty within the CZ but may exercise the control necessary to "(a) prevent infringement of customs, fiscal, immigration or sanitary laws within its territory or territorial seas; and (b) punish infringement of the above laws and regulations committed within its territory or territorial sea."[4]

The second new area delineated by the UNCLOS is a state's exclusive economic zone (EEZ). The EEZ "is an area beyond and adjacent to the territorial sea" in which the state has "sovereign rights for the purpose of exploring and exploiting, conserving and managing the natural resources, whether living or non-living." The nation's EEZ also includes jurisdiction over artificial islands, installations, and structures; marine research; and protection and preservation of the environment. The EEZ may not extend beyond two hundred nautical miles from the state's coastline.[5]

Finally, UNCLOS defines a state's rights on its continental shelf (CS), comprising "the sea-bed and subsoil of the submarine areas that extend beyond its territorial sea" to a maximum distance of 350 nautical miles from the state's coastline. The state has sovereign rights over

the CS "for the purpose of exploring it and exploiting its natural resources," both living and nonliving. The state does not, however, have
any legal rights on the water surface or the airspace above the CS
area.[6]

Thus UNCLOS delineates four areas of national maritime rights,
all measured from the state's coastline: (1) 12 nautical miles: territorial seas, in which the state exercises full legal sovereignty; (2) 24
nautical miles: contiguous zone, in which the state exercises limited
legal sovereignty; (3) 200 nautical miles: exclusive economic zone, in
which the state exercises full economic sovereignty; and (4) 350 nautical miles (maximum): continental shelf, in which the state exercises
limited economic sovereignty.

Two other UNCLOS provisions are particularly important to China's
maritime claims. The UNCLOS definition of an "island" as "a naturally
formed area of land, surrounded by water, which is above water at
high tide" affects Beijing's insular claims in the East and South China
Seas. An island possesses the territorial sea, CZ, EEZ, and CS characteristics of a continental state.[7] The UNCLOS provision for delimiting
the EEZ between states less than four hundred nautical miles apart,
and the CS between states less than seven hundred nautical miles
apart, particularly affects China's maritime territorial claims with
South Korea, Japan, and several Southeast Asian nations. States with
conflicting EEZ or CS claims are urged to "achieve an equitable solution." If they cannot agree, they are obligated to submit the dispute to
UNCLOS-created adjudication bodies for resolution.[8]

A final point in this brief discussion of the UNCLOS needs to be
made. In its effort to resolve old questions of maritime law, the UNC-
LOS raises some new problems, two of which particularly apply to
China's claims in Southeast Asian waters. First is the creation of the
two-hundred-nautical-mile EEZ in a region where multiple national
claims often overlap. One extreme example is the Gulf of Thailand,
where the EEZ claims of Cambodia, Malaysia, and Vietnam theoretically leave Thailand with no EEZ.[9]

Second, the UNCLOS-related right of states to impose navigation
restrictions within their territorial waters allows archipelagic states to
make troublesome claims. Indonesia, for instance, has tried to limit
the freedom of navigation of ships transiting the vital Sunda and
Lombok Straits into the South China Sea.[10]

Many states have included formal reservations when ratifying the

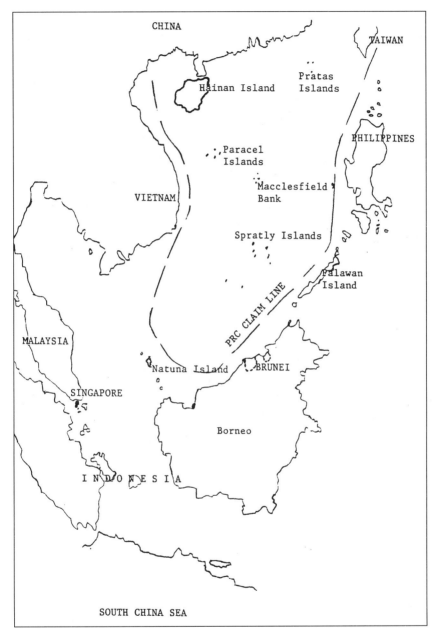

South China Sea   U.S. PACIFIC COMMAND

UNCLOS; China listed five, for reasons including the view that international law historically has been used by western nations for imperialistic purposes against developing countries and that the sea often served as an avenue for the invasion and exploitation of China. The first reservation claimed "sovereign rights and jurisdiction" over China's EEZ and "the continental shelf." This claim appears to contravene both the UNCLOS description of limited sovereign rights over the EEZ and the UNCLOS definition of the CS.

Second, Beijing opposed the UNCLOS-suggested method of delineating contested EEZ and CS claims by applying equidistance criteria, instead favoring bilateral negotiations by the parties concerned. Third, China declared that all boundary disputes would be settled through bilateral consultations, not by reference to the international tribunals recommended by UNCLOS.

Fourth, China attempted to qualify the UNCLOS provision for foreign warships having the right of innocent passage through its territorial (i.e., sovereign) waters. "Foreign ships for military purposes," stated Beijing, "shall be subject to approval by the Government of the PRC for entering the territorial sea of the PRC."

Finally, Beijing reaffirmed its sovereignty over all the islands it had claimed in its 1992 "Law on the Territorial Sea and the Contiguous Zone." These include the disputed "Taiwan and all islands appertaining thereto," as well as the Penghu, Dongsha, Senkaku (Diaoyu), Paracel (Xisha), Spratly (Nansha), and other South China Sea islands.[11] This would remove from discussion exactly the sort of issue UNCLOS was created to address.

Maritime Interests

China's maritime interests have steadily expanded during the past two decades, and now range from the Arctic to the Antarctic. The PLAN's first long-range mission occurred in 1980, when a large task group of ships was deployed to the South Pacific to monitor China's first satellite launches.[12] The first Chinese expedition to the Antarctic occurred in 1984; the sixteenth of these expeditions took place during the 1999-2000 summer season.[13] PLAN units conducted its first Arctic expedition in the summer of 1999, engaging in oceanographic studies and sea-bottom research—both of which have operational implications for the PLAN's ASW capability.[14]

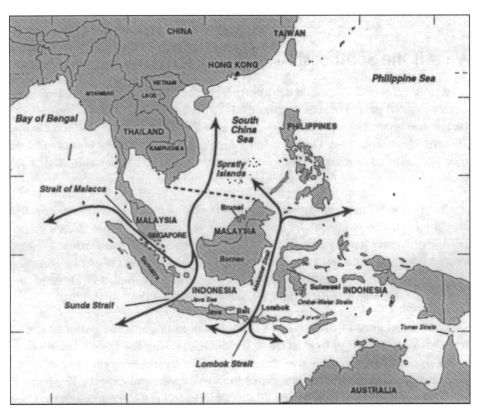

Strategic chokepoints: the Straits of Malacca, Sunda, and Lombok and SLOCs passing the Spratly Islands   INSTITUTE FOR NATIONAL STRATEGIC STUDIES,
WASHINGTON, D.C

China has underlined its interest in Indian Ocean SLOCs by join-ing the Indian Ocean Rim Association for Regional Cooperation (IORARC) as a "dialogue partner." The IORARC was organized to pro-mote regional economic construction; Foreign Ministry spokesman Zhu Bangzao stated that China "will take an active part in coopera-tion projects of the association [and] is also willing to make joint ef-forts . . . in establishing a new international political and economic order."[15]

Taiwan is obviously China's most important maritime issue, but next in importance are its territorial claims in the South China Sea.[16] Larger than the Mediterranean and just as much a maritime cross-roads, the South China Sea stretches from the Taiwan Strait in the north to the Malacca Strait in the south, and comprises the world's second busiest international sea lane.[17] It is rich in oil, natural gas, and fish, and lies at the center of Southeast Asia, scene of the world's highest economic growth rates during the past forty years. Sovereignty claims in the area are also driven by national pride.

The South China Sea contains several hundred small islands, rocks, cays, and reefs categorized as "land features." In geological terms, the South China Sea is a "deep rhombus-shaped basin in the eastern portion, with reef-studded shoal areas rising up steeply within the basin to the south and northwest. A broad, shallow shelf extends up to 150 miles in width between the mainland and the northwestern side of the basin. To the south, off southern Vietnam, the shelf narrows and connects with the Sundra Shelf. . . . Many of the so-called islands in the Spratly area are merely rocky outcroppings that are underwater at high tide."[18] Few are "naturally . . . above water at high tide" and hence "islands" as defined in international law. Most of these are grouped in two archipelagoes: the Paracel Islands in the northwestern South China Sea and the Spratly Islands in the south-central South China Sea.

The Spratlys include more than one hundred islets, reefs, and sea mounts scattered over 410,000 square kilometers, many submerged even at low tide; the Paracels number about two dozen land features. The total land area of the Spratlys is less than three square miles; that of the Paracels is even less. The highest point of land in the former is four meters, on Southwest Cay; that in the latter is fourteen meters, on Rocky Island. Claimants have built artificial structures on some of the subsurface reefs and other territory to qualify them as "islands," although the UNCLOS specifies that an "island" must be naturally formed. All are susceptible to being wiped clean by typhoons, most common in the area from June to November.[19]

There are few real islands of size in any of these groupings. The largest in the Spratlys is Itu Aba (called Taiping Dao by China), about half a square mile in area and the only island in the South China Sea with a natural water supply. About fifty of the Spratlys are occupied by one or another of the claimants. Taiwan occupies only Itu Aba, on which it has built a paved runway. Malaysia has occupied five or six islands, the Philippines seven to nine, China nine to twelve, and Vietnam seventeen to twenty-three.[20] Taiwan also occupies the Pratas Reef group, which lies northeast of the Paracels and is also claimed by China.[21]

The South China Sea may be divided into five primary areas that are in dispute:

1. Eastern Gulf of Thailand, where Thailand, Malaysia, and Cambodia claim overlapping maritime boundaries.

2. Northern part of the Natuna Islands, where Indonesia and Vietnam disagree over ownership of three small islands; this is the area that China may also claim, based on Beijing's 1992 map, discussed below.

3. Gulf of Tonkin, where China and Vietnam make conflicting maritime territorial claims.

4. the Paracel Islands, claimed by China, Taiwan, and Vietnam.

5. Spratly Islands, claimed by China, Taiwan, Vietnam, Malaysia, the Philippines, and Brunei.[22]

Economic Interests

Petroleum is China's preeminent offshore economic interest. The northern and extreme southern parts of the South China Sea have long been a source of oil and natural gas reserves from which China, Vietnam, Brunei, Indonesia, the Philippines, and Malaysia all benefit. The presence of petroleum reserves around the Spratly Islands is problematic, although it inspires numerous territorial claims to those islands.

China's most inclusive counterclaimant to South China Sea energy resources, Vietnam, argues that China is violating both the UNCLOS and Vietnam's continental shelf.[23] Fortunately for Beijing, Hanoi has neither the naval nor the economic strength to contest successfully for those resources. Vietnam's Navy consists of a ragtag collection of old Soviet patrol craft and is no match for the PLAN.

None of the Southeast Asian nations with counterclaims to South China Sea properties want to cast Beijing in the role of villain, precisely because of China's overwhelming naval and economic superiority. In fact, Malaysia signed an agreement with China in June 1999 to "use peaceful means of resolving tensions over disputed waters in the South China Sea."[24] Similarly, Jakarta is trying to wish away its conflicting claims with China over the Natuna Islands and their attendant gas fields.[25]

The region's nations cannot muster enough commonality of purpose to present Beijing with a united front. This reflects current strategic reality and supports China's view that it will get its way in the South China Sea as long as the region's nations are unable to unite in opposition to Beijing.

At present, China, the Philippines, Brunei, Indonesia, Malaysia, and Vietnam are all harvesting energy resources from the South China Sea. Disagreements about maritime boundaries are being negotiated or ignored, except for the most contentious area—the Spratly Islands.

This potentially dangerous situation is kept in check by the fact that meaningful oil or gas reserves have not been found. Several oil companies, including such giants as Phillips, Mobil, Exxon, China National Offshore Oil Corporation (CNOOC), British Petroleum (BP), Amoco, and Shell, have been exploring for oil in the South China Sea since the early 1970s, but with no success in the Spratlys.[26] If commercially valuable petroleum deposits are found, Beijing will undoubtedly adopt an even less flexible position on its sovereign rights to the area, with a modernizing PLAN to enforce its claims.

Fisheries are another vital offshore resource. China has had the largest fisheries industry in the world since 1990, with 41.22 million tons harvested in 1999.[27] The South China Sea is rich in this resource, but in danger of being "fished out." Beijing tries to enforce a fish conservation program through a large fleet of "fishing patrol ships" under the Agriculture Ministry.[28] China's efforts to institute this program have suffered from a lack of cooperation by surrounding nations and its own coastal provinces.[29] The Association of Southeast Asian Nations (ASEAN) is also addressing the issue of conserving Southeast Asian fish stocks, but with little success to date.[30]

Sea lines of communication are increasingly important to Beijing. Ships carry about 85 percent of China's trade, and the third point of the South China Sea's economic value lies in its vital SLOCs. More than half of the world's total merchant shipping passes through the Malacca, Sunda, and Lombok Straits into the South China Sea. More than three times as many ships pass through the Malacca Strait as pass through the Suez Canal, and more than five times as many as pass through the Panama Canal.

Half of this traffic passes near the Spratly Islands; it is dominated by raw materials, particularly petroleum products. Nearly two-thirds of the tonnage transiting the Malacca Strait and half of that passing near the Spratlys is crude oil from the Middle East, 8.2 million barrels per day in 1996, while liquefied natural gas (LNG) shipments through the South China Sea constitute two-thirds of the world's total LNG trade.[31]

Territorial Claims

China, Taiwan, and Vietnam claim all of the Paracels and the Spratlys, while Malaysia and the Philippines claim several of the latter group. Brunei in 1984 established an "exclusive fishing zone" that includes Louisa Reef in the southern Spratlys, but has not officially claimed that bit of land. Indonesia does not claim any of the Spratlys, but the rich oil and natural gas fields surrounding its Natuna Islands extend into the area of the South China Sea claimed by China; hence, it is a very concerned participant in the region's territorial disputes.

The South China Sea has been a primary area of fishing and shipping routes since ancient times for both Chinese seafarers and those of many other nationalities. Hence, the sovereignty claims of China/ Taiwan and Vietnam possess both historical validity and weaknesses.[32]

Vietnam cites the first written claim to the South China Sea islands made according to modern usage, by France in 1933, when its colonial regime in Vietnam established administrative control over the islands. This claim is undercut, however, by China's 1887 treaty with France that included a map showing the Spratly Islands in Beijing's jurisdiction; furthermore, Hanoi twice in the 1950s acknowledged China's sovereignty over these islands.[33]

Japan occupied the Paracel and Spratly Islands from 1938 to 1945, using them as a naval resupply base during World War II. In 1945, they were surrendered to Chinese forces, although the 1951 U.S.-Japanese peace treaty did not specify to whom Japan was formally returning the islands.[34]

Beijing's claim to all of the Spratly (Nansha) and Paracel (Xisha) Islands, as well as others in the South China Sea, is formalized in China's 1992 Law on the Territorial Sea and the Contiguous Zone. In December 1947 the CCP formally announced the incorporation of the Paracels and the Spratlys into Guangdong Province. In 1951, Beijing criticized the U.S.-Japanese peace treaty for not specifying Chinese sovereignty over the islands.[35]

Beijing describes the Spratly Islands as twenty-five islands and "over 230 reef shoals and sand banks" that account for "more than one quarter of China's three million square kilometer marine territory," and explains its policy as "maintaining sovereignty, shelving disputes and seeking common development."[36]

The Chinese (and Taiwanese) historical claims include evidence of Chinese voyages through the area in the Han dynasty (206 B.C.–A.D. 220), nominal administration of the islands during the Tang Dynasty (A.D. 618–906), and Chinese artifacts from that dynasty found on the islands.[37] These claims, by themselves, do not establish sovereignty under modern usage, but Beijing consistently phrases its claims in absolute terms.[38] Furthermore, China uses "straight baselines" to demarcate its territorial claims along all of its coastline and the Paracels, a method contrary to the 1982 UNCLOS.[39] Taiwan also passed the Territorial Sea and Contiguous Zone Law in 1993, in which it claims sovereignty over the same U-shaped line in the South China Sea as does Beijing in its 1992 legislation.[40]

The PLAN defeated a Vietnamese naval group near the Spratly Islands in March 1988, sinking three ships and killing seventy-two Vietnamese, after which it occupied Fiery Cross Reef and continued to militarize the Spratlys. Best known are its activities on Mischief Reef, but Beijing has also occupied Cuarteron Reef (Huayang Jiao), Gaven Reef (Nanxun Jiao or Duolu Jiao), Johnson Reef (Chigua Jiao), Subi Reef (Zhubi Jiao), Kennan Reef (Dongmen Jiao), Loaita Cay (Nanyue Shazhou, Nanyao Shanzhou), North Danger Reefs (Shuangzi Jiao or Gonshi Jiao), and Whitson Reef (Niue Jiao).[41] Significant military outposts have been constructed on Fiery Cross, Gaven, and Johnson Reefs in the Spratlys, in addition to the air base on Woody Island (Yongxing Tai to China; Phu Lam to Vietnam) and other military facilities on Lincoln and Duncan Reefs in the Paracels.[42]

Hanoi cites fifteenth-century historical evidence in support of its claims, but in more modern times lists a series of nineteenth- and twentieth-century factors, particularly France's 1933 claim to seven of the Spratlys. In 1958, however, North Vietnam agreed in a note to Beijing with China's claims "on China's territorial sea." Hanoi has since dismissed this note as resulting from the pressure "when Vietnam had to fight against U.S. intervention and aggression."[43] Vietnam maintains military garrisons on perhaps twenty Spratly land forms, only nine of which naturally remain above water at high tide: Spratly Island (Dao Truong Sa), West London Reef (Da Tay and Con Tay), Amboyna Cay

(An Bang), Pearson Reef (Hon Sap, Phan Vinh, or Dao Vanh Vinh), Sin Cowe Island (Sinh Ton), Namyit Island (Dao Nam Yit), Sand Cay (Da Son Ca), Barque Canada Reef (Bai Thuyen Chai), and Southwest Cay (Song Tu Tay).[44] Vietnam also claims a continental shelf in excess of two hundred nautical miles.

China and Vietnam agreed to settle their contested land border in a treaty signed on 30 December 1999 but still dispute their maritime boundary in the northern Beibu Bay (in the Tonkin Gulf) between Vietnam and Hainan Island.[45] Hanoi bases its claim on the line established by the French in the 1887 treaty with China; Beijing has responded that the boundary should be equidistant between the two nations.[46] Negotiations on this contentious issue continued throughout 2000, with the Sino-Vietnamese Working Group meeting almost twenty times.[47] The two governments announced on 25 December that they had reached agreements "to facilitate mutually beneficial cooperation in . . . offshore fishing and aquatic culture." They also agreed "on the Delimitation of the Beibu Bay [Tonkin Gulf] Territorial Sea, the Exclusive Economic Zone, and Continental Shelves."[48] Although it does not address the most serious issues between Hanoi and Beijing—the Paracel and Spratly Islands—if this agreement holds up under the stress of the disagreements that are certain to ensue, it will relieve China (and the PLAN) of a significant security concern in the South China Sea.

The dispute over the Paracel and Spratly Islands is the most serious in the South China Sea, especially with regard to petroleum reserves. China and Vietnam have twice fought sea battles over these islands, and have come close to blows over oil rigs just west of the Spratlys. Vietnam's view is that "China attacked and seized Vietnam's Paracel Islands," in January 1974 and "in March 1988, after a military attack on Vietnamese freighters, . . . occupied Chu Thap, Chau Vien, Ga Ven, and Tu Nghia reefs." Beijing's May 1992 contract with Crestone, an American oil company, is derided for being based on an "absurd claim" because the area covered by the contract is part of Vietnam's continental shelf. China is further accused of deliberately ignoring the UNCLOS in occupying the Paracels and various Spratly Islands as part of a plan to "monopolize the Eastern Sea by [the] early 21st century."[49]

Vietnam is widely engaged with foreign oil companies to exploit petroleum fields in its claimed territorial waters and on its continental shelf. The first such effort was a 1972 agreement with the Italian company Agenzia Generale Italina Petroli to explore parts of the continental shelf. The French company Compagnie Generale de Geophysique was hired in 1976 to survey offshore areas off the southern Vietnamese coast,[50] and a 1984 joint venture with the Soviet Union to explore Vietnam's southern continental shelf found oil.[51]

Hanoi signed an exploration agreement with the U.S. company, Conoco, in 1992 to explore an area that contravenes that specified in the 1992 China-Crestone contract: Vietnam's Blocks 133, 134, and 135, which overlap China's Wan Bei-21 field.[52] China's April 1994 announcement that it had commenced drilling was followed within hours by Vietnam's announcement that it had signed exploration contracts with American, Japanese, and Russian companies to explore an adjoining field within China's claimed area.[53] This situation has resulted in some minor incidents between the two nations' ships, but none so far have involved loss of life or property.[54]

The record since the September 1997 party congress in Hanoi indicates that Vietnam is slowing economic modernization to avoid risk to communist party rule. Hence, the 1997 reports of oil companies slowing their efforts in Vietnamese waters and the significant decrease in foreign investment during 1998.[55] Seven American and British petroleum companies ended operations in Vietnam in 1999.[56]

The Philippines' claim to various Spratly Islands is based on the 1947 "discovery" and "occupation" of the Spratlys by a Filipino businessman—claims that were not announced until 1956 and were "deeded to the Philippine government" in 1974.[57] An indeterminate number of Philippine troops are stationed on some of the Spratlys claimed by Manila: Commodore Reef (Rizal), Lankiam Cay (Panata), Loaita Island (Kota), Nanshan Island (Lawak), Flat Island (Patag), West York Island (Likas), Northeast Cay (Parola), and Thitu Island (Pagasa), which also contains a short airstrip. The Philippines' territorial disputes in the South China Sea are not just with China but also include disagreements over island sovereignty with Malaysia and Vietnam.[58]

There are two categories of dispute between Manila and Beijing. First, the Philippines' most important offshore petroleum sources, the Malampaya and Camago natural gas and condensate fields, are located in eastern South China Sea waters also claimed by China. Philippine oil exploration in the Spratlys actually preceded Chinese efforts, as Manila granted concessions to Amoco, Salen, and the Philippine Oil Development Company in the early 1970s and 1980s, and drilled wells on Reed Bank (Liyu Tan and Lile Tan). In the late 1980s, the American Kirkland Oil Company received a similar contract.[59]

Second, China and the Philippines have, since 1995, been engaged in a contentious dispute about ownership of land features in the Spratly Islands. As noted, Beijing claims all of the Spratlys; Manila claims nine or ten of the islands. China's actions on Mischief Reef (Meiji Jiao), located just 140 nautical miles from the Philippine island of Palawan, well within the Philippine-claimed EEZ, have received the most attention. Beijing built this reef, normally barely above the sea's surface, into a sizable artificial island. The PLA then constructed buildings, installed communications equipment and possibly sensors, and built helicopter landing platforms and docking facilities.

A similar pattern is emerging on Scarborough Shoals (Huangyan Island), located just 122 nautical miles off Luzon. Chinese fishing boats frequently visit this reef and have been confronted on several occasions by Philippine patrol craft. One Filipino congressman has described these incursions as "just the first step of a Chinese invasion into our territory. The Chinese always start by sending fishing vessels, then they build shelters and before we know it, the soldiers arrive."[60] China has been unbending about its ownership of both Mischief Reef and Scarborough Shoals.

The Philippines lacks an effective navy or air force and cannot stop China's actions, although Philippine leaders have been trying to modernize their military.[61] President Corazon Aquino urged the Philippine Congress in 1990 to fund a $1 billion modernization program, with emphasis on the navy and air force. Her successor, Fidel Ramos, was especially concerned about Philippine claims in the South China Sea and convinced Congress to pass a five-year, $12.6 billion armed forces modernization program—but little of this money was actually allocated or spent on the military.[62]

The Chinese activities on Mischief Reef undoubtedly were a prime reason Manila ratified the Visiting Forces Agreement (VFA) with the United States in 1999, which facilitated renewal of exercises between the two nations.[63] The first joint exercise following the VFA signing took place in January-February 2000, as "Balikitan 2000" involved U.S. and Philippine Air Force and Army units on Luzon and Palawan.[64] This successful exercise has already led one prominent Philippine legislator, senate president Blas Ople, to boast, "I have no doubt in my mind that our American friends in accordance with the treaty obligation, will not hesitate to join us in repulsing any forcible aggression against our territory."[65] President José Estrada emphasized, however, that the U.S.-Philippine exercises were not aimed at "any country, including China."[66]

The Philippine government is trying to follow a delicate line between defusing the situation, stating that no "immediate threat of armed clashes" is present,[67] while still insisting on its sovereignty claims by placing markers on the disputed islands and maintaining patrols by its very few ships.[68] These patrols have harried Chinese fishing boats away from Scarborough Shoals, in two cases "accidentally" sinking PRC boats, on 26 January 2000 boarding other Chinese trawlers, and on 2 February firing warning shots at intruding boats.[69]

These 1999–2000 incidents have led to an exchange of notes between Manila and Beijing, which has treated the contretemps with patience bordering on disdain. While insisting that "the international community universally respects the fact that the Huangyan Island [Scarborough Shoals] is Chinese territory," China urges the Philippines to "stop creating new disturbances, and work with China in safeguarding peace and stability in the South China Sea."[70]

This dispute has illustrated both Beijing's "two-track" strategy in the South China Sea and Manila's helplessness in the face of that strategy. Although the Philippines successfully obtained the support of its ASEAN neighbors following China's January 1995 incursions onto Mischief Reef, Manila's appeals in 1999 to ASEAN and the UN following further Chinese actions in 1998 were rebuffed.[71] The defense treaty with the United States also offers little hope of assistance.[72]

Secretary for Policy Lauro Baja of the Department of Foreign Affairs has described Manila's plight as "a lose-lose situation."[73] Estrada struck the most positive note he could during his May 2000 visit to Beijing, agreeing with President Jiang Zemin that the South China Sea disputes should be "resolved through peaceful means." The two presidents signed five agreements, including the Joint Statement on the Framework for Cooperation Between the Governments of China and the Philippines in the 21st Century.[74]

Other regional nations also have South China Sea interests. Kuala Lumpur bases its claim to South China Sea islands on two legal principles: continental shelf extension and discovery/occupation.[75] Malaysia claims twelve land features in the Spratlys, but three islands —Swallow Reef (Terembu Layang Layang), Ardasier Bank (Terumbu Ubi), and Mariveles Reef (Terumbu Mantanani)—are occupied on the basis that they are part of its continental shelf.[76] Similarly, Brunei's implied claim to Louisa Reef is based on the continental shelf extension principle.[77]

Malaysia has generally been a leader among Southeast Asian nations professing to see no "China threat." Although China's 1995 occupation of Mischief Reef came as a "shock" to Malaysian leaders, they have since reverted to a studiously noncontentious policy with Beijing. Ironically, Kuala Lumpur has also adopted an aggressive policy of occupying and building up the Spratly Islands it claims.

Indonesia has played the leading role in establishing international processes to resolve territorial disputes in the region, beginning with a 1990 "workshop" on the Spratlys.[78] The South China Sea Informal Working Group held its tenth meeting in Bogor in December 1999, the latest evidence of Indonesia's efforts, which were reinforced by Minister of Foreign Affairs Alwi Shihab's "guarantee" that "Indonesia will stay with its commitment to endorse peace, stability and cooperation in the [dispute over the Spratly Islands]."[79]

Jakarta remains concerned, however, about China's 1992 law delineating territorial claims in the South China Sea, which include part of the Natuna gas fields. Beijing emphasized its claim at a 1993 Indonesian-sponsored workshop on the Spratlys, displaying a map that depicted its claim line extending well into Jakarta's claimed EEZ.[80] Even before this law was passed, Foreign Minister Ali Alatas had warned in 1991 that the Spratly Islands dispute might become a "conflict area" for the ASEAN states.

Jakarta queried Beijing about the claim in 1994; the latter then and since has refused to respond, other than to maintain that Chinese sovereignty over the claimed South China Sea area (presumably including part of the Natuna fields) was based on "inheritance from past dynasties." Indonesia refuses to accept this rationale; Jakarta and Beijing have continued to keep this dispute quiet although unresolved.[81] Jakarta is taking military steps, however; four Maritime Region Commands have been established under the Navy, nominally to "focus on development of the country's marine resources."[82]

The PLAN in the South China Sea

China has built an air base on Woody Island, the largest in the Paracels, with an area of 1.1 square miles, located 200 nautical miles southeast of Hainan Island. It has the only paved runway in the islands, along with piers and a ship channel through the surrounding reef. The PLAN has designated Woody Island as "headquarters" for its South China Sea forces. The island is capable of handling current Chinese tactical jets (at least F-6/F-7), with covered revetments for four aircraft and paved apron space for about thirty more; it possesses very limited radar-control facilities and almost no aircraft maintenance capability.[83] China is also building facilities on Lincoln and Duncan Reefs, probably for communications and logistics.[84]

The greater the value placed on maritime interests such as the Spratly Islands, the greater the Navy's potential clout in PLA budget competition and the greater the willingness of the Beijing leadership to authorize naval modernization and growth. Some observers even argue that China's aggressive stance in the South China Sea is being driven by the PLAN, over the objections of the foreign ministry.[85]

One case in point is Beijing specifically telling the Crestone chairman in 1992 that the PLAN would be deployed to protect his activities, if necessary.[86] That same year, PLAN deputy commander Zhang Xusan stated that "it was high time for China to readjust naval strategy and make greater efforts to recover South China Sea oil and gas resources."[87] The conjunction of these three events—territorial claim, oil exploration contract, and naval strategic pronouncement—are a strong indicator in Beijing's increasing interest in maritime strength.

There has even been an element of *lebensraum* in PLAN arguments, taking a lead from Deng Xiaoping's statements at a forum of the CCP Central Committee in 1979 about China's large population and small area of arable land. The PLAN's interest in pushing Beijing's claims in the South China Sea was verbalized in 1984 when Adm. Liu Huaqing, then head of the PLAN, argued that a strong, modern navy was needed for China to secure its rich maritime resources.[88] This line was followed in 1988 and 1989 *Jeifangjun Bao* articles pointing out the value of maritime resources. One highlighted the need to "vigorously develop and use the ocean. . . . The defense of the territorial unity and the protection of the rights and interests of the oceans are significant to the security and development of a country. . . . Every reef and island is connected to a large area of territorial water and an exclusive economic zone that is priceless."

A second article pointed out that the sea was a valuable source of food and minerals; it was "deplorable" that China had not taken advantage of this wealth and "we must give prominent attention to strengthening naval construction, while energetically developing the marine areas. . . . The emphasis on developing the Navy is where the fundamental and long-term interests of the state and the people lie."[89] Concern has been expressed that the PLAN lacks easy access to the open ocean; a variation on this is to draw a ratio between a nation's maritime area and the length of its coastline. Chinese analysts have arrived at a global average of 94 to 100, while claiming that China's ratio is only 30 to 1,000. This may or may not be a meaningful figure, but Beijing is increasing its budget for marine surveying and research to increase the benefits gained from its maritime areas.[90]

Resolving the Disputes

There are legal problems with both the Chinese and the Vietnamese sovereignty claims in the Spratlys. One authority describes them as "incomplete, intermittent, and unconvincing" because none demonstrates "effective control, administration and governance of sovereign territory."[91] The Philippine, Malaysian, and Brunei claims, based on the continental shelf and proximity, have a much stronger case under the UNCLOS than do Chinese, Taiwanese, and Vietnamese claims, which are based on history. In fact, the validity of all these claims is weakened by both the lack of continuity in historic occupancy of the various islands and by the lack of clearly defined national continental shelves in the restricted South China Sea.[92]

At the July 1995 conference of the ASEAN, Foreign Minister Qian Qichen expressed China's willingness to participate in a multinational discussion of the issue, promising to "resolve the dispute over ownership of the Spratly Islands according to international law and UN conventions."[93] China's apparently cooperative attitude in 1995 was probably due to two factors. First, following the PLAN's initial incursions onto Mischief Reef early that year, the Philippines successfully enlisted ASEAN's verbal support against Beijing's actions. This multinational opposition probably surprised the Chinese and caused them to slow their South China Sea actions. Second, when Taiwan President Lee Teng-hui visited the United States in the summer of 1995, Beijing expressed its displeasure through extensive military operations in the Taiwan Strait area.

China may well have "cooled" the situation in the South China Sea

to focus on the higher priority concerns about Taiwan. Since then,
however, Beijing has reverted to a stiffer position, agreeing to peacefully settle the disputes "through bilateral negotiation," as long as the
parties understand that China holds "indisputable sovereignty over
the South China Sea and adjacent water."[94] Some of this may be pos-
turing, but Beijing has been remarkably consistent.

The ten ASEAN nations have agreed on a Code of Conduct (COC)
that includes the following four provisions:

1. Settle disputes on the sovereignty and jurisdiction over the
   South China Sea with peaceful means without resorting to
   force.

2. All concerned parties are urged to exercise self-restraint to
   create a fine atmosphere to settle the disputes.

3. Under the condition that the sovereignty and jurisdiction
   of the countries having direct interests in the region are
   not harmed, discuss the feasibility of cooperation of all
   parties in such respects as navigation, traffic safety,
   marine environmental protection, and measures against
   pirates, drug trafficking, and smuggling.

4. Invite the parties concerned to sign the declaration.[95]

The workshops have developed an infrastructure, including Technical
Working Groups (TWG) to investigate specific areas of contention,
with Groups of Experts Meetings reporting to the TWGs on specific issues. Twenty-six meetings have been held, with every ASEAN member
and claimant state except Taiwan hosting at least one session.[96] The
ASEAN Regional Forum (ARF) also addressed the South China Sea territorial claims issue at the Sixth Annual ARF Meeting, held in Singapore in July 1999. The group's chairman "welcomed the commitment
of all the countries concerned to the peaceful settlement of disputes in
the South China Sea in accordance with . . . the UNCLOS, stressed the
importance of freedom of navigation in this area[,] . . . further welcomed the dialogue in the ASEAN-China Senior Officials Consultations, . . . and the continuing work of the Informal Workshop on Managing Potential Conflicts in the South China Sea, [noting] that ASEAN
was working on a regional Code of Conduct in the South China Sea."[97]

ASEAN discussions have included China's agreement to abide by a
code that would help settle territorial disputes in the region "without

prejudice to freedom of navigation in the South China Sea" and in "accordance with the recognized principles of international law, including the UNCLOS."[98]

Despite this appearance of flexibility, however, Qian Qichen's actual speech at the ASEAN conference included six major points, many of which maintained a uncompromising tone:

1. China has indisputable sovereignty over the Spratly Island and *adjacent waters*.

2. China is willing to hold peaceful talks with concerned countries to resolve disputes properly, in accordance with the principle of national defense law and modern maritime law.

3. China's proposal to "shelve disputes and facilitate joint development" is the most realistic and practical way to resolve the Spratly dispute.

4. China is willing to hold *bilateral consultations* with claimant states, considering it *inappropriate to hold multilateral talks at an international conference*.

5. China has always attached great importance to safety and freedom in international lanes in the South China Sea and believes there should be no problems in this regard.

6. The Spratly disputes do not concern the United States at all, and it has no reason to interfere.[99]

Although some observers have chosen to interpret these remarks as a relaxation of China's attitude, Qian really reinforced Beijing's refusal to engage in multilateral discussions: only bilateral "negotiations" were possible, and even those could occur only under the precondition that China held complete sovereignty over the Spratly Islands.

The most viable proposal for resolving the South China Sea territorial disputes probably remains adoption of the "code of conduct" championed by Indonesia, Malaysia, and the Philippines. Proposals for a South China Sea Code of Conduct came from the "Workshops on Managing Potential Conflicts in the South China Sea," the first of which was hosted by Indonesia in 1990. The tenth workshop met in Manila in November 1999; the eleventh took place in Thailand in March 2000.[100] A COC was also discussed at the sixth China-ASEAN Senior Officials Meeting in Malaysia in April 2000, which established a COC drafting committee of Thai and Chinese representatives. These met in Kuala Lumpur in late May, and their efforts were to be discussed at ASEAN's first foreign ministerial meeting in Bangkok in late July.

In March and May 2000, China and ASEAN agreed on certain measures leading to a COC. Most recently, they announced "working-level" meetings in late August 2000, following Beijing's release of a recommended COC on 15 August. China continues to insist, however, that only the Spratlys are open to discussion; it refuses to agree with the ASEAN position of restricting construction on disputed land features.

Beijing has also issued a new demand, that "military exercises should be restricted in the waters around" the Spratly Islands. This is certainly aimed against joint U.S.-Philippine operations, which have resumed following the 1999 signing of the Visiting Forces Agreement between the two nations. The November 2000 ASEAN summit also failed to reach agreement on a Code of Conduct.[101]

In fact, Qian's speech, the gist of which has been repeated by other Chinese officials on several occasions, simply supports the dual-track policy Beijing is following in the South China Sea. It pursues diplomatic discussions and even proposes economic cooperative schemes—all without for one instant relaxing its insistence that "China has indisputable sovereignty over the Nansha Islands and their adjacent waters." The 30 August meeting was held in Dalian, China, and ended without agreement on the COC. Additionally, a Chinese Foreign Ministry spokesman blamed the ASEAN nations for failing to be "flexible" and hence causing the discussions to be unproductive.

Furthermore, Chinese officials have consistently insisted that the Paracel Islands are excluded from any such discussions, and that the proposed code would not halt construction on contested islands. It has also stated that "China has indisputable sovereignty over the Nansha Archipelago and their adjacent waters," while noting that Beijing would participate in discussions focusing "on issues concerning East Asian cooperation in the financial, scientific-technological, and agricultural sectors"—but not sovereignty issues.[102]

Meanwhile, in parallel with its rhetoric, Beijing continues increasing its presence in the South China Sea islands. The January 1995 Mischief Reef incursions were not pressed immediately, as noted above, but since early 1998 China has expanded its presence on these rocks, using them to build the artificial island that now constitutes a minor naval base. The next target appears to be Scarborough Shoals.

Beijing is able to pursue this two-track policy because, first, it is simply the most powerful military force in the South China Sea. Some of the regional states field formidable forces, but none of them compare individually to the PLAN or the People's Liberation Army–Air Force (PLAAF). Although united ASEAN naval and air forces could counter the Chinese military, organization member states are not able to cooperate to that extent. Furthermore, the general mind-set among the ASEAN states, exemplified by Malaysia, is to act as if China is not a threat because they are not prepared to respond to Beijing as a threat.

Second, Beijing is succeeding in the South China Sea because the only nation that could successfully curtail its efforts, the United States, is maintaining a "hands-off" policy. The U.S. position has been to urge peaceful resolution of the area's territorial disputes, insisting only that freedom of navigation not be restricted. Beijing agrees it has no intention of interfering with this right, and has not attempted to do so, while warning the ASEAN states against conducting military exercises with U.S. forces.[103]

East China Sea

China's maritime territorial disputes with the Republic of South Korea and with Japan include issues similar to those in the South China Sea but are much simpler. Petroleum issues are incipient, as proven oil reserves to date lie well within Beijing's continental shelf, in the Yellow Sea, Bohai (Bo Sea), and shallow coastal waters.

Fisheries are a more troublesome issue, although China has been negotiating with both Korea and Japan to arrive at an equitable division of the area's biological resources. These negotiations so far have established at least temporary measures for resolving the fishing disputes.[104]

China claims the Diaoyutai, a group of five small islands and three rocky outcroppings lying 90 nautical miles northeast of Taiwan and 220 nautical miles west-southwest of Okinawa, also claimed by Japan as the Senkaku Islands.[105] These islands were recognized as belonging to China based on a fourteenth-century claim, until acquired by Japan under the Treaty of Shimonoseki following its victorious war with China in 1895. When the allied powers returned Taiwan to China in 1945, the Senkakus remained with Japan, possibly through ignorance on the part of the allied decision makers, although Tokyo maintains that the islands were always part of Okinawa.

The Senkakus are uninhabited and, except for fisheries long used by both Chinese and Japanese fishermen, have no intrinsic value other than as a symbol of national pride. They do lie on a part of the continental shelf disputed by Beijing and Tokyo; if petroleum reserves are discovered in the vicinity, ownership of the Senkaku Islands/Diaoyutais might carry with it ownership of that oil. In fact, a 1968 UN study suggesting the presence of petroleum reserves stimulated the present dispute.

Ownership of the disputed continental shelf would first have to be resolved, of course, possibly within the UNCLOS framework for settling such disputes.[106] Oil has not been discovered in the immediate vicinity of these islands, but the large deposits elsewhere on the East China Sea continental shelf make discoveries likely. Tokyo argues that the two nations' overlapping EEZs should be divided midway between Japan and China, while Beijing's position is that the boundary lies to the east of the Senkakus.[107]

Beijing and Tokyo seem determined to prevent this dispute from erupting into crisis, especially in view of the disruptive incidents on the Senkakus in 1978, 1988, 1990, and several occurrences from 1996 to the present by rightist groups from Japan, Hong Kong, and Taiwan.[108] Tokyo maintains that it lacks justification for action against private groups landing and building structures on privately owned Japanese territory, while Beijing insists the islands are "historically" and "indisputably" part of China's territory.[109]

China is continuing to send PLAN support ships into the disputed area around the Senkakus, most recently in May 2000, when a Chinese ice breaker–surveillance ship circumnavigated Honshu.[110] Indeed, early in the year the Japan Maritime Self-Defense Force (JMSDF) reported that "a total of fifteen Chinese research ships entered the [disputed] waters on twenty-three occasions during the year, where no such vessels had been seen before."[111] This is probably part of a deliberate Beijing policy similar to the American Freedom of Navigation program, under which U.S. ships deliberately, if briefly, transit seas claimed as sovereign by nations whose claims the United States disputes. The Chinese incursions seem to be increasing in 2000, however, and this raises the potential for a confrontation between one of Beijing's ships and a Japanese warship or patrol plane, which routinely respond to them.[112] These deployments are legal but are an irritant to Japan and have become a matter of high-level interest in both countries. Despite promises by Beijing officials to give Tokyo prior notice of such voyages, they are continuing on an unannounced basis.[113]

Beijing's policy in the Diaoyutais/Senkakus is similar to its strategy in the South China Sea. It is maintaining a rigid position on the sovereignty of the islands, while willing to discuss, preferably bilaterally, peripheral issues of territorial usage. Meanwhile, China insists on keeping to itself definitions of sovereignty, which augurs ill for diplomacy succeeding in resolving East and South China Sea territorial disputes.

Another factor strengthening Beijing's inflexibility over these claims is China's increasing dependence on offshore mineral resources; Beijing's maritime economic stake is large and growing. This combination of extreme sensitivity to sovereignty issues and possible susceptibility to offshore economic pressure, should instigate in Beijing a drive to ensure that the PLAN is fully capable of defending China's interests.

3

China's Maritime Economic Interests

The PLAN's value as an instrument of statecraft is linked directly to the value of China's maritime economic stake. This includes the concentration of the nation's modern economic enterprises in the coastal regions, China's dependence on one of the world's largest fleet of merchant ships, and Beijing's interest in offshore energy supplies, primarily oil and gas.[1]

China is the world's fifth largest investor in offshore mining, and the China Association for Science and Technology describes the increasing requirement for energy as one of the nation's "five challenges" for the twenty-first century.[2] The value of offshore resources will continue to increase for China as its population, the world's largest at 1.3 billion, continues to grow and its economy continues to expand.[3]

Beijing is moving on several fronts to ensure that its burgeoning economy remains supplied with sufficient energy. First are the world's third largest coal reserves, the country's most widely used energy source, providing 71 percent of its energy consumption.[4] Coal, however, has troubling environmental and health effects.[5]

The second front involves offshore petroleum supplies. Another future source of seabed energy may be "natural gas [or methane gas] hydrate." This thick, waxy form of fossil fuel may be found in abundance in the seabed of the South and East China Seas. The technology to recover methane hydrate efficiently does not currently exist, however, primarily because of the depth (more than six hundred meters) at which it lies below the ocean floor and the problem of liquefying it for extraction.[6]

The third front is investigation and use of non–fossil fuel sources of energy, primarily nuclear power, but also including hydroelectric, wind, tidal, and biomass-fueled power.[7] Fourth is importing oil from other nations, and fifth, the large-scale campaign now underway to buy foreign oil fields, or at least their product.

With an annual output of 164 million tons, China is the world's fifth-largest oil producer. Approximately 90 percent of the country's oil comes from the Daqing field, but this source is expected to decline in future years. Other expected major sources, such as the Tarim Basin, have been disappointing. China has been a net importer of total petroleum since 1993. This imbalance will increase as industrialization continues, possibly by as much as five to tenfold.[8]

Offshore drilling is an appealing way for Beijing to make up for shortages in China's energy sources, but the process of exploration, discovery, and recovery of offshore petroleum reserves is lengthy and complex, as is getting the product to market economically. Furthermore, these reserves lie outside Beijing's normal military parameters; any threat to them would have to be met by naval and air forces.

China began large-scale development of offshore fields in 1969, with productive wells in the Bohai's Takang field, while drilling was underway in the East and South China Seas by 1973. Estimates of China's offshore petroleum reserves have varied widely, ranging from a U.S. Geological Survey estimate of 1 billion barrels, to a Chinese estimate of 130 billion barrels.[9] The situation for Beijing is further clouded by claims on portions of the continental shelf by North Korea, South Korea, Japan, Taiwan, and Vietnam. The Philippines, Brunei, Indonesia, and Malaysia also claim some of the potential reserves claimed by China.

Recovery of offshore resources is controlled by the state. Beijing reorganized this sector in the mid-1990s, promoting three state oil companies to the ministerial level directly under the State Economic and Trade Commission. These are the China National Petroleum Corporation (CNPC), the China National Petrochemical Corporation (Sinopec), and CNOOC. China's oil company officials have expressed concern that significant privatizing of state-owned enterprises might leave them unable to compete with foreign firms after China joins the World Trade Organization because WTO membership should force Beijing to remove the protective fence it has built around its oil industry.[10]

Maritime areas are currently providing between 5 and 10 percent of China's oil production and promise to provide more; Beijing is expecting an annual increase of about 20 percent in offshore oil and gas production between 2000 and 2005.[11] In the north, the Bohai seabed is estimated to contain more than 1.5 billion barrels of oil. The East China Sea also contains significant petroleum reserves, with production dating from 1998.[12] Farther south, the area off the Pearl River estuary (near Guangzhou) may produce almost 30,000 barrels per day when it reaches full capacity.[13] Finally, the South China Sea is currently producing oil from its northern areas in the Gulf of Tonkin and near Hainan Island, but suspected larger reserves near the Spratly Islands in the southern part of this sea have yet to be proven.

Natural gas is the second source of fuel from offshore reserves. China's annual consumption of natural gas is estimated to increase 30 billion cubic meters by 2005, and perhaps 50 billion cubic meters by 2010. The country may possess 33 trillion cubic meters of natural gas, of which only 1.7 trillion have so far been found; offshore fields may contain a significant percentage of these suspected reserves.[14] The South China Sea is a major source of this clean-burning, high-quality form of energy, with four separate fields identified. Hong Kong already receives, via pipelines, 3.4 billion cubic meters annually from the Nanyacheng 13-1 field off the coast of Hainan Island, and China is preparing to build its first natural gas liquefaction terminal in Shenzhen, between Guangzhou and Hong Kong, in recognition of the South China Sea's potential.[15]

Two natural gas fields are also operating in the East China Sea, within four hundred kilometers of Shanghai. They currently provide the city with 400 million cubic meters of natural gas annually, a figure expected to increase to 1.2 billion cubic meters by 2010. Further north, a gas field in the Bohai provides 400 million cubic meters of natural gas to a chemical fertilizer plant, and it will increase production to 700 million cubic meters by 2010.[16]

Beijing's reliance on offshore petroleum and natural gas reserves makes their defense a national security issue, and clearly a concern for the PLAN. These energy sources are located throughout China's continental shelf, extending more than 4,000 kilometers from Korea to Vietnam. The shelf is delineated by the 200-meter curve (water depth), 125 to 450 kilometers from China's coastline. This adds up to a huge Chinese continental shelf area of approximately 1.2 million square kilometers.

National Policy

Beijing stated at the end of 1999 that the nation would continue to depend on fossil fuels for the majority of its energy needs.[17] China imported almost 20 percent of its consumption of oil products in 1999, and Beijing is obviously concerned about China's shift from energy exporter to energy importer.[18] This concern was exacerbated by a drop of 3.3 percent in domestic energy production in 1998, while electrical output increased by 2.5 percent.[19] Chen Geng, deputy director of the State Petroleum and Chemical Industries Bureau, cited increased energy demand of approximately 4 percent per year when he listed corrective steps the government was inaugurating:

> The country will continue to exploit domestic and overseas natural gas reserves, to include possible pipelines with Russia.
>
> "Technical innovation" will be used to increase Chinese recovery of petroleum assets. This effort will include a nationally directed program of "science and technology projects" to increase oil and gas development in the twenty-first century. The Bohai fields were cited for increased production as a result of technologically advanced methodology.[20]
>
> The domestic pipeline network will be expanded to speed up the distribution of these expanded energy resources, especially natural gas.[21]
>
> Beijing will initiate a national strategic reserve program, to stockpile fuel in case of emergency.
>
> China will pursue additional overseas petroleum resources, including Central Asia, Russia, Africa, and Latin America, in addition to the Middle East.[22]
>
> Beijing will allow greater profits for the state-owned oil sector companies.
>
> Beijing also promises to deregulate some aspects of its petroleum industry, in an effort to attract more foreign investors.

Chen announced that the government "would no longer set mandatory production targets and get directly involved in product distribution" but would give that decision-making power to company management. The intent is to give freer play to market forces in the energy industry.[23] While seeking new international sources of petroleum, the government also wants to maximize the recovery of China's own energy resources to reduce foreign dependence.

Hence, the early 1999 decision to increase state-directed exploration efforts in offshore areas, especially those thought to contain significant natural gas deposits. CNOOC, China's largest oil and natural gas producer, has the lead in this effort. Promising fields in the South and East China Seas and the Yellow Sea have been identified and prioritized for further development.[24] The president of CNOOC, Wei Liucheng, estimates China's total offshore oil and gas resources at 25 billion tons and 14 trillion cubic meters, respectively. He stated that the company would invest $57.5 million in 2000 to develop additional offshore oil and gas fields, primarily in Bohai and the South China Sea.[25] The company budgeted for a 17.5 percent increase in offshore oil production in 2000, at an investment cost of $556 million.[26]

Offshore Oil Fields

There are seven ocean "basins" wholly or partially contained within China's continental shelf. From north to south, they are the Bohai, North Yellow Sea, South Yellow Sea, East China Sea, Pearl River Mouth, Beibu (Tonkin) Gulf, and South China Sea Basins.[27] Petroleum fields have been found in all of these basins, and the nation's continental shelf has yet to be fully explored.

The Bohai fields currently are China's most important offshore energy resource area, with annual production of 2.1 million tons of oil and 367 million cubic meters of natural gas.[28] "Proven reserves" of 66 million tons of petroleum and 10 billion cubic meters of natural gas are estimated.[29]

The East China Sea is a newer resource of petroleum products for China, especially natural gas. Discoveries indicate reserves of approximately 150 billion cubic meters, which are already providing the primary energy source for Shanghai and "major industrialized cities" in Zhejiang Province.

There are currently six producing gas fields and twenty-three specific gas-bearing structures in the South China Sea.[30] The most productive area for China has been the Pearl River Mouth Basin, in the northern part of the South China Sea. Fields in this area had a total annual output of 13 million tons in 1998, making it the fourth largest source of petroleum for China.[31]

Foreign companies are playing a significant role in all of China's efforts to recover offshore energy.[32] A survey of new major onshore and offshore energy projects in China reveals consistent involvement of non-Chinese companies, usually up to the 50 percent mark. Since 1979, Beijing has "cooperated" with more than fifty foreign companies in exploring for offshore petroleum.[33] Wei emphasized China's continuing need for foreign participation in recovering these resources, noting that China currently has "over 130 contracts with over 70 oil companies from 18 countries and regions" in joint development efforts, with total foreign investments of $6.4 billion.[34]

Beijing is allocating a significant portion of a crucial economic sector to foreign companies, several of them from the United States, which of course maintains the strongest naval presence in East Asia. Hence, the calculus of a Sino-American crisis could involve the United States planning the evacuation of American oil company employees on a Chinese-owned oil platform, located in international waters being defended by PLAN warships. This would not be a comfortable scenario for either navy.

The South China Sea is China's only contested area of known energy reserves. It is an oceanic "lake" surrounded by seven other nations, most of whom claim part or all of the sea's resources.[35] Beijing's ability to garner those resources may rest directly on the ability of its navy to enforce its national claims.

Total oil production from the South China Sea in 1998 was more than 1.3 million barrels per day, from proven reserves of approximately 7.5 billion barrels. Almost all of this came from the uncontested northern area of the sea.[36] There are no proven reserves for the Spratly or Paracel Islands, and no commercially recoverable oil or gas has been discovered there. Geologists and analysts disagree on the presence (and recoverability) of petroleum reserves near these islands, estimates varying widely.[37]

Estimates of the petroleum reserves in the South China Sea range from Beijing's wildly optimistic 213 billion barrels (105 in the area of the Spratlys) to a U.S. estimate of 28 billion barrels (2.1 in the Spratlys).[38] A similar range of estimates exists for natural gas reserves, about which the Chinese are also optimistic, offering an estimate of more than 2,000 trillion cubic feet, whereas the U.S. estimate is a more modest 266 trillion cubic feet.[39] China's belief in these estimates is more important than their dubious accuracy, and Beijing's high expectations strengthen its determination to protect its sovereignty claims in the Spratly Islands.[40]

More than 50 million tons of crude oil have been produced since the first well began pumping in 1990, and production expands annually, as additional wells are installed.[41] The history of the Lufeng 22-1 oil field, located in the northern South China Sea, illustrates the difficulties recovering petroleum reserves from the area: the petroleum in these fields is typically located in high porosity sandstone and is waxy in texture, which requires extraordinary drilling and recovery methods. Additionally, they are located in a prime area of tropical cyclones. These historically have had an average duration of twenty-six hours, generating a wave height of up to eight meters. Force 6 winds and extremely rough seas are also common to the area. Specialized tankers have been designed and built to transport this field's product to the mainland—tankers that presumably would require PLAN protection in times of international crisis.[42]

The western sea area also promises to become a significant natural gas source, with four fields and fifteen gas-bearing structures expected.[43] These fields are expected to provide 3 billion cubic meters of gas by 2005, and 6 billion by 2010.[44]

Beijing's 1992 law brings it into direct contention with the other claimants to South China Sea resources. PLAN forces have regularly deployed to the Paracel Islands since the early 1970s, and to the Spratly Islands since the early 1980s. A military presence had been established on six of the islands by 1989.

Oil Imports and Exports

In addition to using foreign investment and technological know-how to extract energy from offshore reserves, Beijing is pursuing an active campaign to secure energy supplies from international sources, with oil imports growing at an average rate of 9 percent annually since 1993.[45] Dependence on imported oil will increase as the economic growth rate climbs; annual growth rates of 7 percent might require

China to import 45 percent of its petroleum requirements by 2010. Lower growth rates would of course reduce this percentage, but would not reverse China's reliance on imported petroleum.[46]

Beijing's goal is reportedly an annual overseas oil capacity of 50 million tons annually.[47] Transnational oil production has been secured from Southeast Asia, Central Asia, Russia, the Middle East, and Latin America. The CNPC holds oil concessions in Canada, Kazakhstan, Venezuela, Peru, Sudan, Iraq—and the United States, where it purchased ninety-eight old oil wells in Texas.[48] Investments also have been made in the petroleum production industries of Bangladesh, Burma, Colombia, Ecuador, Indonesia, Iran, Malaysia, Mexico, Mongolia, Nigeria, Pakistan, Papua New Guinea, Thailand, and Venezuela.[49] Crude oil imports are primarily from Southwest Asia (53.1 percent) and Southeast Asia (36.1 percent).[50]

Despite Beijing's campaigns to secure energy supplies around the world, the Middle East will remain China's primary source of overseas oil. That region contains the world's largest proven petroleum deposits, with 65 percent of the global total, and also offer the world's lowest recovery cost, one-tenth of that in China, by one estimate.[51] China imported almost 17 million tons of oil from Middle Eastern countries in 1997, more than 40 percent of the total imported, and the total has increased each year since then.[52]

A recent report by China's Strategy and Management Society emphasized the security aspects of this relationship, urging that China adjust its policies in "political, diplomatic, economic, and trade fields" to ensure that "Middle East oil will be provided to China for a long time to come." Direct purchases of oil are being supplemented by Beijing's agreements with Iraq and Iran to exploit specific fields for China's benefit.[53] Continuing dependence on Middle Eastern oil means "China must strategically make appropriate arrangements and preparations in the political, diplomatic, economic, and even military aspects, in order for this supply to be accessible on a reliable and secure basis. [China must be able to] guarantee unimpeded passage through the international oil routes" for this oil. Finally, "militarily speaking, China must make necessary arrangements for the safe supply of energy for itself."[54] The PLAN's role in this mission is obvious.

The use of foreign investment exposes China to foreign influence, an important factor, as energy resources lie at the heart of continued economic growth, which in turn directly affects regime legitimacy.

World Trade Organization membership may further increase dependence on imported oil, because it will then be even less expensive than the domestically produced product.[55]

Relying on foreign sources of energy will also pose strategic problems for China. Russia is unstable and economically bereft; one of the reasons that such huge reserves of oil and natural gas are present in Siberia is that they are expensive and the region lacks the infrastructure for their recovery. Central Asia is also shadowed by political uncertainty, lack of infrastructure, and high costs of doing business. Finally, the Middle East is politically complex, to say the least, and a mix of unreliable dictatorships, religious and ethnic fault lines, and political hot spots.

From a strategic perspective, the problem may be even worse than Beijing believes because the International Energy Agency estimated in March 2000 that China's long-term oil import requirements will actually be three times Beijing's estimates by 2020. Oil imports are expected to increase by approximately 30 percent (to about 45 million tons) in 2000 alone.[56]

Alternate Energy Sources

Coal currently provides about three-fourths of China's energy.[57] In addition to oil and gas, China is pursuing other sources of power, including water, solar, wind, geothermal, tidal, and biomass sources.[58] Commercial nuclear power was inaugurated in 1990, and its use is growing, although at a slow pace, with the three plants currently in operation providing approximately 1 percent of the nation's electricity. The nuclear power industry is strictly governed by the state, under several agencies.[59]

Beijing's long-range goal is to have nuclear power-generating capacity provide approximately 4 percent of China's energy needs by 2050, with more than a dozen provinces participating in this growth cycle.[60] Beijing's plan includes four nuclear power stations that began construction in 2000, all of them located in coastal areas, in recognition of the rapid economic growth occurring in those provinces.[61] This relatively modest increase in nuclear power generating capacity is being pursued with significant Russian assistance.[62] As of December 2000, however, discussions of Sino-Russian ventures in this sensitive field were far from reaching fruition.

No matter what the energy source, distribution of the power produced must be addressed. China's economic imbalance, with energy-
consumers concentrated in the eastern region of the country and
primary energy sources located in northeast and northwest China,
exacerbates the power distribution problem for Beijing.[63] Offshore
energy sources offer a partial solution to this problem of providing
power to Shanghai, Guangdong, and other areas of dynamic economic growth.[64]

Shipping

The PLAN also has a strategic interest in oceanic trade, in view of
China's increasing dependency on foreign trade and energy sources,
and its rapidly growing merchant marine.[65] As much as 50 percent of
China's economy depends on foreign trade, about 90 percent of
which is transported by ship. China's large and growing merchant
fleet calls at more than six hundred ports in more than 150 countries.[66] The maritime environment also directly impacts China's serious and increasing resource problems, especially energy and food,
both of which depend on the sea. China relies on tankers for almost
all its crucial oil imports, while it annually imports millions of tons of
grain by sea.[67]

The PLAN mission most directly tied to this vital economic sector
is SLOC defense. The navy must safeguard sea lanes in Beijing's
claimed territorial waters, which requires a brown/green-water navy
in the Yellow Sea, in the East China Sea west of the Japan-Philippines line, and in the South China Sea. The PLAN may possess the assets to defend its brown-water SLOCs—those within one hundred
nautical miles of its coast—but the next level of SLOC protection includes those sea lanes that extend throughout East Asia, from the Sea
of Japan to the Andaman Sea west of Malacca. The PLAN's ability to
defend these green-water SLOCs is more problematical.[68]

Finally, long-range SLOC protection would involve defending sea
lanes throughout the East China Sea and South Asian waters, including the Indian Ocean, the North Arabian Sea, and perhaps even
the Persian Gulf and Red Sea. The PLAN possesses little ability to
defend SLOCs west of Malacca or in other blue-water areas, and there
is very little evidence that Beijing is moving significantly to improve
this capability.

PLAN operations in the Indian Ocean may not be tasked to a specific fleet, but the South Sea Fleet's area of responsibility (AOR) includes the eastern approaches to the Indonesian Straits—Makassar, Sunda, Lombok, and Malacca—that control the SLOCs into the Indian Ocean.[69] China's primary maritime concern west of Malacca is maintenance of the Indian Ocean SLOCs, vital to China's international trade, highlighted by oil imports from the Persian Gulf.[70] Defending China's SLOCs is a vital national interest for Beijing in view of increasing dependency on foreign trade and energy sources and its rapidly growing merchant marine.

Fisheries

China has been the world's biggest producer of seafood since 1990, with more than 160,000 fishing boats manned by more than one million fishermen.[71] Beijing has worked actively with the UN to develop its recent Fish Stocks Agreement, aiming to prevent areas from being overfished, and has undertaken independent action to conserve fisheries.[72] In view of a 17 percent drop in marine fishing output in 1998 for China, Beijing instituted a plan of "zero growth" for fishing in 1999. This followed a series of annual fishing bans imposed since 1995 along China's coasts, for which Beijing claims "remarkable" results.[73]

China's periodic fishing bans in the Yellow and East China Seas have achieved results, but their effectiveness in the South China Sea has been limited by the lack of cooperation by the other nations bordering that body of water, although Taiwan appears to be cooperating.[74] Furthermore, Beijing's fish-conservation efforts appear not to be welcome by coastal provincial governments that rely heavily on ocean resources.[75] The most recent ban in the South China Sea began on 1 June 2000 and reportedly was being enforced by "296 fishery management ships" under the aegis of the Ministry of Agriculture's Fishery Bureau.[76]

China was a party to fourteen significant fishing disputes between 1994 and 1997, involving Russia, Japan, North Korea, South Korea, Taiwan, the Philippines, Indonesia, Vietnam, and Thailand.[77] Some of these problems have threatened to turn into a "cod war" reminiscent of that between Iceland and Great Britain in the 1970s, especially recent clashes between Chinese fishing boats and Philippine patrol vessels. None have so far directly involved the PLAN.

In addition to disputes over their maritime boundary, China and Japan signed a bilateral fisheries treaty in 1997 but did not reach agreement until May 2000 to implement the pact, beginning 1 June 2000. The treaty establishes a "fisheries zoning line" at 127° 30' east longitude in the East China Sea: six hundred Chinese boats a year will be allowed to fish east of this line.[78] Even before the implementation date, Beijing announced that its fishery administration fleet—not the PLAN—would be responsible for enforcing the pact in the East China Sea.[79]

China is also negotiating with South Korea to establish a bilateral treaty to conserve Yellow Sea fisheries and to continue the Yellow Sea Marine Ecosystem Preservation Project, begun in 1991.[80] The China Maritime Safety Administration (MSA) and the South Korean Ministry of Maritime and Fishery did agree after the Second Sino-Korean Sea Safety Cooperation Meeting in May 2000, to "deepen their understanding of each other's safety rules [to] facilitate bilateral trade."[81] A fisheries agreement is also under negotiation, with talks ongoing.[82]

China is likely to remain a net energy importer. Barring some massive petroleum discovery, the country's dependence on imported oil and natural gas will continue to increase annually. This in turn will increase the importance of the SLOCs over which petroleum products flow. None are more important than those from the Middle East, but none are longer or pose a more difficult problem for a maritime planner. The PLAN is not capable of exerting even presence, let alone control, over these widely flung SLOCs. Beijing will not be able to rely on its Navy to protect its vital SLOCs, unless the PLAN is dramatically increased. There is no evidence of that, however, which means that China will have to engage a range of diplomatic and economic measures to ensure a steady supply of energy resources.

Conserving and maintaining adequate fisheries also poses a complex international problem for China. The PLAN can play a role in the Yellow, East China, and South China Seas, but Beijing will have to rely on diplomatic, economic, and international environmental conservation efforts to ensure its fair share of diminishing ocean protein.

The PLAN's role in China's significant efforts to garner offshore resources has been marginal at most. The Navy has an active oceanographic research program, with major implications for commercial application. It has conducted extensive surveying operations on China's continental shelf, for instance, albeit more likely for operational reasons such as preparing for submarine and ASW operations, than for finding resources.[83] Nonetheless, the PLAN's presence in China's claimed territorial waters underlies the sovereignty that allows China to benefit from the sea's resources.

China has developed a "marine high technology" plan devoted to both military and civilian economic ends. This project entered the "863 Program" in 1996 because of its "far-reaching strategic significance for protecting China's maritime rights and interests, developing a marine economy, furthering marine S&T development, and building a stronger China." The project focuses on technology-intensive maritime territorial investigations, marine petroleum exploration and development, bio-resources development, and marine environmental surveillance and warning. Particularly highlighted is "marine detection technology," including navigation and positioning systems; shipborne radar and global positioning system; and various sensor technology, including satellite optical, electronic, acoustical, and bottom-array systems.[84]

China today is among the most dependent of nations on ocean resources for food, energy, and trade. This places the PLAN in a position of major responsibility for the nation's security and well-being, although its ability to fulfill this responsibility is questionable.

4

PLAN Establishment

The PLAN was downsized as part of Beijing's 1985 decision to reduce the size of the PLA.[1] Its strength was approximately 270,000 personnel in 1995, about 9 percent of the overall PLA's strength. At the end of 1998, PLAN strength was 250,000 personnel, or about 10 percent of the PLA's total strength. This number was scheduled for a further 10 percent reduction by mid-2000 as part of the three-year, 500,000-man cut in PLA strength announced by Jiang Zemin in 1997.[2] This downsizing is part of the effort to reorganize the PLA for future warfare, in which personnel skill and technological competence count more than mass.

This program is solid evidence of Beijing's determination to field a PLA for the twenty-first century. Most important, active duty PLA forces will become quantitatively smaller, with an emphasis on technological quality. A link to Maoist People's War will remain, as reserves and the People's Armed Police (PAP) increase in size. Although the PLA will retain many existing weapons, significant resources will be devoted to developing new tactics and techniques to defeat a high-technology enemy. Hence, only limited amounts of foreign weapons and equipment will be introduced into the forces; the indigenous Chinese defense industry will be the source of the majority of modern weapons. The PLA will try to develop capabilities that emphasize rapid response and joint operations, focusing on precision attack, air operations, naval operations, information warfare, and space operations. This will require developing command and control organizations to better manage the demands of future warfare.[3]

Since the majority of this reduction will affect the Army, the Navy's percentage of overall PLA strength should increase. These points will affect the Navy's administrative and operational practices, but are not likely to require changes to basic fleet organization. Furthermore, comparatively speaking, the Navy is not manpower-intensive but relies heavily on its equipment.

. In fact, downsizing to "buy" quality at the expense of quantity should be favored by the PLAN, since its technology-intensive forces cannot be effective without relatively bright, highly trained crews operating its sophisticated systems. A more capable Navy should gain a larger share of available military resources to support advanced equipment.

Although the PLAN is and will almost certainly remain the smallest of China's conventional armed services, it may exert influence in PLA policy determination out of proportion to its size. This is evidenced by the fact that the PLAN probably receives as much as one-third of the PLA budget, although it comprises no more than about 13 percent of the two million PLA personnel.[4]

PLAN size is only one indicator of its importance in Beijing's view; its strategic missions should make the PLAN commander an important military participant in the national security policy apparatus. While he probably is as influential as his nominal equals—the heads of the PLAAF, the Second Artillery, and China's seven military regions —his actual influence is likely tied directly to specific maritime missions and/or to the degree of crisis felt about the strategic issue of the moment.[5]

PLAN Role

Adm. Shi Yunsheng rose to command of the PLAN through a series of important operational and administrative assignments. He is a naval aviator and served in senior positions in both the North and South Sea Fleets, including command of the PLANAF forces that participated in the 1988 battles against Vietnam in the South China Sea.[6]

Shi has to "wear more than one hat" as PLAN commander. First, as the senior officer in the PLAN, he is responsible for directing the operational tasking of the Navy in accordance with the determination of national security objectives. The most important facet of this responsibility is ensuring that the PLAN is ready to fulfill its role in national tasking ranging from combating piracy to preparing for various operational options regarding Taiwan.

In late October or early November, naval headquarters in Beijing nominates to the CMC countries to be visited by PLAN ships during the following calendar year. Nominations are based on visits the PLAN Headquarters or fleet commanders think will serve Chinese and PLAN purposes. These employment plans are submitted to the First Office of the Ministry of Defense for vetting and, if approved, to the CMC for approval.

After national approval is gained, ship selection and preparation is the responsibility of the Navy offices and fleet headquarters designated by PLAN Headquarters. Typical preparations for a significant foreign deployment would include ship selection from different fleets, to pick the most operationally ready and best looking ships, as well as those with the most proficient commanding officers (CO). An effort is also made to "share the wealth" among the fleets, by rewarding those units that have performed unusually well. Once selected, the ships' COs and crews are "frozen" to ensure continuity throughout the special deployment. Additional crewmen and officers are also usually assigned to increase the number of personnel benefiting from the special deployment (a procedure especially followed in the case of the 1997 PLAN deployment to North and South America). The ships are assigned a dedicated supply officer to help them prepare for the deployment, may receive special training for a particularly long deployment, and their crews receive cultural familiarization lectures.[7]

Second, as representative of the PLAN in Beijing, Shi serves as advocate for his service in the resource allocation process—in PLA budget battles, in other words. His personal effectiveness in this role is not easily discernible, since current major equipment modernization programs such as the acquisition of *Kilo*-class submarines, *Sovremenny*-class destroyers, *Song*-class submarines, Ukrainian-built gas turbine engines, and various foreign weapons and fire-control systems, were initiated before he assumed his present office. Hence, as of mid-2000 the PLAN under Shi's command has not significantly increased the number of ships or aircraft it operates.

Third, and perhaps more significant than continuing equipment modernization, are the organizational changes that have occurred since Shi assumed office in 1997. A particularly significant change is the ongoing restructuring of the training and education establishment, from officer accession to ship-crew training. The PLAN also operates its own academic research institute (the Naval Research Institute) and equipment research institute (the Naval Research Center) in Beijing, which follow the direction of the Navy commander. The Naval Equipment Improvement and Research Center was established in 1983 to conduct research, development, and evaluation of naval equipment. The Research Center develops doctrine and strategy.[8]

The PLAN is emulating U.S. reserve officer training corps (ROTC) programs for producing well-educated, technically oriented candidate officers.[9] Agreements are being signed between MR headquarters and civilian universities located in their respective military regions through which the university receives compensation for producing military officer candidates.[10]

The Navy is pursuing an especially ambitious ROTC-type program, with the goal of producing one thousand officers a year, 40 percent of the PLAN officer corps, from civilian universities by 2010. These civilian university programs will be linked to the military academy structure, probably to maintain control of the ideological as well as the subject-matter content of the "civilian" program.[11]

The Navy is also participating in the general overhaul of PLA service academies, following Jiang Zemin's demand that academy education "strengthen the military through science and technology."[12] In Wuhan, the former Navy Engineering Academy and Navy Electronics Engineering Academy have been merged into the Engineering University of the Navy. The new school, established in June 1999, reportedly awards undergraduate degrees and has graduate programs in thirty-five subjects.[13] The university's thirteen departments seem to focus on advanced technological areas that address the putative "revolution in military affairs" (RMA), including warship kinetic engineering, electronic information and naval arms engineering, and command and electronic warfare engineering.[14]

Fourth, education for ships' crews previously occurred almost entirely aboard ship. Within the past decade, however, the PLAN has created more centralized schools and training facilities to help teach personnel how to operate modern shipboard systems.

These new schools and training centers are operated by each fleet's naval base commands, and have been established to teach engineering, surface warfare, ship handling, aviation operations, submarine warfare, and medical operations, in addition to addressing specific equipment systems. The East Sea Fleet, at least, also has established a petty-officer leadership school, in Shanghai, which draws its students from ship and aircraft squadron personnel who have reenlisted.[15]

Fifth, in the unglamorous but vital area of logistics, the PLAN has been trying to modernize its support systems during Shi Yunsheng's term in office. He has devoted considerable attention to improving the Navy's General Logistics Command. Shi is reportedly building a "modern logistic support system."[16] The new system includes oil and water supply systems for the fleet, as well as improving the capabilities and utilization of surveying, salvage, transport, and hospital ships. Improved ship maintenance is being pursued, as is better support for equipment maintenance and repair.[17]

Shi is also working to implement the PLA's General Logistics Department's plan to establish a joint logistics service for all services in order to improve the timeliness and effectiveness of PLA logistics, including privatization of some parts of the system.[18] Under this plan, currently being implemented to include creation of joint "naval-air-ground rapid-response logistics units," the Navy will remain responsible for specific requirements linked to operations at sea, such as providing shipboard supplies and harbor facilities.[19]

This program includes reorganizing the naval base structure to improve management and the availability of supplies both afloat and ashore. The new logistics organization will apparently continue relying on a three-level structure: PLAN headquarters, fleet headquarters, and naval base.[20] More important than the bureaucratic structure, however, is the way in which operational units interact with the replacement-parts management system. Very little is known about the mundane but important question of how an operating unit in the PLAN obtains replacement parts on both a routine and an emergent basis. If a radar on board a ship fails, for instance, how long does it take for that ship's technician to obtain the necessary replacement part? Is it carried on board the ship? Does it remain in a warehouse at the ship's home naval base or in a warehouse in Beijing? Or does the part have to be shipped from the factory where it is manufactured?

The new logistics system presumably addresses this issue, in addition to aiming to improve provisioning, repair and maintenance, medical care, and technical systems support of naval units and activities in China. There is no firm evidence that the PLAN is establishing such facilities abroad.[21]

Sixth, Shi Yunsheng presumably is expected to wear a joint (or "purple," in U.S. parlance) hat as a senior member of China's military hierarchy. The importance of ensuring the close coordination of efforts by all services—joint warfare—was brought home to the PLA by the allied victory against Iraq in Desert Storm in 1991. To further jointness, Shi must subsume PLAN priorities within national defense plans that may reduce the Navy's share of defense resources.

This "hat" is probably more complex for senior PLA officers than for their foreign counterparts because of the relationship between the CCP and the PLA: maintaining a "party army" strains the process of military modernization. "Red" versus "expert" is an overdrawn expression, but increasing military professionalism is clearly one of Beijing's goals and is not likely facilitated by the continuing priority placed on ensuring an ideologically oriented military loyal to the CCP. In other words, Shi Yunsheng must not only be "purple," he must also be "Red."[22]

Seventh, Shi represents China in his relations with foreign navies. He has traveled to the United States, most recently in April 2000, and in November 1999 he made a trip to France and Egypt accompanied by his East Sea Fleet commander. This may simply represent tasking from the CMC, but it also reflects Shi's personal interest in foreign navies and a degree of cosmopolitanism perhaps not common among all senior PLA commanders.[23]

These seven points indicate that Shi Yunsheng has been an active Navy chief, but evaluating his effectiveness requires information that is difficult to access, given the opaqueness of PLA headquarters. There are factors arguing in favor of his limitations as commander. First, he had a hard act to follow: with the retirement in September 1997 of Liu Huaqing as CMC vice chairman, the PLAN (and its commander) lost an advocate at the highest level of China's defense establishment. Liu certainly wore purple and Red hats, but he is also the father of the current modernizing process in the PLAN. Shi does not have Liu's stature because of his lack of a personal relationship with Jiang

Zemin (Shi must, however, hold Jiang's confidence, because the CMC chairman would have the final vote on selecting the Navy's commander), lack of similar experience in the PLA, and because of his relatively junior rank among the heads of the services.[24] Writing circa 1997, Michael Swaine credits the PLAN with "behaving as a quasi-independent bureaucratic actor . . . pushing for a greater recognition of its institutional viewpoint in the senior levels of the PLA leadership, with significant success . . . as the major . . . proponent of the creation of a technologically sophisticated, operationally versatile blue water force," although he notes that the "pace and direction of naval modernization remains a major subject of debate" among PLA leaders, with the PLAN viewpoint "often challenged by the ground forces orientation of the [General Staff Department] GSD."[25] Within the Navy itself, Shi's effectiveness may be limited by the fact that he has spent his entire operational career in aviation units, and has had no shipboard experience.[26]

Force Structure and Organization

Admiral Shi has categorized the PLAN force structure as comprising five "major arms systems": naval surface vessel units, naval submarine units, naval aviation units, naval coastal defense units, and the Marine Corps.[27]

The PLAN commander is headquartered in Beijing, with the Navy's political commissar, usually his equivalent in rank). Nominally, the commander and political commissar are also equivalent in authority.[28] There are three vice admirals as deputy commanders of the PLAN, as well as two deputy commissars, a vice admiral, and a rear admiral. The former includes personnel affairs among his duties, while the latter serves as PLAN inspector general.[29]

The PLAN headquarters is organized into four departments. The Headquarters and Political Departments are headed by vice admirals, the Logistics and Equipment Departments by rear admirals. A fifth department is formed by PLANAF Headquarters, headed by a vice admiral. Management of the personnel system is an important function within the Political Department, where it is directed by a rear admiral with a direct line of communication to the PLAN political commissar. This office manages the PLAN officer promotion system, which uses a system of committees.

PLAN officers are commissioned at the naval base level. The academy commander (if they are naval academy graduates) signs their diplomas; the commander and the political commissar of the naval base at which they are first stationed following graduation sign their commissions.

A personnel committee at their parent naval base considers officers with the seniority and qualifications to be considered for promotion to lieutenant, lieutenant commander, and commander for promotion. The base political commissar chairs the committee; the base commander (usually a senior captain) has the authority to approve the promotion of those selected. Hence, the promotion system, as it does in most navies, gives a shore commander rather than a seagoing commander the authority to promote or not promote officers stationed in operational fleet units. If the PLAN conforms to common naval practice, however, a seagoing officer's promotability is strongly affected by reports of efficiency from his/her operational commander. Moreover, the base commanders likely have had several successful assignments at sea, or they would not have been promoted to their senior rank and selected for such responsible positions.

The role played by the unit political commissar in officer promotion is important: officer evaluations are undoubtedly based on estimates of both ideological reliability and professional expertise, but the balance between the two is not clear. Some analysts of the PLA believe that professional performance is increasingly important, and that the political commissar's job is increasingly that of a personnel manager and "human resources" specialist, rather than ideological policeman—although that role certainly remains. A committee headed by the fleet political commissar makes selection for promotion to the rank of captain at each of the three geographic fleets. The fleet commander has the authority to approve the promotions of the officers selected.

Promotion nominations to the ranks of senior captain, rear admiral, and vice admiral occur at PLAN headquarters. The PLAN political commissar nominally chairs the selection committee, which forwards the senior captain and various admiral promotion nominations to a CMC-level office or committee for final approval. Promotions to full admiral are rare and almost certainly a matter for the CMC. The entire PLAN officer selection and promotion system for vice admiral and below is overseen by the Committee of the CCP of the Navy for Promotions and Major Policies, chaired by the PLAN commander.[30]

This is a complex process, but not noticeably more so than that employed in other militaries. The promotion system is notable, however, for the important role assigned to the CCP as managers of the PLAN officer corps.

Headquarters Department

The Headquarters Department is arguably the most important of the four PLAN departments in Beijing, as it is through this department that the chain of command runs to the three operational fleets. Within the Headquarters Department are one office and four second-level departments, each headed by a senior captain.

The General Office includes seven departments, among which are Military Strategic Studies, which focuses on long-range planning and strategy; Political-Military Affairs, which is organized into global geographic sections; Military Assistants, which provides and coordinates the activities of administrative and executive assistants to senior PLAN officers in the headquarters; and Operations, which performs the planning function for future fleet operations.

The first of the four second-level Headquarters departments is the Operations Department, which transmits—and probably formulates —operational tasking directly to the three fleets. The third is the Intelligence Department, which is organized into regional divisions— Western Hemisphere, Europe, Asia, West Asia, Africa—and performs the PLAN headquarters intelligence function. There are also Planning and Secretarial divisions. This office probably provides intelligence both up, to the PLAN commander, and down, to the fleet. The PLAN Intelligence Office's relationship to the CMC/PLA intelligence hierarchy is not clear.

The fourth department, Training, contains three sections. These are responsible for PLAN academies (surface, subsurface, aviation) and other officer schools.[31] The Training Department also manages enlisted and officer equipment classroom training and probably is the PLAN's primary point of contact with the GSD for training matters.

The PLAN's Training Department's relationships with the GSD Training Department and with the geographic fleets' Training Departments are unclear. If the PLAN resembles the PLAAF in this regard, it participates in a GSD annual training conference that delineates the next year's training objectives. In past years, the GSD has stressed general themes that run through more specific training tasks. In 1994, joint operations were emphasized; the 1995 plan repeated that emphasis, but added "a call for increased ideological education."

Each service is assigned guidelines in the annual training plan. In 1995, for instance, the PLAN was instructed to "train by separate ship types and flight units at separate levels. Training will focus on individual ships, based on combat mission requirements and actual use of weapons. Strengthen multi-ship, multi-arms and CPX [command and control] training [and] will emphasize training on new equipment. Units with new ships and aircraft will be organized to train together. Units with new equipment will conduct live-firing exercises and annual tests."[32] This seems to provide very useful and practical direction from the PLAN Training Department's perspective: it offers guidance without restrictive control, and allows the PLAN to "flesh out" the annual training plan to ensure that the Navy's operational objectives are met. Headquarters presumably then passes the plan to the geographic fleets for execution—probably following additional modification at that level. Since each fleet faces a different subregion, each should have specific training requirements.[33]

Finally, the Headquarters Department includes the Military Affairs Department, the organization responsible for developing naval doctrine, writing and promulgating regulations, overseeing naval publications in general, and organizational structure (including recruiting). It would logically have a strong relationship with counterpart CMC departments, but that is not clear.

For instance, does the Military Affairs Department receive tasking directly from the CMC, or does its direction come strictly through PLAN headquarters? Does the Military Affairs Department receive input from the fleet and naval colleges? The Naval Command Academy at Nanjing has an operational (experimental) cell with the East Sea Fleet, which would furnish a logical path for recommendations about doctrinal and tactical development to reach PLAN headquarters from the fleet. Additionally, is recruiting coordinated at the CMC level to ensure an equitable distribution of available manpower among the various PLA services?

Political Department

The second of the PLAN's Beijing departments is the Political Department, which serves the PLAN's political commissar as his avenue to fleet and unit commissars. It is divided into at least one office and four second-level departments: the General Office and the Personnel, Propaganda, Cultural Affairs, and Military Court Departments. Each of these organizations is replicated in the geographic fleet headquarters. The Political Department provides, on paper, a duplicative chain of command throughout the PLAN, which may be as much at the service of the PLAN commander as it is the PLAN's political commissar.

Logistics Department

The Logistics Department includes at least nine second-level departments: Headquarters Office and Supply, Financial, Ordnance, Civil Engineering, Communication and Transportation, Medical (divided into Hospitals and Public Health Bureaus), Port Management, Material and Petroleum, and Production Management. These bear the responsibility for ensuring that the Navy's shore establishment supports the operating units. It is also responsible for the PLAN's logistics reorganization currently in progress.

This department has important personnel responsibilities, as well: the Civil Engineering Department is in charge of family housing construction and maintenance. The Financial Department must ensure an efficient pay and benefits structure for Navy personnel. The role of the Medical Department includes both the PLAN medical care system of clinics and hospitals, as well as medical care in operational units at sea and distant installations, such as the South China Sea island outposts.

Equipment Department

The Equipment Department includes second-level departments for Development, Construction, and Repair—each containing specific sections responsible for surface, subsurface, and aviation systems. Additionally, there is an Employment Management Bureau, and Equipment Technology, Equipment Repairs, and Science and Technology Departments, as well as the Center for Equipment Feasibility (probably within the Naval Research Center).[34] This department also manages PLAN weapons and test ranges, including the Underwater Ordnance Testing Ground off Shanghai and the missile and gunnery testing range near the Liaodong Peninsula.

The fifth department is the PLANAF. The chain of command from Navy Headquarters runs through the Headquarters Department to the three operating fleets, but the vice admiral commanding the

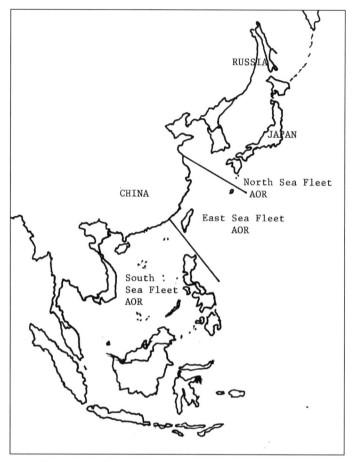

PLAN fleet areas of responsibility   BERNARD D. COLE

Navy's air force reports directly to the Navy commander.[35] He has two rear admirals as deputy commanders; the PLANAF political commissar is a vice admiral and has two rear admirals as deputies.

The Navy's air arm is primarily land-based, although it began shipboard operations in January 1980.[36] While the PLANAF historically has not kept pace with PLAAF aircraft acquisitions, the South Sea Fleet air arm has conducted midair refueling training, albeit more than a year after the PLAAF first conducted these operations. The PLAAF and PLANAF have demonstrated the capability to conduct aerial refueling only after many years of trying. How much longer will it take them to possess the operational capability to refuel numerous aircraft—including at night and in bad weather—when the mission requires refueling to reach their target and return home safely? It may well take several years to develop this level of proficiency on a sustainable basis.[37]

Geographic Fleet Organization

The three operating fleets are organized into air, surface, and subsurface forces. Each is assigned three air divisions of the PLANAF (a division consists of approximately thirty-six aircraft). Each division is composed of four air regiments, which in turn each contain four air groups.[38] The fleet PLANAF arm includes land-based and seaplane patrol planes, bombers, fighters, helicopters, transport, and support aircraft. The fleet air commander is operationally responsible to his fleet commander but receives administrative support from the PLANAF commander headquartered in Beijing. Engineering, maintenance, supply, and training support is provided.

In addition to the aviation arm, each fleet includes large combatants (destroyers and frigates), small combatants (patrol boats), amphibious transports, mine warfare, replenishment-at-sea, and miscellaneous support ships. A senior captain serves as commander of the surface-forces flotilla and a senior captain as commander of the submarine flotilla, with each flotilla organized into squadrons of the same ship-type. Under this system, a squadron is composed entirely, for instance, of *Luda*-class DDGs, or *Jiangwei*-class guided-missile frigates (FFG), or *Ming*-class submarines (SS), and so on. These flotilla commanders report directly to the fleet commander; the flotilla commanders for small craft such as small patrol boat, harbor, and support vessels report to the local naval base commander.[39]

The submarine force was organized in 1951, established its first base in 1952 and submarine school in 1953, both at Qingdao, and began operating in June 1954.[40] The PLAN currently includes six nuclear-powered submarines: five *Han*-class attack boats (SSN) and one *Xia*-class nuclear-powered fleet ballistic missile submarine (SSBN). There is also one conventionally powered SSB, a *Golf II*. The submarine force currently totals approximately fifty-nine operational boats, including the nuclear-powered force. There are four *Kilo*-class boats acquired from Russia since 1995, and a mix of *Song, Ming,* and *Romeo* ships, all diesel-electric-powered submarines of various vintages.[41] The *Song*-class submarine may be the Chinese-built replacement for these boats; the third ship was launched in early 2000.

The PLAN's submarines are organized into six or seven flotillas. The 2d, 12th, and 62d are part of the North Sea Fleet and include all six nuclear-powered submarines. The 22d and 42d Flotillas are stationed with the East Sea Fleet and include China's four *Kilo*-class boats, while the South Sea Fleet deploys the 32d and possibly a second flotilla. The *Ming*-class submarines are assigned to this fleet.[42]

The PLAN's newest indigenously produced surface ship is the *Luhai*-class DDG, the *Shenzhen*.[43] The first of two *Sovremenny*-class DDGs purchased from Russia, the *Hangzhou*, reached its new home port of Zhoushan in early 2000, with the second ship of this class reportedly undergoing sea trials, preparatory to arriving in China late in the year.[44] Other surface forces include two *Luhu*-class guided missile destroyers and fourteen operational *Luda*-class DDGs, including the three newest models, one *Luda III* and two *Luda II*s.[45] Additional large surface combatants include a mix of approximately six *Jiangwei*-class and twenty-four *Jianghu*-class guided-missile frigates.

Smaller craft include several hundred vessels, ranging from modern missile-equipped *Huang*-class patrol boats to small riverine combatants—some of which are assigned to the PAP, the MSA, the Customs Service, or the maritime militia.

The PLAN amphibious force is capable of embarking perhaps one mechanized infantry division, approximately twelve thousand troops and their equipment, for a relatively short voyage.[46] It includes thirteen landing-ships-tank (LST), six of them the relatively modern *Yuting* class and seven the *Yukan* class. Two additional *Yuting*s are currently under construction. There are also approximately forty smaller landing-ships-mechanized (LSM) of various classes and ages, as well as six *Qiongsha*-class troop transports (two of which have been converted to hospital ships).[47]

Several of the combatants, including the *Luda*-class DDGs, have minelaying racks installed, but mine warfare (MIW) forces in the PLAN do not appear to receive a high priority, which is surprising in view of the efficacy of mine warfare in various Taiwan scenarios. The PLAN has just one dedicated minelayer, the *Wolei*, and approximately fifty-eight mine sweeping craft, at least half of them in the reserve force and of questionable operational readiness.[48]

Each fleet's AOR includes naval bases and subordinate naval garrison commands. These are important organizations, with extensive geographic reach: they provide "hotel" and other logistics services to fleet operating units, including training and education, maintenance, and general administrative support.[49]

Command Relationships

China is divided into seven military regions (MRs), each commanded by a lieutenant general. The PLAN commander (and the PLAAF commander) rank at the same level as the MR commanders. Each fleet commander serves as deputy commander of the MR most geographically closest to his command's AOR. A vice admiral commands the North Sea Fleet and serves as a Jinan MR deputy commander, but his authority during wartime is unclear: would he function as a true, joint deputy commander, or merely be the deputy in charge of naval forces? Furthermore, what is the relationship between the North Sea Fleet commander and the Shenyang and Beijing MR commanders? Does he, for instance, maintain liaison offices in their command centers? Similarly, what arrangements are in place for coordinating PLANAF and PLAAF operations in the MR?

There is a great potential for fractured command and control, leading to reduced operational effectiveness, if a proven system is not in place to coordinate among Navy, Army, and Air Force commands in a given MR. The fleet commander's relationship with the MR PLAAF commander, also a MR deputy commander, is unclear as well.[50] The MR commander probably determines seniority between his two deputies.

Command relationships within the MRs during peacetime are further clouded by the PLAN and PLAAF commanders' dual chains of command: administrative and operational, with the MR commander—invariably a ground forces officer—not in control of both chains. The MR commander's scope of authority may be further complicated by the status of special units, such as quick-reaction forces, which are operationally tasked by the GSD.[51]

Command relationships are theoretically clarified during wartime and during major exercises, when one or more MRs forms a "front," as during the 1979 Vietnam incursion. Officers from Beijing headquarters staffs augment the front. These officers no doubt are supposed to ensure compliance with Beijing's orders and are empowered to relax or sustain constraints on the front commander's freedom of action: in the 1979 case, these issues included how far he could move forces into Vietnam and to what degree "hot pursuit" was authorized.[52]

North Sea Fleet

The North Sea Fleet is headquartered at Qingdao, on the southern coast of the Shandong Peninsula, with other major bases at Lushun and Xiaopingdao. Smaller facilities are located at Huludao (including nuclear submarine construction and support), Weihai, Qingshan, Lianyungang, Lingshanwei, Dahushan, Changshanqundao, Liushuang, Yushan, Dayuanjiadun, and Jianggezhuang, the last serving as the fleet's submarine home port. Important shipbuilding facilities are located at Dalian. PLANAF facilities are located at Luda, Qingdao, Jinxi, Jiyuan, Laiyang, Jiaozhou, Xingtai, Laishan, Anyang, Changzhi, and Shanhaiguan. The Liangxiang airfield just outside Beijing is in the North Sea Fleet's AOR, but as the home field for the PLAN's fleet of executive aircraft (the "VIP" squadron), it is controlled by PLAN headquarters in Beijing.[53]

The fleet's AOR extends from the Korean border (marked by the Yalu River) to approximately 35° 10'N latitude. This area corresponds roughly to the Shenyang, Beijing, and Jinan MRs or, described another way, includes the Bohai and northern half of the Yellow Sea. The AOR's coastline is divided into nine coastal defense zones. The North Sea Fleet's forces include three submarine, three surface combatant, one amphibious, and one MIW squadrons, as well as the Bohai Training Flotilla and hundreds of small patrol and auxiliary craft.

As is the case with all three fleets, the North Sea Fleet's command structure closely resembles PLAN Headquarters in Beijing. Command and other positions are assigned two ranks: they may be filled by an officer holding the "primary" rank (vice admiral for a fleet commander, for instance) or by an officer holding the "auxiliary" or "secondary" rank (rear admiral for a fleet commander). The fleet's political commissar is a vice admiral, as are the three deputy commanders and two deputy political commissars. The fleet aviation commander is also a rear admiral. The fleet's Lushun and Qingdao Naval Bases are commanded by rear admirals, while the garrison commands at Dalian and at Weihai's seaport, Liugongdao, are commanded by senior captains.

East Sea Fleet

The East Sea Fleet is headquartered at Ningbo, with other major bases at Shanghai, Fujian, and Zhoushan (where the newly acquired *Sovremenny*-class DDGs are homeported). Smaller facilities are located at Chenjiagang, Dinghai, Wusong, Xinxiang, Wenzhou, Sanduao, Xiamen, Quandao, and Xiangshan (submarines, including all four *Kilo*-class subs, are homeported at the last).[54] Important shipbuilding facilities are located at Shanghai (for surface ships) and inland on the Yangtze River at Wuhan (for submarines). PLANAF facilities are located at Ningbo, Shanghai, Luqiao, Shitangqiao, Danyang, and Daishan.

The fleet's AOR reaches from approximately 35° 10'N down to 23° 30'N latitude, corresponding roughly to the Nanjing MR, or to the littoral areas of the southern half of the Yellow Sea, all of the East China Sea, and the Taiwan Strait. Its coastline is divided into seven coastal defense zones. Assigned units include two submarine, two surface combatant, one amphibious, and one MIW squadron, as well as over two hundred small patrol and auxiliary craft, including those that patrol the Yangtze and other riverine waters.

The East Sea Fleet is commanded by a vice admiral who also serves as a Nanjing MR deputy commander; its political commissar is also a vice admiral. The three deputy fleet commanders are rear admirals, as are the two deputy political commissars and the fleet aviation commander. Base commanders for Fujian, Shanghai, and Zhoushan are rear admirals, while a senior captain commands the Xiamen Naval Garrison.

South Sea Fleet

The South Sea Fleet is headquartered at Zhanjiang, with other major bases at Yulin and Guangzhou. Lesser facilities are located at Hong Kong, Haikou, Shantou, Humen, Kuanchuang, Tsun, Mawai, Beihai, Pingtan, Sanzhou, Tang Chian Huan, Longmen, Bailong, Donguon, Baimajing, and Xiachuandao. PLANAF facilities are located at Lingshui, Foluo, Haikou, Sanya, Guiping, Jialaishi, and Lingling. The fleet's AOR stretches from approximately 23° 30'N to the Vietnamese border, equating to the Guangzhou MR, or the littoral areas of the South China Sea and the Beibu Gulf. Its coastline is divided into nine coastal defense zones.

The fleet's most important operational responsibility is the South China Sea, with significant support facilities on Woody Island and on Fiery Cross, Lincoln, and Duncan Reefs. The fleet's responsibility for the contested Paracel and Spratly Islands, and Macclesfield Bank, explains the presence at Hainan's Lingshui airfield of the PLANAF's long-range B-6 Badger (Soviet-designed Tu-16) aircraft. The base on Woody Island in the Paracels is the only South China Sea facility capable of supporting tactical aircraft, with a paved airstrip.[55]

The South Sea Fleet is home to the PLAN's newest indigenously produced surface combatant, the *Luhai*-class guided-missile destroyer. It also includes one MIW, one amphibious, one or two submarine, and two surface combatant squadrons, as well as perhaps three hundred patrol and auxiliary craft, including those based at Hong Kong and on the MR's rivers. Additionally, the fleet includes one of China's three major replenishment-at-sea ships, the *Nanchang*.

The South Sea Fleet—significantly, not the East Sea Fleet facing Taiwan—also deploys the majority of China's newer amphibious ships, including all four *Qiongsha*-class troop transports, both hospital ships, ten of the fifteen *Yuting*-class and *Yukan*-class LSTs, and all four of the *Yudao*-class LSMs.[56]

China's Marine Corps is stationed in the South Sea Fleet's AOR. The corps is composed of two multiarm brigades of approximately 6,000 personnel each, organized into 750-man battalions. Each brigade includes infantry, artillery, armor, engineer, communications, antichemical, antiarmor, and amphibious scout personnel.[57]

The corps' primary mission is amphibious warfare; the South China Sea is its anticipated operating theater and the Marines man the island outposts of that sea. The Marine Corps does not have a single commander, but each brigade reports directly to the fleet commander. This system would seem to hinder both joint operations and employment of the Corps as a single force. Furthermore, in wartime the Marine Corps, as a rapid reaction force, would likely be tasked directly by the GSD, further fracturing the chain of command.[58]

The vice admiral commanding the South Sea Fleet serves as a Guangzhou MR deputy commander; another vice admiral is the fleet political commissar. The three deputy commanders are rear admirals, as are the two deputy political commissars. The fleet's PLANAF forces are commanded by a rear admiral; the Marine Corps brigades by senior captains. The fleet's naval bases at Yulin, Zhangjian, and Guangzhou are commanded by rear admirals, although the Yulin commander is senior to his counterparts.[59] Senior captains command the naval garrisons at Shantou and Xisha.

PLANAF Operations

One important but obscure relationship is that between PLANAF and PLAAF components. Does the PLAAF assume operational control of PLANAF units in time of war, for instance, to increase the efficiency of coastal air defense? Are PLANAF units wholly responsible for the defense of naval bases and other facilities, or can they call on PLAAF assistance? Or are the two air components in the midst of the same command and control imbroglio that has dogged the American military for so many years? The preliminary, general response to these questions is that although over-water flights have now become routine for the PLAAF, there are still very limited joint flight operations occurring between the two "air forces."

One of the factors in this situation is the organization of China's coastal air defenses, including the way responsibility for continental air defense is assigned by the CMC. Ideally, the coastline would be divided into air defense sectors commanded by a joint commander with authority to call upon both PLAAF and PLANAF resources, but this does not appear to be the case.

From north to south along China's coast, air defense is assigned by the proximity of airfields, rather than by service. The North Sea Fleet's PLANAF contingent has the responsibility from its northern border down to about the Shandong Peninsula; the PLAAF then assumes air defense responsibility to a point south of Shanghai, although that city is located in the heart of the PLAN's East Sea Fleet AOR. The PLANAF resumes air defense responsibility for a brief stretch south of Shanghai, but the PLAAF then has the mission for most of Fujian Province's coastline, which places it on the front line against Taiwan. The PLANAF resumes air defense for most of the South Sea Fleet AOR, including the South China Sea.[60]

This system, based on geographical sectors rather than service capability or doctrine, indicates that not only are joint maritime flight operations not routinely employed, but joint doctrine for such operations has not been systemically developed by the two "air forces." Indeed, PLAAF operations over water likely concentrate on classic air intercept and pursuit operations, while PLANAF operational doctrine concentrates on fleet support missions, such as surveillance and ASW. Nevertheless, U.S. military surveillance aircraft operating off the coast in the East Sea Fleet's AOR are often intercepted by PLANAF F-7 fighters.[61]

Coast Guard

China does not have a formally organized coast guard, but the functions normally assigned to that service—maritime safety, customs enforcement, environmental protection and the like—are the responsibility of several organizations. Beijing organized a maritime militia in the early 1950s as part of the effort to defend the fishing fleet and coastal trade against depredations by KMT naval forces. This force consisted largely of fishing trawlers armed with machine guns and hand-held weapons. They were controlled by local CCP branches, and when on a mission carried party representatives.[62] In 1955, Beijing organized Public Security Force sea units; they were responsible for guarding ports, rivers, and the fishing fleets. Ironically, these duties often took them further to sea than the PLAN. Naval district defense units were also organized, and tasked with cooperating with the Army for inshore coastal defense.[63]

There is a gap in our knowledge about the development of these forces. China currently deploys several maritime auxiliary forces, all of them semimilitary to a degree. These include the Customs Service, the State Oceanographic Bureau, the Public Security Bureau's Maritime Section, the Border Security Force's Maritime Command, the Ministry of Public Security's Frontier Guard Detachment, the MSA, and a maritime militia. The Customs Service may be the most professional of these organizations, although all use a collection of more than two hundred patrol craft of various classes, many of them seagoing.[64]

The State Oceanographic Bureau is responsible for research and environmental protection, including enforcement of the Marine Environmental Protection Law of the PRC, passed in December 1999.[65] This law assigns responsibilities to several organizations, although they have additional duties, as well.

State Environmental Protection Administration:
a consolidated supervisory and managerial department for national environmental protection work.

State Marine Administration: supervision and management

of the marine environment and organization of investigations, monitoring, lookout, evaluation, and scientific research of the marine environment.

State Maritime Affairs Administration: supervision and management of nonfishing and nonmilitary shipping pollution of the marine environment.

State Fishery Administration: supervision and management of pollution to the marine environment by nonmilitary ships inside fishing port waters and fishing boats outside fishing port waters.

Military Environmental Protection Department: supervision and management of pollution to the marine environment by military ships and boats.[66]

Other craft are in the Coastal Regional Defense Forces, comprising twenty-five thousand personnel. This force is probably part of the Naval Coastal Defense System, which includes a system of coastal observation posts spread along China's coastline, coastal cruise missile and artillery sites, coastal patrol boat squadrons, and a network of coastal radar and communications stations.[67]

The recently established Maritime Safety Administration operates under the Communications Ministry in Beijing. Fourteen of a planned twenty offices had been set up by the end of 1999. The MSA is reportedly charged with supervising the "management of navigation marks, the surveying of sea-routes, and the inspection of ships and maritime facilities," with a special focus on shipboard safety.[68] Its ship salvage responsibilities are carried out through the semiprivate China Salvage Company, which also provides afloat and air SAR assistance.[69]

Finally, the Frontier Guard Department is "in charge of administering social order of vessels along the coasts." Rumors have surfaced that some of these vessels have been involved in piracy and other illegal acts in China's coastal waters, perhaps evidenced in guidance to this force to "strictly abide by law-enforcement procedures [and not] to levy fines which are beyond their authority, or which are too excessive."[70]

Doctrine and Organization

Maritime warfare is by nature multidimensional, a characteristic becoming steadily more complex as information-age developments are adapted for naval use. PLAN organization still conforms, however, to classic naval force structure—surface, subsurface, and air components operating almost entirely along traditional "vertical" administrative and operational chains of command.

Effective doctrine should also reflect and affect organization. The PLAN's current fleet and shore establishment organization, for instance, does not appear to reflect a significant attempt to conform to developments in modern warfare commonly attributed to "information warfare" or the "revolution in military affairs." In fact, recent fleet exercises indicate that only in the past five years or so has the PLAN begun trying to master the integrated, joint maritime warfare developed by Western navies half a century ago. The experimental work possibly underway in the Naval Research Center, the Naval Research Institute, or the Nanjing Command Academy's experimental cell located with the East Sea Fleet may lead to such changes.

The PLAN today is logically organized, with an emphasis on maintaining and improving its operational forces. Its basic organization is a mixture of geographic and mission-oriented commands typical of large navies. The three operational fleets are organized geographically, but are also oriented toward historic and potential threats. All operate in the shadow of U.S. naval and air power.

The North Sea Fleet faces a complex theater involving Russia, Korea, and Japan. The East Sea Fleet's AOR centers on Taiwan but also includes the Senkaku (Diaoyu) Islands. This fleet presumably is tasked with primary planning and execution responsibility for naval action against Taiwan. The fleet itself possesses inadequate assets to execute any significant action against Taiwan, but under a wartime "front" command would probably be empowered to take operational control of aircraft, surface and subsurface ships, and other resources from its sister fleets. The South Sea Fleet also faces a complex operational situation, with its AOR including the South China Sea's operational and political problems, as well as unanswered questions about the long-term value to China of possible seabed resources in the area.

Naval headquarters in Beijing, not to mention the CMC, would of course play a very close supervisory/command role in any such military operations against Taiwan. It is also possible that in the event of such a very major military engagement, one of the other fleets, most likely the North Sea Fleet, would simply be combined with the East Sea Fleet. Moreover, the distances between adjacent PLAN fleets are quite short, generally just one to three days of steaming at moderate speeds, unlike the situation with the U.S. or Russian navies, where the distances between the ports and operating areas of the major fleets are generally measured in thousands of miles and weeks of cruising time.

There are no significant geographic obstacles to quick or frequent PLAN interfleet transfers, although the presence of foreign naval bases throughout East Asia, from Petropavlosk in Russia to Singapore, certainly may constrain such operations. Still, the primary obstacles to PLAN interfleet operations are probably lack of common operational doctrine and nonstandard procedures and tactics, along with lack of practice in working together.[71]

The PLAN's Beijing organization is unremarkable, reflecting the usual requirements for administering a large maritime force. Its bureaucratic structure consists of departments dedicated to "standard" naval functions and requirements, although the political department and attendant structure certainly distinguishes it from Western navies. What is less clear than the internal PLAN structure is the organization's relationship with the PLA's general staff departments and the CMC, the operational chain of command from that body through PLAN headquarters to the operational units, and the Navy's role in PLA strategic planning.

Adm. Shi Yunsheng's June 2000 promotion to full admiral might indicate greater recognition of the PLAN's increased importance by Beijing; more likely, it merely recognizes his successful career and longevity in service. Shi Yunsheng appears to be exercising effective command of the PLAN, focusing his efforts on improving education and training; maintenance, fleet support, and the Navy's ability to attain its strategic objectives.

PLAN organization has evolved undramatically since its founding fifty years ago, when it was formed as an East China force in reaction to the Kuomintang threat from the sea. The relative strengths of the North, East, and South Sea fleets has not varied startlingly over time, but changes are discernible during various periods when Beijing identified national security concerns with the United States, the Soviet Union, Taiwan, or the South China Sea. Future concerns with India or with stronger Southeast Asian naval forces would likely result in a similar shift in emphasis, with the South Sea Fleet receiving more modernized ships and aircraft, and expanded shore facilities. The extent of such a shift, however, would depend on the criticality of concern for Taiwan and possible intervention by U.S. naval and air forces.

PLAN fleet organization is marked by some interesting factors. First, the different fleets have also been assigned responsibility for specific platforms, such as submarines or amphibious ships, probably for reasons of assigned missions or for ease of maintenance and operation. Second, concentrating all ships of a class in the same fleet simplifies maintenance, training, and support in general of that class, but has the potential to reduce those ships' utility if they have to be assigned to a different fleet. "Type commanders" are apparently not utilized: this system assigns to a rear or vice admiral responsibility for maintaining and training all the ships in a specific type—destroyers, submarines, amphibious ships, and so on.

Third, as previously noted, the issue of fleet interoperability—the degree of standardization of administrative and operational procedures, communications, and tactics—is not clear. Fourth, the relationships among CMC, PLAN headquarters, MR, and fleet headquarters are generally unknown. Fifth, the operating fleets' role in doctrinal development is not completely understood.

Currently, the East and South Sea Fleets appear to be receiving the bulk of new PLAN ships and aircraft, although accurate counting is difficult. This would be a logical development, given the strategic priority of the Taiwan and South China Sea issues. That said, the presence of the very strong, modern Japanese and South Korean navies means that China will be cautious about diverting too much strength from the North Sea Fleet. In the near-term, the three fleets should remain balanced, with each deploying the surface, submarine, and aviation assets required to accomplish its tasking. Competition for resources among the fleets and, within the fleets among the surface, submarine, and aviation branches will also continue.

China's first major efforts to organize a modern navy in the second half of the nineteenth century occurred at roughly the same time as Japan's effort. Both nations sought the technological and organizational expertise of outsiders; they bought and reverse-engineered foreign ships and systems while developing an indigenous military-industrial infrastructure. Japan succeeded, because it also developed a coherent organization that enabled the Navy to function effectively as an instrument of the national security structure. China failed in the nineteenth century in part because of inadequate organization; the current PLAN looks more promising.

The Navy's organization is determined to a significant extent by the ships and aircraft it operates. The goal is maximum effectiveness of these units, modified by geography, perceived threats, and the international and domestic political considerations. PLAN organization will change, furthermore, as the Navy grows and modernizes—as new ships and aircraft are deployed.

5

Ships and Aircraft of the PLAN

Naval authors in China have recently emphasized the value of technological advances, including a shift "from platform-centric to network-centric . . . strategy based on the speed of command."[1] This refers to a theory held by the U.S. Navy that future fleet operations will be conducted not by individual ships acting on the basis of their own sensors, weapons, and communications and control systems, but by groups of ships operating as members of a cooperative network. The ships, aircraft, and even shore stations will be linked by computers and operate in a coherent "network-centric" environment, passing information back and forth and functioning as a single entity.

The PLAN, however, is still very much "platform-centric," almost wholly dependent on individual ship and aircraft operations. These platforms constitute the naval power available to China to secure its territorial claims in the East and South China Seas.

China's Navy has depended mainly on Soviet/Russian platforms since its inception in 1950, when it commissioned its first patrol boats, soon followed by small combatants (frigates and corvettes) and submarines. This dependence continues, as the PLAN in February 2000 received its first *Sovremenny*-class DDG from Russia.

During the past decade or so, the PLAN has added to its ranks about one DDG, one submarine, and three FFGs each year, a modest program of naval growth. China's Navy does have indigenously produced ships, of course, but these are almost all derivations of Soviet/Russian designs. The *Luda*-class DDG, for example, is based on the old (c. 1940s) Soviet-designed *Kotlin*-class destroyer. China's newer *Luhu*-class DDG is a modernized version of the *Luda*, while the even newer *Luhai* is simply a larger *Luhu*. In fact, only the three *Song*-class submarines, nine *Jiangwei*-class and four later modifications of the *Jianghu*-class frigates, the twenty-five *Houxin*- and *Houjian*-class missile patrol boats, and the two *Fuqing*-class replenishment-at-sea (RAS) ships are indigenously designed and constructed—and even these rely heavily on foreign-designed/produced engineering, weapons, and sensor systems. The Navy Weapons Assessment Research Center reported in 1990 that since its establishment in 1983 it had "gathered and translated" more than five million words "from foreign naval materials" and written "sixty-six investigative reports on foreign vessels."[2]

A similar dependence on foreign designs marks the PLAN's submarine fleet. China has yet to design and construct a successful submarine; the *Song* class may be the first, although it apparently incorporates French hull construction and sonar technology, and although launched in 1994, it may not yet be operational, as of mid-2000.[3] The single *Xia*-class fleet ballistic missile boat (SSBN) conducted a successful missile-firing exercise in 1988 but has only infrequently been at sea since then.[4]

The New PLAN (1950)

The PLA had little time to rest after its victory in 1949. China needed a navy, and Beijing quickly moved to create one, with the Soviet Union as its source in early 1950. Initial Soviet assistance included four old submarines, two destroyers, and a large number of patrol boats. The new PLAN also acquired various ships captured from or turned over by the Nationalist Chinese Navy, including ex-Japanese and U.S. vessels.[5] These comprised a cruiser, about ten corvettes, forty ex-U.S. landing craft, and several dozen miscellaneous river gunboats, minesweepers, and yard craft as part of a total force of approximately 183 ships.[6]

Table 1. The PLAN, 1955

Ship Type	Number	Source
Light cruiser	1	ex-KMT *Huang Ho*
Destroyers	2	ex-Soviet *Gordy*
Frigates	12	ex-Japan, UK
Gunboats	16	ex-U.S., UK, Japan
Minesweepers	2	ex-U.S.
LSTs	4	ex-U.S.
LSMs	28	ex-U.S.
Supply ships	4	ex-U.S.

China has struggled to establish a comprehensive shipbuilding industry, adopting a three-step plan in 1951 that was based on obtaining Soviet technology, transitioning to "semi-indigenous production," and then proceeding to indigenous production.[7] The Department of Ship Construction was established in September 1952, centralizing shipbuilding facilities previously under MR control. This followed the PLAN commander's call to "build a repair and construction system from top to bottom."[8] A series of research and development institutes were created in 1957 and 1958; the disruptions of the Great Leap Forward and the GPCR were followed by the establishment of the Navy Weapons Assessment Research Center and the Navy Equipment Verification Center, both in 1983.[9] Table 1 shows the PLAN in 1955, following Soviet assistance during the PRC's first five years.[10]

A large shore-based infrastructure, including shipyards, naval colleges, and extensive coastal fortifications, was also built with Soviet help.[11] The high point of the cooperative period with the Soviets was the February 1959 "New Technology Agreement," which provided for China's purchase of additional conventionally powered submarines, torpedo boats, and missile boats.[12]

The PLAN had grown considerably by 1960 (see table 2),[13] but had made only limited strides toward modernization. The force centered around eight ex-Soviet destroyers, two dozen old Soviet submarines, and a motley collection of foreign-built patrol boats, landing craft, and yard craft. The 1953 and 1959 agreements with the Soviet Union provided China with the means to build submarines, surface ships, minesweepers, and patrol boats. However, the only vessels built in China by 1960 were some of the patrol boats, in part because Mao Zedong's priority on constructing a nuclear-powered submarine monopolized PLAN financial resources.[14]

Table 2. The PLAN, 1960

Ship Type	Number	Source
Destroyers	8	ex-Soviet *Gordy, Riga*
Frigates	12	9 ex-Japan, 3 ex-UK
Gunboats	27	14 ex-Soviet, 8 ex-Japan, 3 ex-UK
Minesweepers	17	10 ex-Soviet ocean, 7 ex-U.S., Japan coastal
Submarines	26	ex-Soviet W, S, M-V
LSTs	12	ex-U.S.
LSMs	28	ex-U.S.
Supply ships	3	ex-U.S.

Soviet assistance ended in 1960. China began building an indigenous Navy, but as table 3 shows,[15] had made little progress by 1970. The domestic and international events of the 1960s, marked by the split with the Soviet Union and the onset of the Cultural Revolution, hamstrung PLAN modernization throughout the decade and well into the 1970s.

The PLAN had moved into the missile age by 1970, however, deploying a Soviet-designed ballistic missile submarine, as well as more than thirty other submarines. The Navy still included a collection of assorted Soviet, Japanese, U.S., British, Canadian, and Italian-built destroyers and escort vessels inherited from the KMT or Japanese navies, and its most modern craft were ten Soviet-built patrol boats armed with cruise missiles. More than four hundred Chinese-built patrol craft, some of them hydrofoils and most armed with torpedoes, rounded out the fleet.[16] The 1970s PLAN focused on building submarines and antiship missiles.

Although heavily dependent on Soviet designs, Chinese-built warships were prominent in the PLAN for the first time in the 1970s: *Luda*-class guided-missile destroyers, frigates, and fast-attack missile boats had all joined the fleet. The submarine force included the first Chinese-built nuclear-powered attack submarine, as well as about sixty conventionally powered boats.[17]

By 1980 (see table 4),[18] Deng Xiaoping had strongly endorsed the "four modernizations," with the PLA last in the budgetary queue, and accepted PLA efforts to raise its own capital by engaging in China's civilian economic sector. This priority continues to frame PLAN modernization programs, although the termination of PLA commercial involvement, if it has actually occurred, must be further constraining the Navy's budget resources. Significant modernization steps by the

Table 3. The PLAN, 1970

Ship Type	Number	Source
Destroyers	4	ex-Soviet *Gordy*
Frigates	16	4 *Jiangnan*, 4 ex-Soviet *Riga*, 8 ex-Japan
Missile boats	10	ex-Soviet *Osa*, *Komar*
Minesweepers	24	20 ex-Soviet ocean, 5 ex-U.S., UK coastal
Submarines	35	ex-Soviet G, W, R, M-V
LSTs	20	ex-U.S.
LSMs	29	ex-U.S.
Supply ships	8	ex-U.S.

Table 4. The PLAN, 1980

Ship Type	Number	Source
Destroyers	11	7 *Luda*, 4 ex-Soviet *Gordy*
Frigates	16	5 *Jianghu*, 2 *Jiangdong*, 5 *Jiangnan*, 4 ex-Soviet *Riga*
Missile boats	161	OSA, *Komar* (ex-Soviet, Soviet design)
Minesweepers	17	ex-Soviet, Soviet design T-43
Submarines	87	
SSN	2	*Han*
SSB	1	*Golf* (Soviet design)
SS	84	2 *Ming*, 62 *Romeo*, 20+ *Whiskey* (Soviet design)
Amphibious vessels	43	
LST	15	ex-U.S.
LSM	21	2 *Yuling*, 19 ex-U.S.
Supply ships	about 40	PRC-built, ex-U.S.

Navy will require either a reordering of the four priorities, or special allocations to the PLAN for the construction or purchase of more modern systems and platforms.

The PLAN in 2000: Submarines

The PLAN maintains a large submarine force, with modernization proceeding slowly. The bulk of the force is composed of thirty to forty improved versions of the 1950s Soviet-designed *Romeo*-class submarine.

These boats are seldom seen at sea, possibly because of a lack of trained crews, and have only rudimentary ASW capability.[19] China has built nineteen *Ming*-class submarines, an improved *Romeo* design. The *Ming*s, in turn, are supposed to be succeeded by the *Song* class.

Song construction may fall victim to additional purchases of Russian submarines. China has acquired four *Kilo*-class subs, two of them the "export" model and two of them the quieter and more capable design produced for the Russian Navy. Although a 1970s design, the *Kilo* is still a very capable, quiet submarine—if properly maintained and operated. The PLAN appears to be experiencing problems learning to operate and maintain these boats. Crew training has not gone well; serious problems with the propulsion batteries have developed, and the submarines are returning to Russia for all but routine maintenance.[20]

While there are several reports that China will acquire additional *Kilo*-class subs, in view of these problems the PLAN may decide either to continue building the *Song* class or purchase one of the *Amur*-class submarines, the Russian follow-on design to the *Kilo*. Although two *Amur* hulls were reported under construction, Russia has stopped work on both ships as a result of budgetary problems and a lack of foreign orders.[21]

The six different models planned for the *Amur* family are apparently being designed to compete with the popular German series of export submarines. Although conventionally powered, the largest of the *Amur*s, the *Lada* class, will be equipped with an air independent propulsion system (AIP). This system has long promised to revolutionize conventional submarine capabilities by extending maximum submerged operating time from the *Kilo*'s four days to as long as forty days. AIPs fall into two broad categories: fuel-burning heat engines, which reuse a combination of oxygen and the products of engine combustion, and electrochemical engines, which transform chemical energy into electrical power by using hydrogen and oxygen.[22]

Russia is working hard to develop AIP technology, and the proposed *Lada* class will employ a "fuel cell" using liquid oxygen and hydrogen. Some AIP system variants have been tested at sea by Australia, Russia, and Sweden, with the latter actually operating three submarines equipped with AIP "Stirling" engines that enable them to operate submerged for as long as two weeks. The Stirling engine is limited by speed and depth considerations, however, and a practical, operational AIP system has yet to be produced.

One former PLAN commander claimed that "the development of nuclear-powered submarines is the chief objective of this century," and the PLAN currently has six nuclear-powered submarines, the *Xia*-class SSBN and five *Han*-class attack submarines (SSN).[23] These vessels were built in China to Soviet designs, but have not been entirely successful. The *Xia* has seldom been seen at sea, while the *Han*s are relatively noisy and have suffered from frequent engineering problems.[24]

China is moving to augment these boats with a new SSN, designated the Type-093, and a new SSBN, designated the Type-094.[25] Both will almost certainly rely on Russian design and engineering assistance. The first Type-093 is under construction, with a possible commissioning date of 2005, but a start date for the Type-094 is undetermined.[26] Predicting the length of time it will take for China to deploy new submarines is chancy, given Beijing's poor track record: the *Han* was begun in 1958, but did not go to sea until 1974.[27] Hence, there are not likely to be significant changes in the composition of China's submarine force during the next decade, barring a large-scale purchase of foreign boats.

The PLAN submarine force is improving its weapon suites more rapidly than its ships.[28] Recent purchases of Russian wire-guided and wake-homing torpedoes provide very capable weapons that are difficult for surface ships to counter. Beijing has also reportedly purchased Soviet-designed rocket-propelled torpedoes from Ukraine.[29]

Surface Combatants

The most numerous and largest ships in China's Navy are its surface combatants, described as the "vital" or "main" PLAN component. Even the Chinese evaluate their newest warships "on a par with foreign warships of the 1980s"—but that is an optimistic estimate.[30]

The most recent and potent addition to China's surface fleet is the *Sovremenny*-class DDG. The first of two purchased is homeported in Zhoushan, near Ningbo in the East China Sea Fleet's AOR. The second ship was delivered to China in November 2000.[31] Probably purchased for $420 million each, the *Sovremenny* DDGs are capable warships, designed by the Soviet Union in the early 1970s for surface warfare.[32] Its primary armament is the formidable Moskit missile, designed to attack surface ships.[33] Each *Sovremenny* carries eight of these missiles, with no on-board reload capability. The Moskit has a range of more than eighty-seven nautical miles and carries a 300-kilogram conventional warhead.[34] The missile's lethality rests for the most part on its speed and flight profile: immediately following launch to a probable altitude of several hundred feet, the missile descends to "sea-skimming" altitude—below twenty meters above the ocean's surface. As it closes the target, the Moskit accelerates to a speed as high as Mach 2.5. This final part of the flight profile is complicated by the missile's ability to conduct radical evasive maneuvers, possibly "a series of sharp S-shaped maneuvers, with overload as much as 15 Gs," to complicate the fire-control solution for the target's defensive systems.[35] The first twenty-four Moskits were delivered to China in April 2000; the second group of twenty-four was scheduled for delivery by the end of 2000.[36]

The *Sovremenny* is also capable of firing the Moskit's successor currently under development, the Yakhont, which may have almost twice the range, 162 nautical miles, but a smaller warhead, 200 kilograms.[37] Beijing has not yet purchased the Yakhont but will probably do so. The *Sovremenny*'s capabilities in other warfare areas are much less formidable. Its only AAW missile system fires the SA-N-7 "Gadfly" or SA-N-17 "Grizzly" missile. Although superior to any previous PLAN AAW system, these missiles are essentially "point defense" weapons: their maximum range, 13.5 to 15 nautical miles, is too short to allow significant area air-defense coverage.[38] Four 30-mm rapid-fire guns provide even shorter-range air defense.

ASW capability is equally unimpressive, depending on a medium frequency, hull-mounted active sonar, and a weapons suite composed of torpedoes and mortars. The most significant ASW system on the *Sovremenny* is its two Ka-28 helicopters, which are equipped with sonars and other submarine-detection systems, and armed with torpedoes.[39]

These weaknesses in AAW and ASW do not detract from the *Sovremenny*'s potent capability in combating surface ships, but highlight the fact that it was not designed by the Soviet Union to operate alone. The ship is intended to form part of a large, multimission task group. Operation of these ships in wartime will have to be very carefully orchestrated to prevent their quick destruction by aircraft or submarines. The PLAN is trying to purchase additional *Sovremennys*.[40]

China's first DDG was the *Luda*-class ship, which joined the PLAN in 1971. The Navy currently has sixteen *Luda*s, in three subclasses. The fifteen ships of the *Luda I* and *Luda II* subclasses are armed with the old, but still capable Hai Ying-2 (HY-2) anti–surface ship missile (SSM) system, with a range of 51 nautical miles. The SSM on the one *Luda III* was upgraded to the Ying Ji-1 (YJ-1), a shorter range (23 nautical miles) but more reliable missile.[41] The *Luda*s were constructed without an antiaircraft (AAW) missile system, although two of them have been retrofitted with the French-built Crotale point-defense system, with a range of 7.5 nautical miles against incoming air targets.

The *Luda*s all have the typical PLAN ASW suite: medium or high frequency, hull-mounted sonar; Soviet-designed mortars/depth charges; and (in this case, Italian-designed) torpedoes. At least one of the ships has been modified to carry two French-built Z-9A Dauphin helicopters. The sole *Luda III* also is equipped with a variable-depth sonar.[42] These are still useful ships, and represent an important PLAN transition to the missile age, but suffer from significant defects in terms of turn-of-the-century naval technology such as systems integration, ASW suites, and air defense.

The PLAN took a significant step forward in the mid-1990s with the *Luhu*-class DDG. Although only two of these ships have been built, they are China's first gas turbine-powered warships, with engines purchased from the United States. In other respects, however, the *Luhu* represents only incremental advances over the *Luda* across the spectrum of naval warfare capabilities.

The two *Luhu*-class DDGs, *Harbin* and *Qingdao*, are armed with the YJ-1 SSM missile, which has a range of twenty-two nautical miles, and the Crotale AAW missile, which has a range of seven nautical miles. Four 30-mm gatling guns offer short-range air defense, and the ship is equipped with U.S.-built dispensers of super rapid blooming offboard chaff (SRBOC).[43] A French-designed Tavitac combat integration system and a logically designed combat direction center enhance the *Luhu*'s combat effectiveness.[44] The *Luhu*s are both equipped with Zhi-9A helicopters, as lead components in an ASW suite that includes a hull-mounted, medium-frequency sonar, Italian-designed torpedoes, and Soviet-designed mortars.

The small size of this class may be due to China having acquired only five LM-2500 marine gas-turbine engines from the United States, before the post–Tiananmen Square sanctions halted such sales.[45] Each *Luhu* is equipped with two of these engines, and China was forced to look elsewhere for gas turbines for additional ships. This may have led directly to the design of China's newest warship, the *Luhai*-class DDG, the first of which, *Shenzhen*, was commissioned in 1999.

The *Luhai* is significantly larger than the *Luhu*-class DDGs, displacing 7,940 tons to their 4,200. The *Shenzhen* is armed with the YJ-2 SSM, similar to the YJ-1 carried by the *Luhu* but with a greater range (sixty-six nautical miles). AAW defense is similar to the *Luhus*—the Crotale AAW missile system and gatling guns, as is the ASW suite—medium frequency sonar, torpedoes, mortars, and two Ka-28 helicopters. *Shenzhen's* larger size may have been dictated by the need to install Ukrainian-built gas turbine engines, which are larger than the *Luhus'* LM-2500s, but the additional volume offers valuable room and stability as the PLAN modernizes the ship with improved weapons and sensor systems.

China has attributed significant stealth characteristics to the *Luhai* —"its special invisibility feature is even more prominent"—but pictures of *Shenzhen* do not support this claim, although the ship may have a lower radar signature than previous Chinese-built ships. The ship's superstructure includes too many "corners" that could have been eliminated to reduce radar reflectivity. There are also several items of deck equipment, including boat davits, guns, and even the anchor housing area that do not appear designed to reduce the ship's radar signature. Furthermore, the *Luhai* is not "painted" with a radar-absorbent coating, although this is relatively easy to apply.[46]

The PLAN's newest guided-missile frigate is the *Jiangwei* class, of which two subclasses have been built. The first *Jiangwei* was commissioned in 1991; eight more have joined the fleet. At 2,250 tons displacement, this ship is much smaller than China's destroyers, but a capable escort. The *Jiangwei I* subclass is armed with the YJ-1/2 SSM and Hang Qi-61 (HQ-61) AAW system. This latter missile is a Chinese-built point defense weapon, with a range of 7.5 nautical miles, apparently reverse-engineered from the Crotale system. The *Jiangwei II* subclass differs in substituting the Crotale for the HQ-61—apparently because the indigenous system was unsatisfactory. Additional air defense is provided by gatling guns and SRBOC chaff launchers.[47]

The *Jiangweis* are powered by German-manufactured/designed diesel engines and have the typical PLAN ASW suite: a hull-mounted medium-frequency sonar and ASW mortars, but lack torpedoes. They embark a single Z-9A helicopter and have well-designed combat direction centers equipped with the Tavitac combat integration system.[48]

The *Jiangwei* class, still being produced, represents a significant step forward from the older *Jianghu*-class frigates. Twenty-eight *Jianghus* were commissioned between the mid-1970s and 1996. They are diesel-powered and armed with four HY-2 SSMs for surface warfare, but have neither AAW missiles nor gatling guns. Their ASW suite is limited to the typical hull-mounted, medium-frequency sonar, mortars, and depth charges. The ships lack torpedoes and helicopters, except for one ship of the class, *Siping,* which was converted to include a flight deck for a Z-9A helicopter, Italian-built ASW torpedo tubes, and two gatling-gun installations.[49]

This ship's numerous portholes indicates a lack of air conditioning, which would adversely affect the performance of on-board electronic equipment during operations in tropical or subtropical waters. The *Jianghus'* most serious shortcoming, however, is the lack of a combat direction center in most ships of the class.[50] A warship lacking this most basic element of system integration—installed in U.S. ships during the second half of World War II—is essentially unable to operate in a modern naval environment.

The PLAN's origin as a coastal defense force and the Soviet influence has meant an early and continuing reliance on relatively small warships, usually displacing less than 500 tons. Currently, the PLAN includes perhaps sixty Chinese versions of the old Soviet-designed *Osa*-class and *Komar*-class patrol boats firing SSMs with a range of twenty-five or forty-five nautical miles. These boats, counted in the hundreds a few years ago, are being phased out; replacing them are the five *Houjian*-class and twenty (to date) *Houxin*-class patrol boats. Both are armed with twenty-five-nautical-mile YJ-1 SSMs, although the *Houxin* is a modification of the forty-year-old *Hainan*-class gunboat. These are essentially coastal craft, with the *Houjians* homeported in Hong Kong, but certainly capable of operating in the South China Sea and the waters around Taiwan in times of calm to moderate weather. The PLAN also includes about 250 smaller patrol boats armed with guns or torpedoes.

Also small in size but with significant potential are mine warfare ships. Mines are the most cost-effective means of naval warfare, especially in littoral waters. Hence, it is surprising that China, with its self-proclaimed defensive maritime strategy, has not made a larger investment in this warfare area.

The PLAN includes only one dedicated minelayer, although almost any naval surface ship, as well as most merchantmen and fishing trawlers, can deploy mines in a rough fashion. China also has a small mine-clearing force, based on twenty-seven Soviet-designed *T-43* oceangoing and eight coastal minesweepers. There are also forty-six remote operated minesweepers, almost all of them in the Navy's reserve force (as are an additional thirteen *T-43*s).[51] The PLAN's mine inventory may include as many as one hundred thousand mines, but almost all of these are very old models. It may, however, be acquiring rocket-propelled mines from Ukraine.[52]

The PLAN earned its first laurels fighting the Taiwan Navy among the islands of China's coastal waters in the early 1950s, actions that focused on launching or repelling amphibious operations. Despite this experience, the PLAN in 2000 is not able to deploy a large amphibious force. Thirteen modern LSTs form the heart of this force. The seven *Yukan*-class LSTs were constructed between 1980 and 1995; they can embark 200 troops and ten tanks. The six ships of the more modern *Yuting* class are slightly larger (embarking 250 troops and ten tanks) and have a large helicopter deck on the fantail.

The PLAN also includes "landing ships-mechanized" (LSMs). There are eleven modern ships of the *Yudeng* and *Yuhai* classes, with only the latter still in production. Older LSMs include thirty-one *Yuliang*-class ships, each embarking three tanks and a limited number of troops.

Amphibious operations pose three basic problems. First, how are forces transported to the objective? The PLAN apparently intends augmenting its amphibious lift with merchant ships. Civilian vessels have participated in amphibious exercises since at least 1994, and the Navy has a program for refitting merchant ships for possible use as amphibious lift, but history shows that using civilian troop lift is very problematic.[53]

Second, how is control of the sea gained sufficiently to ensure safe transport? Here, China must employ its surface fleet, from patrol boats to DDGs, to protect the ships transporting invasion forces, and to ensure logistical support of the force after it lands. Mine warfare could also play a significant role in answering this question. Given the strength of the Taiwan Navy, however, the PLAN will not easily be able to establish this control.

Third, how is control of the air gained sufficiently to ensure both the safe transport of the invasion force and its defense after the initial landing? Here, China must be able to call upon the resources of the PLANAF, the PLAAF, and shore-based ballistic and cruise missiles. The lack of joint PLANAF-PLAAF training, and Taiwan's small but modern air force, will pose a serious challenge to Chinese attempts to gain control of the air.

The PLAN includes numerous supply and support ships, but only three of them are capable of replenishment at sea, supplying warships when they are underway in the open ocean. Each of the three fleets is assigned one of these "AORs," either *Nanyun* (South Sea Fleet) or one of the two *Fuqing*-class ships (North and East Sea Fleets). These are relatively large ships (thirty-seven and twenty-one thou-sand tons displacement, respectively), capable of refueling two ships simultaneously.

Although two additional *Fuqing*s were built, one was sold to Pakistan and one was converted to the civilian merchant fleet, indicating that the PLAN is not concerned about further increasing its ability to conduct underway replenishment.[54] This is a strong sign that China is not moving to expand further into blue-water naval operations.

The PLAN also includes five much smaller cargo ships (4,300 to 8,800 tons displacement), and several dozen small oilers, many of them in the merchant fleet but apparently available for Navy tasking. These ships range from 530 to 2,300 tons displacement, and are not designed for underway replenishment. The Navy also has several other auxiliaries, including twelve submarine support ships and a small repair ship (converted from an old U.S.-built LST), as well as more than forty oceangoing tugboats. Troop transports include the four *Qiongsha*-class ships, each capable of embarking four hundred troops and all stationed in the South Sea Fleet.

Beijing continues to deploy a robust fleet of survey and research ships, led by four large (eighteen thousand tons displacement) "space event ships," which entered service between 1979 and 1999 to support China's space program.[55] An additional forty-seven ships serve multiple purposes, from exploring the ocean floor to intelligence gathering. The most modern are the two *Wuhu*-class surveillance ships, launched in 1997 and equipped with a flight deck. Some of these research vessels are operated for the Academy of Sciences, as are about two dozen other ships assigned to the Ministry of Communications or the Hydrographic Department. Additionally, as many as eighty fishing trawlers may be used for offshore surveillance, although their ties to the PLAN (if any) are not clear.[56]

Ballistic Missiles

The Navy's role in China's national nuclear deterrent force has been limited to its single *Xia*-class SSBN, with its eight Ju Lang-1 (JL-1) intermediate-range ballistic missiles. The JL-1, a solid-fuel, nineteen-

Table 5. Chinese Antiship Cruise Missiles

Designation	Range	Mach	Warhead	Altitude	Guidance	Remarks
S/HY-1*	40 km	1.3	400 kg	100–300 meters	I-band active radar	On older ships
HY-2/C-201	70 km	1.3	513 kg	100–300 meters	Active radar	
C-601	100 km	.9	510 kg		Active radar	B-6 launched
C-611	200 km	.9	510 kg		Active radar	Air-launched
HY-3/C-101	50 km	SS**	513 kg	100–300 meters	Cm-wave active radar	Ship-launched
YJ-1/C-801	40 km	SS	165 kg	50 meters cruise, 5–7 meters terminal	Cm-wave radar	Ship- and air-launched
YJ-2/C-802 (aka YJ-1)	120 km	.85	165 kg	50 meters cruise, 5–7 meters terminal	Mm-wave radar	Ship- and air-launched
YJ-6	50 km	.85	165 kg	50 meters cruise, 5–7 meters terminal	Mm-wave radar	Air-launched
YJ-8	40 km	.85	165 kg	50 meters cruise, 5–7 meters terminal	Mm-wave radar	Sub-launched
SS-N-22	160 km	2.5	300 kg	20 meters	Active radar	Complex terminal maneuvers

*Missile identification/parameters vary among different sources. **Supersonic hundred-kilometer-range, nuclear-capable missile, is due to be replaced by the Ju Lang-2 (JL-2), with an expected range of twelve thousand kilometers and possibly capable of carrying multiple, independently targetable nuclear warheads. The JL-1 took sixteen years to develop and deploy; the JL-2 will be a modification of the Dong Feng-31 (DF-31), which had its first test firing in 1999 and should be ready for maritime testing within the decade—well before the Type-094 SSBN is ready to go to sea.[57]

China's indigenous cruise missile development program dates back to the late 1950s, before which the PLAN had been operating the SS-N-2 Styx surface-to-surface missiles provided by the Soviet Union. Later purchases of the French-built Exocet missile provided an additional model to Chinese designers. Long-range—more than two hundred kilometers—cruise missiles are under development, and will include models launched from submerged submarines.[58] China has developed the capability of designing and manufacturing cruise missiles with close to state-of-the-art features. (See table 5.)[59]

The PLAN's short- to medium-range surface-to-surface missiles include the Shang You-1A (SY-1A), a version of the Soviet-built Styx, with a range of 70 kilometers. This missile has been widely exported and is in service on *Luda* destroyers, *Jianghu* frigates, and older missile patrol boats. Its successors, the YJ-1 and Ying Ji-2 (YJ-2), have a range of 40 and 120 kilometers, respectively, and are similar to the Exocet. They are in service on later *Jianghu* and *Luda* ships, on *Jiangwei* frigates, *Luhu* and *Luhai* destroyers, and newer (*Houjian*- and *Houxin*-class) missile patrol boats.[60] Two of the *Han*-class submarines may have been modified to launch either the YJ-1 or YJ-2 while submerged.[61]

Naval Aviation

The PLAN's own "air force," the PLANAF, is one of the world's largest naval air arms. It currently fields twenty-seven regiments, each with twenty-four to twenty-five aircraft. Total PLANAF strength is uncertain, as discussed in the previous chapter, but numbers approximately eight hundred aircraft. This number is likely to be reduced by about two hundred over the next decade, as the PLANAF continues to phase out its F-6, A-5, and B-5 aircraft. Since it was formed in 1952, its pattern of aircraft acquisition indicates that it is a "poor cousin" to the PLAAF. The PLANAF had yet (as of August 2000) to begin operating the

Su-27, although this aircraft, China's most modern, has been flown by the PLAAF for several years.[62] The PLANAF's front-line tactical airplanes include several-hundred F-6, F-7, and F-8 fighter-bombers and the A-5 strike aircraft.

The naval air force's missions include fleet air-defense, at-sea reconnaissance and patrol, ASW, electronic countermeasures, transport, mine laying, rescue, and vertical assault.[63] The PLAN's surveillance aircraft include six SH-5 amphibians and six maritime versions of the Soviet-designed Y-8 (AN-12) transport, which are capable of rudimentary ASW operations. The PLANAF also retains about fifty B-6 aircraft; twenty of these are able to carry antiship cruise missiles, while the remaining planes are used for surveillance and general utility missions.[64]

The most serious PLANAF shortfalls are in effective fixed-wing ASW aircraft, as well as the lack of tankers and command and control aircraft. The PLAAF is currently acquiring both of these latter aircraft types; eventually, the PLANAF will be able to take advantage of their services, but because of cost probably will not own its own assets.[65]

This highlights the PLANAF's lack of status both relative to the PLAAF and, within the PLAN, to the surface and subsurface communities. The PLANAF will probably not be able to afford either the Su-27 or the Su-30 as its next generation air-superiority aircraft; the F-10 might fill that role, but it is still unproven, despite more than ten years of development. Another important modernization issue is selecting a long-range strike aircraft to replace the B-6, although these will probably not be completely phased out for another decade. The PLANAF probably views the FBC-1, a strike aircraft that has been under development for more than a decade and is able to carry two to four C-801 antiship cruise missiles, as the B-6's successor.[66]

A particularly important element within the Navy's aviation arm is composed of helicopters (helos). The PLAN was the first Chinese service to operate helos, beginning with delivery of twelve French-built Super Frelons in 1977–78. France agreed to Chinese production of these helos as the Z-8, intended primarily for ASW, but it was not until 1994 that aircraft development was finally completed for these helos to be manufactured in China. About thirty-two of these aircraft have been produced; they reportedly operate from the following ships: the *Nanyun*-class and *Dayun*-class replenishment ships, the *Dajiang*-class submarine support and oceanographic research-class ships, and the *Xianyang Hong*–class surveillance ship. These helos have also been observed escorting Chinese submarines, especially those that are nuclear-powered and engaged in ASW operations.

China has also built the French-designed Dauphin (Z-9) helo in a Navy version, with as many as eighty-eight produced since 1980. These are operated from the *Luhu*-, *Luda II*-, *Jiangwei*-, and *Jianghu II*–class destroyers and frigates, as well as by the training ship *Shichang*. The latest Z-9s are equipped with dipping sonars and may also serve as a data link between missile-firing warships and the YH-8 SSM when attacking over-the-horizon targets (OTHT).[67]

The PLAN does not have any aircraft carriers in commission, under construction, or under negotiation for foreign purchase, despite continuing speculation in the press.[68] China has acquired four aircraft carriers during the past quarter-century: ex-HMAS *Melbourne* was purchased from Australia, nominally for its scrap value. The ship was scrapped, but only after engineers had measured the ship and learned what they could about carrier construction and operations from the hulk. Three ex-Soviet carriers, the *Minsk, Kiev,* and *Varyag,* have also been purchased by Chinese companies, supposedly for conversion to casinos. All three are decrepit hulks—*Minsk* and *Kiev* were two of the Soviet Union's first carriers and have been inactive for several years before being sold to Chinese interests. The *Varyag,* a unit in the Soviet's newest and largest classes of aircraft carriers, is equipped with a "ski jump" bow to facilitate fixed-wing aircraft operations. Its construction began in a Ukrainian shipyard in 1985; the 1989 collapse of the Soviet Union halted its construction ten years ago.[69] Neither the *Minsk, Kiev,* nor *Varyag* are viable candidates for refitting. As a result of their long periods of inactivity, their hulls and decks must be heavily corroded, their propulsion machinery seriously deteriorated, and their installed weapons and sensor systems, if still installed, beyond repair.[70]

China will eventually acquire large ships capable of operating fixed-wing aircraft, and there is some evidence that the PLAN has conducted training in simulated carrier operations for pilots and relatively senior officers.[71] Recent press reports advocating a PLAN carrier usually describe a forty-to-fifty-thousand-ton displacement ship, perhaps similar to the French-built *Charles De Gaulle,* as part of a special PLA construction program designated the "998 Plan."[72] The carriers would probably be constructed in China, since the only non-American shipyard with experience in constructing large (more than fifty thousand tons displacement) aircraft carriers is the Chenormorsky facility in Ukraine, which "has no carrier orders, no obvious prospects, and thus no active work force," and Russian yards in Severodvinsk and Saint Petersburg, neither of which has engaged in carrier construction since 1992.[73]

None of the reports of PLAN carrier acquisition have been confirmed, and there is no evidence that carrier construction is either underway or planned for the immediate future.[74] In February 1997, the president of the Spanish shipbuilding company Bazan, which built Thailand's small carrier, visited China to give a "sales pitch" to senior PLA and civilian defense officials. His visit was unsuccessful and serves as an indicator that China does not intend, at least in the near-term, to acquire aircraft carriers.[75]

Shortcomings

The PLAN recognizes its equipment deficiencies, as well as the difficulties it faces correcting them. The director of the General Armament Department, Gen. Cao Guangchuan, complained that "because of low pay, it was difficult for his department to retain top-quality scientists and researchers," and that "the task of developing the Navy's armaments is arduous."[76] The PLAN surface forces suffer in at least four areas.

AAW

First is the lack of effective *area* AAW defense—the ability to defend not just individual ships, but groups of ships. The *Luda* class has no surface-to-air missile (SAM) system at all; the *Luhu* and the *Luhai* classes are equipped with the French-built Crotale or its Chinese version, the HQ-7—a "point-defense" system.

A point-defense system is designed to defend its own launching ship; an "area-defense" system has the capability to defend a formation of ships. The key to this difference is the area-defense system's range, and its ability to detect and process multiple targets simultaneously, especially targets with a crossing component in their fire-control solution. The five *Jiangwei II*–class ships are equipped with the Chinese version (HQ-7) of the Crotale.[77]

ASW

Second are the PLAN's ASW suites. Despite promising developments using satellite-based radar to find submarine wakes and airborne lasers to detect submarines at depth, sound transmission through water (sonar) remains the most reliable way to detect a submarine. Transmitting sound through the water, however, does not occur in a straight line; the sound is "bent" by water depth, salinity, currents, and temperature. Sonar is also less effective in most coastal waters, due to decreased water depth, increased ship traffic, and mixture of fresh and salt water.

There are two operational sonar methods. Active sonar uses "echo ranging" to find a submarine by bouncing an audible signal off the hull. The ship transmitting an active sonar pulse can be detected at about twice the distance it can detect a submarine, however. ASW helicopters and aircraft can also employ active sonar. A better detection method is passive sonar, using hydrophones to detect the distinctive sound pattern—the "acoustic signature"—of a submarine. Passive sonar does not reveal the ASW ship's location, but requires a quiet ship, one that generates as little noise as possible.

Another way to categorize sonar is by frequency. Lower frequency active sonars are capable of extremely long-range detection but are most useful on the open ocean. High-frequency sonars have a shorter operational range but more definition than low-frequency systems; they are useful in coastal waters. It is possible for a ship to be equipped with both a relatively low-frequency sonar for detecting a submarine, and a high-frequency sonar to be used in shallow water or when attacking a submarine.

Finally, sonar may be mounted on the hull of a ship (either active or passive), towed behind it on a long cable (passive), or towed on a shorter cable as a "variable-depth sonar" (again, either active or passive). The latter two systems allow the sonar to be placed below thermal layers in the water, enhancing the range and probability of detecting submarines. It may use both active and passive means, and is usually more effective in the open ocean rather than in coastal waters.

PLAN ships make almost exclusive use of hull-mounted, active, medium-frequency sonars. This probably represents a financial and operational compromise, since this sonar type is the least expensive and simplest to operate of the various types discussed above. Only the two *Luhu*s are equipped with towed, variable-depth sonar although this also uses active, medium-frequency sound transmission.[78] Detecting submarines, especially from a surface ship, is a very difficult process and the PLAN is not taking advantage of available ASW technology, some of it forty years old.

China's Navy also lacks significant airborne and, apparently, seabed ASW resources. There are only a dozen old aircraft assigned to the ASW mission; China does not appear to have deployed bottom listening arrays in its coastal waters.[79]

Systems Integration

Third, effective operation in these complex mission areas, AAW and ASW, and in modern naval warfare in general, requires the effective integration of shipboard, airborne, and shore-based systems. There is limited systems integration in China's surface ships, and only basic central combat direction systems.[80] The PLAN is beginning to make progress in this crucial area of integrating the sensor, weapon, and command and control functions, but it appears that even China's newest ships have only partially integrated, automated sensor and weapon systems.[81] The combination of foreign and Chinese-built units within the same system—a French-built missile system with a Chinese air-search radar, for instance—complicates the integration problem.

Maintenance and Supply

Fourth, all the PLAN front-line combatants suffer from the foreign origin of many of their weapons and sensor systems, and in some cases their propulsion plants. Countries of origin, either design and/or manufacture, include France, Italy, the United States, Ukraine, and, especially, Russia and the Soviet Union. This makes maintenance training and supply support difficult. The *Luhu* class, for example, incorporates "more than forty advanced foreign technologies."[82]

Further problems result from different ships of the same class having different components or even different systems: stocking the adequate replacement parts, acquiring the correct test equipment, and training maintenance technicians are significantly complicated by a lack of commonality within and between systems. These complications commonly result in reduced system efficiency and hence warship lethality. PLAN writers recognize the benefits of systems integration and equipment commonality, and its absence may be due to

budgetary limitations, the mix of indigenous construction and foreign purchases, and the small number of ships in most PLAN
classes.[83]

Although PLAN commander Shi Yunsheng has claimed that the
"CPC leadership" believes "building a powerful People's Navy" is the
"major task of our Army building," there is little evidence that this is
little more than oratory.[84] Hence the PLAN's officer and enlisted personnel face increased requirements to get the most out of their ships
and aircraft.

Kilo-class SS   U.S. NAVAL INSTITUTE

Ming-class SS   U.S. NAVY PHOTO, COURTESY A. D. BAKER, III

Romeo-class SS

Luda-class DDG

Luhu-class DDG, *Harbin,* underway and approaching anchorage.

Luhu-class DDG showing the variable-depth sonar at its stern.

Fuzhou, China's most modern warship, one of two *Sovremenny* class DDGs purchased from Russia, steams to its new homeport while its crew mans the rails.   DEREK FOX

Jiangwei-class FFG   H&L VAN GINDEREN

Jianghu-class FFG

Jiangwei-class FFG, probably *Huaibei,* at anchor. Note telescoping hangar in the closed position.

Yukan-class LST

Fuqing-class AOR, *Fencang,* one of the PLAN's three replenishment-at-sea ships at anchor.

Luda II–class DDG *Zhuhai* at anchor during 1995 naval review in Indonesia.

Luda-class DDG refueling from a *Fuqing*-class AOR.

T-43-class oceangoing minesweeper

Nancang (*Nanyun 953*) AOR

Shichang-class multipurpose ship

B-6 (Tu-16) bomber

B-5 (Il-28) bomber

Zhi-8 (Super Frelon) helicopter

Z9 Dauphin helicopter on board *Luhai*-class DDG, *Qingdao*. The prominent "nose" probably contains radar or electronic-warfare equipment; also note the French-built RAST (recovery-assist-securing-traversing) system on deck.

H&L VAN GINDEREN

Left quarter view of Z9 Dauphin helicopter, looking forward on board *Luhai*-class DDG, *Qingdao*. The French-built Z9 is capable of launching antiair and antiship missiles.

H&L VAN GINDEREN

SH-5 amphibian

6

Personnel, Education, and Training

Discussion of PLAN modernization typically focuses on hardware—on new ships, submarines, missiles, and airplanes. That technological emphasis is understandable, but it too often overlooks the key factor in naval effectiveness: the personnel who man and operate the hardware. Addressing the Central Military Commission in 1999, Jiang Zemin stated, "We must place education at academies and universities in a strategic position among our development priorities. . . . We cannot do without high-quality talented military people. . . . Our goal [is] giving priority to developing military academies and universities and our goal of accelerating the cultivation of high-quality talented military people."[1]

This chapter will address the human factor in the Chinese Navy as it enters the twenty-first century. The PLAN is still overwhelmingly a male-dominated organization, although women play a role in shore administration and training billets, and are also active in the Marine

Corps.[2] The PLAN's manning structure will be discussed progressively: the first topic is the recruitment of officers and enlisted personnel. Second is a discussion of force structure and leadership considerations. Next, in order, are comments about PLAN schooling, training, and exercises. The sixth topic is discussion of the role played in PLAN manning by ideology, with a view to evaluating the issue of professionalism and political reliability in China's Navy.[3] When Jiang Zemin praised the military academies, for instance, he emphasized that they were responsible for "maintaining high ideological unity."[4]

PLAN Manning

The PLAN remains, in terms of manpower, the largest navy in the Pacific.[5] It was organized in 1950 with an initial strength of 450,000. In 2001, following completion of the 500,000 reduction in PLA manning announced by Jiang Zemin in 1997, personnel in the PLAN will number approximately 225,000.[6] Almost half this total is in the operating forces.[7] Of this number, approximately 25,000 man the PLAN air force and 12,000 the Marine Corps. Hence, about 75,000 are responsible for manning approximately 164 ships and submarines.[8] This gives a personnel-to-ship proportion of roughly 460, not significantly different from Japan's Maritime Self-Defense Force (415), or the navies of Korea (432), and Taiwan (420), indicating that the PLAN is utilizing its manpower relatively efficiently.[9]

The number and quality of naval personnel are central factors determining the force's efficiency and potential. Despite the draw-down in overall naval strength in recent years, certain PLAN "communities" have almost certainly been improved in terms of their personnel's qualifications and intellectual capability. These include the submarine force, especially the nuclear-powered boats; aviation units flying improved aircraft, such as the F-8II; and shipboard crew members who maintain and operate electronic and missile systems.

The Marine Corps is one arm of the PLAN that has continued to grow during overall PLA downsizing. The corps was organized as an infantry brigade, augmented by integral armor, artillery, engineer, and other supporting elements, totaling six thousand personnel.[10] Interestingly, Marine Corps officers are drawn from the PLAN and are able to move back and forth between naval and marine units during their term of service.[11] The corps began expanding in late 1998 and today includes two augmented brigades, totaling about twelve thousand personnel.[12]

The number of PLA personnel has been reduced to *increase* rather than *decrease* military power, as China seeks to fund state-of-the-art technology at the cost of low-skilled ground troops.[13] The drive to substitute personnel quality for quantity applies particularly to the PLAN, since naval systems are technologically intense, become operational only after long periods of research and development, and demand operating personnel who are intellectually capable and the product of extensive training.

The PLAN's manning problem is difficult; it is no longer practical to recruit young workers with little education. Today's technologically intense naval systems require recruits with sufficient education and potential to learn how to maintain and operate complex engineering, sensor, and weapons systems.[14] This demand has not been ameliorated by the absence of systemic assignment policies in the PLAN. Although naval personnel tend to remain in the same fleet and even in the same home port for long periods of time, there are no set terms for sea duty or shore duty. Assignments apparently are made based almost entirely on service needs. Even officer tour lengths are not standardized; although most ship commanding officers are in command for three to four years, in some cases this tour has lasted seven years.[15]

The advent of the revolution in military affairs has not, in PLA eyes, reduced the importance of the human element in warfare. Increased personnel expertise, in conjunction with technologically advanced systems, is described in the importance of "the organic integration of man and weaponry."[16] Modern warfare is understood to require educated, technologically competent personnel. "Human factors will be of primary importance" is how this is phrased in one recent PLA article,[17] while Jiang Zemin has argued that "manpower is a decisive factor in determining the outcome of war."[18]

The Navy faces tough competition attracting both officer and enlisted recruits, since the best-qualified young high school and college graduates have attractive opportunities in the private sector.[19] The PLAN has been trying to reduce the percentage of recruits in its force from more than 80 percent to 65 percent, and pay has also been increasing steadily during the past decade, with as much as a 100 percent increase for some ranks in 1999–2000.[20]

China's military conscription system targets males from eighteen to twenty years old and females eighteen and nineteen years old. Males up to the age of twenty-two may also enlist if they have a college education. All males must have completed at least junior school; females must be high school graduates. The winter 2000 Conscription Order emphasized this requirement.[21]

Recruiting is conducted on a county basis, with the number of recruits determined by unit needs. For instance, a particular naval unit would be assigned to a specific area, and authorized by PLA headquarters to recruit a specific number of recruits. The unit sends two or three junior officers as a "selecting team" to that county, where they join with the two or three personnel manning that county's People's Armed Forces Department to form a "recruiting team." Draft-age candidates are "called up" for physical and mental examinations; the preapproved number of recruits is selected from those who pass. Hence, each county's quota of recruits is determined by the needs of the military unit to which it is assigned in a given year.[22]

Enlistments have also been shortened from three years (for the army) and four years (for the Navy and Air Force) to two years for all services, as part of a 1999 overhaul of the enlisted rank structure. The PLAN, however, still requires a three- or four-year obligation, if the recruit is going to attend a technical training course before or immediately after reporting to his or her first operational unit. This policy illustrates the Navy's need for extensive technical training for its recruits.[23]

PLAN "boot camp" lasts twelve weeks and focuses on physical training and basic military orientation. Recruits then move on to their first duty assignment or for further training. Enlisted training and education typically occurs aboard the first operational unit or is conducted by a Base Command within one of the three geographic fleets. Each fleet command has a training directorate, with responsibilities that likely include training standardization and prioritization. These include "floating schools" in such specialties as engineering, medical, surface warfare, aviation, and submarine warfare. There is apparently no formal coordinating body among the three fleet training directorates, other than the chain of command from one fleet up to PLAN headquarters in Beijing and then back down to another fleet. The PLAN does not have established "type commanders," admirals with large staffs dedicated not to fleet operations but to ensuring that ships and aircraft of a particular class or type are maintained and trained to meet Navy-wide standards of operational excellence.[24]

The long-expressed PLA desire to emulate the U.S. Reserve Officer Training Corps (ROTC) programs for producing well-educated, technically oriented candidate officers is being implemented.[25] Agreements are being signed between MR headquarters and civilian universities by which the university receives compensation for producing military officer candidates.[26] The Guangzhou MR, for example, has a agreement with Wuhan University under which students who are selected by the PLA receive military training during summer and winter vacation periods in return for "national defense scholarships." The program is open to qualified undergraduate and graduate students who sign an agreement to join the PLA after graduation.[27]

The Navy is pursuing an especially ambitious ROTC-type program, establishing "science and technology cooperative ties" with more than one hundred colleges in twenty provinces and municipalities.[28] The "Chinese navy plans to recruit about 1,000 officers from non-military universities and colleges yearly beginning this autumn in an effort to meet its need for command and technical talent. . . . [These officers] will account for 40 percent of all naval officers by the year 2010."[29] The aim is to increase the educational level of naval officers, in recognition of the technological demands of leading a modern navy.[30] This program apparently continues to receive strong CMC support.[31]

The naval academies are the traditional source of new officers, and they are now trying to recruit new students who already hold civilian degrees, in an attempt "to cultivate more high-caliber officers for the Navy."[32] An effort is also underway to regularize the system of commissioning enlisted personnel, with the stipulation that "outstanding compulsory servicemen" must be vetted for "political and ideological firmness, professional and technological competence, a high cultural standard, and a fine physical and mental quality."[33]

PLAN officer candidates are also recruited directly from the civilian population. The military academies have sought as many as five thousand entrants annually, with the Navy giving priority to "outstanding student cadres" whom are willing to volunteer for submarine service.[34] Academy candidates are required to take the nationally administered Unified College Entrance Examination, usually in late June. The military academies (and other "special schools") have first choice of the successful applicants, before the other universities select; student preferences are of secondary consideration. New cadets are admitted on a provincial basis, almost always to the service academy in or nearest their native province.[35]

The PLAN has difficulty retaining highly trained enlisted and officer personnel. Again, China's rapidly growing economy offers attractive alternatives to sea duty and military discipline, particularly to the highly trained technicians the PLAN most wants to retain. At the end of the first enlistment, a sailor may reenlist for an additional three-year tour, followed by a succession of two four-year obligations, a five-year reenlistment, and, finally, a nine-year obligation. Total service is limited to thirty years or until the sailor reaches the age of fifty-five. To reenlist, the individual must be devoted to the national defense cause, be competent for the job, possess a desired skill, be a lower secondary or higher school graduate, and be physically healthy.[36] In most cases, a volunteer for reenlisting remains and receives additional training at his or her original unit.

The great majority of sailors leave the Navy after fourteen to eighteen years, which does not enhance development of a mature, experienced body of senior noncommissioned officers (NCOs). PLAN officers understand this problem and current training reforms instituted by Adm. Shi Yunsheng include the development of technically competent NCOs who are also effective leaders.[37] Civilian employees form an important element of PLA manning. They perform technical and specialist functions, mostly in schools, hospitals, and administrative centers, and comprise as much as 25 percent of total PLAN active-duty strength.[38]

Regulations and Structure

The PLAN's rank structure is similar to that of other navies, except that the senior officer who heads the Navy is nominally only a vice admiral (two-star rank in the PLAN), although the rank of full admiral (three-star insignia) does exist. There is currently only one other flag rank active, that of rear admiral (one-star insignia). Other officer ranks are senior captain, captain, commander, lieutenant commander, lieutenant, lieutenant (j.g.), and ensign. Enlisted draftee ranks run from seaman second class to seaman first class after one year of satisfactory duty. Volunteer enlisted personnel, including draftees who reenlist after their initial tour of service, are ranked as petty officers, grades 1 through 6. Petty officers grades 1 and 2 are "junior petty officers," those in grades 3 and 4 are "intermediate petty officers," and those who occupy grades 5 and 6 are "senior petty officers." Promotion through the enlisted ranks is based both on professional qualifications and time in service.[39]

This rank structure was overhauled in the 1999 reform of thirteen PLA Regulations on Military Service. A particular target of the restructuring was the NCO corps, which was "too narrow and . . . too small," especially in comparison to the "armed forces of some developed countries, a situation which is not conducive to winning local wars under conditions of modern technology." The new NCO corps continues to focus on promoting technicians, but also includes promotions for administrative, training, and operational specialists. Additionally, female sailors are now offered the opportunity to qualify for previously forbidden technical specialties.[40]

Professional Military Education

PLAN leaders have recognized the importance of training and education since their service's founding. The initial 1950 plan for organizing the Navy included schools to address command, submarines, fast boats, gunnery, aviation, joint service, political cadre, logistics, mechanical engineering, and naval engineering. The PLAN school structure has waxed and waned during the ensuing fifty years, across four broad phases.

The first period lasted from 1950 to 1960, when Moscow's influence was at its peak and the PLAN's curricula were based on the Soviet model. This included the study of service regulations, ordinances, and rules; damage control; biological-chemical warfare defense; ship building techniques; reconnaissance; navigation; gunnery; communications; electronics and counterelectronics; radar; and mechanical engineering.[41]

There then ensued a second, ill-defined period during which the PLAN leadership tried to absorb the lessons of the Korean War, the advent of nuclear technology, and the unsettled leadership situation involving the Peng Dehuai affair. The third period, marked by the GPCR, was as disastrous for naval professional education as it was for the PLA. The fourth period began after Deng Xiaoping's rise to power in the late 1970s. Deng instituted significant reforms; reorganization and consolidation of the PLA education system followed. In 1975, Deng Xi-aoping stated that "peacetime education and training should be considered a matter of strategic importance."[42] Finally, the founding of the National Defense University in Beijing in 1985 heralded a notable professionalization of military education in China.

The PLA initiated major changes in its education system's organization and curricula in 1998. The new program was undertaken by the CMC in the belief that "warfare is changing from a traditional mechanical war to an informationalized one," and that the "key in competing for strategic initiatives in the new century [is] the establishment of a new military educational system." This passage is evidence of apparent PLA belief in and understanding of an ongoing RMA: war by machine is being superseded by war conducted on the basis of controlling information. The CMC criticized the academies for many problems, "intensively manifested in the large number of colleges, the small scale of individual colleges, the dispersal of educational resources, low training standards, and the low profit of running schools."[43] Senior leadership comments consistently address the importance of political reliability, as well.

Jiang Zemin's 1999 remarks about the importance of the PLA's academies emphasized selecting cadres "who are strong in politics and good at education" as academy leaders. He also urged adequate funding for the academies "at the same pace as the increase in defense expenditures," while ensuring that teaching facilities and equipment "are ready to provide academies with new weapons and technical accoutrements."[44]

Gen. Fu Quanyou further described the military education system as designed to produce "strategist-type staff officers who are sharp-minded, knowledgeable, and enterprising and innovative. . . . Expert-type technical personnel [must be] proficient in professional work, command consummate skills, and have all-round qualities." Trainers must be "able to explain things, do things, teach things, and conduct ideological and political work."[45]

In April 2000, the CMC published the "Essentials for Reform and Development of Military Universities and Schools," which aims to define military education for the twenty-first century.[46] The new plan applies to both military schools and civilian universities participating in "ROTC." The "essentials" specify three types of programs: undergraduate degree programs for officer trainees, continuing education in engineering for serving officers, and "reading-for-degree" and postgraduate courses, also for active-duty officers.

tive to "focus training and education on high-tech conditions." This directive also linked higher education to officer promotion in the PLA. The campaign appears to be bearing fruit; recent statistics show that senior PLAN officers are both younger and better educated than their predecessors.[60]

Adm. Shi Yunsheng described his service's program to build "a new education system" covering combat command tactics, engineering technology, logistic management, political work, and rank and file education. He also described a "naval commander training system at four levels": technological, tactical, joint tactical, and campaign.[61]

This educational infrastructure is linked to PLAN officer advancement and eligibility for specific positions. Shipboard officers must complete the appropriate course of instruction before assuming designated duties. Ship and aviation squadron commanding officers must satisfy educational requirements, as well as demonstrate political reliability and operational expertise. Commanders are subject to a four-part qualification progression before taking command: they must satisfy requirements at the technological, tactical, joint tactical, and campaign levels.[62] These involve both practical and theoretical examinations, including "a wide range of professional knowledge and skills on thirty-four professional and academic subjects."[63]

The Navy has moved to link classroom education and operational training, with both addressing combat command tactics, engineering technology, logistics management, political work, and enlisted education and training. Although detailed information about career progression in the PLAN is scarce, officers probably follow a path similar to their American counterparts. A PLAN submariner, for example, takes about ten years of commissioned service to reach the position of executive officer, and another three to five years to receive a commanding officer assignment at sea.[64]

The first fruit of the 1998 military school reorganization was the Naval Engineering University, which opened in Wuhan in June 1999. This university, the PLAN's only "comprehensive university," one of just five such in the PLA, was formed by combining the previously independent Navy Engineering Academy and Navy Electronics Engineering Academy.[65] The new university is organized into thirteen departments, including warship kinetic engineering, electronic information, naval arms engineering, management engineering, communications engineering, and command and electronic warfare engineering. The curricula focus on integrating information technology with weapons systems, and with "tackling the key problem of [fus]ing and joining electronic information to weapons systems."[66] This sounds very much like an attempt to apply the theory of the putative RMA to the reality of naval operations.

Although the emphasis of recent revisions and innovations has focused on officer education, enlisted personnel have not been neglected. The most recent innovation established the All-Army Propaganda and Cultural Information Network, using Internet technology to enable centralized education among different bases and units. This system's ability to provide enlisted personnel with political education was lauded—another indicator of the leadership's concern with political reliability.[67]

Training

Training ships' crews previously occurred almost entirely aboard ship. Within the past decade, however, the PLAN has created more centralized facilities to teach personnel how to operate modern shipboard systems. These new schools/training centers are operated by each fleet's naval base commands to teach engineering, surface warfare, ship handling, aviation operations, submarine warfare, and medical operations, in addition to addressing specific equipment systems.[68]

Navies typically follow one of two general training models. The U.S. model maximizes the amount of training conducted under operational conditions—at sea and in the air. The Soviet/Russian model maximizes the amount of training conducted ashore and in port, not at sea. This difference is most easily quantified in the number of days a ship spends at sea in a given year, or the number of pilot flying hours per year. That said, the increasing availability of sophisticated shore-based trainers that accurately simulate real-time operational conditions has blurred the distinction between the two general training models.

The Chinese Navy historically has followed the Russian model; during the late 1950s, the PLAN translated more than one hundred Soviet naval training manuals, and published guidelines for conducting training at sea.[69] They emphasized a cautious, step-by-step approach to training—not surprising for a new navy. Today, however, PLAN surface ships apparently still only spend about twenty-four days underway each year, and its tactical pilots fly no more than 120 hours per year, both extremely low levels by U.S. (and other Western) standards.[70]

Some of this shortfall could be made up if the PLAN used a sophisticated shore-based training infrastructure, but that is still at a very basic level of development.[71] One recent exercise for destroyer commanding officers demonstrated this pattern. "The traditional training method," this report claimed, "was marred by overemphasis on duration and number of exercises to the neglect of training efficiency and by overemphasis on physical agility and skills to the neglect of brainpower."[72] Increased training efficiency is obviously laudable, but operating effectively at sea is in fact physically demanding; operating at sea requires training at sea.

Operating so infrequently in a real-world environment means that a ship's crew has to relearn basic procedures each time its ship gets underway, or its aircraft takes off. This establishes a training matrix with restricted potential. A warship's crew, for instance, that has to dedicate the first 25 to 50 percent of each underway training period ensuring that its crew remains proficient at basic individual and single-ship level tasks, will have considerable difficulty establishing crew proficiency at a level of complex, integrated, joint operations.

The 1985 shift in strategic focus to "high-tech wars on the periphery" has affected PLAN training and exercising. The shift from inshore to offshore defense requires a corresponding shift in at-sea training, to include open ocean navigation, seamanship, logistics, and operations, especially surveillance, command and control, and multiship formation training.

Coordinated training among subsurface, surface, and aviation units recognizes the increasing role played by technological advances in maritime operations, which depends on automaticity and integrated operations. Hence, the PLAN is expanding its exercise infrastructure and regimen, to include more multi-unit operational training, although the degree to which the above requirements are actually exercised is not clear. The PLAN explains the requirement for a new training paradigm in a historical context, claiming that "each major mass-scale military training campaign has invariably [been] accompanied . . . by the study of new knowledge [including] studying cultural knowledge in the 1950s and 1960s; studying science in the 1980s; and studying high technology at present. . . . The ongoing mass-scale campaign of military training with science and technology [requires that] to train soldiers, it is imperative to let them practice using their equipment."[73]

This new training program must also, in the PLA view, be integrated with developing technologies and instituted throughout the training infrastructure: "When the new equipment is still in the stage of preliminary research, military academies and schools should already introduce related courses; while the new equipment is being produced after design finalization, military academies and schools should be equipped with it first and incorporate it into the curriculum; as the new equipment arrives in units, the relevant mainstay personnel responsible for its command, operation, and maintenance should take up their positions with the arrival of the equipment, and . . . training provided to the units in a timely manner."[74]

This idea was stated more simply more than a decade ago, when the PLAN commander justified "long-distance training in the oceans" by stating that "the Navy belongs to the sea. . . . It is necessary to undergo training [on] the oceans, [and] become adapted to a life at sea for long period of time."[75] Gen. Fu Quanyou has illustrated possible conflict between "down to earth" exercises and budgetary concerns by noting the importance of "simulated training," "on-base training," and "training management," as opposed to training under battlefield conditions.[76]

The ability to train more at sea is supported by the recently commissioned, ten-thousand-ton-displacement training ship named *Shichang*. Previous PLAN training ships were devoted to officer surface training; *Shichang* is designed to take advantage of modular installations that enable it to serve interchangeably for surface navigation training for up to two hundred people, or to embark two to three helicopters for aviation training. It can also serve as a supply ship or a hospital ship, with the appropriate modules installed.[77] The vessel may also have the capability to serve as a fleet command and control ship. *Shichang*'s first voyage was reportedly a training cruise for reserve PLAN personnel. It has also participated in major exercises since then, including a July 2000 East China Sea Fleet operation dedicated to logistics training utilizing civilian shipping and a November 2000 exercise, apparently with the North Sea Fleet, that included navigation training, convoying, and civilian mobilization exercises.[78]

Individual ship training is a prerequisite to more advanced, multi-ship training exercises. Each of the PLAN's three fleets has a "vessel training center" where all new and overhauled ships receive training and certification before assuming combat duties with the operating fleet.[79] A small sampling of individual and small-unit training reveals a "building block" approach, with training progressing both in complexity and scope until a unit is qualified to join fleet-level operations. Such "building block" events include training in small-craft maneuvering, sea-lane interdiction, reconnaissance, submarine positioning and navigation, landing ship formation steaming, Marine Corps landing drills, weapons and sensor systems exercises, and aviation unit familiarization with new equipment. This training is conducted by shore-based "teaching staff" who both train and evaluate operational personnel, including assessment of commanding officers.[80]

The PLAN claims to be trying to make its training more realistic. The Nanjing and Guangzhou MRs, for instance, are credited with conducting "in-depth studies" on joint amphibious operations, with the Navy emphasizing "naval blockade, underwater surprise-defense, and mining of harbor piers," and the air force including in its training "low-altitude maritime attack" against ships. Throughout, the concern is to ensure that "training is as close to real combat as possible."[81] The fact remains, however, that the PLAN has not been observed significantly increasing the number of days it spends training at sea.

PLAN efforts to modernize its advanced training are marked by three characteristics. First is its experimental nature: post-exercise analysis is used to evaluate standardized exercises and derive doctrinal and tactical improvements. Second, joint and combined arms operations are emphasized, often with "blue" (i.e., enemy) and "red" forces opposing each other. Third, despite the assertions about the RMA and the importance of injecting "science and technology" into training, the PLAN continues to emphasize the importance of man over machine and technology.[82]

The PLA seems uncertain how best to mix the human element with "the application of science and technology," and learn to operate "under information conditions." Have PLA perceptions of the RMA affected its education and training? The General Staff Department's Officer Training Bureau's director has written that RMA has five features: (1) changing the components of the armed forces, especially in the campaign formation between different services; (2) introducing new combat means; (3) generating much larger combat space; (4) creating new modes of operations; and (5) inventing new methods of combat engagement.[83]

A long series of articles in *Jiefangjun Bao* shows concern with combined training, and sees the use of training simulators as a means both to save money and to enhance training, but does not seem certain about how to do so.[84] One rather extreme PLA view is that "we should bring true the change from 'two armies pitted against each other in front of each's [*sic*] positions' into 'confrontation on the net.' On a high-tech battlefield, network confrontation is more important than firepower confrontation."[85]

Information warfare (IW) and what the U.S. Navy calls "network centric warfare" has been strongly emphasized in various articles, but most repeat "buzzwords" without offering realistic links between concept and operational practice: "The main contents of training . . . are: basic theory, including computer basics and application, communications network technology, the information highway, digitized units and theaters, electronic countermeasures, radar technology, . . . together with . . . IW rules and regulations, IW strategy and tactics, and theater IW and strategic IW; information systems . . . information weapons . . . simulated IW . . . protection of information systems, computer virus attacks and counterattacks, and jamming and counter-jamming of communications networks."[86]

On a more prosaic level, PLAN training has focused on "multidimensional attacks against targets on the ground from the air and sea," with classroom courses on "sea-crossing landing operations."[87] Technical training has been modernized, to include logistical and other support facets of maritime warfare.[88] Furthermore, it is not clear that training is conducted with the same methodology and to the same standards in all three fleets.

Although the PLAN headquarters' Training Department should ensure Navy-wide uniformity, there are probably significant differences among the three fleets' training regimens, which would negatively impact standardization and complicate interfleet operations. Each fleet obviously is commanded by a different admiral, faces different strategic and operational environments, and deploys different ships and aircraft.

Exercises

Identifying and analyzing PLAN exercises is hindered by China's concern for secrecy. One source claimed that the Navy "successively held

as many as a hundred large-scale blue-water combined training programs and exercises" between 1979 and 1999.[89] An excellent 1996 study
identified ninety-six significant (division size or larger) PLA training exercises conducted between January 1990 and November 1995, a high
number of such training events, about sixteen per year.[90] The Navy participated in thirty-six of these, with half of that number also involving
the army and/or air force.

Fifteen of the thirty-six were characterized as "combined arms exercises," and fifteen of the thirty-six involved amphibious training.
The exercises were conducted fairly equally among the three different fleets, with the North Sea Fleet conducting thirteen, and the East
Sea and South Sea Fleets ten each. Some of this training probably involved units from more than one of the fleets operating together, but
that information was not available. One interesting facet is that despite appearing to be oriented primarily toward amphibious warfare,
the South Sea Fleet only engaged in approximately the same number
of amphibious training exercises, six, as did the East and North Sea
Fleets, five each. The PLA may also have established a dedicated amphibious warfare training area in the East Sea Fleet AOR.[91]

The PLAN has not engaged in many complex, joint, interfleet exercises. The most sophisticated exercise examined in this study was conducted in November 1995 on Dongshan Island, in conjunction with
and to influence Taiwan's legislative elections. Apparently, "a ground
force element of at least regimental size conducted an amphibious
landing supported by perhaps a battalion of amphibious tanks and six
or more transport helicopters with assault troops." Air support by Su-
27s and A-5 aircraft, airborne operations, PLAN fire support, and multiple landing beaches were all part of the exercise, which also demonstrated a "viable command and control system." The authors of the
study perceptively noted, however, that the exercise was a public relations event, and demonstrated PLA limitations as well as capability
conducting joint and combined-arms warfare.[92] The "jointness" of PLA
exercises is a common refrain in Chinese reports, including statements
by army and air force commanders.[93]

Furthermore, one major exercise had to be curtailed—"its amphibious landing phase was defeated resoundingly and realistically
by bad weather"—although the PLAN declared the exercise a success.
One Western observer has noted the important and troubling conclusion that while China evaluates some exercises as successful, most
other observers do not: "The gap between China's and the outside

world's perception of the consequences of China's coercive exercises is one of the most dangerous aspects of the Taiwan situation."[94]

The PLAN appears to have continued this training pace since 1995, which indicates serious intent to improve its ability to conduct amphibious, combined arms, and joint operations. The even spread of exercise types among the three fleets, another characteristic that has continued, indicates China's intent to develop fleets with relatively balanced capabilities—and perhaps reflects Beijing's opinion that none of the three fleets operates in a more threatening theater than the other two.

The following significant PLAN exercises have been identified from open-source reports. It is not an exhaustive list, but serves as a useful indicator of the pace and scope of naval training exercises in recent years.

The June 2000 exercises are particularly interesting as a strong indicator of the PLAN's interest in doctrinal development. They emphasized "securing beachheads, executing rapid maneuver along front lines, rapid establishment of air defenses, and securing logistics in conjunction with the use of antiaircraft artillery and landing vessels." Exercise goals included making an amphibious assault, ensuring logistics support, and moving inland, all in the face of enemy air superiority—a Taiwan scenario, in other words.

The above compilation does not include a unique series of humanitarian-oriented exercises that have been conducted in the Hong Kong area since the early 1980s. These "sea and air rescue exercises" (SAREX) have been conducted primarily by the U.S. Coast Guard and its Hong Kong counterpart. Since 1997 these annual exercises, usually conducted in January, have included participation by U.S. Navy and PLAN units. In 1999 and 2000, the SAREX participants included representatives from Vietnam's nascent coast guard.[95] A similar, but much larger exercise was recently conducted among units from Beijing, Hong Kong, and Macao.[96]

Jiang Zemin, as CMC chairman, frequently calls for the increased application of science and technology to training exercises, a call the PLAN is heeding. A "naval-aeronautical-antisubmarine" exercise in April 1999 demonstrated the North Sea Fleet's efforts to exercise many of the values described in the new combat regulations. Command and control of forces ashore, in the air, and at sea was exercised by the fleet's naval "Air Force Command Center," while the use of the satellite Global Positioning System was cited as an example of incorporating

Table 6. PLAN Exercises, 1995–2000

Date	Exercises	Fleet
January 1995	Joint Combined Arms (JCA), logistics, sea transport ops	North Sea Fleet
June 1995	JCA, amphibious ops	East and North (?) Sea Fleets
June 1995	JCA, amphibious ops	South Sea Fleet
August 1995	JCA, including missile, gunnery, ASW, AAW ops	North, East, South Sea Fleets
October 1995	JCA, including amphibious, ASW ops	East and South Sea Fleets
November 1995	Amphibious ops	East and South Sea Fleets
March 1996	JCA, including amphibious, airborne, hovercraft, helicopter ops: curtailed by bad weather	East Sea Fleet
October 1996	JCA, including amphibious, airborne ops	East Sea Fleet
July 1997	JCA, including amphibious, submarine, and submarine mining ops	South Sea Fleet
June 1998	Submarine ops	North Sea Fleet
April 1999	ASW ops (subsurface, surface, air units)	North Sea Fleet
July 1999	JCA, including militia, reserves, and "civilian vessel mobilization and acquisition" ops	East and North Sea Fleets
August 1999	Submarine ops	East Sea Fleet
September 1999	JCA, including amphibious, airborne, Special Operating Forces, unmanned air vehicles, militia, and reserves with "10,000" mobilized (and armed) civilian vessels[a]	East and South Sea Fleets
January 2000	"Light vessel" ops, including replenishment at sea, command and control	East Sea Fleet

[a] Widely reported series of exercises, announced by Zhang Wannian as intended to demonstrate the PLA's capability to ensure Taiwan did not achieve independence.

Table 6. PLAN Exercises, 1995–2000 *continued*

Date	Exercises	Fleet
April 2000	JCA, including amphibious, mine warfare, surface warfare, submarine, air, reserve, and militia ops[b]	North, East, South Sea Fleets
May 2000	"Light vessel" ops, including navigation, cover and deception, surface warfare, logistics[c]	East Sea Fleet
June 2000	JCA, amphibious, air defense, logistics ops	South Sea Fleet
June 2000	Joint, mine, antiair, amphibious, mine warfare ops[d]	North Sea Fleet
July 2000	Joint, amphibious, communications, "integrated" ops	East Sea Fleet

[b] Announced as a "rotational combat exercise," designed as "much closer to actual combat."[97] A significant exercise, described in "Three Fleets Join Forces and Over 1,000 Fighters Dispatched Within an Hour," *Hong Kong Tai Yang Pao*, 1 May 2000, in FBIS-CPP20000501000027, as a "super exercise." Despite the obvious hyperbole in this report, the exercise was one of the few involving all three PLAN fleets. Li Nien-ting, "The PLA Conducts Sea-Crossing Surprise-Attack operation Exercise," *Sing Tao Jih Pao*, 20 February 2000, in FBIS-CPP20000221000015, reports a PLAAF exercise conducted with a PLAN "submarine unit" and PLA antiaircraft artillery units, but this probably refers to the same exercise noted above.

[c] Chi Yongbo, Xu Gangyao, and Si Yanwen, "Light Cavalry on Sea Moves from Inshore Waters to Offshore Waters," *Jiefangjun Bao*, 17 May 2000, 2, in FBIS-CPP20000517000048, dwells on the personnel limitations—food and water, navigational capability, seaworthiness—of operating small combatants on the high seas.

[d] Li Tianhong and Liu Xueming, "PLA Army Vessel Units Have Transformed from Focus on Transportation Duties and Guarantee to On-the-Sea Mobile Combat," *Jiefangjun Bao*, 4 June 2000, 1, in FBIS-CPP20000605000090, is notable for concentrating on the role of ships manned by army troops; this is not unique to China (the U.S. Army, for example, mans more "ships" than does the U.S. Navy), but provides an additional source of amphibious shipping to PLAN strategists.

"science and technology" into the exercise.[98] The exercise was "live," with operational units participating in all phases of training; doctrinal impact was achieved through post-exercise analysis and a "lessons learned" process, aided by the use of collated, computerized "radar and command guidance" information.[99]

This exercise demonstrates PLAN efforts during the past five years to focus on translating the "science and technology" logo into meaningful exercises. The 1999 Navy Military Training Working Conference focused on this problem, touting the development of "analogous" multifunctional training systems for surface and subsurface warfare, to include simulated missile, gun, and torpedo targets that are "increasingly more scientific and closer to the requirements for actual combat."[100] Here too, however, the PLAN seems to be focusing on ways to compensate for the lack of training at sea with real systems.

Ideology and Professionalization: Politics at Sea

Chapter 1 included a discussion of the history of the crux of civil-military relations in China, training personnel who are both ideologically "sound" and professionally competent. At one level, this becomes a question of allocating training hours: for instance, how many hours each week does a newly commissioned naval officer aboard a *Luhai*-class destroyer spend studying Marxism-Leninism-Maoism, as opposed to studying the maintenance and operation requirements of the sonar system for which he is responsible?[101]

Reorganization of military schools and the attempt to modernize their curricula and ties to the operating forces are evidence of the torch having been passed from the revolutionary generation to that which is leading the Navy into the twenty-first century. The old ideological struggle in the PLA between political reliability ("Red") and professional knowledge ("expert") has been decided in favor of the latter.

While the question of political reliability is still an issue with China's leadership, it is likely no more than a marginal concern in the everyday operation of the PLAN. Modernization has been explicitly embraced and has been accompanied by increasing professionalization. This in turn means that an officer will become a specialist as his or her career progresses, since the increasing complexity of modern, technologically intense sensor and weapons systems demand increasingly specialized knowledge. Such knowledge is gained only through schooling and repeated operational tours in the same warfare specialty, and/or with the same system. "Warfare specialties" include air/antiair, surface/antisurface, submarine/antisubmarine, mine, electronic, engineering, and command and control.[102]

Another aspect of this question is PLA officers' view of themselves "as chief protectors of China's territorial interests and national honor."[103] The PLA may never directly govern China, but the PRC's history is one of close military-civilian rule; from 1949 until the 1990s the nation's rulers were both military and civilian figures. Jiang Zemin is the first truly civilian ruler of China since 1911.

The increasing professionalization in the PLAN does not necessarily detract from its loyalty to the CCP, of course, but that appears to be a matter of serious concern to the leadership in Beijing. Today's officer corps is undoubtedly more technologically oriented and professionally educated than at any time since 1949. It also is the product of a distinctly military career. This might be expected to lead to an increasingly strong sense of cohesiveness and esprit among officers, including strong nationalistic leanings. That in turn does not require a choice of loyalty to state vice party, but the National Defense Law of 1997 suggests that choice has been made—in favor of the state. "Paradoxically," however, in the words of Ellis Joffe, "professionalism has intensified, rather than reduced" the involvement of PLA leaders determining Beijing's policies, especially with respect to Taiwan.[104]

The organization for exercising political control in the military has not, on paper, changed since the founding of the PLAN, but the reality is different, since military and political elites are no longer identical.[105] This role in turn may be contributing to a separation of the officer corps from the CCP, a separation exacerbated by the generally much-reduced role of the party throughout Chinese life. In the early years of the PLAN, the commissar had to approve the commanding officer's orders. This became a particular point of contention following the Korean War.[106]

Political education in the PLA emphasizes the importance of party supremacy over the military.[107] President Jiang Zemin, Defense Minister Chi Haotian, Gen. Zhang Wannian, and other leaders repeatedly emphasize the PLA as a party army. The frequency of such statements indicates both discomfort with a perceived lack of political awareness in the PLA and belief that the Chinese military must remain a party army.

In a long article in 1999, Gen. Chen Bingde, then commander of the Nanjing MR, repeatedly emphasized the revolutionary character of the PLA, the importance of "ensuring eternal political qualification. . . . Giving top priority to strengthening ideological and political work. . . . Accepting the absolute leadership of the party. . . . Further improve and strengthen ideological and political work in the Army

. . . [and] study in depth how to effectively do ideological and political work in the Army."[108]

The political commissar represents the party in PLAN operational units. His importance as military decision maker has been reduced as increasingly complex systems and technology characterize the Navy. The commissar's original role in a Leninist military was to serve as co-commander of the unit, with a perhaps determining voice in operational decisions. This role has changed, however, and current political commissar duties focus on several important but essentially non-operational areas. This in turn probably represents a reduction in the importance of the PLA's General Political Department in the functioning of the PLAN at the fleet level and below.

Political commissars are also more highly educated and trained than in past years. They face professional military education requirements similar to their "professional" counterparts, including attendance at National Defense University courses.[109] A unit's political commissar is still an important individual possessing significant duties.[110] These focus on personnel management and include assigning personnel work and housing, looking after their morale and welfare, serving as party educators with local reserve and militia units to ensure that their training conforms to CCP dictates, and helping to find employment for the large number of personnel demobilized as a result of recent force reductions.[111] The commissars also must champion various PLA reforms, such as Jiang Zemin's "five sentence prescript."[112]

The current role of the political commissar in the PLAN is primarily that of educator in CCP and navy theory ("political work") and regulations, personnel officer, and counselor; his position as party representative still carries weight.[113] These duties were summed up in a recent *Jiefangjun Bao* article:

> It is difficult to raise great enthusiasm for troop training in science and technology and more difficult to continue it persistently. . . . [But improving] the purposefulness of the political work in the training can sweep obstacles from the path. . . . When troop training reforms face frustrations, a boost of enthusiastic encouragement can often help officers and soldiers rise again with force and spirit to overcome difficulties. . . . Political officers at all levels should conscientiously study the essence of the CMC's directive, arduously study and master the laws and characteristics of the troop training in science and tech-

nology . . . We should go far into the training ground . . . regarding the
political work in the process of the troop training.[114]

Political commissars are further admonished to "take the top responsibility for the military modernization construction on the precondition of adhering to the principle of 'politically qualified.'"[115]

⌒⌐

The PLAN serves a nation with a rapidly expanding economy and an
increasingly well educated population. The positive aspects of this
situation include a pool of better educated and intellectually qualified personnel from which officers and enlisted personnel may be
drawn for service in a navy that is increasingly dependent on sophisticated technology. The situation also has negative aspects, however,
given the reduced motivation for young men and women to elect
naval service rather than entry into the booming economy.

Once in the Navy, personnel are subject to an apparently logical,
progressive structure of education and training. The education-
training-exercise paradigm established by the Chinese Navy is coherent on paper, but hampered by the short service term of recruits, the
decentralized administration of training, and the apparently ill-
defined operational objectives for the PLAN as a whole. Furthermore,
the priority assigned ideological training in the Navy is unclear, but
certainly continues to affect professional development.

While public assessments by the PLAN inevitably laud operational
training and exercises in the highest terms, an undertone of dissatis-
faction is apparent. The frequent admonitions to educate, train, and
exercise in accordance with the dictates of high technology and modern methods evidences this feeling.

Significant in this respect is the account by two senior captains
who served as on-scene observers of one of the U.S. Navy's most advanced, complex exercises, RIMPAC 98. In an interview published in
Jiefangjun Bao, these officers were unable to restrain their enthusi-
asm for several aspects of the operational expertise they witnessed,
including equipment such as advanced automation, information pro-
cessing technology, and night-vision systems. On the personnel aspects, they emphasized the "rigorous and regular personnel training"; the ability to operate at sea for extended periods, "whole-staff,
whole-system, whole-function, and whole-course training"; the ability of equipment to operate continuously for long periods; personnel
and equipment safety awareness and programs; frequent and contin-

uing personnel education and training; systematic equipment maintenance procedures and practices; delegation of responsibility to lower-ranking officers and enlisted personnel; and shipboard cleanliness. Perhaps most telling was their emphasis on having witnessed consistent "specific efforts in a down-to-earth manner instead of shouting empty slogans."[116]

This report highlights both the limits of our knowledge of PLAN operations and readiness and a tentative conclusion that China's Navy has a very long way to go before becoming a twenty-first-century force. Whether and when the PLAN achieves that status will depend in large part on the national priorities set by Beijing and the national maritime strategy it follows.

7

Doctrine and Operations in the PLAN

Doctrine is defined in the United States as "fundamental principles by which the military forces or elements thereof guide their actions in support of national objectives [and which] is authoritative but requires judgment in application."[1] It provides the crucial bridge between strategic intent and operational effectiveness. Doctrine is nominally driven by anticipated missions, perhaps illustrated by scenarios to which military planners respond.

The *Chinese Naval Officer's Manual* lists the following operational missions for the various PLAN warfare communities.

Surface Fleet

attack enemy warships
antisubmarine warfare
amphibious warfare
mine warfare
coastal defense

maritime surveillance
merchant ship convoys
logistics
search and rescue

Submarine Force

attack enemy naval bases and coasts	maritime patrol and reconnaissance
strategic nuclear strikes	logistic lift
mine warfare	search and rescue
interdicting enemy logistics	

PLAN Air Force

attack enemy naval installations	antisurface warfare
	anti-air warfare
defend PLAN surface and submarine forces during offensive operations	maritime reconnaissance
	early warning
	communications
antisubmarine warfare	logistic lift
amphibious warfare	search and rescue
mine warfare	

Marine Corps

forward base seizure	coastal defense[2]
amphibious warfare	

These lists contain some unusual features. One is that "strategic nuclear strikes" is given as the first mission for a submarine force apparently incapable of executing it. A second is assigning "logistic lift" to submarines, a mission long abandoned by other navies. Third, no mention is made of electronic warfare as a mission. Fourth, ASW is not assigned to the submarine force. And finally, no mention is made of special operations or joint operations for any element of the PLAN. This list of missions does illustrate, however, that modern maritime warfare is multidimensional and becoming steadily more complex as information-age developments are adapted for naval use.

Operational Doctrine

The PLAN has operated successfully on several occasions since it was founded in 1949. Doctrine, however, has often followed rather than preceded operations. The PLAN learned from its failures and successes in the Taiwan Strait in the 1950s and was successful against the South Vietnamese Navy in 1974 and against the Vietnamese Navy in

1988 in the South China Sea. The reorganization of the Marine Corps is evidence of the PLA's development of operational doctrine for power projection.[3] The Marines contributed six hundred troops to the 1974 takeover of the Paracels; major amphibious exercises continue. Marine units are also training with airborne forces and to operate from submarines.

Innovative operational doctrine can compensate for some material shortfalls. The chief lesson of Desert Storm and Kosovo for the PLAN, where U.S. superiority in military technology and operational power was graphically demonstrated, may well be that Chinese maritime power for at least the next fifty years will lack the capability for successful direct confrontation with U.S. forces. Instead, the PLAN will have to rely on speed, mobility, flexibility, and initiative in a contest with the United States. A logical step in such a conflict would be to gain the initiative through preemption. This does not necessarily require a "bolt from the blue" but could be achieved by seizing the initiative at a time of significant naval weakness on the part of the adversary.

Chinese strategists are justly proud to trace their heritage back to Sun Zi's *Art of War*, a compilation of writings from sixth century B.C. China. The author focused on the moral and intellectual aspects of war rather than on physical measures. While there is nothing unique to that heritage in avoiding an enemy's strength, a PLAN strategist could be expected to advocate military action in East Asian waters at a time when the U.S. aircraft carrier homeported in Japan is deployed to the Persian Gulf. Immediately available U.S. maritime power would be further limited at a time when the carriers homeported in the United States were engaged in long-term maintenance or not "worked up" for their next deployment. Another way to reduce U.S. resources would be to instigate a crisis on the Korean Peninsula to absorb Okinawa-based Marines and the U.S. air forces in Japan and Korea.

Operational doctrine, however, should also be linked directly to capabilities. The PLAN is aware of this increasing complexity, but has yet to demonstrate the capability to operate in that environment. A recent director of the PLAN's Research Institute described future maritime conflict scenarios in futuristic terms of three "theaters"—space, undersea, and electromagnetic: "Land-based arms will be sharply improved [and] will be able to powerfully strike and intercept formations at sea, . . . In sea-air combat, electronic warfare and missile strikes, particularly long-distance strikes by warships, their carrier-based aircraft, and aerial combat fighters, will become the essential forms. . . . The appearance of underwater aircraft carriers and undersea mine-laying robots, and even the construction of seabed military bases, will sharpen surface-undersea combat. In sea-space combat, space-based methods and forces are going to have a very conspicuous status in future naval warfare."[4]

Clearly, the PLAN wants to participate in the RMA; systems acquisition, personnel education and training, and fleet exercises address capabilities that fall under the RMA rubric. The military-industrial and PLAN infrastructures are not yet capable of implementing them, but given the inherent uncertainties of an RMA, Chinese efforts in that direction should not be discounted.

One of the PLA's recently revised regulations, perhaps the most important in terms of warfighting capability, is the Chinese PLA Program for Combined Campaigns.[5] This regulation connotes a strategy-doctrine-operational art-tactics progression that could describe twenty-first-century PLAN capabilities. Throughout, the "Combined Campaigns" regulation emphasizes the importance of standardization and of science and technology, since these "have now become the key factor in deciding upon the outcome of a war."

At the strategic level, entering "a new stage of historical development," the PLA must learn from "several recent local wars" (presumably including U.S. campaigns in Iraq and Kosovo). The regulation requires the PLA to "strive to take the initiative" in war, while further refining "the People's War strategy and the People's War tactics." This apparent modernization process may indicate a final break with the Maoist doctrine of fighting a "People's War at sea." The early PLAN resorted to a form of guerrilla war at sea because of its operational focus on inshore waters, its lack of oceangoing warships, and the dominance of leaders with an Army background. Today, "People's War" seems to mean not so much guerrilla war as it does finding the personnel capable of learning to fight a war under modern "high tech" conditions.

Doctrinally, the regulation first delineates "the principle of unity" —emphasizing that the "new-generation PLA" regulations must "uphold a unified combat ideology," to include training and tactics. Second, the "Combined Campaign" regulation applies to both single-service and joint combat operations: naval units "will have clear-cut combat regulations to abide by and a unified combat ideology to follow in different types of combat operations launched at different levels."

The locus of doctrinal development within the PLAN is not obvious, however. It is not clear, for instance, that the Navy's Beijing headquarters has a determinative position in promulgating doctrine, especially in view of each of the geographic fleets having its own training department. Discussion with PLAN officers indicates that significant doctrinal development occurs at the fleet and/or military region level, which could lead to significant differences among the operational fleets.

This leads directly to considerations of "readiness," defined as a measure of a particular ship, squadron, or even fleet's ability to carry out various assigned tasks effectively. A fully combat-ready navy unit would be sufficiently trained to be able to carry out successfully all assigned missions. Hence, "readiness" is a measure of a navy's training, doctrine, and administration processes. We have little information about PLAN combat-readiness on a continuing basis, although specific exercises, such as those conducted in the vicinity of the Taiwan Strait in 1995–96, evidenced a very respectable level of readiness by the East Sea Fleet and associated units.

Third, at the operational level, the new regulation addresses local war fought under high-technology conditions. This in turn has yielded "tactics with Chinese characteristics," including a new command system that applies to logistic support, political work, information war, "an electronic confrontation battle," and "an anti–air raid battle." These tactical elements have been "given full scope" in PLAN training activities. The importance of science and technology is again underlined, with those factors embodied in training activities that emphasize the use of simulators, joint campaigning, the systematic application of force, and a combat environment "in light of an information war and a digitized battlefield."

This, and the other new regulations promulgated by the CMC in 1999, show a firm appreciation of the basic characteristics of modern warfare, demonstrated or at least foreshadowed in the Persian Gulf War and the allied campaign in Kosovo. The regulations also reflect PLA frustration at China's laggard pace in being able to operate at the new level. This Combined Campaign regulation, for instance, closes with a call for "optimizing" new weapon development and "developing a batch of offensive means capable of simultaneously serving as a deterrent 'trump card'" in combat operations. It further calls for the "informationalization" of "existing PLA weaponry and equipment [to heighten] PLA combat effectiveness as quickly as possible."

The PLAN is trying to implement the new regulations through increasingly intense and advanced operational training and exercises. PLA strategy, doctrine, and tactics may, as a result, play a stronger role in achieving China's national security goals.

PLAN research and development efforts appear focused on creating a modern navy capable of carrying out at least a green-water maritime strategy, but China's research and development still suffers from fifty years of violent political changes that rent the educational and scientific fabric of the country. China currently is capable of building capable warships, but ships built in 2000 on a 1970 technological base are obsolete when their hulls first hit the water. They are not necessarily ineffective but must be employed conservatively and imaginatively.

Beijing's recent naval purchases, especially from Russia, demonstrate its determination to speed the pace of naval modernization—and possibly its frustration at China's inability to develop its own important naval systems.[6] The ships and systems acquired in the past twenty years are credited with giving China "a significant main naval fighting force" but one inadequate "to have all-around (three-dimensional) control of blue water." The PLAN leadership seems to understand what it needs to achieve its strategic goals.[7]

Senior Chinese strategists appear to understand the U.S. Navy's overwhelming superiority to the PLAN and its determinant role in maritime Asia. Two examples are submarine-launched ICBMs and fleet air defense. First, China may have once, in 1988, successfully launched a missile from its single ballistic-missile submarine; the United States in March 1999 conducted its eighty-first consecutive successful launch and flight to target of an ICBM, in that case a Trident D-5. Second, the PLAN's newest warship, the *Luhai*-class destroyer, and its prospective *Sovremenny*-class ships purchased from Russia, are equipped with only a very limited air-defense missile system; the United States is already developing the follow-on to Aegis, even now far more capable than any other AAW system in the world.[8]

Despite this situation, more junior planners and PLAN officers no doubt are laboring to find an operational schema that will allow them to defeat, or at least sidestep, U.S. naval and air power. This is not an easy task, since the U.S. naval forces in East Asia normally include two aircraft carriers, approximately twelve cruisers and destroyers, several of them armed with the Aegis system, two to four nuclear-powered submarines, four to six underway-replenishment ships, and an amphibious ready group. Centered around a forty-thousand-ton displacement helicopter carrier, this group includes two other ships and supports the Marine brigade on Okinawa. Air assets include Navy and Marine Corps air wings, as well as the Fifth, Seventh, and Thirteenth Air Forces.

Specific scenarios are almost certainly used for planning purposes. SLOC defense is one scenario, or rather, strategic ambition, that might appeal to naval planners. Expanding or building PLAN and PLANAF bases in the Spratly Islands and on Burmese territory would provide a starting point for a major Chinese role in controlling the Malacca and associated straits. It would place the PLAN astride the points vital to China's increasing dependence on offshore petroleum resources and, indeed, to the economic life of East Asia.

Operational Implications

China's ability to exercise power at sea is key to its operational doctrine. Naval power requires the ability to exercise not just sea denial, but the ability to control or significantly affect events ashore from sea-based units. The objective may be a continent or a small island; the means can range from a demonstration offshore to launching cruise missiles, to landing special operations forces from a submarine, to a full-scale amphibious invasion.

The first requirement facing the PLAN is developing the ability to transport and support forces at sea, over time. China has never possessed a robust capability to transport and land troops under combat conditions, and the PLAN currently does not appear to be making a dramatic effort to correct this deficiency.[9]

China's large and growing merchant fleet means that each of the three fleets has access to enough civilian vessels to embark several divisions of troops. Mobilization of some of these assets has been exercised, but the existence of a regularized, practiced system of mobilization of these assets is problematical.[10] Arguments that civilian shipping can be used in a successful amphibious assault against Taiwan are unconvincing.[11]

Second, if China's 1992 law claiming the South China Sea as sovereign waters is to be enforced, the PLAN will have to be able to implement Article 10, which asserts that "foreign naval vessels . . . must obtain China's permission before proceeding through the South China Sea" and foreign submarines must surface and fly their country's flag. If they do not comply, Beijing "can order the eviction of foreign naval vessels" from its waters.[12] The PLAN does not possess this capability, and it has no modernization or expansion programs that will lead to its ability to "evict" a well-managed naval force from the South China Sea.

The PLAN has frequently demonstrated its ability to deploy and maintain ships in the South China Sea, both on routine operations and in exercises.[13] In mid-October 1996, for instance, the PLA reportedly conducted a fifteen-day exercise "seizing islands."[14] This drill, as well as those conducted in the vicinity of Taiwan in 1995 and 1996, is clear evidence of the PLAN exercising in support of national strategic objectives: the linkage between training and/or exercising and maritime strategy is more significant than the technological complexity of the actual training. These exercises do not, however, demonstrate that the PLAN is capable of fulfilling its Article 10 responsibilities against naval and air power wielded by an alerted, determined opponent in the South China Sea.

The third twenty-first-century PLAN requirement is to possess the technological sophistication and personnel expertise required to accomplish its strategic goals. Adm. Shi Yunsheng has listed five attributes of a modern navy, all of which pose a challenge to the PLAN: (1) strengthened "research on naval strategies," (2) "vigorous development of high-tech equipment," (3) train personnel "with modern and scientific and technological qualities" to operate its "modern equipment," (4) effective "medium and long-term" plans, and (5) "modernization of the main equipment of the navy."[15]

Shortfalls in meeting these objectives may be at least partially compensated for by innovative operational doctrine. The RMA, which was demonstrated in Desert Storm and dramatically emphasized during the U.S. campaign in Kosovo, appears to offer such an opportunity to some PLA strategists. One has written, for instance, that "cruise missiles are the vanguard, aerial strength is the main power, and the ground, sea, air, space, and electromagnetism are integrated. This will become a basic mode for the recent and future high-technology regional war."[16]

There is little evidence that China has progressed very far in developing operational capability in this possible future realm of warfare, but the PLAN has in fact made significant strides in certain areas, such as cruise missiles. Table 6 shows that the Chinese Navy now deploys a large family of very capable antiship missiles.

Fourth, the use of maritime militia forces continues to receive attention as a means of supplementing fleet manning, as noted in chapter 5. The use of militia at sea, couched in Maoist terms, is potentially useful in a coastal defensive scenario: "Maritime militia guerrilla warfare under high-tech conditions include carrying out feints to deceive and confuse the enemy, conducting harassment raids on enemy targets on the sea, and carrying out blockades, blocking, striking, and bombing to destroy the enemy's island (or coastal) facilities." The author, the Fujian MR commander, characterizes guerrilla warfare at sea as requiring thorough planning and preparation, "scientific organization," unified command and close coordination, stealth, seizing the initiative, and fast-paced operations. His further emphasis on "rational use" perhaps indicates the practical limits of this concept.[17]

The fifth requirement the PLAN faces are financial, industrial, and technological limitations integrating the RMA; nuclear deterrence may receive renewed priority. China has built two strategic missile submarines, neither of which was operational in 2000. These ships are capable of launching the CSS-N-3 intermediate range ballistic missile (IRBM), which has a range of seventeen hundred kilometers.[18]

China is planning to build a follow-on class to the *Xia*, the Project-094 boat, almost certainly with Russian assistance. This effort has the potential to alter radically the strategic maritime picture in the Pacific. A Project 094 armed with the new JL-2 ICBM (a maritime version of the DF-31 under development in mid-2000) would for the first time enable China to put a strategic deterrent to sea that would credibly threaten the United States. The new SSBN may go to sea during the next decade.[19]

Sixth, any effective naval force requires air power, and no aspect of PLAN modernization attracts more interest and generates more concern than indications that the PLANAF is becoming dramatically stronger. This has several aspects.

Aircraft carriers would be seen as providing China with air cover for the long-range power projection needed to seize and hold disputed territory such as the Spratly Islands. Also, a PLAN carrier force operating east of Taiwan would place that island's air defense forces in the middle of an attack from two fronts, if the PLA were able to coordinate carrier-based attacks with shore-based attacks from the mainland.[20]

The arrival of U.S. carriers in the Taiwan area in March 1996 frustrated PLAN strategists. Never did Beijing more directly feel the effectiveness of aircraft carriers as political instruments. Furthermore, senior PLA officers appreciated the operational importance of two versus one carrier: if one U.S. carrier had been deployed, it would have constituted a diplomatic signal; two carriers were sent, however, which constituted an operationally effective force able to fly air-strike missions twenty-four hours a day for several days.[21]

The 1996 crisis forcefully reminded the PLA of American command of the seas in East Asia, and that the PLAN's ability to carry out missions opposed by the United States is nil, unless a way is found to nullify American sea power. Indeed, Chinese acquisition of a carrier in the near future, in conjunction with the purchase of anticarrier *Sovremennys*, might indicate that the United States' 1996 action spurred China's naval modernization on a scale similar to that followed by the Soviet Union after the embarrassment of the 1962 Cuban Missile Crisis. If the Soviet Navy's very impressive Okean exercises in 1975 is the bench mark, a similar blue-water demonstration by the PLAN could be expected by about 2005, but there is little evidence that the PLAN is moving toward that goal.

Aircraft carriers are a means, not an end, however, and PLAN strategists who favor large carriers are likely pursuing the wrong objective. The "end" is correcting the PLAN's most crucial shortcoming—the lack of air power at sea. Shore-based air power offers the PLAN a second and probably more efficacious route to winning control of maritime air space. Fuel limits and air control are the two key ingredients in effective maritime air power, especially if the aircraft launch from shore bases and have to operate hundreds of miles from the coast.

China is developing the capacity to refuel tactical aircraft in the air; Chinese press coverage of the October 1999 parade marking the PRC's fiftieth anniversary included pictures of a close formation of an aerial tanker and two tactical aircraft. The latter were not actually "hooked up" to the tanker, but the PLAAF and the PLANAF have both successfully conducted air-to-air refueling.[22]

Air control is the second of these basic requirements. Given the strong influence of Soviet doctrine in the PLA during the past fifty years, it is logical to assume that PLAAF and PLANAF air control follows the relatively rigid Soviet model of very close control. That may not be a disadvantage if PLAN operational missions are tightly focused on limited offshore tasking, such as coastal patrol and ship surveillance, and sector-limited air defense. The employment of maritime air power becomes more demanding, however, in other operational scenarios such as ASW, amphibious assault operations, and area defense. The summer 2000 Israeli refusal to complete the sale to China of its first dedicated airborne air control platform (AWACs), an Israeli-modified IL-76 Russian aircraft mounting a Phalcon radar, means that Beijing's air forces still lack this basic capability. Beijing has apparently agreed to purchase from Moscow Russian-built A-50 AWACs, a less capable aircraft.[23]

A third factor in deploying air power over the ocean is the joint relationship between the PLANAF and the PLAAF. Numerous interviews with PLA officers indicate that interservice flight operations are not common. The effects of the lack of joint flight operations between the two "air forces" may be ameliorated, since the PLAAF has increased its over-water flights since 1996, to the point that such maritime operations are now (2000) routine. Additionally, the PLA has assigned coastal air defense missions by service.[24]

This system, based on geographical sectors rather than service capability or doctrine, indicates that not only are joint maritime flight operations not routinely exercised, but that joint doctrine for such operations has not been systemically developed by the two "air forces." Indeed, PLAAF operations over water likely concentrate on classic air intercept and pursuit operations, while PLANAF operational doctrine focuses on fleet support missions, such as surveillance and ASW.

In sum, PLA budgetary limitations are likely to continue to prevent the PLAN from acquiring aircraft carriers for the next decade, although a radical change in China's strategic view could change that situation. Reasons for this decision include the high costs of both acquiring and operating an aircraft carrier. A carrier requires such a large financial and personnel investment that it embodies the state: loss of a carrier in combat would be not just a ship lost, but a national loss. Hence, a carrier requires a fleet of other ships for its protection. These ships must provide a very robust capability to defend the carrier against all surface, subsurface, and aviation threats. The carrier also requires replenishment-at-sea ships to keep it (and its escorts) supplied with fuel, ordnance, and other supplies.

PLAN acquisition of a carrier would adversely affect China's diplomatic standing, since other Asian nations would view with deep concern such evidence of Beijing's regional ambitions. Most importantly, the PLAN is currently focused on Taiwan as its overwhelmingly dominant national security issue, and an aircraft carrier is not viewed as especially useful in strait scenarios.[25]

The seventh PLAN requirement is defending China's SLOCs, a vital national interest for Beijing. The first level of SLOC defense is safeguarding the sea lanes in Beijing's claimed territorial waters, which requires a brown/green-water Navy in the Yellow Sea, East China Sea west of the Japan-Philippines line, and in the South China Sea. The PLAN already possesses most of the assets to defend its brown-water SLOCs—say those within one hundred nautical miles of its coast.[26] The next level of SLOC protection includes those sea lanes that extend throughout East Asia, from the Sea of Japan to the Andaman Sea west of Malacca. The PLAN is currently unable to defend these green-water SLOCs.[27]

Tactical Environment

Again, specific opponents are almost certainly used as planning "strawmen," as the "blue forces." The PLAN does not have any realistic ambition of matching U.S. naval power in the next half-century, but it is surely viewing other regional navies with a calculating eye. Russia's Pacific fleet normally includes eight SSBNs, perhaps sixteen modern nuclear-powered attack submarines, a nuclear-powered guided-missile cruiser (reportedly inactive), no more than a dozen other guided-missile cruisers and destroyers, at least a dozen minesweepers, six LSTs, but apparently no underway replenishment ships. This nominally significant fleet suffers from a lack of logistical support and is of doubtful readiness.[28]

The most formidable Asian navy is the euphemistically named Japan Maritime Self-Defense Force (JMSDF). As discussed earlier, the PLAN will not be a match for the Japanese Navy for at least the next two decades—assuming, of course, that Japan does not decide to halt its naval developments.

That hardly seems likely; Tokyo is continuing to build on what is already the most modern and powerful naval force in Asia other than the U.S. Seventh Fleet. Furthermore, the United States is working to ensure the technological modernity of Japan's Navy, which already includes Aegis-equipped ships, modern (if conventionally powered) submarines, air-capable surface ships, and a modern maritime air arm trained and equipped to operate out to one thousand nautical miles from the home islands. This extends Tokyo's maritime reach from the Bering Sea to the Luzon Strait, between Taiwan and the Philippines.

Japan's maritime power includes one of the world's leading shipbuilding industries, largest fishing fleets, and one of the world's strongest commercial fleets. Furthermore, Japan is modernizing its combat ships and aircraft at a steady pace. Thus, it will remain the most powerful Asian Navy, and more importantly, will maintain a position from which it can easily expand and further modernize rapidly to fill in behind any U.S. withdrawal from the region.

Japan clearly has the financial, personnel, industrial, and technological-scientific resources to become Asia's dominant maritime force. It would take only the perception in Tokyo that the strategic situation in East Asia is changing dramatically—a significantly decreased United States military presence, for instance, or a dramatically more capable PLAN—for Japan to seek such dominance to ensure vital SLOCs.

The PLAN would also have a difficult time opposing the Republic of Korea Navy (ROKN). Seoul is modernizing and expanding its Navy, although ROKN planning scenarios probably look toward Japan rather than China as a likely opponent. The ROKN already includes almost forty surface ships armed with either Harpoon or Exocet surface-to-surface missiles. Even the few remaining ancient ex–United States *Sumner-* and *Gearing*-class destroyers can outshoot many PLAN combatants. South Korea also deploys eight modern conventionally powered submarines, with more on the way, as well as a significant mine warfare and special warfare force. Equally important is the fact that this small country is currently more capable than China of producing state-of-the-art military technology.

Taiwan is modernizing its Navy as determinedly as is China, albeit without the crucially important submarine construction. Most troublesome for Taiwan's exercise of naval power is, quite simply, geography. The island's propinquity to the mainland will make it difficult for Taipei to counterbalance Beijing's air power. In other words, the future promises a degree of Chinese air superiority that will cancel out any Taiwanese superiority at sea.

Taiwan's Navy currently includes just two relatively modern submarines, built in 1980. Efforts to acquire more units have failed in the face of Chinese protests to potential sources, such as France, Germany, and the Netherlands, but Taiwan has been more successful in acquiring surface ships. Seven very old ex–United States *Gearing*-class destroyers have been equipped with the capable Standard (MR-1) AAW missile system and are joined by six modern *La Fayette*–class missile ships of French design, eight FFG-7 type guided-missile frigates of U.S. design being built in Taiwan, and eight ex-U.S. *Knox*-class frigates. A follow-on class of FFGs is also planned.

Other Asian nations, especially Indonesia, Singapore, Malaysia, and Thailand, are also modernizing their navies, although these efforts are still constrained by the effects of the economic disaster that struck in July 1997.[29] Only the Philippines and Vietnam are not modernizing their navies.

Indonesia is, for at least the third time, trying to expand its Navy in recognition of its inherently maritime nature as an archipelagic nation, exacerbated by the increasing need to guarantee communications between Jakarta and outlying provinces subject to secessionist movements. Beijing's territorial ambitions in the southern South China Sea also concern the Indonesians.

Indonesia's effort, based on the purchase of six Harpoon-equipped corvettes from the Netherlands and sixteen ex-East German corvettes, has apparently been productive, since the Indonesian Navy already included two modern conventionally powered submarines and eight capable surface ships, most armed with surface-to-surface missiles. The Navy also includes a large patrol/coastal force, necessary for a nation of almost countless islands, stretching across several thousand miles of Southeast Asia's southern rim.

Jakarta still faces a complex maritime strategic situation: the Navy must defend the coastal waters and oil fields; safeguard Indonesian territorial and maritime claims against the Philippines, Malaysia, and other neighbors; and enforce Indonesian sovereignty over oil and natural gas fields in the South China Sea against possible Chinese encroachment. Finally, the Navy plays an important role in maintaining national unity in very trying times.

Singapore continued to modernize its armed forces throughout the recent economic slowdown. The island-state is creating a centralized, coherent, joint defense system with a naval arm of missile-firing surface combatants, submarines, and shore-based air power.[30] Malaysia's efforts to increase its naval strength have slowed, although new surface combatant vessels are being acquired; plans to deploy submarines are now on hold. The first of a new class of missile-armed corvettes joined the Malaysian Navy in March 2000, and Kuala Lumpur simultaneously announced that the submarines might still be acquired.[31]

Bangkok has halted naval modernization because of the 1997 economic crash. Thailand continues to benefit from its close military relationship with the United States, however, highlighted by the biannual "Cobra Gold" exercises and supported by defense agreements between the two nations.[32] Material improvements to Thailand's Navy continue to be "on hold," however.

Thailand continues to play a wily international game, and has purchased significant quantities of arms from Beijing, including six frigates now armed with Harpoons or the Chinese version of Exocet.[33] The two countries signed the Plan of Action for the 21st Century in February 1999. The plan includes mutual visits by senior officials, and increased trade and cooperation in science and technology, in addition to "reviving existing arms purchase plans."[34]

The Thai Navy also includes two Harpoon-armed *Knox*-class frigates leased from the United States and two other Harpoon-armed corvettes, but its most significant warship is a small aircraft carrier. The *Chakri Naruebet* was built in Spain in 1997, displaces about twelve thousand tons, has a "ski jump" flight deck with two aircraft elevators, and can embark a combination of twelve helicopters and vertical-takeoff-and-landing (VTOL) type aircraft. The carrier has a nominal mission of SAR and humanitarian operations and reportedly is equipped with quarters for the royal family.

Hence, Thailand is the only Asian Pacific navy with integral sea-based air power, although it has operated the carrier only infrequently.[35] This capability positions Thailand to take the lead in any confrontation between the Southeast Asian nations and an outside power—such as might develop with China over South China Sea territorial claims. Thailand has no claims in that sea, however, and her obvious attempts to remain friendly with China limit the possibility of Bangkok assuming a strong leadership role.

The Philippines, despite its status as China's primary disputant in the South China Sea, simply does not have a Navy (or air force) of any significance. Manila's periodic declarations that the Navy will be modernized and expanded have come to naught. Reasons for this inaction include a weak national treasury, weak national leadership, political maneuvering among civilian parties, an uneasy civil-military relationship dating back at least to the end of the Marcos regime in 1986, and a lack of national strategic goals. These factors contribute to the legislature's refusal to finance a large Navy, while resurgent rebellions by the New People's Army in the north and Islamic groups in the south force the military to concentrate on internal security. There are few resources available for contesting maritime territorial claims.

Manila's mutual defense treaty with the United States may be reinvigorated by the Visiting Forces Agreement passed by the Philippine Senate in 1999, but that treaty probably does not apply to the islands disputed with Beijing. Furthermore, Manila has been steering a rudderless path in the face of China's campaign to solidify its presence in the Spratly Islands.

Vietnam's recent agreement with India for the two nations' navies and coast guards to "launch joint training and exercises" may improve Vietnamese naval strength.[36] The Hanoi government has not indicated any plans for significant modernization plans for its navy, however, and that force will remain very limited at least in the near-term.

India's formidable Navy, composed largely of Soviet-designed ships, submarines, and aircraft, but including a British-built aircraft carrier, poses a major counterforce to any Chinese ambitions to extend a naval presence into the Indian Ocean—and makes such ambitions impractical for at least the next decade. Despite recent warming of Sino-Indian relations, Beijing is wary of Indian naval ambitions, and New Delhi interprets Beijing's activities in Burma as evidence of a policy to establish a presence on the western approaches to the South China Sea, in spite of recent joint statements to "resolve to maintain peace along [their] borders."[37]

A new naval doctrine was announced in December 1999 that envisions an Indian Navy in 2010 built around two aircraft carriers, and cruise missile-firing submarines and long-range maritime patrol aircraft. Indian naval plans have included 1999 visits to the Persian Gulf and the Mediterranean Sea, and exercises with South Korea, Vietnam, and Japan in late 2000. This latter deployment included a port visit to Shanghai, despite clear Indian concerns about PLAN activities in Burma.[38]

Australia deploys a small but extremely professional and capable force of surface combatants, submarines, and aircraft. It is one of the few Asian navies with the capability to support itself at sea over long distances. Its neighbor, New Zealand, offers equally professional naval personnel, but successive governments in Wellington seem determined to reduce the Navy to a very small force.

In sum, indigenous Asia-Pacific navies include the extremely formidable JMSDF and the rapidly improving ROKN. Singapore, Malaysia, Indonesia, and Thailand all have modern navies, but only by operating in concert could they pose a challenge to the PLAN. The political situation in Southeast Asia makes that unlikely.

Given Korea and Japan's distance from the contentious South China Sea, and the constitutional and historical factors that inhibit Tokyo, China faces no naval force south of Taiwan with which it need be seriously concerned—other than the U.S. Seventh Fleet, assisted by Australia. That is a formidable force, however, since U.S. naval forces in East and Southwest Asia usually include two aircraft carriers, four nuclear-powered submarines, a dozen cruisers and destroyers, many of them equipped with Aegis, four underway replenishment ships, and an amphibious ready group. This group includes a very large (about forty thousand tons displacement) helicopter carrier and two other large amphibious ships, operating in support of the Marine brigade based on Okinawa. Air assets include two Navy and one Marine Corps air wings, and three numbered U.S. Air Forces.

This situation provides parameters to PLAN officers developing operational doctrine, who can focus on two general factors: the advent of the RMA and the U.S. naval presence in the Asia-Pacific. These are significant factors, but may well be imposing a syllogism over the development of maritime doctrine in China:

> Any mission must be couched in terms of PLAN capability to execute it;
>
> no traditional naval mission can be completed without U.S. dispensation;
>
> hence, the PLAN must devolve nontraditional means for carrying out its assigned missions.

If PLAN strategists are in fact engaged in this sort of strategic "Easter egg hunt," they will fail to develop effective operational effectiveness, all the talk of RMA and Sun Zi notwithstanding.

Taiwan

PLAN planners face one urgent scenario: the potential employment of PLAN force against Taiwan. Chinese political and senior military leaders certainly would prefer peaceful reunification, but the spring 2000 election of a Democratic Progressive Party (DPP) government and Beijing's refusal to renounce the possible use of force both mean PLAN planners are working hard to develop efficient and effective plans for employing naval force against Taiwan. These plans probably cover the gamut of maritime operations, from submarine and air surveillance of Taiwanese ship traffic, to a full-scale amphibious invasion of the island.

PLAN operational thought about Taiwan seems to be focusing on three alternative military courses of action: amphibious assault, blockade, and "deterrent strike."[39] An amphibious assault from the sea is, of course, the classic military attack to capture an island. This is a difficult, complex operation to carry out successfully, requiring the attacker not merely to match the defender's forces, but to outnumber them by a 5 to 1 ratio.[40] In 1944, U.S. Army planners believed that an assault on Taiwan was insupportable, requiring seven infantry divisions, approximately 150,000 combat troops, plus 220,000 supporting personnel.[41]

PLAN planners will have to take into account the typically bad, changeable weather in the Taiwan Strait and the lack of suitable landing beaches on either of the island's coasts. The strait is subject to high winds and seas, often above those forecast, and is susceptible to typhoons during most of the year. The lack of beaches is compounded by the presence of wide areas of mud flats, tidal ranges of up to fifteen meters, and complex currents.[42]

PLAN officers also have to face the usual plethora of military planning issues. These range from the manning status of ships to the troop-carrying capacity of individual landing craft; from the availability of aircraft bed-down sites on the mainland to the availability of the communications frequencies and troop rations required for extensive operations at sea.

One vital factor, viewing the present platforms and capabilities of the Chinese and Taiwan militaries, is that the PLAN would have a very difficult time establishing control of the Taiwan Strait. Without sea control, at least for the period required for specific maritime actions against Taiwan, there is little that the PLAN surface fleet can accomplish. Hence, PLAN plans have to proceed with the assumption that it may not be able to defeat the Taiwan Navy—a factor that poses significant operational difficulties. To surmount this problem, PLAN planners are no doubt seeking a way to neutralize their potential adversary, perhaps through surprise and deception, special operations and psychological warfare, and information warfare.

Even more important than these issues is, of course, the U.S. role. Clearly, for the foreseeable future, the PLAN will not be able to conduct significant operations on or above the sea without U.S. acquiescence.

This does not mean, however, that the PLAN is hapless in the face of active U.S. opposition. For one thing, ASW is so difficult that the United States will not be able completely to foreclose PLAN submarine operations. For another, China might launch military action against Taiwan at a time when U.S. forces are not on alert, and when no U.S. aircraft carrier battle group (CVBG) is operating in the Western Pacific. The potential U.S. role provides impetus for PLAN planners to devise a way to present Washington with a fait accompli, to achieve military victory before the United States is able to intervene decisively.[43] The PLAN would then be able to carry out specific missions against Taiwan with minimal U.S. naval interference, at least for a short period, perhaps ten days.

An effective air and sea blockade would affect Taiwan severely. PLAN submarines and mines could provide the main means of enforcing a closure of the island's two significant commercial ports, Keelung and Kaohsiung. Furthermore, Beijing could claim that mines laid around Taiwan were within China's territorial waters and hence did not violate international law, as long as the appropriate warnings to mariners were issued. Beijing could further announce that merchant ships scheduled to call at Taiwan's ports had to first stop at a mainland port to embark a pilot who would safely navigate the ship through the minefields.

Taiwan's weak minesweeping force consists of four relatively new (c. 1990) coastal mine hunters obtained from Germany and eight ex-U.S. and ex-Belgian minesweepers that are forty to fifty years old.[44] China's dedicated mine warfare forces are also small, but mines can be laid by almost any surface ship, as well as by aircraft. Significantly, PLAN surface combatants are required annually to exercise laying mines, which is not a common practice in most navies.

Mines are easy to distribute and difficult to counter. Not only is mine sweeping laborious, but just the announcement that mines have been laid will play havoc with insurance rates and commercial shipping to the island.

Finally, even a U.S. decision to assist Taiwan in breaking a Chinese blockade would pose several problems to Washington. First, the U.S. Navy has a limited mine-clearing capability, and, except for two small ships located in Japan, these ships and helicopters could not arrive in the Taiwan area without significant delay.[45] Second is the legal problem of minefields laid in China's claimed territorial waters. Third, would the United States decide to attack the mainland sources of the mines and their distributors? That would constitute escalation on a grand scale.

The third military Chinese option is the one most often discussed in the media: the use of ballistic missiles, and perhaps manned aircraft, to bombard Taiwan. China's missile launches in the spring of 1996 of course contribute to the discussion of this option, but to be effective, a missile barrage must overcome significant hurdles. First is topography: Taiwan is a large, mountainous island, not a "billiard table" target.

Second, the mainstays of China's present missile inventory, the M-9 and M-11, have moderately sized warheads, five hundred and eight hundred kilograms, respectively. More important, their accuracy, probably 120 to 600 meters, is not particularly impressive as measured by circular error of probability (CEP), which equals one-half the distance around the aim point within which the missile should be expected to land.[46] An M-9 or M-11 missile aimed at an airfield, for example, would probably hit the airfield, but hitting the intersection of two runways or the control tower would largely be a matter of chance. Their accuracy will improve as the PLA improves its access to state-of-the-art GPS technology. China is developing land-attack cruise missiles, which are generally more accurate than ballistic missiles, but typically carry smaller warheads.

China's missile force could inflict great death and destruction on Taiwan and its people, but by themselves, and despite expected improvements in accuracy, even several hundred of these missiles would not be able to force the Taipei government to surrender, given strong popular will on the island. This is the second and most important strategic question: How strong is the Taiwan population's will to resist?

For the next ten to twenty years: China cannot transport a sufficient force across the strait for a successful amphibious assault; Taiwan is too big to be bombed into submission by manned bombers and ballistic missiles; and the island could stockpile enough energy resources, obtain sufficient supplies by air, and prevent implementation of a complete blockade to make that option work—if the will to resist is present.[47]

What course of action will Beijing select to resolve the tough strategic questions posed by Taiwan and the South China Sea? The Navy provides the weapons and manpower, and develops the operational doctrine to operate at sea, but this must be framed by a coherent maritime strategy.

8

China's Maritime Strategy

A senior strategist at China's Academy of Military Science recently cited defense as the continuing, central theme in both continental and maritime strategy in China. Lt. Gen. Mi Zhenyu claims that although imperial China fought sea battles, the "basic format in ancient times was 'land as primary, sea as secondary.'" He then argues that today "equal consideration is given to 'land and sea,'" and that Beijing considers "the ocean as its chief strategic defensive direction." Mi avers that "China's political and economic focus lies on the coastal areas [and] for the present and a fairly long period to come, [its] strategic focus will be in the direction of the sea."[1] Coloring this modern construction is the onerous legacy of Mao Zedong's People's War. In the words of one longtime observer of Chinese military thought, "A considerable portion of all Chinese military writing still must pay homage to the heritage of People's War."[2]

The classic maritime strategic concept is "Command of the Sea," most simply defined as the ability to use the sea while denying its use to an adversary. "Sea Control" is a lesser but powerful concept, defined as a nation's ability to "command" a discrete ocean area for a limited period of time—sufficient to achieve limited strategic goals. The counterpoint to Sea Control is "Sea Denial": denying an adversary use of a discrete maritime area without necessarily using it oneself. All of these concepts require a nation to be effective in the air, as well as on and beneath the ocean surface. Sea Denial in littoral waters is a particularly attractive option for even a small naval power, if it has access to mines, missiles, small surface ships and submarines, and shore-based aircraft—as does the PLAN.[3]

A number of factors influence modern naval strategy-making, including

Training and education programs leading to professional specialization of the officer corps

National naval leadership

Naval systems and platforms costs, capabilities, and sustainability

National scientific and industrial infrastructure for research, development, and production of naval warfare technology and systems

The ability to derive doctrine and tactics

The ability to administer and operate command and control tactical units beyond individual ships

Sources of intelligence, and its production, analysis, and dissemination

Service-wide naval strategic planning

The place held by naval strategists in the national strategy-making structure.[4]

We will use this list as a measure of China's development of a maritime strategy.

Maritime strategy should reflect Colin Gray's dictum that "man lives on the land, not on the sea, and conflict at sea has strategic meaning only with reference to what its outcome enables, or implies, for the course of events on land."[5] Gray cautions, however, that in all the history of war, "the enemy who is confined to a land strategy is in the end defeated."[6] In other words, a maritime strategist must remember that Command of the Sea, Sea Control, and Sea Denial are all means and not an end. They serve only to promote a nation's ability to project power ashore, to directly affect events on the land.

Strategy, Politics, and Geography

The current Chinese campaign to modernize its military follows the sea change in strategic thinking that occurred in 1985, when expectations of global nuclear war or large-scale conflict with the Soviet Union gave way to a focus on small, local wars on China's periphery.[7] Five types of local, limited wars are envisioned: small-scale conflicts in disputed border areas, conflicts over disputed islands or ocean areas, surprise air attacks, deliberate incursions into China, and counterattacks by China against an aggressor or "to uphold justice and dispel threats."[8]

This was an extremely important shift for Chinese maritime strategic thought. The PLAN shifted from a general strategy of coastal defense to one of offshore defense. The Navy also moved from Army acolyte to prominent participant in possible operational scenarios, including threats from Japan, Taiwan, and India, and dealing with contentious maritime claims.

Although historically focused on continental security concerns, China has rarely ignored its maritime boundaries. China's emperors had built a formidable force for employment on rivers and along the coast as early as the twelfth century; the early-fifteenth-century voyages of Zheng He to the east coast of Africa and the Persian Gulf constituted a major accomplishment. The late-Qing and Republican regimes had neither the organization nor the resources to develop a strong navy. Furthermore, none of these governments developed a coherent or durable maritime strategy.

PLAN Strategy, 1949–1960

Soviet naval advisors brought to China the Soviet "Young School" of maritime strategy, which emphasized coastal defense by a Navy of small surface craft and submarines. The Young School had developed in the Soviet Union shortly after World War I, based on conditions particular to postrevolutionary Russia:

A new regime that was under military and political attack by several capitalist countries and had not completely quelled domestic fighting.

A regime that *expected* to be attacked by capitalist nations, with amphibious attack a current fact and future threat, especially from "the ultimate bastion of imperialism, the United States."[9]

A navy that was in disarray, and almost entirely manned by captured or defected former enemy personnel.

Budgetary shortages that limited the amount available to spend on expensive naval systems.

Lack of an industrial infrastructure to produce indigenously modern naval armaments.

A maritime frontier hemmed in by adversarial fleets and bases.

These conditions also applied to China in 1949, as did the additional problem of no recent maritime tradition. The Young School concept was attractive to early PLAN strategists, since it required a defensive Navy that would be relatively inexpensive to build, and could be quickly manned and trained.[10] Furthermore, the concept was analogous to guerrilla war at sea.

The Soviet Union sent an initial cadre of five hundred naval advisors to China in 1950; there were between fifteen hundred and two thousand by 1953. These advisors paralleled the Chinese chain of command from Beijing headquarters to individual ships and squadrons, thus providing the means for inculcating Soviet naval doctrine throughout the new Navy. "Large numbers" of Chinese officers, including the new head of the PLAN, Gen. Xiao Jingguang, received training in the Soviet Union. Xiao was twice a student in Moscow and spoke fluent Russian; he was both "an excellent administrator" and "a staunch Maoist who could be counted upon to adhere to whatever line the chairman espoused."[11]

Although its maritime strategy in the early 1950s was primarily defensive, Beijing worked to develop the offensive capability to recover the offshore islands still occupied by the KMT, a campaign expected to culminate in the conquest of Taiwan.[12] When he inspected PLAN units in February 1953, during the Korean War, Mao Zedong justified the need for "a strong navy for the purposes of fighting against imperialist aggression."[13] In December of that year, he assigned the PLAN three priority missions: eliminate KMT naval interference and ensure safe navigation, prepare to recover Taiwan, and oppose aggression from the sea. Chinese and Taiwanese forces resumed amphibious attacks and counterattacks, which ended in Beijing's possession of all the significant offshore islands except Quemoy, Matsu, and of course Taiwan. The PLA also succeeded in stopping most of the attacks on merchant and fishing vessels, as well as the Taiwanese raids on the mainland. In less than a decade, the PLAN had been organized, sent to sea, and proven effective as a Soviet-style coastal defense force, while adhering to the rubric of People's War.

The Korean War did not change Beijing's belief that relatively short-range defensive sea forces could counter the American invasion threat; no blue-water Chinese Navy was planned after 1954. The Navy's attempts to modernize, with an emphasis on technology and technical training, took place under a brown-water defensive strategy.

Attempts in the 1950s to develop a specific and perhaps independent strategic role for the PLAN fell victim to the triumph of politics over technology. Throughout the ideological turmoil of the late 1950s and the 1960s, Beijing invested heavily in a determined effort to develop nuclear weapons, missiles, and the nuclear-powered submarines from which they could be launched.[14]

A New Situation, 1960–1976

Despite the drive to produce modern strategic weapons, Mao's concept of People's War continued to guide the small Navy as well as the other branches of the PLA, as did adherence to the Young School—modified by some significant naval developments. By the end of the decade, relations with the Soviet Union had deteriorated to the point of armed conflict along the Amur River. The former ally was now the enemy, and the former enemy, the United States, would soon be China's strategic ally.

The massive Soviet threat in the 1960s and the PLA's lack of mobility drove China's national security strategy to continue fielding very large ground forces, supplemented by a coastal Navy. The PLAN's brown-water role was modified only by the development in the 1960s of nuclear-powered attack and ballistic missile submarines that later joined the fleet from 1970 to 1991.[15]

The Navy continued to follow a strategy of coastal defense during the GPCR, which meant serving as an extension of the Army and little modernization. People's War held that technology and weaponry were insignificant compared to the effect of revolutionary soldiers imbued with Mao's ideology.

After the Great Proletarian Cultural Revolution

PLAN strategic missions still fell under the Young School during the 1970s. Assistance to the Army; offshore patrol against criminal activities such as smuggling, piracy, and illegal immigration; life-saving; and safety of navigation were the Navy's missions. Beijing also perceived its ancient antagonist, Japan, reemerging as a strong maritime force.

Meanwhile, the Soviet Navy in the 1960s and 1970s underwent a dramatic change under the leadership of Adm. Sergei Gorshkov, partly from the impetus of the Cuban Missile Crisis's demonstration of Soviet maritime weakness. Under Gorshkov's guidance, the Soviets attempted to build a worldwide fleet to match that of the United States. This fleet's missions in time of war would be defense of offshore areas, countering an adversary's strategic strike systems, sea control in fleet ballistic missile (FBM) operating areas, strategic nuclear strike, disrupting an adversary's SLOCs, and protecting friendly SLOCs.

Gorshkov's maritime strategy also included specific peacetime tasks: showing the flag, gaining international respect, supporting economic interests, managing crises, limiting an adversary's options, exercising local sea control, and use in local wars.[16]

A similar naval metamorphosis did not occur in China, but the growth and modernization of the Soviet Navy heightened Beijing's concern. People's War was no longer deemed adequate as maritime strategy; Chinese planners began thinking about projecting naval power against potential Soviet actions beyond the immediate coastal arena.

Concern about Soviet aggression rose in concert with continued determination to ensure the viability of Beijing's territorial claims throughout East Asia. Taiwan was the most important of these, but China was also concerned about its claims in the East and South China Seas.

Beijing ended the 1970s with a limited strategic view of the maritime environment. Deng Xiaoping reemphasized the Navy's role as a coastal defense force, a view retained throughout the first half of the

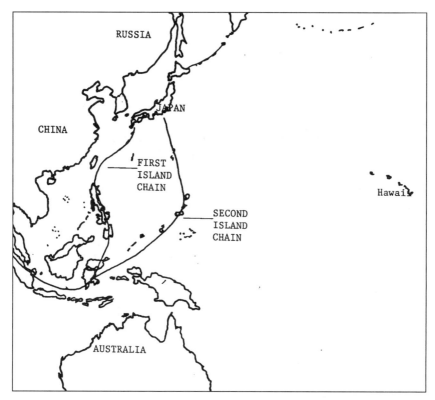

RUSSIA

JAPAN

CHINA

FIRST
ISLAND
CHAIN

SECOND
ISLAND
CHAIN

Hawaii

AUSTRALIA

Adm. Liu Huaqing's island chains

BERNARD D. COLE

1980s. At that point, the Navy came to be viewed as something more than an adjunct to the ground forces. China's coastal concentration of economic interests and military bases, its widening maritime interests and increased budget resources after 1979, did give rise to increased interest in a stronger Navy. China also completed developing a seaborne nuclear deterrent force, based on Mao's earlier declaration that the Navy had to be built up "to make it dreadful to the enemy."[17] Although the single SSBN China deployed about 1980 was a national rather than a naval asset, the *Xia* gave the PLAN a nuclear deterrent mission for the first time.

Liu Huaqing's Vision

The chief architect of China's emerging maritime strategy in the 1980s was Gen. Liu Huaqing, commander of the PLAN from 1982 to 1987 and then vice chairman of the Central Military Commission to September 1997. As early as 1982, Liu directed the PLAN's Naval Research College to elaborate a strategy of "offshore defense." By offshore, Liu meant the ocean area from China's coast to approximately the "First Island Chain," defined by a line through the Kurile Islands, Japan and the Ryukyu Islands, Taiwan, the Philippines, Borneo, and Natuna Besar.[18] Liu observed that "the strategic position of the Pacific is becoming more important [and] as China is gradually expanding the scale of its maritime development, the Chinese Navy will have to shoulder more and heavier tasks in both peacetime and war." He argued that "the scope of sea warfare operations has extended from the limited space of air, the surface, the water, and coasts, to all space from under the sea to outer space and from the sea inland. . . . In order to safeguard China's coast, resist possible foreign invasion, and defend our maritime rights and interests, it is only right and proper that China should attach great importance to developing its own navy, including 'emphatic' development of its submarine force."[19]

Liu wanted to change the maritime element of China's national strategy from coastal defense to "offshore active defense."[20] This strategy included stubborn defense near the shore, mobile warfare at sea, and surprise guerrilla-like attacks at sea.[21] These three tenets continued to pay homage to Maoist concepts of warfighting, but were significant because of Liu's emphasis on moving China's maritime defense seaward.

"Offshore" in this construct has been variously defined, ranging from 150 to 600 nautical miles, but Liu delineated two strategic maritime areas the nation must be able to control.[22] The first of these, under Phase One of the strategy, includes the Yellow Sea, facing Korea and Japan; the western East China Sea, including Taiwan; and the South China Sea.[23] These fall within China's defined area of vital national interests: territorial claims, natural resources, and coastal defense. The area is also delineated by the First Island Chain, with 2000 the goal for establishing Chinese control of this area.

The second strategic maritime area, under Phase Two of Liu's strategy, is delineated by the "Second Island Chain," a north-south line from the Kuriles through Japan, the Bonins, the Marianas, and the Carolines, and would mean Beijing's control of all of East Asia's vast ocean areas, nominally by 2020.[24] China's ability to control this area would require very significant national resources for its Navy and Air Force. Even then, two conditions would have to occur. First, the United States would have to withdraw its military presence from the region. Second, Japan would have to sit idly by in the face of U.S. withdrawal, and not engage in an arms race with Beijing to ensure continued Japanese maritime superiority.

The third stage of Liu's maritime strategy is the PLAN becoming a global force by 2050. A step toward this goal occurred in the spring of 1997, when within a three-month period China deployed multiship task groups composed of warships and logistics support vessels to Southeast Asia, and to North, Central, and South America. This significant accomplishment was the widest-ranging Chinese naval deployment since the voyages of Zheng He.

Ironically, defining "phases" of maritime theaters by fixed geographic boundaries reveals a strong continentalist perspective, even in the mind of China's most prominent post-1949 admiral. It violates the central tenet of classic maritime strategy that while the soldier thinks of terrain and theaters, the sailor of necessity thinks in wider terms, outside immediate physical limits—there is no "terrain" at sea.[25]

Liu's emphasis is understandable, however, given his Army background and early Soviet training and the continuing influence of Soviet/Russian naval strategic thought in China. By the mid-1980s, Soviet maritime strategy had settled on a division of its coastal waters into defense zones out to about 2,000 nautical miles. Liu Huaqing's maritime "phases" almost certainly owe their origin to the earlier Soviet "zones," the innermost of which was called the "area of sea control." The second zone was the "area of sea denial"; the third was a broad region for long-range reconnaissance and submarine interdiction. The first and second Soviet zones, extending seaward 1,500 nautical miles, closely match Liu's two island chains, the second of which lies about 1,350 to 1,500 nautical miles from China's coast.

The similarity between the Chinese and Soviet maritime strategic concepts is sharply drawn in an article by Liu's successor as PLAN commander, Zhang Lianzhong. In 1988 he identified three maritime defense areas for the PLAN:

> [First,] the exterior perimeter [encompasses] the seas out to the first chain of islands. This region will be defended by conventional and nuclear submarines (some of which will be armed with anti-ship missiles), by naval medium-range aircraft and by surface warships. The submarines will play a dynamic role to ensure defense in depth, including the laying of mines in the enemy's sea lines of communication. The middle defense perimeter extends 150 miles from the coast and

comes within, but in most cases does not reach, the first chain of islands. Anti-ship aircraft, destroyers and escort vessels will carry the
main burden in this area. The interior defense perimeter extends to
sixty miles from the coast. This will be the theater of operations for the
main naval Air Force, fast-attack boats and land-based antiship missile units.[26]

Scenarios

Liu's strategy outlines a possible direction for future modernization
and growth. It delineates control of vast oceanic expanses, a very difficult task simply by virtue of the geography, not to mention that
other nations would object to Chinese hegemony over such a large
portion of the earth's surface. Of course, the PLAN is currently incapable of executing its missions within even the First Island Chain, although the target year has arrived. Recent PLAN deployments to the
Western Hemisphere were just a small step; there currently is no
hard evidence that China's national leadership has decided to shift its
budget priorities to the extent necessary for realization of Liu
Huaqing's Phase Two by 2020.[27]

Liu directed study and elaboration of his strategic concepts,
which emphasized naval missions well to seaward of the coastal zone
that formed the basis for past PRC maritime strategy.[28] He was no
fool and this three-phase strategic progression may well have been
designed primarily for domestic consumption, to win resources for
the PLAN. Liu would have been following a path similar to that of
naval expansionists in turn-of-the-century America and Germany as
they built modern navies in conjunction with their nations' rapidly
expanding economies.

PLAN modernization requires a well-articulated offshore mission,
supporting China as the strongest maritime power in East Asia and
as a major power in the Pacific. A direct line may be drawn from
Sergei Gorshkov to Liu Huaqing: the former was an instructor at the
Voroshilov Naval Academy in Leningrad when the latter was a student at the school.[29]

The PLAN has not been tasked with all of the "new" Soviet maritime strategic objectives of the 1970s. It has no "FBM operating areas"
to control, for instance, and its "strategic nuclear strike" capability is
almost non-existent—but both of these missions will be applicable if

China succeeds in building and deploying three or more new (Type 094) ballistic missile submarines.[30] The PLAN has, however, adopted peacetime strategic missions almost identical to those outlined by Gorshkov—who cited the American threat as his basic justification for a strong Navy. Writing in 1975, he accused the United States of following an "oceanic strategy" of aggression against the Soviet Union.[31] Chinese strategists today use similar words; the Soviet-Russian maritime strategic influence remains strong in China's Navy.

Maritime Strategic Interests

In the Fourteenth Party Congress political report, in 1992, General Secretary Jiang Zemin described the PLA's mission as defending the unity, territorial integrity, and maritime rights and interests of the homeland. This was the first time Jiang had addressed "maritime rights and interests."[32] He later pledged the PLAN "to safeguard the sovereignty of China's territorial waters, uphold the country's unity and social stability and create a safe and stable environment for the nation's economic development."[33]

Any list of strategic goals for the PLAN would include defense of China's maritime borders. Recent diplomatic accomplishments have resulted in at least nominal resolution of border disputes with all of its continental neighbors, allowing Beijing to focus on maritime disputes. Vice Adm. Cheng Mingshang, PLAN vice chief in 1991, argued that the Navy was vital to China's national security as "the tool of the state's foreign policy. . . . An international navy can project its presence far away from home. It can even appear at the sea close to the coastal lines of the target countries. . . . This has made the navy the most active strategic force in peacetime, a pillar for the country's foreign policy and the embodiment of the country's will and power."[34] Liu Huaqing also cited the concentration of modern economic interests and growth in the special development zones clustered along China's seaboard as economic justification for a strong PLAN. He stated that "the Chinese navy must live up to the historical responsibility to grow rapidly up into a major power in the Pacific area in order to secure the smooth progress of China's economic modernization."[35]

In the fall of 1995, Jiang Zemin described China as "a continental power, and a coastal power as well." He noted the coastal region's "dense population, with its scientific, technological, and economic levels," stating that "the ocean as a natural protective screen covers this region of strategic significance. . . . We can be sure that the development and utilization of the ocean will be of increasingly greater significance to China's long range development. This being the case, we must see the ocean from a strategic plane, and . . . set out new and higher requirements on navy building. We must . . . step up the pace of navy modernization to meet the requirements of future wars."[36]

China's North Sea Fleet was responsible for countering any southward movement of the Soviet Pacific Fleet between the 1960 split with the Soviet Union and that empire's dissolution in 1989.[37] Although this is no longer a significant mission, the North Sea Fleet still faces a difficult maritime situation: Russia, South Korea, and Japan all possess capable navies, although Russia's fleet is only a shadow of its former self.

Japan looms very large on China's horizon. Ancient disputes and rancor combined with World War II grievances and suspicion of future Japanese aggression create an edgy relationship. It is inherently a maritime relationship, given the seas that lie between the two nations as a natural barrier to any but seaborne or airborne interaction. Beijing's evaluation of Tokyo's intentions must also take into account the alliance with the United States, especially with respect to the implications of the 1998 security guidelines as they may apply to Taiwan. If Tokyo and the United States interpret those guidelines' reference to "waters surrounding Japan" as including Taiwan, then China would face a much more complicated situation in the strait.

Taiwan of course is the essence of Beijing's strategic concerns. Despite concern about the United States, China refuses to renounce the use of military force to ensure the reunification of Taiwan. Beijing must count on the PLAN for policy options ranging from intimidation to outright invasion. The East Sea Fleet presumably has local planning responsibility for contingency operations involving Taiwan, and also has been tasked with executing the many diplomatic missions. Naval headquarters also assigned the East Sea Fleet responsibility for several recent significant deployments to Southeast Asia and to the Western Hemisphere.[38]

The South China Sea is second only to Taiwan as a PLAN concern. This contiguous sea embodies important economic, political, and nationalistic strategic issues for Beijing; Liu Huaqing noted the PLAN's mission to secure the "vast resources" of this sea.[39] The National People's Congress passed the Law of the Territorial Sea and Contiguous Zones in February 1992, midway through his tenure as China's senior uniformed officer. This act claimed for China essentially all of the South China Sea, ocean as well as land areas.

Chinese strategic concern about India centers on the nuclear threat recently demonstrated in the successful testing of nuclear weapons and missiles. This capability, combined with the Sino-Indian border dispute and Beijing's concern for its ally, Pakistan, gives India a special position in China's strategic view. Another factor of concern to Beijing must be India's desire to be involved in the South China Sea, recently evidenced in New Delhi's agreement with Hanoi for mutual naval training events.[40]

China has been active in Burma, primarily because of Beijing's concerns about the heavy flow of illegal drugs across the border into Yunnan Province, but also perhaps as a reflection of concerns about Indian intentions.[41] The regional press has reported three Chinese approaches in Burma. First is the sale of military equipment amounting to as much as U.S.$1.2 billion since 1990, and accompanied by military and technical advisors. This has ranged from small arms to oceangoing warships, including ten *Hainan*-class coastal patrol craft and six *Houxin*-class missile boats.[42]

Second, Chinese military personnel have been reported in Burma, building and improving maritime facilities at Hainggyi, Akyab, and in the Mergui Islands off Burma's isthmian coast.[43] Third, there have been reports of Chinese activity at what may be electronic monitoring facilities on the Cocos and Hangyi Islands in the Andaman Sea. Such facilities would provide Beijing's naval commanders with intelligence on Indian and other naval forces in the Indian Ocean.[44]

Most recently, China and Burma have announced a "framework of future bilateral relations and cooperation." This statement addresses increased trade and economic relations; forestry, tourism, culture, judicial cooperation; joint attacks on transnational issues; and general regional cooperation.[45] Military issues are not discussed in this agreement, however, which is similar to those China has signed with Malaysia and Thailand.

There is no hard evidence that China is establishing a naval presence in the eastern Indian Ocean, but the rationale for a PLAN presence in these waters is obvious: maritime concerns arising from China's dependence on trade and imported petroleum, and fears that an unfriendly India could control the Indian Ocean's SLOCs on which China depends.

Continued development of China's economy in the twenty-first century depends on reliable sources of energy.[46] This imported petroleum comes primarily from the Middle East, over sea lanes that pass through the Indian Ocean, and the South and East China Seas. These routes also pass through several geographic "choke points," including the Luzon and Taiwan Straits, the Strait of Malacca, and the Strait of Hormuz.

China can project almost no naval control over these choke points, except for the Taiwan narrows, but the PLAN may want to correct this deficiency, beginning with a naval presence in the western approaches to the SCS. Beijing believes a strong PLAN is vital to resolving all these (and many other) issues of national security concern.[47]

A Blue-Water Navy?

Fulfilling Liu Huaqing's three-phase strategy would require task groups of missile-firing, power-projection capable ships supported by nuclear-powered submarines and maritime air power.[48] The homage still paid to People's War probably amounts to little more than "political correctness" but may also come from recognition of China's lag in military technology and the continuing need to seek advantage from the nation's vast manpower. Liu and current Chinese leaders want a Navy that is both technologically advanced and politically dedicated.

Completing the third phase of Liu Huaqing's strategy—global maritime power—would require China's leaders to adopt as a national goal construction of a very large Navy during the next fifty years. This maritime strategic objective, if distant in accomplishment, or even chimerical, may still serve the PLAN in domestic budget battles.[49]

Liu's naval strategy is comprehensive, focusing on missions concerning Taiwan, asserting China's claims to offshore territories and natural resources, defending the homeland against invasion, and strategic deterrence. Strategy, however, is a starting point for national security, not its consummation. A viable maritime strategy will have to grow beyond Liu Huaqing for the PLAN to become a modern, power-projecting force. Senior military and civilian leaders will have to embrace the concept and allocate the resources to provide the PLAN with the capability to fulfill strategic goals.

PLAN Strategic Capabilities

Adm. Shi Yunsheng has attributed several features to China's twenty-first-century Navy: first, an "'offshore defense' strategy"; second, "making the navy strong with science and technology, narrowing the gap between it and other military powers"; third, "more advanced weapons," including "warships, submarines, fighters, missiles, torpedoes, guns, and electronic equipment"; and fourth, trained personnel and "more qualified people."[50] Although logistics and sustainment at sea, and information warfare, are missing from this list, it illustrates the PLAN commander's appreciation for how far his force has to go to "improve its capacity to win a war at sea."[51]

China faces five major maritime security situations in Asia: Japan, Taiwan, the South China Sea, India, and vital SLOCs. The Navy seeks a greater role within the Army-dominated PLA and in the national security policy process. Casting the United States as the adversary facilitates these efforts, given U.S. naval dominance throughout East Asia.

The PLAN offers China's leaders a flexible, ready instrument for applying power, and Beijing has not hesitated to use the PLAN: witness the 1974, 1988, 1995, and 1998–99 actions in the South China Sea. "Offshore Defense" is a maritime strategy with clear offensive implications: Beijing is moving its strategic line seaward from the coast, demonstrating that the Navy has a key role in China's twenty-first-century strategy. Insofar as the PLAN is concerned, a strategy of "offshore defense" includes missions to contain and resist foreign aggression from the seas, defend China's territory and sovereignty, and safeguard the motherland's unification and marine rights.[52]

These strategic objectives translate into complex and difficult specific missions:

Preparing for operations against Taiwan

Defending Chinese claims in the East and South China Seas[53]

Maintaining a strategic deterrent force against the United States (and possibly India, Russia, and Japan)

Protecting vital SLOCs—some lying a great distance from China

Serving as a diplomatic force.[54]

Beijing's developing maritime strategy seeks to encompass both modern technology and Maoist doctrine, as in "the use of strategy can reverse the balance of combat strength." The ideal maritime strategy will overcome recognized shortcomings in doctrine, equipment, and training.

The PLAN is a long way from being the dominant naval power in East Asia, however, even apart from the U.S. maritime presence. The JMSDF is certainly superior to the PLAN, and the ROKN would be a very difficult opponent. Even the Taiwan Navy would not be a pushover for the PLAN. Clearly, a wise maritime strategist in Beijing would not, in the event of conflict, pose the PLAN "one-on-one" against any of these modern naval forces.

A more thoughtful strategy would be required for the PLAN to achieve specific goals in the face of opposition by the U.S. Navy, the JMSDF, the ROKN, or the Taiwan Navy. One aspect of such a strategy would almost certainly be employment of information warfare methods to counter the advanced military technological superiority of these fleets—a capability more discussed than demonstrated in China.

Another strategic step in such a conflict would be to gain the initiative through preemption. This does not necessarily require a "bolt from the blue," but could be achieved by seizing the initiative at a time of significant naval weakness on the part of the adversary."[55]

One of the PLAN's leading strategists describes the sea as the "new high ground of strategic competition" and urges PLAN attention to five areas of international rivalry: ocean islands, sea-space jurisdiction, marine resources, maritime strategic advantage, and strategic sea-lanes. The seas are described as both "a protective screen" but also as "a marine invasion route." Naval missions are seen as first, coastal defense; second, control of the "sea space," which is "four dimensional," including air, surface, subsurface, and the seabed. The Asia-Pacific region is described as a "priority region of maritime strategic competition." Control of the seas involves many areas such as political, economic, diplomatic, "science and technology, and military. . . . Military control of the seas means achieving and defending national unification, defending national maritime territorial sovereignty and maritime rights and interests, protecting legitimate maritime economic activities and scientific research, and ensuring a peaceful and stable climate for national reform, opening, and coastal economic development, by dealing with possible maritime incidents, armed conflicts, and local wars. . . . Our Navy has an inescapable mission. . . . The 21st century is going to be a maritime one. . . . We will have to make our maritime strategy a key part."[56]

The PLAN's strategic responsibilities are challenging. First, the distances involved in securing the South China Sea are daunting to a Navy weak in air power, amphibious lift, and logistics sustainment. Second, the opposition posed by Taiwan makes any assault on that island a significant military as well as political problem. Third, in the Japanese Navy, the PLAN would face a superior adversary. To be effective, China's maritime strategy must compensate for the PLAN's material shortcomings and its lack of operational experience. That said, the PLAN today is a formidable force within littoral East Asia, and is viewed in the region as a vehicle for aggression.[57]

Given the continued presence of peaceful borders to the north and west, Beijing's national security priorities for at least the next decade will lie to the maritime east and southeast. The PLAN must be able to control East Asian seas to accomplish Beijing's strategic aims, but China faces significant hurdles in its weak technological and industrial infrastructure and resource availability. Deploying even a regionally dominant Navy will be difficult.

The PLAN has other twenty-first-century naval missions. First, establishment of an effective nuclear deterrent force at sea as the core of a maritime strategy for the new millennium. Second, maintenance of a naval presence throughout East Asia, using port visits to the nations of Northeast and Southeast Asia, with an occasional foray to Southwest Asia and the Western Hemisphere. Within this general policy of presence, the PLAN will be focused, as part of a joint force with the PLAAF, on specific objectives that in turn require a credible power-projection force, with enough amphibious and logistics capability to take and hold disputed territory in the East and South China Seas. A third mission is pursuit of SLOC defense (likely avenues are expanding a presence west of Malacca and diplomatic efforts in Southwest Asia). Finally, the question of Taiwan will dominate national security strategy discussions. PLAN strategists will have to ensure that their force remains a key player in plans to coerce Taiwan's reunification but do so in a manner that will not consume all modernization efforts. Given present and probable future budget resources, it would not be in the PLAN's interest, for example, to build a massive amphibious force.

The first stage of Liu Huaqing's reported strategy—to control China's adjacent seas out to the First Island Chain, is reasonable and attainable within the next twenty years, but only first, if Beijing changes the national prioritization of resource allocation necessary to build a modern maritime force and second, if Japan and the United

States allow it to occur. It is extremely unlikely that Japan and the United States would allow the balance of naval power to shift in Beijing's favor. Also, there is currently insufficient evidence to conclude that China is reordering its national modernization priorities.

Comparison to Germany's late-nineteenth-century naval building "dash" to catch up to Great Britain's Navy is not a valid analogy in China's case. Imperial Germany already possessed in the late 1890s an industrial-technological-scientific infrastructure equal and perhaps superior to its competitor, Great Britain; China fails to match this status vis-à-vis the United States, Japan, or even South Korea.[58]

Earlier in this chapter, I listed nine factors that affect a nation's development of a maritime strategy. How does China measure up?

First, training and education programs are receiving increasing attention as the professional specialization of the officer corps increases. Modern training and education systems and methodology are being adopted, but suffer from time devoted to political education and resource limitations.

Second, PLAN modernization is focusing on naval systems and platforms costs, capabilities, and sustainability, as new systems and platforms are bought on the global market and produced in China. Resource limitations, relatively weak indigenous infrastructure, and a low starting point all hamper this effort.

Third, the national scientific and industrial infrastructure for research, development, and production of naval warfare technology and systems is improving, but remains inadequate to support rapid design and buildup of state-of-the-art systems from drawing board to operational force; hence the continued reliance on foreign purchases.

Fourth, the ability to derive doctrine and tactics is uncertain, but clearly advancing, as evidenced in publications, military education and training, and exercises, especially those focused on joint operations, and integrated systems employment. Fifth, the ability to administer, operate, and command and control tactical formations is improving, as demonstrated by current administrative streamlining and recent long range deployments of small flotillas, but is still a question mark at the fleet and theater level.

Sixth, intelligence—sources, production, analysis, and dissemination—probably absorbs major resources in the PLAN, but its role and influence are unclear. Seventh, service-wide naval strategic planning appears to be ongoing, with apparent focus on not matching a potential adversary's (i.e., the United States) strengths but avoiding those strengths. Eighth, national naval leadership is probably weaker following Lui Huaqing's retirement. Finally, there seems no evidence that naval strategists hold an enhanced position in the national strategy-making structure, but their status is likely to rise in proportion with the degree of crisis in maritime situations, such as Taiwan or the South China Sea.

China is pursuing a maritime strategy consciously designed to achieve near-term national security objectives and longer-term regional maritime dominance through both combatant and merchant fleets. In the near term, Beijing is building a Navy capable of decisively influencing the operational aspects of the Taiwan and South China Sea situations, should diplomacy and other instruments of statecraft fail. Building or expanding PLAN and PLANAF bases in the Spratlys or on Burmese territory would provide a starting point for a major Chinese role in controlling the Malacca and associated straits, key to the economic life of East Asia.

Power-projection ashore, with its emphasis on littoral warfare, also tends to lessen the traditional importance placed on "blue-water operations," ironically at the very time when China seems focused on developing a Navy specifically for that arena. The term in the maritime strategic lexicography that most closely describes Beijing's maritime ambition is "sea denial." China is planning a Navy capable of ensuring the accomplishment of regional strategic objectives, despite possible interference by the United States. Historically, this is the classic maritime strategic option followed by continentalist powers, such as Wilhelmine Germany and the Soviet Union.

A less well known term that describes Beijing's naval ambitions is "flotilla defense," used by Sir John Fisher, Great Britain's first sea lord in the early years of the last century. Fisher was concerned that Britain's large fleet of battleships would not be able to operate safely in the narrow seas surrounding Britain in the face of the torpedo threat from submarines and small surface craft. Hence, he advocated flotilla defense as a way to safeguard the nation from invasion and attack. Fisher wanted to use submarines and torpedo-launching small craft to defeat attempts by large enemy ships to attack British ports and shore points.[59]

If the flotilla defense concept is applied to the relatively constricted Chinese coastal waters within the First Island Chain, then China, like Britain circa 1907 and the Soviet Union in the 1920s, is still building a Navy capable of nothing more than expanded coastal defense. The area to be defended has been increased from a few miles to more than two hundred, and the primary weapons of choice may be cruise and ballistic missiles vice torpedoes, but the concept is little changed.

Further maturation of the PLAN as an important instrument of national security will depend on how China's rulers view naval power and maritime economic interests. The value to the nation of its rich offshore mineral and biological resources, and its dependence on seaborne trade and transportation, are clearly understood in Beijing. Whether the utility of a strong, blue-water Navy in China's national security strategy is equally understood is not clear. There is little evidence that China's historic dependence on continental power has changed.

Conclusion

Imperial China for the most part ignored the sea, except for brief periods and specific campaigns. Republican China was simply too preoccupied with the civil war and Japanese invasion to focus on naval development. The Communist regime installed in 1949 has maintained a traditional Chinese attitude toward its Navy as a secondary instrument of national power.

Mao apparently recognized in 1950 that organizing a navy to extend Beijing's rule to Taiwan required a coherent effort to develop expertise in amphibious warfare, seaborne logistics, and maritime air power. His campaign to organize such a navy was aborted because of the Korean War and thereafter limited by domestic political events, especially the disastrous Great Leap Forward. Later, naval development was all but frozen during the 1960s by the Sino-Soviet split and the GPCR. Only at the end of the 1970s, after the end of the GPCR and the post-Mao power struggle, was the PLAN in a position to "take off."

This did not happen, although the PLAN did benefit from a close and relatively open relationship with the United States in the 1980s. China purchased advanced naval systems, including LM2500 gas turbine engines and Mk 46 ASW torpedoes. The sanctions that followed the June 1989 Tiananmen Square massacre ended U.S. naval assistance, and China has since turned to Europe, Israel, and especially Russia for naval assistance.

Currently, Beijing is paying more attention to its maritime problems and the PLAN is receiving at least its share of China's defense budget, but the PLA remains dominated by the Army. As it enters the twenty-first century, the Chinese Navy still owes a good deal to its history, which has been marked by some notable consistencies. Although the maritime element of China's national security has never held top priority in Beijing's strategic calculations, it has rarely been ignored.

Furthermore, Chinese naval efforts have been closely linked to the nation's economic development. China's economic boom of the past quarter-century has been concentrated in the coastal cities and provinces; the increasing concentration of industrial, technological, commercial, informational, and even agricultural wealth within approximately a five-hundred-mile coastal belt is reason to spur naval expansion and modernization. Beijing is addressing this strategic situation not by developing a large, modern navy, however, but by directing future development toward China's western provinces.[1] Granted, this campaign's motivation is primarily social, reflecting concern that continued internal development and orderliness require a greater dissemination of wealth throughout China's society, but it is an indicator of Beijing's limited strategic view of its Navy.

China's requirements for naval power are also driven by increasing dependence on offshore energy sources, both continental shelf petroleum deposits and foreign imports. The PLAN is responsible for ensuring the availability of these energy supplies in time of conflict. The Navy, however, neither has the present force nor is it receiving the resources for future development that will enable it to ensure China's continued access to foreign and offshore energy resources.

China's dependence on overseas trade for so much of its national wealth is another economic concern presenting the PLAN with a classic maritime mission. The overwhelming majority of this trade is carried by Chinese and foreign ships over sea lanes that crisscross the world. The security of such global SLOCs can never be assured, although some degree of guarantee can be provided by a nation with a navy strong enough to deter would-be disrupters.

The PLAN does not possess the forces in either range or capability to defend China's SLOCs other than those immediately off its coast. Actually, there is no need for China to devote significant resources to defending any but local SLOCs, so long as the United States continues following its policy as self-designated guardian of the world's sea lanes. This is especially true given Washington's emphasis on defending the SLOCs most important to China's import of petroleum from Southwest Asia and the Middle East.

The PLAN is more capable of ensuring the security of China's insular territorial claims in the South and East China Seas, but it lacks the force both in numbers and capability to force the reunification issue with Taiwan. Naval exercises are focusing on classic amphibious training, although Beijing is not building a navy capable of extended, large-scale assault operations. Furthermore, the PLAN continues to lack a reliable source of offshore air power; it has no fixed-wing-capable ships, only nascent in-flight refueling capability, no airborne air control, and very limited joint operational capability with the PLAAF. All of these factors must be corrected before the PLAN is capable of operating in anything but a defensive, brown-water environment against a twenty-first-century navy.

Chinese naval development since the early nineteenth century has been marked by significant interaction with foreign navies. Qing Dynasty modernization efforts drew on Japanese, German, British, and American naval professionals as advisors, administrators, and engineers. This trend has continued under the People's Republic of China, with a sporadic but enduring reliance on Soviet/Russian advisors, strategy, equipment, technology, and engineers.

Russian maritime strategic and material influence continues in the PLAN, but a continuing, close relationship between the two countries is unlikely. The history of Sino-Russian relations since the thirteenth century argues against a long-term alliance between the two nations: the two countries have rarely engaged in a friendly relationship from the time the Mongol "Golden Horde" swept across the Russian steppes. More recently, Moscow and Beijing have been antagonists for the past 150 years except for relatively brief periods: 1919 to 1924, 1945 to 1960, and from about 1989 to the present.

China recognizes and may be uncomfortable with its Russian

relationship, but Beijing is obviously willing to profit by Moscow's economic distress and international problems. The two nations' strategic situations also retain some similarity, based not on ideology but on geography and history. Both China and Russia have always been primarily continentalist in their strategic outlook.

In fact, Russian president Vladimir Putin recently spoke of a new naval doctrine with the following priorities: guaranteeing Russia's access to the world's oceans, preventing discriminatory actions against Russia or its allies, preventing domination of oceans important to Russian state interests, and helping to settle disputes over the use of the world's oceans on terms advantageous to Russia.[2]

Substituting "China" for "Russia" makes this doctrine equally applicable to Beijing's maritime circumstances. China's continued reliance on foreign sources results from the ready availability of advanced Russian and other foreign systems, and the apparent realization that the Chinese military-industrial complex (CMIC) is either not capable or is unwilling to research, design, develop, and produce many of the modern naval systems the PLAN wants and needs. This may result from lack of dedicated technological expertise, research and development facilities, manufacturing plant, more profitable private sector markets, or all of the above. As a result, China enters the new century with the naval sector neglected when a company, even a state-owned enterprise, has a better profit opportunity elsewhere.

Another question about the PLAN's future arises because naval doctrine development in China is not transparent. PLAN descriptions of recently conducted exercises use the right labels—joint warfare, systems integration, coordinated subsurface-surface-aviation operations, centralized command and control—but the actual practice of these elements of modern naval warfare is problematical, given the Navy's training regimen and equipment limitations.

Foreign analysts must remember, however, that while the PLAN has never engaged in a major campaign or combat at sea, and may find itself badly outgunned, its personnel's dedication, courage, and resourcefulness should not be doubted. Furthermore, Beijing's record of using military force to "teach lessons" means that the PLAN may be ordered forth in situations not anticipated by foreign opponents.

By one count, China employed force 118 times internationally between 1949 and 1992.[3] Moreover, Beijing's willingness to resort to force even when significantly outgunned should impart a cautionary message for strategists viewing China's possible reactions to specific issues, especially Taiwan's efforts to resist reunification. In other words, China will continue to be constrained by U.S. (and perhaps Japanese) naval force, but will employ the PLAN in situations involving sovereignty claims.

The "Next" PLAN

Yu Guoquan, director of the Department of Naval Equipment Technology and Warships Division in 1995, outlined a version of twenty-first-century naval systems. The fact that his writing more or less regurgitates American naval authors does not detract from its possible impact within the PLAN. New naval weaponry, he wrote, would have six features:

1. Improved reconnaissance and observation, precise targeting, and better weapon-sensor integration would result in quicker reaction time.
2. Increased lethality.
3. Increased mobility and speed, and hence shorter engagements.
4. Improved protective and survival systems.
5. Increased emphasis on electronic jamming and targeting.
6. Naval warfare will be fought in all dimensions.[4]

China is pursuing multiple paths to acquiring a modern navy: indigenous construction, reverse engineering of foreign ships and aircraft, and outright purchase of foreign platforms.[5] All of these methods have drawbacks. First, despite fifty years of experience, China still is struggling to establish an efficient military-industrial complex for the research, development, manufacturing, testing, and support of modern military systems. One observer recently noted problems plaguing this infrastructure, including inadequate funding, lack of horizontal integration, inadequate integration with the civilian commercial sector, technology absorption problems, and lack of skilled experts, managers, and labor.[6]

Today, PLAN ships are built by a process involving the Navy, a state-owned enterprise, and private industry. The first step is the expression by the Navy of the need for a specific ship, with desired characteristics. The origins of such requests is not clear; the Naval Research Institute and Naval Research Center in Beijing probably contribute, as perhaps does the Naval Command College in Nanjing and the fleet commanders. Once a request for a new ship is approved by the PLAN, the PLA, and the CMC, it is passed to the China Shipbuilding Corporation (CSC), a state-owned enterprise. The CSC works with the Navy to finalize the design, and then negotiates the shipbuilding program with a shipyard, which may be privately owned. PLAN construction representatives are stationed at the shipyard as liaison during the construction process.[7]

A second drawback is that China has a problematic record for re-verse-engineering foreign systems, taking an average of fifteen years to proceed from sample platform to series production.[8] Third, while foreign purchases, such as the recent acquisition from Russia of *Kilo*-class submarines and *Sovremenny*-class DDGs, make headlines, China is not likely to devote the massive amounts of hard currency necessary to purchase a complete navy abroad. To do so would impact Beijing's current emphasis on the growth of the domestic economy and civil infrastructure. Furthermore, reliance on foreign arms purchases both retards the growth of the Chinese defense industry and to an extent mortgages the military to the originating country for maintenance, training, and spare parts.

Another drawback to Beijing's current policy is that the multiple paths lead to inefficiencies, not just in acquiring new platforms and systems but in producing a coherent force able to operate effectively at sea. A force including so many disparate types and modifications of systems, with the attendant complexities of training, maintenance, and spare parts support will be operationally limited.

There are several reasons for China's multipath approach to navy building. First, domestic military and political concerns limit available resources. Second is what history indicates will be a fairly transitory friendship with Russia. Third is the questionable health of the Chinese economy.[9] Fourth, China's military-industrial infrastructure has far to go to reach twenty-first-century capabilities. Finally, naval planners face China's lack of maritime tradition: voyages half a millennia ago do not constitute a useful heritage when the intervening centuries have been devoted to introspective nationalism.

Building a navy in this inchoate fashion significantly increases the complexity of training, manning, and maintaining the fleet. Just managing an effective parts supply system for a fleet of many different ship types is difficult, as is outfitting and supporting it logistically. Further, purchasing military equipment abroad is a questionable option in the long term. Nations rarely sell their most capable front-line weapons to others, and not every nation can produce such weapons, no matter how well-intentioned. For instance, modern SSN design and manufacture lie within the capability of even fewer: the United States, Russia, and perhaps France. Additionally, buying a modern force takes investment that could otherwise be devoted to building an indigenous infrastructure, and in the long run will limit the nation's military potential.

The Future Force

PLAN growth depends directly on resources allocated by the government. A global or blue-water navy can be built only if one of two decisions is made. First, within the PLA the Navy is accorded a greatly increased percentage of available funding, perhaps half or more of the total. This is hardly likely in the Army-dominated PLA. Second, Beijing would have to reorder its four modernization priorities to place the military first or second on the scale, with most of the resulting increase allocated to the Navy. Third, major increases in Beijing's military expenditures depend on continued economic growth. Absent growth of at least 5 to 7 percent, the leadership will certainly keep the military budget at the bottom of the national spending priorities list. To do otherwise would jeopardize popular countenance of the Communist government, support that depends on a flourishing economy.

By 2010, the PLAN will probably number approximately seventy modern surface combatants, two old ballistic-missile submarines, and twenty to thirty modern attack submarines.[10] The new Type-094 SSBN almost certainly will not be in commission by 2010, which means that the PLAN's role in China's strategic nuclear deterrent force will remain limited to the fifty-year-old *Golf II* submarine and the forty-year-old *Xia*, neither of which appears to be operational.

The first Type-093 SSN should be in the water by the end of the decade, which means the PLAN will in theory deploy six nuclear-powered attack boats, although its ability to maintain the operability of all five *Han*-class submarines is problematic: one to four are currently believed to be operational.[11] The Navy's attack submarine force will also include approximately thirty very old *Romeo*s, less than twenty *Ming*s, and perhaps six *Song* class. The PLAN undoubtedly wants to buy more *Kilo*s or the new *Amur*-class submarines from Russia, but faces budgetary limitations that dictate indigenous production or foreign purchases, but not both in significant numbers. The PLAN will probably purchase eight more Russian boats by 2010, assuming Beijing makes the necessary funding available.

The amphibious and logistical force will be more modern, but current building efforts make it unlikely that the PLAN will include more than approximately two dozen amphibious ships of two thousand tons displacement or larger, and three modern replenishment-at-sea ships.

The PLANAF faces resource and doctrinal competition within the PLAN among the different warfare communities (surface, subsurface, aviation, Marine Corps), and with the PLAAF. The PLANAF does not appear to occupy a strong position in these bureaucratic battles. A large conventional aircraft carrier will not be deployed, but one air-capable ship similar to the "through deck cruisers" built by the Soviet Union will be acquired by the PLAN. China's ability to provide effective air cover to the fleet at sea will continue to depend on shore-based units, with a long-term goal of acquiring one large, fixed-wing-capable ship for each of the three fleets.

The Marine Corps may add a third brigade, but its amphibious assault mission will keep it tasked to the South Sea Fleet. The Corps' role as a "rapid reaction" unit probably means, however, that its operational assignments are determined more by the CMC General Staff Department than by the South Sea Fleet commander.[12]

Force Trends

Although prospective PLAN numbers are small compared to the U.S. Navy, they are large by Asian standards, and reflect several specific factors. First, Beijing's number one "national security" priority will remain retention of power by the CCP. This requires a continued emphasis on fostering a strong and growing economy, which in turn means military budget resources will not dramatically increase.

Hence, the PLAN will continue to acquire new vessels, aircraft, and systems in small numbers. It also means that China's military-industrial complex will remain more interested in profit maximization than in production of military systems. Today's PLAN is being modernized the same way Li Hongzhang tried to create a Chinese navy more than a century ago, by following three different approaches: indigenous production, purchases abroad, and reverse engineering foreign systems. It did not work particularly well then, and is not likely to work any better in the twenty-first century.

Second, the PRC has built a navy composed of relatively small ship classes. Most Western naval observers focus on the disadvantages of this practice, but it may fit well with China's diffuse military-industrial complex and PLAN budgetary limitations. The acquisition of rapidly succeeding small ship classes will likely continue.

Third, Beijing's number one maritime strategic goal of defending China against seaborne invasion is not urgent, given the absence of any such threat. More specific strategic maritime concerns, including the South China Sea, brown-water SLOC defense, and the preservation of offshore resources, require capable naval forces, but Beijing is not allocating the resources to build the PLAN to the level required to fulfill those objectives. Even the determination to reunite Taiwan with the mainland has failed to spur dramatic naval expansion.

Fourth, the Chinese polity is undergoing a significant recharacterization; the revolutionary generation of military-civilian leadership is all but extinct. Current and future leaders will be *either* civilian or military, barring the unlikely rise of a military officer to national leadership. The PLAN will continue assuming a more professional character, a process that may isolate the PLA from China's population. Defense Minister Chi Haotian discussed this as a concern of the national leadership, in September 1998.[13]

Summary

China's strategic view, budgetary limitations, foreign relations, and domestic political situation all indicate that the PLAN will continue to be modernized as a regional rather than a global navy. From Beijing's perspective, the PLAN must be able to prevent any other Asian navy interfering with China's national security objectives, and to at least give pause to U.S. maritime intervention. A globally capable PLAN would have to be able to project power around the world, from the western Pacific to the western Atlantic, clearly an ambition beyond China's goals for the twenty-first century.[14] Of course, even a regionally capable PLAN would have to be included in calculation of global strategic forces, given East Asia's size, population, and economic importance.

This would be heightened by increased Chinese maritime presence at a few particularly sensitive political-military points, such as

the Malacca Strait. Early indicators of such intent might be the relationship with Burma, especially the activities in that nation's coastal
and island areas, and the "satellite tracking station" in Kiribati,
which establishes a Chinese presence in the central Pacific.[15] The
PLAN has also built a solid record of naval presence, with visits to
more than twenty countries in the 1990s, a program normal to a nation of China's geographic, economic, political, and cultural importance.[16] Recent success in resolving border disputes with its continental neighbors has freed Beijing to pay more attention to maritime
boundary issues.

Further maturation of the PLAN as an important instrument of national security will depend on how naval power and maritime economic interests are viewed in Beijing. The value to the nation of its
rich offshore mineral and biological resources, and its dependence on
seaborne trade and transportation, are clearly understood by the
PLAN. Those interests are categorized as "five rivalries" over "ocean islands, sea space jurisdiction, marine resources, the maritime strategic
advantage, and strategic sea lanes."[17]

The U.S. fleet remains the determinant factor in East Asian maritime crises. It will continue to fill that role for as long as the United
States has the will to keep it there. Beijing recognizes this dominance,
and there is no evidence that PLAN arguments for blue-water naval capability have received support within PLA headquarters or the CMC.

Chinese military tradition does not include deploying forces outside China.[18] Dramatic naval expansion would require the national
leadership to reorder its modernization priorities list, which in turn
would demand continued economic growth. The statement of military modernization by then-Defense Minister Xu Xiangqian in October 1979 is worth quoting: "The modernization of national defense
cannot be divorced from the modernization of agriculture, industry,
science and technology and, in the final analysis, is based on the national economy. . . . Blindly pursuing large-scale and high-speed development in building national defense will invariably and seriously
hinder the development of the national economy and will harm the
base of the defense industry."[19]

Economic priorities and the "requirement to defend the world's
longest land border with the most nations over every known type of
terrain and climate" mean that China will not fulfill Liu Huaqing's
ambition for a blue-water navy.[20] Instead, Beijing wants a navy capable of ensuring coastal defense and the success of discrete, well-de-

fined campaigns to enforce sovereignty claims. Taiwan and the South China Sea are the two scenarios that top the list of potential maritime conflicts. China requires the ability to prevail in an area one hundred to two hundred nautical miles off its coast, for a period of ten to thirty days, although the Spratly Islands require the ability to project maritime power out to about six hundred nautical miles. This means a PLAN able to prevail inside the First Island Chain, which it is currently unable to do against the United States or Japan, and with only a fair chance of success against South Korea or Taiwan. To increase its Navy's effectiveness in even these limited areas, China will have to deploy modern submarines, guided-missile destroyers and frigates with effective antisubmarine warfare and air-defense systems. These ships will have to be supported by land-based air power with airborne warning and control and aerial refueling to extend both endurance and combat effectiveness.

Beijing believes its national security objectives can be attained by modernizing its current naval force structure. Consequently, China is not investing the major resources required to build the large capital ships and supporting auxiliaries necessary for extended blue-water operations. Beijing apparently does not believe current maritime concerns are serious enough to change China's historic dependence on continental power, or to build a modern maritime force that will dominate the Asia-Pacific.

NOTES

Introduction

1. Deng, *Chinese Maritime Activities,* provides a well-written history of this topic.
2. See "China's Sea Route to West Asia Begins in Xuwen," *Xinhua* (Beijing), 21 June 2000, in Foreign Broadcast Information Service (hereafter cited as FBIS), China, 1999, Serial 0421, for archaeologists' theory that trading voyages may have departed from Guangdong Province as early as 200 B.C., two hundred years before the "Silk Road" was established.
3. Needham, *Science and Civilization in China,* discusses these and related developments in his massive work.
4. Deng, *Chinese Maritime Activities,* 41.
5. Forage, "Foundations of Chinese Naval Supremacy," 3.
6. Ibid., 70.
7. Lo, "Emergence of China as a Sea Power," 491.
8. Forage, "Foundations of Chinese Naval Supremacy," 6–7.
9. Ibid., 19–21, provides a fascinating account of two battles between Song and Yuan naval forces.
10. Fairbank, "Maritime and Continental in China's History," 15.
11. Forage, "Foundations of Chinese Naval Supremacy," 500–501, provides an interesting description of these early weapons.
12. E. L. Dreyer, "Poyang Campaign," provides a thorough, thoughtful description and analysis of the Ming campaign.
13. For an interesting if Eurocentric interpretation of the role maritime mobility played in European imperialism, see Raudzens, "Military Revolution or Maritime Evolution?"
14. Deng, *Chinese Maritime Activities,* chaps. 2 and 3, describes Zheng He's voyages in terms of China's economic progress; Fairbank, "Maritime and Continental in China's History," 16–17, provides an interesting discussion of the reaction of the Ming rulers with extensive references.

15. Fairbank, "Maritime and Continental in China's History," 16.
16. Spence, *Search for Modern China,* 53–54, describing Taiwan in terms which might be still used by PLA planners.
17. See Juo, "Self-Strengthening." The classic study of this movement is Wright, *Last Stand of Chinese Conservatism.* Fairbank, "Maritime and Continental in China's History," 220, relates one famous case of corruption: the diversion of perhaps $50 million in naval construction funds to the building of the Empress's Summer Palace in Beijing, complete with a large boat made of marble.
18. The most detailed description of the Sino-French naval war is in Wright, *Chinese Steam Navy,* 59–66. A briefer description is Spence, *Search for Modern China,* 221. The French had eight warships and two torpedo boats; the Chinese had eleven warships and several other craft, but all were made of wood. The French also destroyed the Chinese shore installations. Wright claims that the Chinese nonetheless won a victory of sorts: international opinion was much impressed that because of the performance of Chinese armies against the French operating from Tonkin, Beijing had for the first time brought a western attack to a standstill, and the war was settled by arbitration.
19. Swanson, *Eighth Voyage of the Dragon,* 96–102, discusses these developments.
20. Wright, *Chinese Steam Navy,* 85–105, provides a detailed description of the Sino-Japanese battles. Japanese success was simplified by the fact that the Weihaiwei forts' guns were designed only to defend against threats from seaward; Japanese forces took advantage of the same mistake in 1941, when it was repeated by the British in Singapore.
21. Swanson, *Eighth Voyage of the Dragon,* 223.
22. China was only one of several countries modernizing their navies at this time: Great Britain, Germany, France, Italy, Russia, Japan, the United States, and even Austria-Hungary were all expanding their fleets. Those that came to grief—China, Germany, Austria-Hungary—all failed to develop meaningful strategic and operational frameworks for their new navies. Tyler, *Pulling Strings in China,* tells some colorful stories about another, more successful maritime force developed in China during the late nineteenth century: the Revenue Service established as part of the Customs Service long supervised by Sir Robert Hart. British seamen officered most of the ships of this service. Tyler also states that he was on board the Chinese flagship at Weihaiwei in 1895, and characterized that navy as "a monstrously disordered epicyclic heterogeneity."
23. "Chinese Navy," 1302.
24. See Cole, *Gunboats and Marines,* 89–90, for an account of the Wanhsien affair. See Swanson, *Eighth Voyage of the Dragon,* 157, for an account of

the 1929 incident: the "Chinese" naval forces were actually those of Zhang Xueliang, the Manchurian warlord (the "Young Marshall") who had recently sworn allegiance to Chang Kai-shek's Nationalist government. The Chinese account of this battle quoted by Swanson ends with a Soviet victory due to superior firepower, including air strikes.

25. The United States, for instance, used just two navy transports and a commercial passenger liner to move a regiment of Marines from the United States to the Far East, then between the Philippines and China, and between north and south China, as crises waxed and waned.

26. Unless otherwise specified, distances will be given in nautical miles, one of which equals approximately 1.2 statute miles.

27. Quoted in *Xinhua,* 21 April 1999, in FBIS-CHI-99-0421.

28. Kearsley, *Maritime Power and the Twenty-First Century,* 17.

29. Downing, "China's Evolving Maritime Strategy, Part 1," 130.

30. Chen Wanjun, "Interview with Sr. Capt. Yu Guoquan (Director of Division of Ships, Dept. of Armaments & Technology, PLAN)," *Jianchuan Zhishi* (Beijing), 7 July 1995, 2–3, in FBIS-CST-96-014, 54.

31. Xu Zuzhi, "Chinese Navy Has Truly Become a Great Wall at Sea," *Zhongguo Xinwen She* (Beijing), 1 October 1999, in FBIS-CHI-99-1005.

32. Zhang, *Mao's Military Romanticism,* 46–54, provides a useful description of the beginnings of the PLAN.

33. Rosinski, quoted in Simpson, *Essays on Maritime Strategy,* 25.

34. Li, "PLA's Evolving Warfighting Doctrine," 402, notes that "since the mid-1980s, China has claimed sovereignty over three million square kilometers of maritime territory (China's land territory is 9.6 million square kilometers). . . . This territory covers 320 kilometers of continental shelves and exclusive economic zones, and extends 1,600 kilometers to include the whole of the Nansha (Spratly) Islands."

35. Quoted in Cha Chun-ming, "Chinese Navy Heads Toward Modernization," *Ta Kung Pao* (Hong Kong), 11 April 1999, p. B-6, in FBIS-CHI-99-0418.

36. One can buy the ships and systems that make up a navy, but they are almost worthless without the infrastructure to maintain and support them, as well as the operational know-how to employ them effectively.

37. Speech at Geneva, 26 March 1999, quoted in *Xinhua,* 26 March 1999, in FBIS-CHI-99-0326. Also see Luo Renshi, "What is New About the 'New Gunboat Policy,'" *Jiefangjun Bao* (Beijing), 20 May 1999, 5, in FBIS-CHI-99-0526, who attributes this American policy to a "Gulf War syndrome" replacing the "Vietnam War syndrome."

38. *Xinhua,* 6 April 1999, in FBIS-CHI-99-0406.

39. Dong Guozheng, "Security Globalization is Not Tantamount to Americanization," *Jiefangjun Bao,* 24 May 1999, 5, in FBIS-CHI-99-0602.

40. See, for instance, Li Donhang, "Dangerous Attempt to Resist Multipolarization Process," *Jiefangjun Bao*, 26 May 1999, 5, in FBIS-CHI-99-0604; Li Li, "Monster of Dark Civilization and Conspiracy Strategy—Commenting on Cox Report," *Jiefangjun Bao*, 29 May 1999, 4, in FBIS-CHI-99-0604; Zhang Dezhen, "On U.S. Eurasian Strategy," *Renmin Ribao* (Beijing), 4 June 1999, 6, in FBIS-CHI-99-0605.

41. See Krepon, *Chinese Perspectives*, for the sophistic arguments by four Chinese authors that China should not be held to international norms of "transparency" in national security matters, since the country is still a "developing nation."

42. Jen Hui-wen, "Jiang Zemin Talks Again on Strengthening the Army Through Science and Technology," *Hsin Pao* (Hong Kong), 16 April 1999, 16, FBIS-CHI-99-0417; Li Dan, report of Zhang Wannian speech in *Cheng Ming* (Hong Kong), 1 April 1999, 21–22, in FBIS-CHI-99-0414. FBIS characterizes this source as a magazine with a "tendency to sensationalize."

43. Yan Youqiang and Chen Rongxing, "On Maritime Strategy and the Marine Environment," *Zhongguo Junshi Kexue* [*China Military Science*] (Beijing) 2, 20 May 1997, 81–92, in FBIS-CHI-97-19.

44. Ibid.

Chapter 1. The PLAN's Heritage

1. PLAN vice commander Zhou Xihan, 1957, quoted in Muller, *China's Emergence as a Maritime Power*, 47. Also see Zhang, *Mao's Military Romanticism*, 48.

2. Wortzel, "Beiping-Tianjin Campaign of 1948–49," chart 1, points out that by July 1949 the PLA actually included seventy-seven "naval vessels." Hanrahan, "Report on Red China's New Navy," 847, describes the Nationalist contribution to this force as "twenty-five vessels ranging from LCTs to destroyers, representing an estimated one-fourth of the total Nationalist naval force."

3. Gen. Zhang Aiping, quoted in Hanrahan, "Report on Red China's New Navy," 848.

4. Quoted in Zhang, *Mao's Military Romanticism*, 51.

5. Ibid., 46–54. Muller, *China's Emergence as a Maritime Power*, 13: about 2,000 former Republic of China naval personnel who defected to the communist regime in 1949 formed the core of the nascent PLAN.

6. The reverse also occurs. My conversation with Qingdao Garrison DCOS for Militia and Reserve Affairs in May 2000 involved a long discussion with a PLA "senior colonel" who had spent the previous twenty-two years attaining the rank of senior captain in the PLAN; his transfer to the army came about because of his expertise as an engineer.

7. He Di, "Last Campaign to Unify China," 8. This article is probably the most complete account of this period's PLAN activities connected with the Taiwan Strait islands. Its author works at the Institute of American Studies of the Chinese Academy of Social Sciences and presumably had good access to PLA archives while researching this article.

8. Blackman, *Jane's Fighting Ships: 1955–1956*, 152–55, provides these numbers, but they should be treated only as estimates.

9. Swanson, *Eighth Voyage of the Dragon*, 196.

10. He, "Last Campaign to Unify China," 2, points out that the date for assaulting Taiwan was postponed by Mao several times, as PLA failures against various offshore islands emphasized the additional time required to prepare for a successful, large-scale amphibious assault. Muller, *China's Emergence as a Maritime Power*, 16, gives the planned invasion date as August 1951.

11. He, "Last Campaign to Unify China," 4. Marolda, "U.S. Navy and the Chinese Civil War," 139, states that by spring 1950 Beijing "had assembled a motley armada of 5,000 vessels . . . freighters, motorized junks, and sampans" to use for the invasion of Taiwan; this force was to be manned by "30,000 fishermen and other sailors."

12. See Donovan, *Tumultuous Years*, 206, for Truman's decision to reposition the Seventh Fleet, and 214–18, for a good account of administration thinking (Truman, Acheson, Bohlen, et al.), which demonstrated that the leadership's primary concern was not for Korea and China, but for the Soviet threat to Western Europe. Truman's announcement, "I have ordered the Seventh Fleet to prevent any attack on Formosa. As a corollary of this action I am calling on the Chinese Government on Formosa to cease all air and sea operations against the mainland. The Seventh Fleet will see that this is done," is in State Department, *Public Papers of the Presidents*, 492. The Chinese reaction is in Mao Zedong, "Speech Delivered at the Eighth Meeting of the Government Council of the People's Republic of China (28 June 50)," quoted in Ch'en, *Mao*, 115.

13. Quoted in Marolda, "U.S. Navy and the Chinese Civil War," 119–20.

14. Israel, "Dwight D. Eisenhower," 3015: Eisenhower, in his 2 February 1953 State of the Union Address to Congress, commented that "since the 'Red Chinese' had intervened in the Korean War, he felt no longer any need to 'protect' them from an invasion by. . . . Chiang Kai-shek."

15. Swanson, *Eighth Voyage of the Dragon*, 187.

16. *Dangdai Zhonggun Haijun* (Beijing: China Social Services Publishing House, 1987), translated as *China Today: The People's Navy*, in FBIS: JPRS-CAR-90-014, 16 July 1990, 7. This very interesting history of the PLAN will be referred to hereafter as *People's Navy*.

17. Ibid., 10, also notes that the Soviet ships, designed for a northern climate, were limited when operating in the East and South Sea Fleets'

warmer waters, which is still a concern with the *Sovremenny*-class DDGs currently being purchased by China.

18. *Case of Peng Teh-huai*, 164–65. The quote about the navy is in Swanson, *Eighth Voyage of the Dragon*, 206–8.

19. Quoted in *People's Navy*, 13.

20. Chang and He, "Absence of War in the U.S.-China Confrontation," 1514, describe this action during which "10,000 PLA troops . . . overwhelmed 1,086 [Kuomintang] soldiers."

21. Torda, "Struggle for the Taiwan Strait," describes these early battles, which included PLA successes as well as failures. Also see Huang, "Evolution of the PLA Navy," 3, for a tabular summation of the PLAN's warfighting efforts during this period. Chang and He, "Absence of War in the U.S.-China Confrontation," 1504, 1510, document this (n. 7, n. 8).

22. Other islands remained under Taipei's control, including the Penghus, just off the southwestern Taiwan coast, and the Pratas Islands and Itu Aba in the South China Sea. Taiwan attacks on the mainland continued into the 1960s. These naval campaigns are addressed by Li, "PLA Attacks and Amphibious Operations." Also see Huang, "PLA Navy at War, 1949–1999," for a detailed description of PLAN combat actions.

23. *People's Navy*, 36–37; Allen, Krumel, and Pollack, *China's Air Force Enters the 21st Century*, 205 n. 11: little open-source information is available about PLANAF assets; a reasonable assumption is that the navy's air arm has usually flown the older variants of the same aircraft flown by the PLAAF. The authors provide a useful description of PLA aircraft acquisition programs in Appendix E, 221–29.

24. Swanson, *Eighth Voyage of the Dragon*, 205.

25. The PLAN submarine bases were established with the assistance of Soviet advisers; during discussions with the Allies in the 1940s and with Mao in 1950, Stalin had expressed interest in establishing a Soviet submarine base at Port Arthur (Lushun).

26. Swanson, *Eighth Voyage of the Dragon*, 236.

27. Presumably, the United States would have come to Taiwan's defense had the PRC tried to take advantage of the American preoccupation with Vietnam by attacking the island, but the GPCR was even more of a preoccupation for Beijing.

28. Blackman, *Jane's Fighting Ships: 1970–1971*, 610, credits the Soviet Navy with just four large (four thousand tons displacement) amphibious ships, and eighty smaller (six hundred to one thousand tons) vessels, and these were spread out among all of the Soviet Union's four fleets.

29. *People's Navy* repeatedly emphasizes the deleterious effects of the GPCR.

30. See Lewis and Xue, *China's Strategic Seapower*, 206–23, 231, 236: even Zhou Enlai was unable to protect completely these programs.

31. O'Donnell, "Analysis of Major Developmental Influences," 42, lists the PLAN's Political Commissar, chief operations officer, the East Sea Fleet commander, two deputy commanders, and two Fleet Political Commissars among the "120 senior naval officers and thousands of lower ranking personnel [who] were purged."

32. Lewis and Xue, *China's Strategic Seapower*, 147–48, 223.

33. Blackman, *Jane's Fighting Ships: 1970–1971*, 61–66: the PLAN also included more than thirty other submarines, a collection of assorted foreign-built destroyers and escort vessels (Soviet, Japanese, U.S., British, Canadian, and Italian), and more than four hundred Chinese-built patrol craft, some of them hydrofoils and most armed with torpedoes.

34. FBIS reports cited in Muller, *China's Emergence as a Maritime Power*, 154.

35. Lewis and Xue, *China's Strategic Seapower*, 223, discuss Hua's decision; Deng is quoted, 224.

36. The most memorable expression of this factor was by Lt. Gen. Henry Stackpole, USMC, commander of the Third Marine Expeditionary Force on Okinawa, who was quoted in Fred Hiatt, "Marine General: U.S. Troops Must Stay in Japan," *Washington Post*, 27 March 1990, p. A-14, as describing the United States as "a cap in the [Japanese] bottle."

37. Cheung, *Growth of Chinese Naval Power*, 28. China's Marine Corps had been disestablished in 1957 as "unnecessary." The concentration of amphibious forces in the South rather than the East Sea Fleet may reveal the PLAN's attitude—ambivalent at best—toward the very difficult task of conducting an amphibious assault against Taiwan.

38. Moore, *Jane's Fighting Ships: 1976–1977*, 100–109. The PLAN also included the first Chinese range-instrument ships for tracking guided-missile flights, and the first Chinese-built amphibious transports.

39. Muller, *China's Emergence as a Maritime Power*, 171.

40. Deng Xiaoping, "Speech at an Enlarged Meeting of the Military Commission of the Party Central Committee," cited in Godwin, "Change and Continuity in Chinese Military Doctrine," 23.

41. Wilhelm, *China and Security in the Asian Pacific Region*, 42.

42. Ibid., 32ff.

43. Liu had worked for Deng on two previous occasions. Lewis and Xue, *China Builds the Bomb*, 50, 51.

44. Liu's accomplishments are summed up in Wilhelm, *China and Security in the Asian Pacific Region*, 43.

45. See, for instance, Leifer, "Chinese Economic Reform and Defense Policy"; Garver, "China's Push Through the South China Sea," 1019–22.

46. See Lewis and Xue, *China's Strategic Seapower*, for the best account of the development of the fleet ballistic missile (FBM) and JL-1 programs. A successful 1982 launch was made from a submerged platform; a 1985

attempt from the *Xia* failed; a 1988 attempt succeeded. The *Xia* itself apparently has been a failure, never operating on a regular basis. Moore, *Jane's Fighting Ships: 1999–2000,* 115, reports the "rumor" that a second boat of this class may have been built but lost in a fire before it went to sea. There is also a rumor that the *Xia* may have been overhauled in 2000 in preparation for joining the fleet.

47. Lt. Gen. Mi Zhenyu, PLA, "A Reflection on Geographic Strategy," *Zhongguo Junshi Kexue* (Beijing) [*China Military Science*] 1 (February 1998): 6–14, in FBIS-CHI-98-208.
48. Fairbank, "Maritime and Continental in China's History," discusses these factors at length.
49. Whitson with Huang, *Chinese High Command,* 473: "On balance, it is evident that the evolving Russian model of military ethic and style, especially on the issues of military role, commander authority, and strategy, has been the most important European influence to alter traditional Chinese perspectives."
50. Xu Zuzhi, "Chinese Navy Has Truly Become a Great Wall at Sea," *Zhongguo Xinwen She* (Beijing), 1 October 1999, concisely recaps PLAN equipment and significant events.
51. Blasko, "New PLA Force Structure," 260.

Chapter 2. China's Maritime Territorial Interests

1. Quoted in Schram, *Political Thought of Mao Tse-tung,* 276.
2. See Ball, "Military Acquisitions," 88–89. Taiwan duplicates China's claim to all the Paracel Islands.
3. United Nations, UNCLOS, Art. 2.
4. Ibid., Art. 33.
5. Ibid., Art. 56.
6. Ibid., Arts. 76–78. A nation's CS does not automatically extend out to 350 nautical miles, but is subject to technical definition based on gradient and seabed composition.
7. Ibid., Art. 121, also makes an important distinction between an island and a "rock," which by definition "cannot sustain human habitation or economic life" on its own and which has no EEZ or CS. Although not specified, the inference of this article is that a "rock" which can sustain human life is considered an "island." The moot point is whether a land formation with neither natural water nor food supply qualifies as a "rock" or an "island."
8. Ibid., Art. 83 and Sec. 15.
9. "Thailand, Vietnam Enter New Era of Cooperation," *Nation* (Bangkok), 12 August 1997, A4, in FBIS-EAS-97-224, reports an agreement between Thailand and Vietnam on their maritime boundary; "Thailand, Malaysia

Disband Anti-Communist Committee," *Bangkok Post,* 16 May 1999, in FBIS-EAS-99-0516, reports the resolution of Thai-Malaysian land border issues, and "Malaysia Country Analysis Brief," Energy Information Administration (EIA), 3, describes the development of the "Malaysia-Thailand Joint Development Area in the Gulf of Thailand; but the *Bangkok Post,* 30 April 1999, in FBIS-EAS-99-0430, reports continuing inability to resolve maritime boundary issues with Burma.

10. "East Asia: Straits Challenge," U.S. Pacific Command Virtual Information Center, 10 February 2000, 2.

11. This discussion of Beijing's ratification of UNCLOS is based on Sik et al. 1997, 211–30.

12. Parker, "China's Overseas Bases," 1. Also see "Kiribati Oppositionist on PRC Satellite Station," Melbourne Radio Australia, 20 August 1999, in FBIS-EAS-98-233. Beijing's 1997 agreement with Kiribati to establish a satellite-tracking station on the islands allows China to monitor missile launches from America's Kwajalein launch facility.

13. "Vice-Premier Greets Scientists in Antarctic via Satellite," *Xinhua,* 2 February 2000, in FBIS-20000202001021.

14. See, for instance "Arctic Expedition Persists Through Terrifying Waves," *Xinhua,* 26 July 1999, in FBIS-CHI-99-0726, and "Chinese Arctic Expedition Starts 27-Hour Research," *Xinhua,* 28 July 1999, in FBIS-CHI-99-0728.

15. "Spokesman on PRC Joining Indian Ocean Organization," *Xinhua,* 25 January 2000, in FBIS-20000125000826. "Dialogue Partners" are states "with a special interest or capacity to contribute to this Association." Others in this category include Japan and Egypt. The association's full members are Australia, Bangladesh, India, Indonesia, Iran, Kenya, Madagascar, Malaysia, Mauritius, Mozambique, Oman, Seychelles, Singapore, South Africa, Sri Lanka, Tanzania, Yemen, and the United Arab Emirates. France was recently refused admittance as a full member and will probably reapply to become a dialogue partner.

16. "Taiwan" is used to include the other islands controlled by Taipei, such as Quemoy and Matsu.

17. EIA, *South China Sea Region,* provides a useful description of the South China Sea.

18. Jian, "Multinational Oil Companies," 592, provides the geological description. UNCLOS is the current authority; it also declares that "rocks that cannot sustain human habitation or economic life of their own shall have no exclusive economic zone or continental shelf" (Art. 121, Sec. 39).

19. There was a sample of this in 1995, when "Concrete Claims," *Far Eastern Economic Review,* 20 December 1995, 14, reported that "a Chinese reef-building expedition in the [Spratlys] in early November went badly

wrong after hurricane-force winds and frigid temperatures wrought havoc with the naval personnel. . . . The ship returned from its 10-day mission with half of the 100 crew suffering from pneumonia and assorted injuries."

20. The disparity in numbers of islands occupied by particular countries is due to conflicting reports by various sources.

21. Bodeen, "Taiwan Military Uses Pratas Islands," reported the belligerent claim by Gen. Chang Cheng-chung of the Taiwan army that "we're keeping the necessary force [on Pratas Reef] to keep communist China away." Despite this statement, less than two months later Taipei announced it was replacing its marines on Pratas with personnel from the newly organized Coast Guard (Maubo Chang, "ROC Replacing Troops, Not Retreating from South China Sea," *Taiwan Central News Agency*, 9 December 1999, in FBIS-19991209001133). The most recent press report, "Taiwan Defense Ministry: No Troop Withdrawal from Dongsha," *Chung-Kuo Shih-Pao* (Taipei), 28 January 2000, 4, in FBIS-20000205000020, is a rather defensive statement emphasizing that the replacement of marines by Coast Guard personnel "is not a withdrawal of troops" or reduction of "the original combat capacity." "Su Chi's Statement on the Planned Military Withdrawal from Spratly and Paracel [*sic*] Islands," *China Times*, 19 November 1999, p. 1, quotes the chairman of Taiwan's Mainland Affairs Council stating that the Coast Guard is also scheduled to assume Itu Aba garrison duties.

22. Catley and Keliat, *Spratlys*, 7, offer these divisions.

23. Nguyen Hong Thao, "China's New Advance Into the Eastern Sea in 1998," *Tap Chi Quoc Phong Toan Dan* (Hanoi), December 98, 66–68, in FBIS-19990406000155, contains a summary of Vietnam's position.

24. "China and Malaysia Agree to Boost Defense Co-operation in the South China Sea," *Alexander's*, 19 July 1999.

25. Johnson, "Drawn into the Fray," 153–61, examines the Natuna disagreement in detail, including Jakarta's attempt to ignore the problem.

26. Jian, "Multinational Oil Companies."

27. "PRC to Revise Fisheries Law," *Xinhua*, 3 July 2000, in FBIS-CPP20000703000139.

28. "Chinese Officials Greet Fishing Patrol in Spratlys," *Xinhua*, 2 February 2000, in FBIS-20000202000897, reports that China has "more than 2,200 fishing patrol ships and boats, with over 30,000 fishing law enforcement personnel."

29. See chapter 7, below. Manny B. Marinay, "Manila Proposes Declaring Spratlys 'Common Fishing Ground,'" *Manila Times*, 20 February 2000, in FBIS-SEP20000220000015, reported that Philippine Defense Secretary Orlando Mercado "suggested" designating the disputed islands as a "common fishing ground" for the claimant nations. This proposal would seem to fit with Beijing's previous statements about joint eco-

nomic exploitation of the Spratlys, while deferring resolution of the sovereignty issue.

30. The second meeting of its "Fisheries Consultative Group on Sustainable Fisheries Management in Southeast Asian Region" was held in Kuala Lumpur in March 2000. Valencia and Van Dyke, "Vietnam's National Interests," 229–48, discusses the complex fisheries claims.
31. EIA, *South China Sea Region*, 4. Noer with Gregory, *Chokepoints*, provides a thorough breakdown of the merchant traffic through the South China Sea, by cargo and by ship ownership. This source also estimates costs of using alternate routes in the event the Malacca or other straits cannot be used.
32. Valencia, Van Dyke, and Ludwig, *Sharing the Resources*, provide the most complete discussion of the various national claims to the Spratly Islands.
33. Leifer, "Chinese Economic Reform and Defense Policy," 7.
34. Ibid., 5.
35. Discussed in Catley and Keliat, *Spratlys*, 25–35. The two island groups were transferred to Hainan Province in 1988.
36. Deng Xiaoping, quoted in "Nansha Islands—The Facts," *China Daily*, 8 May 2000, in FBIS-CPP20000508000027. This article also describes the Spratlys, in a gross overstatement of the petroleum reserves that may be located there, as a "second Persian Gulf."
37. Valencia, Van Dyke, and Ludwig, *Sharing the Resources*, 20–21.
38. See, for instance, Chinese Foreign Ministry spokesman Sun Yuxi, *Zhongguo Tongxun She* (Hong Kong), 16 January 1999, in FBIS-CHI-99-025: "China has indisputable sovereignty over the Nansha Islands and the contiguous maritime area." Also, Defense Minister Chi Haotian, "Chi Haotian Reiterates PRC Stand on South China Sea Issue," *Xinhua*, 15 September 1999, in FBIS-CHI-99-0915: "the South China Sea has been China's territory from ancient times and . . . China has had indisputable sovereignty over the Nansha Islands and their adjacent sea areas."
39. Harrison, *China, Oil, and Asia*, 200, concludes that "China does have solid evidence of its presence there dating back to the thirteenth century," but LeGrand, "Memorandum," 1: "All of the straight baselines within the Chinese declaration are excessive and not in accordance with international law." Beijing applies "straight baselines" for its mainland and offshore islands, but has not stated that they apply to the Spratlys. Valencia and Van Dyke, "Vietnam's National Interests," 221, point out that Vietnam also claims straight baselines, claiming much of the Tonkin Gulf as internal waters. "Straight baselines" are sovereignty claim lines that are drawn directly ("straight") from one geographical point to another, rather than in conformance to the coastline; this enables a country to claim a much larger expanse of maritime area as sovereign territory.

40. Lin, "Taiwan's South China Sea Policy," 323–39, describes Taipei's claims. Chen, "Comparison Between Taipei and Peking," 54–58, asserts that while Beijing and Taipei hold the same claims to the South China Sea, Taipei is pursuing a more restrained policy. Finally, Taipei issued a "White Paper on Maritime Policy," *Taiwan Central News Agency*, 22 June 1999, in FBIS-CHI-99-0622, which "stresses the ROC's jurisdiction over the disputed Spratly Islands in the south China Sea" but notes that it is "willing to jointly develop the region's natural resources with neighboring countries." Taiwan has not played a constructive role in settling the South China Sea territorial disputes but has preferred to ride Beijing's rigid coattails: as a former senior naval intelligence officer in Taiwan said to the author, "What do we have to lose?"

41. Valencia, Van Dyke, and Ludwig, *Sharing the Resources*, 22, estimate that about 260 Chinese troops were stationed on nine reefs in the Spratlys in 1993.

42. Author's discussions with U.S. analysts. Valencia, Van Dyke, and Ludwig, *Sharing the Resources*, 11, report that China may have also drilled an oil well ("Nanyang #1") on Fiery Cross Reef.

43. Leifer, "Chinese Economic Reform and Defense Policy," 32. Hanoi's entire coastline, twenty-five hundred kilometers, fronts the South China Sea. Harrison, *China, Oil, and Asia*, 200–201 discusses these Vietnamese claims in detail.

44. Valencia, Van Dyke, and Ludwig, *Sharing the Resources*, 31.

45. "Let Us Build the Vietnam-China Border of Peace and Friendship," *Voice of Vietnam*, 31 December 1999, in FBIS-19991231000206, reported that the Land Border Treaty was signed in Hanoi on 30 December 1999, and that Vietnam and China would continue negotiating the "sea border issue." Despite the exclamatory reports in the Chinese and Vietnamese press, Barry Wain, "Hanoi and Beijing Take a Step Closer," *Asian Wall Street Journal*, 12 May 2000, points out that the two nations had merely "set about jointly demarcating the 1,290-km frontier, a task likely to take several years."

46. Khalilzad et al., *United States and a Rising China*, 29. An equidistant line would seem to be in accord with the UNCLOS, but at variance with China's own reservation to the treaty.

47. "China, Vietnam Hold Talks on Border Issues," *Xinhua*, 23 February 2000, in FBIS-CPP20000223000124, reported that Chinese and Vietnamese assistant foreign ministers had begun discussing "how to further negotiations on demarcating Beibu Bay." The Vietnamese government's views are quoted in Tran Cong Truc (Chairman of Vietnam's Government Border Commission), "SRV Minister Discusses land Border Agreement with China," *Tap Chi Quoc Phong Toan Dan* (Hanoi), 1 February 2000, 35, in FBIS-SEP20000314000061.

48. See "SRV-PRC Working Group Discusses Demarcation of Tonkin Gulf in Beijing," Hanoi Voice of Vietnam, 8 November 2000, in FBIS-SEP20001109000027, for a brief account of these meetings. The December 2000 agreement is in "'Text' of Joint Sino-SRV Statement on All-Round Cooperation in New Century," *Xinhua*, 25 December 2000, in FBIS-CPP20001225000065.

49. Thao 1997; Studeman 1998, reports a March 1992 clash "of which the intensity is not known" between Chinese and Vietnamese force on Da Ba Dau Reef [Whitson Reef in English, possibly Niue Jiao in Chinese]. Valencia, Van Dyke, and Ludwig, *Sharing the Resources*, 94, report a Crestone "Open letter to the Citizens of the Socialist Republic of Vietnam," written with Beijing's approval, which proposed a joint Chinese-Vietnamese drilling effort in this area. Hanoi rejected this offer; Crestone's rights were bought out by another American oil company, Benton Oil Corporation, in 1996.

50. Harrison, *China, Oil, and Asia*, 204.

51. Studeman 1998, 2.

52. EIA, 1987, 2.

53. Leifer, "Chinese Economic Reform and Security Policy," 13.

54. Ibid., 10, identifies clashes in 1993 and 1994. This ironic situation—two American companies competing at the behest of China and Vietnam—would place the U.S. government in an interesting situation should losses of American life or property occur.

55. "Exploration Sags Off Vietnam," 32: "The petroleum industry in Vietnam is currently becalmed." *Alexander's*, 30 June 1999: Vietnam's offshore oil and gas production rose in 1998 and 1999, however, with oil being exported to Japan, Korea, Thailand, the United States, European nations, and, ironically, to China. Vietnam is also building its first oil refinery, in a joint venture with a Russian company.

56. Leifer, "Chinese Economic Reform and Security Policy," 34.

57. Valencia, Van Dyke, and Ludwig, *Sharing the Resources*, 34, also note that Manila announced in 1995 that it was installing "lighthouses" on Nares, Recto or Marie Louise Bank, Seahorse Bank, and Jackson Atoll.

58. See, for instance, "Malaysia Building Up Military Off Philippine Island," *Philippine Star* (Manila), 20 August 1998, 20A, in FBIS-EAS-98-232; Paolo Romero, "Philippine Army Spots 3 PRC, 2 SRV Ships off Spratlys," *Philippine Star*, 26 May 2000, in FBIS-SEP20000526000058; Manny B. Marinay, "Philippine Planes Spot 5 PRC, 3 SRV Vessels in Spratlys," *Manila Times*, 16 May 2000, in FBIS-SEP20000516000057, are just three of an almost constant stream of reports of Manila's concerns about foreign vessels in its claimed South China Sea territories.

59. EIA, 1987, 2; Valencia, Van Dyke, and Ludwig, *Sharing the Resources*, 11.

60. Roilo Golez, 21 January 2000, quoted in Parker, "Conflicting Territorial Claims," 14. Parker, "Scarborough Shoal," describes in detail Chinese activities on this reef that is also claimed by the Philippines and Cathy Rose A. Garcia, "Manila Verifying Reports of PRC Activities in Scarborough," *Manila Business World,* 17 February 2000, in FBIS-SEP20000217000053.

61. Schmetzer 1998, quotes a Philippine naval officer as admitting, "We can only go and look. We don't have the capacity to do anything else. . . . We don't have patrol boats good enough to scare the Chinese, let alone force them to leave."

62. Storey 1999, 104–5, discusses the Philippine Congress's actions. The then-chief of the Philippine armed forces described this program to the author in the spring of 1997 but commented, "I don't expect to see a peso of it."

63. Defense Secretary Orlando Mercado, quoted in ibid.

64. "Philippine-U.S. Joint Military Exercises Open 31 Jan," *Quezon City BMA-7 Radio-Television Arts,* 31 January 2000, in FBIS-20000206000252, reported that the exercise would initially involve 50 Philippine and 40 U.S. military personnel, although follow-on phases would involve considerably more troops.

65. Quoted in Macon Ramos-Araneta, "Philippine Senate President: 'Ready for War' with U.S. Ally," *Manila Times,* 6 February 2000, in FBIS-20000206000427; Ople is referring to the 1952 U.S.-Philippine Mutual Defense Treaty, but that treaty may not include the South China Sea islands.

66. Quoted in "Military Exercises with U.S. Not Aimed at China," *Manila Business World,* 4 November 1999, in FBIS-EAS-99-1104.

67. Philippine armed forces chief, Gen. Angelo Reyes, quoted in Aurea Calica, "Philippine Army Chief: No Threat of Clash Over Spratlys," *Philippine Star,* 20 December 1999, in FBIS-1999120000002. Also see Aurea Calica, "Manila to Forward Spratlys Poaching Evidence to Beijing," *Philippine Star,* 9 February 2000, in FBIS-20000209000083, report that "photographs of dynamite and corals seized from Chinese fishing boats last Jan. 25 will be sent to China to justify Navy patrols off Scarborough Shoal." Philippine complaints about both Chinese and Vietnamese fishing boat incursions continue, as reported in Paolo Romero, "Philippine Navy Spots Two More Chinese Vessels in Spratlys," *Philippine Star,* 1 March 2000, in FBIS-SEP20000301000010; Rocky Nazareno, "RP to Revive Claim over Mischief Reef," *Philippine Daily Inquirer,* 2 April 2001, in FBIS-SEP20010402000026.

68. Sandy Araneta, "Philippine Military to Put Up Markers in Spratlys," *Philippine Star,* 23 December 1998, in FBIS-19981224000007.

69. These late 1999 and early 2000 incidents were widely reported in the Philippine, Chinese, and foreign press. See, for instance, "Spokesman

urges Philippines Not to Detain Fishing Vessels," *Xinhua,* 3 June 1999, in FBIS-CHI-99-0603; "China Says Filipino Navy Chasing PRC Fishing Boats," *Agence Française-Presse* (hereafter cited as *AFP*), 5 November 1999, in FBIS-CHI-99-1105; "Philippine Navy Ship Chases 4 PRC Boats," *Philippine Daily Inquirer,* 26 January 2000, in FBIS-20000126000248; "Philippine Navy to 'Step Up' Patrols in Scarborough Shoal," *Philippine Daily Inquirer,* 27 January 2000, in FBIS-20000127000286; Cynthia D. Balana and Christine Avendano, "Manila Assured No New Chinese Structures in Spratlys," *Philippine Daily Inquirer,* 28 January 2000, in FBIS-20000128000224; and "Philippines to Probe Shooting Incident in Spratly Shoal," *Quezon City BMA-7 Radio-Television Arts,* 4 February 2000, in FBIS-20000204000458. Also see "Philippine Navy Fires Warning Shots," Internet:http://search.yahoo.com.sg/search/news_sg?p=Philippine+navy&n=10. At the same time, Philippine Minister of Defense Orlando Mercado "ruled out future arrests of Chinese fishermen" because it is "a very tedious function." He said that the Philippines would instead "be preventive in our actions." ("Philippine Defense Chief Rules Out Future Arrests of Chinese," Internet: www.insidechina.com/news/php3?id=132395). Maricel V. Cruz, "Manila Protests Presence of PRC Boats in Spratly Shoal," *Manila Times,* 16 January 2000, in FBIS-20000116000060.

70. Foreign Ministry spokesman Zhu Bangzao, quoted in "Spokesman Urges PI Stop Creating 'New Disturbances,'" *Zhongguo Xinwen She,* 27 January 2000, in FBIS-20000127000944. This mantra was repeated on 1 and 3 February 2000, in the same Beijing paper, and at a 3 February press conference. "PRC Punishes Three Captains for Illegal Digging in Coral Reefs," *Xinhua,* 23 May 2000, in FBIS-CPP20000523000140, reports a rare action in which China agreed with Philippine charges, and punished three fishing boats that "illegally dug coral reef around Huangyan island [Scarborough Shoals]."

71. Ching, "Manila Foiled in Spratly Row," 33; "Manila Said Not Getting ASEAN Aid in Mischief Reef Issue," *Manila Business World,* 13 April 1999, in FBIS-EAS-99-0413; "ASEAN Members Said Unhappy with Manila on Spratlys Issue," *Manila Business World,* 26 April 1999, in FBIS-EAS-99-0426, reports that "even some of our ASEAN friends are either mute, timid or cannot go beyond espousal of general principle of peaceful settlement of disputes and polite words of understanding given in the corridors of meeting rooms."

72. The South China Sea islands are probably not covered under this 1955 treaty. See "U.S. Defense Pact Does Not Cover Spratlys," *AFP,* 13 February 1999, in FBIS-FTS19990213000133, quoting Philippine officials; Juliet L. Javellana and Christine Avendano, "Estrada Calls for 'Stronger' Security Ties with U.S.," *Philippine Daily Inquirer,* 4 December 2000, in FBIS-SEP20000518000063.

73. Cited in Kiko Cueto, "Manila Said in 'Lose-Lose' Situation on Chinese Fishermen," *Abante* (Manila), 9 February 2000, in FBIS-20000209000074. The Philippines is faring no better in its territorial disputes with Vietnam and Malaysia. See John McLean, "Philippines Protests at Vietnam Spratly 'Attack,'" *BBC Online Network*, 28 October 1999, for an account of an incident in which Vietnamese forces allegedly fired at a Philippine air force plane. "Fighters Trail Philippine Plane Over Spratlys," Reuters, 1 November 1999, in Yahoo! Headlines, reporting an incident when a Philippine plane surveyed new Malaysian structures on "Pawikan Shoal," which is also claimed by Manila. [Note: "Pawikan Shoal" is not listed on any of the three Spratly Island charts available to the author; possibly this report refers to Louisa Reef (Terumbu Semarang to Malaysia).] Kuala Lumpur rejected Manila's protest in this case, as it had in earlier cases concerning Investigator Shoal [Terumbu Peninjau] and Erica Reef [Terumbu Siput].

74. Quoted in Tan Guoqi, "Jiang Zemin, Estrada Hold Talks on Ties, South China Sea, WTO, One-China Issues," *Xinhua*, 16 May 2000, in FBIS-CPP20000516000147, and "Manila, Beijing Vow to Solve Spratlys Dispute 'Peacefully,'" *Manila Times*, 18 May 2000, in FBIS-SEP20000518000063.

75. Leifer, "Chinese Economic Reform and Security Policy," 36.

76. Parker, "Conflicting Territorial Claims," 9.

77. Leifer, "Chinese Economic Reform and Security Policy," 38.

78. Leifer, "Chinese Economic Reform and Defense Policy," 17, reports "a minor international scandal in 1993" resulting from the PLAN endangering the right of innocent passage, ostensibly while countering smuggling attempts.

79. Santo Darmosumarto, "China's Stance on South China Sea," *Jakarta Post*, 18 December 1999, in FBIS-19991218000030.

80. Quoted in "Indonesia to Help Maintain Security in South China Sea," *Jakarta Post*, 7 December 1999, in FBIS-19991206001856.

81. Johnson, "Drawn into the Fray," 153, quotes Indonesian Foreign Ministry spokesman Irawan Abidin as saying, "We didn't want to make a big fuss out of it," thus nicely summarizing Indonesia's very tentative approach to disputed issues with China.

82. See Whiting, "ASEAN Eyes China," 305–7, for a good discussion of this disagreement; Whiting notes that in September 1996, Indonesia "held its first prominent military exercises around the [Natuna] islands in five years." Also, Indonesian Navy Chief of Staff Admiral Achmad Sutjipto was quoted in "Indonesian Navy to Set Up Four Maritime Region Commands," *Jakarta Antara*, 17 February 2000, in FBIS-SEP20000217000078.

83. Hoffman 1971; author's discussions with U.S. analysts, November 1999: the PLA base on Woody Island has a paved runway twenty-seven hundred meters long.

84. Ibid., *1999 World Factbook.* There are also unpaved runways on several Spratly Islands—Spratly Island itself, Southwest Cay, Thitu Island, and Nanshan Island, according to Valencia, Van Dyke, and Ludwig, *Sharing the Resources,* app. 1, 227–34, which provides the most complete description of the individual Spratly Islands. The lack of complete knowledge about these islands is indicated in the descriptions in Valencia, Van Dyke, and Ludwig: for instance, on 233, "Sin Cowe Island may consist of two sand cays, 4 m and 2.5 m high. If so, it may be that one of these is actually the elusive Sin Cowe East Island; sources are unclear on this. Has fringing reef that is above water at low tide. [One source] claims that this feature is occupied by China, but more recent sources (e.g., *Far Eastern Economic Review,* 13 August 1992) state that the island is still occupied by Vietnam. PRC Scientific Station in Paracels Becomes Operational," *Xinhua,* 27 December 1999, in FBIS-19991227000472, reports "an observation networks station on crustal movement [for] earthquake forecast" had begun operation on Woody Island [Yongxing Tai]: such a facility may be more oriented toward bottom surveys, probably with ASW application. Also see "Conditions Improved for PLA Soldiers on Spratlys," *Xinhua,* 19 April 2000, in FBIS-CPP20000419000003, for indications that assignment to one of the miniscule Spratly garrisons must be very low on the PLAN personnel-assignment priority list, despite resupply by helicopter and the provision of "dish antennas, high-efficiency refrigerators, Karaoke equipment, and VCRs." Xiong Lei and Chen Wanjun, "Soldiers Make Reefs Home," *China Daily,* 8 May 2000, in FBIS-CPP20000508000028, paint an even grimmer picture, although praising the PLAN garrisons for "raising pigs and chickens" and growing vegetables "on soil shipped from the mainland."

85. See, for instance, Whiting, "ASEAN Eyes China," 312; Chung, "Spratlys and Other South China Sea Islands Disputes," 6; *Kyodo News Service,* 27 February 1992, FBIS-EAS-92, 15–16, cited in Studeman, "Calculating China's Advances," n. 37; and Lewis, Hua, and Xue, "Beijing's Defense Establishment," 87–109.

86. Klintworth, "China's Naval Ambitions," 13.

87. Quoted in Catley and Keliat, *Spratlys,* 83.

88. Garver, "China's Push Through the South China Sea," 1022.

89. Quoted in ibid., 1018–20. Muller, *China's Emergence as a Maritime Power,* 168–74, describes the development of maritime strategy in China during the 1970s.

90. Singh, "Continuity and Change," cites a figure of "nearly 800 million yuan" dedicated in the Ninth Five-Year Plan (1996–2000) "to be spent on marine technology, with marine environment, sea water utilization, accurate survey of the continental shelf, utilization of marine energy, and a comprehensive survey of the Polar region and the Spratlys being the

thrust areas." Also see "China's Domestic Maritime Regulations Internationalized," *Xinhua*, 30 November 2000, FBIS-CPP20001130000177.

91. Cordner, "Spratly Islands Dispute," quoted in Valencia, Van Dyke, and Ludwig, *Sharing the Resources*, 39.

92. Mark Valencia, conversation with author, Honolulu, Hawaii, November 1999; Valencia pointed out that continuous occupation, preferably for at least fifty years, is considered the legal standard to establish ownership. Hence, the drive by claimants to build facilities—to "occupy"—the various bits of reef and land that form the Spratly Islands and other areas of the South China Sea. That is, they are actively pursuing a policy of "ownership is nine-tenths of the law," no one more so than Beijing. Taiwan, the Philippines, and Malaysia have included announcements of tourist attractions on some of the Spratlys (or Pratas Reef, in Taipei's case), with Malaysian President Mahathir actually visiting a "resort" on Terembu Layang-Layang (the Malaysian name for Swallow Reef) in 1995. Also see Parker, "Conflicting Territorial Claims," 17. Additionally, there have been reports that both Beijing and Taipei are planning tourist facilities on "their" islands; for example, "To Turn Hainan into a Manor Tourist Province, the Paracel Islands Are to Gradually Open to the Outside World," *Ming Pao* (Hong Kong), 1 April 1998, A14, in FBIS-CHI-98-091.

93. "Beijing Eases Hard-Line Position in Dispute Over Spratly Islands," *Washington Post*, 31 July 1995, p. 16; Leifer, *China in Southeast Asia*, 14.

94. Chinese Foreign Ministry spokeswoman Zhang Qiyue, quoted in "FM Spokeswoman Discusses South China Sea Issue," *Xinhua*, 18 May 2000, in FBIS-CPP20000518000111.

95. "ASEAN Agrees on Code of Conduct for Territorial Disputes in the South China Sea," *Alexander's*, 21 February 2000. Also see Lu Jianren (Chinese Academy of Social Sciences), "Security Cooperation Among ASEAN Countries and Some Points of View," *Ta Kung Pao*, 7 July 1999, p. C-1, in FBIS-CHI-99-0727. Although the COC discussions focus on the South China Sea disputes, there are other maritime issues to which it would also apply: disputes exist between Thailand and Malaysia, Malaysia and Singapore, Malaysia and Indonesia, Vietnam and Malaysia. For the latter's support for a COC, see Sa-Nguan Khumrongro, "Malaysia Said to Favor 'Code of Conduct' to Solve Spratly Dispute," *Sunday Nation* (Bangkok), 10 October 1999, in FBIS-EAS-99-1010.

96. Ibid., 10. Taiwan attends these meetings, albeit as "Chinese Taipei."

97. Quoted in ASEAN, "ASEAN Chairman's Statement," 2.

98. Quoted in He Chong, "China Reiterates Bilateral Talks Should Be Held to Resolve Issues of Sovereignty Over the Nansha (Spratly) Islands in Accordance with International Law and the Law of the Sea," *Zhongguo*

Tongxun She, 6 August 1995, in FBIS-CHI-95-151. Also see "Beijing Adopts Moderate Stance on Spratlys in Philippine Talks, *FBIS Trends*, 23 August 1995, 34.

99. Tadashi Utsunmiya, "Draft Code of Conduct Around Spratlys Drawn by China Revealed," *Sankei Shimbun* (Tokyo), 16 August 2000, in FBIS-JPP20000816000018.

100. Liu Zhenyan, "ASEAN, PRC to Quicken Drafting of Spratlys Code of Conduct," *Xing Xian Ribao* (Bangkok), 29 April 2000, in FBIS-SEP20000501000055.

101. Xiao Rui, "Spokesman on South China Sea Code of Conduct," *Zhongguo Xinwen She*, 26 November 1999, in FBIS-19991128000072, quotes Zhu Bangzao. Also see "China's Sea Change," 6. The Singapore failure, "because of lingering differences," is reported in "Code of Conduct for South China Sea Not to Be Signed," *Bangkok Post*, 22 November 2000, in FBIS-SEP20001122000016.

102. Rui. A good analysis of the difference in Chinese and Southeast Asian positions is given in Wain, "China, ASEAN Meeting Demonstrates Deep Divisions." Zhu Bangzao, "Foreign Ministry Spokesman Answers Questions Raised by Journalists," *Xinhua*, 30 August 2000, in FBIS-CPP20000830000120; also see "ASEAN Empty-Handed After Spratlys Talks," 2000, Internet: www.atimes.com/china/china/htm on the failure of the meeting. China's premier refused to moderate his country's position in November 2000, as reported in "PRC's Zhu Calls for Peace in South China Sea, Makes No Mention of Spratlys," *AFP* (Hong Kong), 25 November 2000, in FBIS-CPP20001125000018. Also see "Codes of Conduct Unlikely to Be Signed," 8 November 2000, 6, Internet: www.insid-echina.com/news.

103. Sa-Nguan Khumrungroj, "PRC Official Warns ASEAN Against Boosting U.S. military ties," *Nation* (Bangkok), 15 March 2000, in FBIS-SEP20000315000021, issued this warning on the eve of the Bangkok ASEAN meeting, demonstrating a typically heavy Chinese diplomatic hand.

104. See "ROK, China Resume Fishing Talks in Beijing," *Korea Times*, 8 March 2000, in FBIS-KPP20000308000078: "Korea and China initialed a draft fisheries agreement in November 1998" which agreed on temporary EEZ boundaries, but also "ROKG to Intensify Watch Against PRC Boats Violating EEZ," *Seoul Yonhap*, 1 June 2000, in FBIS-KPP20000601000093, which quotes Maritime Affairs and Fisheries Minister Lee Hang-kyu that "he expects an increase in the number of Chinese fishing boats illegally operating in the [Korean] EEZ," as "the China-Japan fisheries treaty went into effect." Also see "Japan, China Plan Talks on New Fishery Pact," *Jiji Press* (Tokyo), 5 April 2000, in FBIS-JPP20000405000014, which

announced the beginning of the latest in a series of discussions to activate "a new bilateral fishery accord," based on "a provisional zone created as a result of a territorial dispute over the Senkaku Islands."

105. Chapman, "Senkaku-Daioyutai Island Dispute," 1.
106. UNCLOS, Art. 83, states, "The delimitation of the continental shelf between States with opposite or adjacent coasts shall be effected by agreement on the basis of international law, . . . If no agreement can be reached within a reasonable period of time, the States concerned shall resort to the procedures provided [herein]" which include submitting the dispute to "conciliation" (Annex 5), the International Tribunal for the Law of the Sea, the International Court of Justice, or a special arbitral tribunal.
107. Japanese Defense Agency official cited in "Japan Concerned by PRC Ships' increasing Activities," *Sankei Shimbun* (Tokyo), 18 April 2000, in FBIS-JPP20000418000045.
108. See Down and Saunders, "Legitimacy and the Limits of Nationalism," 127–33, for a detailed review of the 1990 and 1996 incidents.
109. Chapman, "Senkaku-Daioyutai Island Dispute," 6–7. "Japan's Rightists Build Shrine on Diaoyu Islands," *Xinhua*, 29 April 2000, in FBIS-CPP20000429000040, repeated a Sankei Shimbun report of a 20 April incident in which "a right-wing group" of students built a shrine on the islands. He Chong, "Japanese Rightwing Forces Again Cause a Political Situation on Diaoyu Island," *Zhongguo Tonxun She*, 14 May 2000, in FBIS-CPP20000514000055, contains a vitriolic condemnation of Japan's "fallacious reasoning and absurd theories" about the islands.
110. "Japan Voices Concern [about] Chinese Naval Activities Around Japan," *Kyodo*, 19 June 2000, in FBIS-JPP20000619000101 and "Japan Seeks Advance Approval for PRC Naval Research Ships," *Yomiuri Shimbun* (Tokyo) 20 June 2000, in FBIS-JPP20000620000053, report Japan's protest of this and other Chinese maritime surveillance activities, and request for prior notification of certain Chinese ship transits; China dismissed the protest and the request. Also see Chapman, "Senkaku-Daioyutai Island Dispute," 4–6, and "Chinese Ship Spotted Within Japanese EEZ," *Sankei Shimbun*, 5 February 2000, in FBIS-20000205000010, reporting a ship described by Japan's Maritime Safety Office (MSO) as the *Dong Tiao 232*, possibly a "missile monitoring support ship."
111. Quoted in "Chinese Naval Presence Rising Off Japan," *Japan Times*, 22 March 2000. "Japan Concerned by PRC Ships' Increasing Activities," *Sankei Shimbun*, 18 April 2000, reported that in May alone, "thirteen frigates and missile escort patrol boats were spotted, and in July, the missile destroyers and missile frigates were operating in this sea area.
112. See, for instance, "Isle Issue, Taiwan Threaten Ties Between Tokyo, Beijing," *Yomiuri Shimbun*, 8 August 1999, for a report that "PRC ocean re-

search ships have conducted 25 surveys in the territorial waters and exclusive economic zone near the Senkaku Islands."

113. "China Vows to Stop Maritime Activities Near Japan," 14 September
2000, 1, Internet: www.insidechina.com/news. "PRC Official Comments
on Activities by Research Vessels Near Japan," *Nihon Keizai Shimbun*
(Tokyo), 7 September 2000, in FBIS-JPP20000907000043. Japanese re-
action is given in "Government Irritated at China's Naval Operations,"
Sankei Shimbun, 7 August 2000, 7; Gillian Tett and Michael Nakamoto,
"Define Borders," *Financial Times* (London), 14 September 2000, p. 1;
"Japan Calls in Chinese Ambassador over Spy Ship," 8 September 2000,
Internet: www.insidechina.com/news.

Chapter 3. China's Maritime Economic Interests

1. The following state-owned enterprises are referenced in this chapter:
Chinese National Offshore Oil Corporation (CNOOC), Chinese National
Petrochemical Corporation (SINOPEC), China National Petroleum
Corporation (CNPC), China National Star Petroleum (CNSP), China
Offshore Oil Bohai Corporation (COOBC), China Offshore Oil Nankai
East Corporation (COONEC), and the China Petroleum Engineering
Construction Enterprise Group (CPECEG).

   Note on data: There appear to be few objective sources on offshore
petroleum production. It is not an attractive subject for the general
press and few scholars specialize in the subject, especially in its geopolitical implications. Hence, the observer must survey reports issued by
Chinese and foreign oil companies. Since most of the former are state-
owned enterprises, their data may be subject to political influence, and
thus reflect what I call the "Great Leap Forward" syndrome: everything
China does must be reported as superior to any other nation's efforts.
One sees, for example, reports that China "recorded an astonishing 80
percent success ratio for offshore wildcat drilling last year" ("China's
Offshore Oil Sector Profitable"), and that while "the world generally allows an error rate of 5% in exploration work, China has it down to
0.2%" (Wang Xiaomu, deputy head of the China National Oil and Gas
Group's Geophysics Office, quoted in "China Has Very High Success
Rate in Drilling," *Alexander's*, 11 June 1999).

2. Zhou Guangzhao, chairman of the association, "Scientist Outlines Five
Challenges for PRC in 21st Century," *Xinhua*, 24 May 2000, in FBIS-
CPP20000524000031. The other four challenges listed are the aging
population, agriculture, the environment, and "the information sector."

3. "On China as Huge Potential for Small Hydro-Electric Power Projects,"
Xinhua, 21 June 2000, in FBIS-CPP20000621000090, includes a report

by the Rural Electrification Institute that an estimated 75 million Chinese still have no access to electricity.

4. Zhang Shuo, Wang Ruiwu, Wang Hao, and Li Debo, "PRC's Coal Production," *Zhongguo Meitan [China Coal]* (Beijing), 1 May 1999, 14–16, in FBIS-19991223001689, forecast production in 2000 of 1.365 billion tons, not significantly more than 1997 production of 1.325 billion tons. Also see "PRC Should Expand Overseas Oil Exploration, Build Reserve," *Xinhua*, 9 May 2000, in FBIS-CPP20000509000180, states that by contrast, "in developed countries, coal's share averages 26 percent."

5. Wu Wenyue and Song Yang, "Analysis of Coal Supply, Demand," *Zhongguo Meitan*, 1 May 1999, 21–23, in FBIS-20000120000370, reports significant problems in China's coal industry, including wildcat mining, provincial protectionism, internal competition among State-Owned Coal Enterprises, disorganized transportation networks, and moving from a state-dominated to a free-market system.

6. "China to Prospect Seabed Natural Gas Hydrate," *Alexander's*, 11 June 1999; *Xinhua*, 5 July 1999, in *Alexander's*, 8 September 1999, reported that "China has decided to prospect for seabed natural gas hydrate." "Chinese Discover Natural Gas-Hydrate in Paracels," *Xinhua*, 12 April 2000, in FBIS-CPP20000412000014, notes that the Tibetan Plateau may also contain gas hydrate, but fails to address the inability to recover it. Charles Johnson of the East-West Center, conversation with author, Honolulu, Hawaii, November 1999, addressed these difficulties, which are also discussed in "Japan in Attempt to Recover Vast Reserves of Gas Hydrate," BBC report in *Alexander's*, 21 February 2000, which reports that this Japan National Oil Company effort was experimental.

7. "Inner Mongolia Develops Wind Power," *Xinhua*, 21 February 1999, in FBIS-19990221000040; "World Bank Finances Renewable Energy Project in China," *Alexander's*, 19 July 1999; "PRC, EU to Build Tidal Energy Power Station," *Xinhua*, 7 January 1999, in FBIS-19990107000153; "China to Build World's First Tidal Power Station," *Xinhua*, in *Alexander's*, 19 July 1999; "Hebei Farmers Benefit from Straw Gasified Power for Lighting," *Xinhua*, 12 March 2001, in FBIS-CPP20010312000163.

8. Smil, "China's Energy and Resource Uses," 943; Energy Information Administration, "China," EIA, 1999, reported that the Tarim fields, located in China's remote northwest, were producing only eighty thousand barrels daily, and noted the high cost of transporting that oil to China's primary markets, in the eastern part of the country. "CNSPC Discovers Oil in Tahe Oilfield North of Tarim Basin," *Alexander's*, 24 December 1999, reported that while "this find is giant for CNSPC. . . . Foreign exploration in [the] Tarim Basin has been largely disappointing." The "five to ten-fold" increase estimate is in "China's Oil Imports Will Grow Ten-Fold in the Next Decade," *Zhongguo Tongxun She* (Hong Kong), 12 September 1999, in FBIS-1999101300113. Also see Gong Zhengzheng, "Ex-

perts Push for Oil Reserve to Protect Against Unexpected Shortages,"
China Daily, 20 August 2000, in FBIS-CPP20000820000004.

9. Harrison, *China, Oil, and Asia,* 32. Estimates, in billions of barrels, are
1.0 (U.S. Geological Survey), 18.7 (three U.S. oil companies), 30.0 (independent U.S. researcher), 33.8 (Japanese geologists), 44.3–57 (CIA), and
20.3–40 (Soviet geologists). These widely varying results result in part
from differences in methodology used to reach the estimates.

10. "China Oil Industry Questioning Its Ability to Survive International
Competition," *Alexander's,* 28 May 1999. China's two largest oil companies are China National Petroleum Company (CNPC) and China Petrochemical (SINOPEC), which contributed almost 30 percent of the nation's total profit from SOEs in 1998.

11. "PRC Boosts Oil, Gas Production in Bohai, South China Sea," *Xinhua,*
11 April 2000, in FBIS-CPP20000411000151.

12. "PRC Verifies Major Oil, Gas Field in East China Sea," *Xinhua,* 3 February 2000, in FBIS-FTS2000203000508, reports discovery of a new oil
field, Chunxiao Number 3, with a daily yield of 1.2 mcm of natural gas
and 880,000 cubic meters of crude oil.

13. Ibid. The China National Star Petroleum Corporation (CNSP) is the second largest state-owned offshore oil-production company.

14. *Alexander's,* 24 December 1998, 1.

15. Ibid., 22 November 1999, notes that Chinese companies, led by the
CNOOC, will own 65 percent of this project, with foreign firms invited
to bid for the remaining 35 percent.

16. "Profile of China's Oil Industry," 1999, 1–3, Internet: www.firstsearch.
oclc.org/FETCH.

17. "China Increases Oil, Gas Production," *Xinhua,* 8 January 2000, in
FBIS-2000010800418; "China Accelerates Energy Development to Basi-
cally Meet the Demand," *Alexander's,* 19 July 1999.

18. Chen Geng, deputy director of the State Administration of Petroleum
and Chemical Industries, cited in "China's Oil Import Exceeds 40 Million
Tons in 1999," *Xinhua,* 23 February 2000, in FBIS-CPP20000223000013.

19. "Statistics Show Production of Energy Down 3.3 Percent," *Xinhua,* 2
February 1999, in FBIS-19990201001750, notes that crude oil production decreased by 0.7 percent and that of natural gas by 0.6 percent.

20. "Science Said Paying Off for China's Oil Resources," *Xinhua,* 9 January
2000, in FBIS-20000109000265, also claimed that the Bohai contains
"oil deposits of nearly 8 billion tons, and an annual crude output of over
69 million tons."

21. Valencia, "Energy and Insecurity in Asia," 88, shows a map depicting a
web of "Trans-Asian Gas Pipelines" that would include Central Asia,
Russia, Mongolia, China, North and South Korea, Japan, Taiwan, In-
dochina, and Australia. The first phase of this Japanese proposal carries
an estimated price tag of $48,023 million, in 1996 U.S. dollars.

22. Shao Qin, "Experts Urge PRC Oil Strategy to Maintain Oil Supply," *China Daily*, 10 January 2000, in FBIS-20000110000012. Hu Jianyi, "a renowned expert with the Beijing-based Research Institute of Petroleum Exploration and Development," was also cited in this account. There is even a report of China reaching into the Mediterranean: "Milosevic to Sell Refinery to China," *Belgrade Radio B2-92*, 20 January 2000, in FBIS-20000120001507.

23. Chen Geng, quoted in "Oil Giants Get More Power in Bid to Ease Fears Among Foreign Investors," *South China Morning Post* (Hong Kong), 10 December 1999, in FBIS-19991210000166.

24. "PRC Speeds Up Offshore Natural Gas Development," *Xinhua*, 29 April 1999, in FBIS-CHI-99-2282. "China to Launch massive Offshore Oil, Gas Development," *Xinhua*, 18 January 2000, in FBIS-20000118000461, included a national goal of 40 million tons of oil production by 2005.

25. 'Official': Offshore Oil Sector to Increase Profitability," *Xinhua*, 18 January 1999, in FBIS-19990118000426. In "China's Offshore Oil Sector Profitable," 21, CNOOC announced on this same day that its had made a profit of 700 million yuan (about $87.5 million) in 1998. Four days later, CNSPC announced 1998 profits of 245 million yuan (about $29.5 million), an increase of 13 percent from 1997. "CNOOC Offers 2.0 bn Shares," *Alexander's*, 9 December 1999, reports that CNOOC is also China's first major oil company with an overseas listing, reportedly offering two billion shares in Hong Kong and New York. Note that this estimate is considerably lower than others.

26. "CNOOC Plans to Produce 19 mm Tons Crude Oil in 2000," *Alexander's*, 27 April 2000.

27. EIA, *Petroleum Resources of China*, 66ff., provides a brief geological description of China's offshore basins.

28. "China's Bohai Sea Has Great Potential," *Alexander's*, 12 March 1997. These estimates come from the China National Petroleum Corporation (CNPC). This report also quotes an unnamed CNPC official describing the newest oil field (the Chengdao field) as having been "difficult to explore" and requiring innovative technology for exploitation.

29. "Offshore PRC Oilfields to Pump 300,000 Tons of Crude," *Xinhua*, 19 May 2000, in FBIS-CPP20000529000128.

30. "Profile—China's Oil Industry," *Asia Pulse*, August 1999.

31. "New Oil Well Producing in South China Sea," *Asia Pulse*, January 1999.

32. See, for instance, "Shell Is First Foreign Company to Take an Active Role in Gas Extraction in China," *AFP*, in *Alexander's*, 22 November 1999, report that Shell has signed a contract with CNPC for 50 percent stake in a $3 billion deal for gas extraction, pipeline construction, and power generation in Shaanxi and Inner Mongolia; "Chevron to Invest $45 Million in PRC's Offshore Oil Exploration," *Xinhua*, 4 April 2000, in FBIS-CPP20000404000076 and "Chevron to Expand Exploration in Chinese

Oil Fields," *China Daily*, 5 April 2000, in FBIS-CPP20000405000024, report that Chevron has invested in oil exploration and production in the South China Sea since 1990, has invested $90 million in shore facilities, and is "preparing to sink more oil wells" in the Bohai and the East and South China Seas. A survey of new major onshore and offshore energy projects in China reveals consistent involvement of non-Chinese companies, usually up to the 50 percent mark.

33. "China's Largest Offshore Oilfield Found in Bohai Sea," *Xinhua*, 1 February 2000, in FBIS-FTS20000201000037.

34. "PRC Offshore Oil Profits Total 700 Million Yuan in 1998," *Xinhua*, 15 January 1999, in FBIS-19990115000437. "China's Offshore Oil Sector Profitable" cited "a senior China National Offshore Oil Corporation (CNOOC) official" that "China gave priority to offshore oil exploration" in 1998. Also see "Oil Exploration in the South China Sea: What is the International Business Interest in This Region?" U.S. Pacific Command Virtual Information Center, 24 June 1999: American companies currently investing in China's oil exploration efforts in just the South China Sea include Crestone, Exxon, Mobil, Conoco, Arco, Amoco, and Vaalco. Other foreign investors include Royal Dutch Shell, Phillips Petroleum, Alcorn International, and BP.

35. Taiwan, the Philippines, Indonesia, Brunei, Singapore, Malaysia, Vietnam.

36. Austin, *China's Ocean Frontier*, 262, notes that this area contains "two of the biggest PRC offshore gas fields in the South China Sea," Yacheng 13-1 and Dongfang 1-1.

37. Ibid., 3. In November 1999 I interviewed two analysts who, using similar geological data, came to opposite conclusions about the presence or absence of significant petroleum reserves in the Spratlys.

38. U.S. Geodetic Survey (USGS), in USCINCPAC Memo of 15 September 1999. One optimistic estimate of SCS petroleum reserves, 55 billion tons, is in *Xinhua*, 5 September 1994, in FBIS-CHI-94-172.

39. Leifer, "Chinese Economic Reform and Security Policy," 44; Blanche and Blanche, "Oil and Regional Stability," 513. See EIA, "South China Sea Region," 3–4, for the USGS estimate for South China Sea natural gas is 266 trillion cubic feet.

40. A good account of China's activities in the South China Sea is Valencia, *China and the South China Sea Disputes*. Also see Hiramatsu, "China's Naval Advance," 124–32.

41. "South China Sea Oil Fields Produced Over 50 mm Tons in Eight Years," *Alexander's*, 27 October 1998.

42. Brief descriptions of some of this technology is in "Lufeng 22-1," BP Amoco announcement, 18 October 1999, 1–3, Internet: www.offshore-technology.com/projects/lufeng/index. This field is a joint venture between CNOOC and Staatoil of Norway.

43. "Shell Invests $3 Billion for Gas Development in PRC," *Xinhua*, 29 September 1999, FBIS-19990920999635, reported that "the South China Sea Petrochemical Project, co-funded by Shell Group and several large Chinese enterprises[,] . . . has a total investment of 4.5 billion U.S. dollars."

44. "CNOOC Launches Massive Offshore Gas Development," *Xinhua*, 24 October 1999, in FBIS-19991024000092.

45. Troush, "China's Changing Oil Strategy," 3; Austin, *China's Ocean Frontier*, 256; Zhao Shaoqin, "China Exploring Overseas Business," *China Daily*, 8 September 1997, 5, in FBIS-FTS1997090-8001529, all say 1993; Fesharaki, "Review of China's Petroleum Demand," says China became a net petroleum importer in 1996. "China's Crude Oil Imports in 1st Quarter Double 1999's," *Xinhua*, 16 May 2000, in FBIS-CPP20000516000101, reported a large "spike" in crude oil imports in the first quarter of 2000, when they increased by 120 percent over the first quarter of 1999.

46. Troush, "China's Changing Oil Strategy," 2.

47. "China Expects to Import 50 Million Tons of Oil in 2000," *Xinhua*, 21 November 2000, in FBIS-CPP20001121000078. "China Is Actively Exploring International Oil Markets," *Xinhua*, in *Alexander's*, 19 July 1999, reports that Chinese companies have acquired "share-holding, operational and leasing rights of oilfields in Peru, Canada, Thailand, Kuwait . . . Sudan and Russia [as well as] Central Asia," according to Qin Anmin, president of the China Petroleum Engineering Construction Enterprise Group (CPECEG). "Australia to Supply LNG to China," *Alexander's*, 24 December 1998, reports a smaller deal: Guangzhou Province has signed an agreement with Western Australia to acquire 3 million tons of liquefied natural gas (LNG) annually, beginning in 2005.

48. Troush, "China's Changing Oil Strategy," 3. "PRC Making Headway in Overseas Oil Market," *Xinhua*, 14 July 2000, in FBIS-FTS19990714000885, reports that "an oilfield, a long oil pipeline and an oil refinery China built in Sudan has gone into operation," a CNPC project servicing the Muglad Oilfield, with an annual production capacity of up to 10 million tons.

49. The agreement with Caracas includes a total Chinese investment of at least $850 million, most of which purchases the yearly output of Venezuela's Maturin and Maracaibo oil fields. Also see "China Busy to Win Security of Supply for a Growing Economy," *Alexander's*, 27 April 2000. Also see Fesharaki, "Review of China's Petroleum Demand," 8–9. Patrick O'Donoghue, "China Plans to invest in Oilfields," *Caracas Vheadline*, 25 June 1999, in FBIS-19990625001738, reported that China was investing $500 million dollars to develop these oil fields, expanding on an earlier $358 million investment. "Government, China Ink Orimulsion Accord," *Venezuela Online News* (Caracas), 17 April 2000, in FBIS-LAP20000418000003, reports a further Chinese investment of $300 million to build a plant in Venezuela to produce "orimulsion," a "water-

based heavy petroleum emulsion" used chiefly in Italy and Denmark. "Venezuela to Export 480,000 tons of Orimulsion to China," *Xinhua*, 6 March 2000, quoted in *Alexander's*, 27 April 2000, reports that China will import $200 million worth of this product annually.

50. Austin, *China's Ocean Frontier*, 258.
51. "China Increasingly Reliant on Imported Fuel Supplies," *Alexander's*, 7 August 2000.
52. Fesharaki, "Review of China's Petroleum Demand," provides these figures for 1996.
53. Lelyveld, "Iran," reported that the primary Chinese company involved in the proposed joint pipeline-construction project, CNPC, had withdrawn from the arrangement because of financing difficulty.
54. China Strategy and Management Society on 1998–99 international situation: "China's Cooperation with the Middle East on Energy," quoted in *Ta Kung Pao* (Hong Kong), 17 March 1999, p. B-1, in FBIS-19990330000566. "Iran, China Firms to Discuss Pipeline Funding," Reuters, 18 January 2000, reports a proposal for a joint Sino-Iranian construction of a $360 million pipeline from the Caspian coast to Tehran.
55. Jasper Becker, "Future of PRC Refineries in WTO Discussed," *South China Morning Post*, 17 January 2000, p. 3, in FBIS-2000117000240, notes that even without the effect of WTO, China's oil imports may soon equal a third of domestic production.
56. "China's Long-Term Level of Oil Imports Will Outstrip Expectations," *Alexander's*, 27 April 2000.
57. "Nuclear Energy Should Stay on Track," *China Daily*, 7 December 1999, in FBIS-19991206001946. Note 4, above, states that coal provides 71 percent of China's energy needs; China to Develop Own Advanced Nuclear Reactors," *Xinhua*, 7 April 2000, in FBIS-CPP20000407000128, cites 75 percent for this dependency.
58. "China Speeds Up Development of New Energy Sources," *Xinhua*, 26 January 2000, in FBIS-FTS20000126000710, reports "recoverable wind energy sources of 160 million kw, geothermal sources of 3.5 million kw, tidal sources of over 20 million kw, and 300 million tons of biomass available for conversion to methane gas." I am indebted to Dennis Blasko for the information about China's nuclear energy industry: state organizations include the State Commission for Science, Technology and Industry for National Defense (COSTIND), the China Atomic Energy Authority (CAEA), the State Environmental Protection Agency (SEPA) and the National Nuclear Safety Administration (NNSA), the State Development & Planning Commission (SDPC), the Ministry of Science and Technology (MOST) and the Nuclear Safety Center, the China National Nuclear Corporation (CNNC), and the China Nuclear Engineering-Construction Group Corporation.

59. Wang Shibin, "Let Nuclear Energy Bring Benefit to Mankind," *Jiefangjun Bao*, 27 March 2000, in FBIS-CPP20000328000036. CNNC was established in July 1999 and is classified as a "national defense" industrial corporation. It includes 246 industrial enterprises, scientific research and design institutes, and other units. It is a "cradle to grave" organization, responsible for the treatment and disposal of nuclear energy, material, fuel, radioactive waste; it also oversees uranium mining and the research, development, construction, and operation of nuclear energy facilities. Finally, CNNC is responsible for related cooperation with foreign countries.

60. "PRC to Complete Beijing-Based Nuclear Reactor in 2000," *Xinhua*, 17 September 1999, in FBIS-CHI-99-0917. The provinces are Shandong, Fujian, Hainan, Jiangxi, Hunan, Hubei, and Sichuan.

61. Xu Yuming (deputy director of the State Atomic Energy Agency), quoted in "Priority to Costal Areas in Developing Nuclear Power," *Xinhua*, 24 May 1999, in FBIS-19990524001080; Ju Chuanjiang, "Shandong Nuclear Power Plant to Cost $3 Billion," *China Daily*, 30 December 1999, in FBIS-19991230000022, reports that a plant scheduled to begin construction in Shandong in 2003 will cost $3 billion. Jia Baoshang, deputy director of Qin-Hua University's Institute of Engineering Physics, is quoted in "China to Build Twenty Nuclear Power Plants by 2020," *ITAR-TASS*, 19 May 2000, in FBIS-CEP20000519000017, as stating that ten nuclear plants were under construction in 2000, but he may have been counting individual nuclear reactors within each "nuclear power station."

62. "Nuclear Energy Should Stay on Track." Mikhail Kozyrev and Ivan Safronov, "Moscow Has Offered Beijing Nuclear Assistance in Space," *Kommersant* (Moscow), 31 May 2000, in FBIS-CEP20000601000053, notes the visit of Sergey Adamov, head of Russia's Ministry of Atomic Energy to Tianwan, "the biggest of the projects in the Russian-Chinese nuclear program. This entire program of nuclear cooperation should be viewed skeptically, in view of the lack of follow-through on proposals for Sino-Russian cooperation on pipelines and other agreements in the petroleum sector.

63. See, for instance, "Sichuan Power Station Ready to Send Electricity to East," *Xinhua*, 19 February 2000, in FBIS-CPP20000219000038. Anecdotal evidence of the problems with energy distribution in China was provided by an engineer for a large American company that constructed coal-burning power generating stations in Fujian Province: he stated that coal could be purchased more cheaply and shipped more reliably from Australia than from northeastern China.

64. "China Steps Up Offshore Gas Development," *Xinhua*, 3 March 2000, in FBIS-CPP20000303000076.

65. Hugar, "Sea Dragon Network," 6, cites "China's Shipping Prospects," *Cargonews China*, 1 May 1997. Internet: web3.asia1.com.sg/timesnet/

data/cnc/docs/cnc0287.htm, 15 June 1997, reports that the value of this trade grew by twenty percent between 1991 and 1995. Hugar, "Sea Dragon Network," 22, also reports that foreign oil imports grew by 100 percent from 1994 to 1996.

66. Hugar, "Sea Dragon Network," xvi, 70.

67. Hugar, "How Far Will the Dragon Swim?" 48, discusses China's SLOCs. Hugar, "Sea Dragon Network," 27, notes that "China imports five percent of its grain consumption, or 75 million metric tons . . . primarily from Australia, Argentina, Canada, and the United States." Downing, "China's Evolving Maritime Strategy, Part 1," 129–33, discusses China's need to import food; its ability to feed its still growing population is hampered by the low proportion of its land (about 10 percent) that is arable.

68. One of the contentious points about Liu Huaqing's first two strategic stages is their southwestern delineation by the Indonesian Archipelago, since a line drawn through Sumatra extends this area of Chinese aspirations *west* of the Malacca Strait. This infers Beijing's ambition to control that strait, one of the world's most crucial, and one whose fate directly affects the national interests of both Southeast Asian and Indian Ocean nations.

69. Hugar, "Sea Dragon Network," presents the best account of the current reach of China's merchant shipping industry. Particularly useful is his discussion of the ports and shipping routes used by China around the world, which shows the significance of the Indian Ocean.

70. Ibid., 6, 8, reports that the value of this trade grew by 20 percent between 1991 and 1995, and that foreign oil imports grew by 100 percent from 1994 to 1996.

71. Austin, *China's Ocean Frontier*, 264, 266. "PRC Ministry to Regulate Border Security of Coastal Ships," *Xinhua*, 6 April 2000, in FBIS-CPP20000406000064, reported that "at least 310,000 coastal ships and over 1.1.6 million fishermen went to sea last year." "Bejing Hosts 3rd World Fisheries Congress," *Xinhua*, 31 October 2000, in FBIS-CPP20001031000088, reported that "over 400 overseas researchers from more than 50 countries" attended this quadrennial meeting, hosted by the China Society of Fisheries.

72. Scully, "International Perspectives."

73. "China Reaches Goal of Zero Growth in Fishing," *Xinhua*, 8 January 1999, in FBIS-20000108000411.

74. "South China Sea Fishing Ban Underway," *Xinhua*, 1 June 1999, in FTS-19990601000669; "Survey Cites Effectiveness of Fishing Ban," *Xinhua*, 15 June 1999, in FBIS-CHI-99-0615. Deborah Kuo, "Taiwan Fishery Urges to Avoid PRC-Designated Area for Restocking Resources," *Taipei Central News Agency*, 26 May 2000, in FBIS-CPP20000526000078, reports the Kaohsiung Fishery Affairs Department calling for local fishing boats to follow the mainland's fishing guidelines.

75. Valencia, *Maritime Regime for North-East Asia*, 99.
76. "PRC Begins Summer Fishing Ban in South China Sea," *Xinhua*, 1 June 2000, in FBIS-CPP20000601000167.
77. "Clashes Over Fish in Pacific Asia, 1994–1997." Zhao Huanxin, "China's Fishing Industry Preparing for Challenges of WTO Entry," *China Daily*, 1 November 2000, in FBIS-CPP20001101000016, notes Beijing's concern about entry into the WTO having adverse affects on China's fishing industry.
78. "More on Japan-China Fisheries Taking Effect in June," *Kyodo English*, 27 February 2000, in FBIS-JPP20000227000024.
79. "Li Ruihuan Hopes to Resolve Fishing Dispute," *Kyodo*, 10 December 1999, in FBIS-19991210000245; "Tokyo, Beijing Aim to Put Fishery Agreement into Force," *Jiji Press* (Tokyo), 21 January 2000, in FBIS-20000122000031; "Japan-China Fishery Talks Fail to Reach Agreement"; *Jiji Press*, 27 January 2000, in FBIS-FTS20000127001051; and "Japan, PRC Fishery Talks 26–27 February Aim to Break Deadlock," *Jiji Press*, 22 February 2000, in FBIS-JPP20000222000042, discuss the repeated bilateral meetings about the treaty. Zhao Huanxin, "PRC Fleet to Monitor Fishery Agreement with Japan," *China Daily*, 24 May 2000, in FBIS-CPP20000524000016, also reported that this was the first international agreement signed by Beijing under the UNCLOS.
80. "ROK, China to Hold Yellow Sea Environment Meetings," *Seoul Yonhap*, 17 January 2000, in FBIS-20000117000085, and "ROK, PRC to Hold Working-Level Fisheries Talks 25 Jan," ibid., 21 January 2000, in FBIS-20000121000707. "N. Korea Not to Attend Japan Sea Rim Summit," *Kyodo* (Tokyo), 25 October 2000, in FBIS-JPP20001025000080, reports Pyongyang's refusal to participate "due to various circumstances."
81. "China, South Korea Enhance Maritime Safety Cooperation," *Xinhua*, 9 May 2000, in FBIS-CPP20000509000092.
82. "ROKG, China to Hold Fisheries Talks in Beijing on 18 April," *Seoul Yonhap*, 17 April 2000, in FBIS-KPP20000417000040, reports that these negotiations started in November 1998; the next session was scheduled for July 2000.
83. Hiramatsu, "China's Naval Advance," 130.
84. Mo Jie and Chen Bangyan, "Marine Geology High Tech development Strategy," *Zhongguo Dizhi* [*Chinese Geology*] (Beijing), June 1997, in FBIS-CHI-98-013.

Chapter 4. PLAN Establishment

1. See Nan Li, "Organizational Changes in the PLA," 330, who also notes that all headquarters were reduced by 25 percent as part of this reduction.

2. The 270,000 figure is contained in Kuan Cha-chia, "Commander Jiang Speeds Up Army Reform, Structure of Three Armed Services to Be Adjusted," *Kuang Chiao Ching* 305 (16 February 1998), in FBIS-CHI-98-065, 6 March 1998. PLAN strength is given as 230,000 by IISS 1999, 187, but the number 250,000, and the 10 percent cut in manpower, is from my interviews in October 1999. Blasko, "New PLA Force Structure," 263–64, notes that China's July 1998 Defense White Paper states that PLA ground forces will be reduced by 19 percent, naval forces by 11.6 percent, and air forces by 11 percent, which would equal a reduction of about 418,000 ground forces, 31,000 naval personnel, and 52,000 air force personnel.

3. Blasko, "New PLA Force Structure," 262–63.

4. Wang Shichang, "Face the Ocean, Challenge the Giant Waves," cited in Huang, "Chinese Navy's Offshore Active Defense Strategy," 9. These figures do not address national defense expenditures that are not included in the nominal PLA budget, such as foreign purchases of Su-27 and Su-30 aircraft, *Kilo*-class submarines, and *Sovremenny*-class destroyers. Other defense costs that may not be included in the PLA budget include pensions, research and development, and training conducted at civilian schools.

5. See Swaine, *Role of the Chinese Military,* 43–71, who discusses a wide range of participants in the national security policy-making process, including those heading up institutions such as the National Defense University (NDU) and Academy of Military Science (AMS), and retired senior officers.

6. Shambaugh, "China's Post-Deng Military Leadership," 27.

7. PLA officers, interviews with author, discussed his operational responsibility in gaining authorization from the national policy-making apparatus for tasking the Navy wants to execute—such as a multiship deployments to foreign nations—by presenting it as beneficial to China in order to gain official sanction.

8. Li and Yang, *Overview of the Chinese Armed Forces,* 232. David M. Finkelstein of the Center for Naval Analysis (CNA) discussed with the author the different missions of these two organizations: the Hai Jun Jun Shi Xue Shu yan Jiu Suo and the Hai Jun Zhuangbei Lun Xheng Yan Jiu Xhong Xin.

9. I first discussed with PLA officers implementing an ROTC-like program in China in 1993; discussions since then between U.S. and PRC National Defense University (NDU) faculty typically occur at least twice a year and have almost always included ROTC as a topic. The current, highly successful American Naval ROTC (Holloway) program was initiated in 1946 and established units at prominent U.S. universities to produce officers educated in technical and engineering curricula.

10. Senior PLA officer, interview with author. See Xiang Jiajun and Zhang Xuanjie, *Xinhua*, 28 May 1999, in FBIS-CHI-99-0601, for the report that the "Second Artillery Corps signed an agreement with the Northwest Engineering University in Xian today to cultivate cadres for guided missile troops" and will "supply a certain number of outstanding university and graduate students for the Second Artillery Corps every year," with the Corps establishing a "national defense scholarship" at the school to "encourage and fund" likely students. Also see Liu Jianxin, *Xinhua*, 28 October 1999, in FBIS-CHI-99-1103, for the report that the "Guangzhou Military Region and Wuhan University have signed an agreement on jointly training military cadres. . . . This military region will . . . expand the selection of outstanding personnel from institutions of higher learning across the country. . . . All major military regions and armed services have separately designated one local university to be the designated school for training their own cadres."

11. *Xinhua*, 17 August 1999, in FBIS-CHI-99-0817; *Xinhua* (Hong Kong), 21 June 1999, in FBIS-CHI-99-0622, repeats a *Jiefangjun Bao* report note about linkage with military academies; controlling an "ROTC" student's academic "major" has long been a concern in the U.S. Naval ROTC program. This report also notes that the number of academies are being reduced in the interest of making individual schools larger and more efficient. The *Straits Times* (Singapore), 20 June 1999, "China Sets Up Defense Campus," reported that the PLA "has set up a new National Defense Science and Technology University" in Changsha, and "directly under the command of the CMC" will offer a wide range of courses at the general staff college (0-5/0-6) level.

12. "Put Military Academy Education in a Strategic Position of Priority Development," *Jiefangjun Bao*, 23 June 1999, in FBIS-CHI-99-0629. During the past year there have been numerous reports of military academy reform.

13. Li Xianfang and Liu Haiyang, "PRC Navy Forms Engineering University in Wuhan," *Xinhua*, 17 June 1999, in FBIS-CHI-1999-0617.

14. Rear Adm. Shao Zijung (college president), quoted in *Xinhua*, 7 August 1999, in FBIS-CHI-99-0826: "Navy Engineering College Is Aimed at Developing New Naval Military Talent."

15. Senior PLA officers, conversation with author; Xu Sen, "Building a Modern Naval Battlefield—Overview of the Naval Vessel Training Center," *Jiefangjun Bao*, 15 September 1999, 6, in FBIS-CHI-99-0923.

16. Xu, "Building a Modern Naval Battlefield," 244–45.

17. Quoted in Huang Caihong, Chen Wanjun, and Zhang Zhao, "China Enhances the Navy's Comprehensive Strength—Interview with Naval Commander Vadm Shi Yunsheng," *Liaowang* 16 (Beijing) (19 April 1999): 13–15, in FBIS-CHI-99-0513. Referred to hereafter as "Shi Interview."

18. "Zhang Wannian Steps Up Military Logistics Reform," *Xinhua*, 9 December 1999, in FBIS-FTS19991209000883, cites Zhang's statement that "it is imperative for the military to commercialize its logistics in this period of modernization."

19. Jianxiang Bi, "Managing Taiwan Operations," 11. "Shi Interview" describes "naval port cities" being designated as central distribution points in the new logistics system.

20. *People's Navy*, 126; Huang Caihong, Chen Wanjun, and Zhang Zhao, "The PLA Navy Has Enhanced Comprehensive Combat Effectiveness," *Xinhua*, 19 April 1999, in FBIS-CHI-99-0423. Even in the logistics area, Shi has been able to build on his predecessor's work: the PLAN's most significant overseas deployment to date, the three-ship visit to the Americas in 1998, which occurred before Shi was appointed to command the navy, is cited as evidence of the navy's enhanced logistics capability by Cheung, "Reforming the Dragon's Tail," 237.

21. There has been considerable speculation in the open press, especially among Indian analysts, that China has established facilities at Burmese coastal and island sites to support a PLAN presence, but U.S. and Taiwan analysts do not support these accusations.

22. See Mulvenon, *Professionalization*, for the best current analysis of the ongoing professionalization of the PLA's senior officer corps.

23. My conversation with U.S. Navy analysts in November 1999 included the suggestion that Shi and Yang visited France to discuss purchase of a follow-on to the Exocet antiship cruise missiles previously acquired by China and used as the model for the Chinese-built C-800 series missiles; the visit to Egypt was conjectured to be in connection with a possible multiship PLAN deployment to the Mediterranean advocated by Shi. As noted above, this (November) was about the timeframe for such proposals to be forwarded to the Defense Ministry by the Naval Headquarters. Author's discussion with Admiral Shi's U.S. escort officer for his April 2000 visit to the United States revealed that Shi was most interested in U.S. naval aviation programs; command, control, communications, computers, intelligence, surveillance, and reconnaissance (C4ISR); officer and enlisted recruitment, retention, and training programs; and USCG roles, missions, and relationship with the USN.

24. Shi, appointed PLAN commander in September 1997, was finally promoted to full admiral in June 2000. This promotion may merely represent his longevity and distinguished career, but Swaine, *Role of the Chinese Military*, 45, does identify Shi as one of "the most influential (and vocal) bureaucratic players in formulating and supervising critical components of policy."

25. Ibid., 47.

26. This would be a significant problem in the U.S. Navy, among others; an officer of such narrow experience would not be selected to head the U.S. Navy. Historically, there have been very effective heads of Navy with very limited or no seagoing experience (Alfred von Tirpitz, in early-twentieth-century Germany, for instance), but they are the exception. Evaluating the durability of Shi's influence on PLAN modernization and strategic development requires knowledge of how many and influential are his acolytes in the officer corps, especially at the flag-officer level.

27. Quoted in "Shi Interview." Also see Ren Yanjun, "Forging a Shield of Peace for the Republic—Part 1 of Roundup on 50 Years of Achievements in Army Building," *Jiefangjun Bao*, 6 September 1999, 1, 2, in FBIS-CHI-99-0911; and Xu Zuzhi, "Backgrounder on National Day Celebrations," *Zhongguo Xinwen She* (Beijing), 1 October 1999, in FBIS-CHI-99-1002. These press accounts all make a point of citing Shi's role in PLAN modern developments, leading to "greatly improved combat capability."

28. Seniority among officers of the same rank is based on "date of rank": if an officer is promoted to vice admiral on 1 June and a second officer is promoted to the same rank a day later, the first will always be senior to the second, so long as they both are vice admirals. This is not to say, however, that the second officer may not be assigned to a billet in which he is more influential than his nominal senior: the billet may dictate influence, if not "seniority."

29. PLAN organization and office holders' ranks are identified through the *Directory of PRC Military Personalities,* October 2000, U.S. analysts, and PLA sources.

30. This discussion on promotions is based on my interviews with two PLAN senior captains; additional information sources are certainly desirable.

31. The PLAN political commissar/PLAN Political Office probably controls the curriculum at the Political Academy in Qingdao, following PLA General Political Department direction.

32. This discussion draws on Blasko, Klapakis, and Corbett, "Training Tomorrow's PLA," 494–97.

33. For instance, the South Sea Fleet would logically require an annual training regimen that devoted particular attention to amphibious operations. A partial survey of annual, fleet-level training exercises, however, does not show the South Sea Fleet spending significantly more time on amphibious training than the North and East Sea Fleets. So perhaps the fleets faithfully execute the annual training plan as it is passed down from the GSD through the PLAN Training Office.

34. Finkelstein and PLA officers, conversations with author. The PLAN also operates many supporting activities, including oceanographic research facilities; see "Key Ocean Study Established in Hangzhou," in *Xinhua*, 7 November 1999, in FBIS-CHI-99-0079.

35. U.S. Pacific Command (USCINCPAC) sources show the PLANAF reporting not directly to the Navy Commander but through the Headquarters Department.

36. Chen Wanjun and Sha Zhiliang, "Newsletter: Commanding the Winds and the Clouds Between the Sea and the Sky—A True Picture of the Shipborne Aircraft Unit of the People's Navy," *Xinhua*, 21 April 1999, in FBIS-CHI-99-0502, reported that a PLANAF helicopter unit began training for shipboard operations in the late 1970s, with the first successful operational flight occurring on 3 January 1980. Despite this article's purple prose, a 1980 date "fits" with the development of the PLAN's first helicopter-capable combatant, the *Luda II*–class DDG *Jinan*, which began construction in 1977.

37. Sae-Liu, "Chinese Expand Aerial Refueling Capability," reported that "PLA Navy fighters conducted their first aerial refueling mission in late March," using a PLAAF H-6 tanker while PLAAF refueling exercises have been conducted since at least late 1998. This is just the tip of the iceberg; at the April 2000 CNA conference on the PLAN the leading U.S. authority on China's air forces, Kenneth Allen, listed some of the questions to which we have no answer: how many hours does each pilot fly, annually and what kinds of missions are exercised; do the pilots train in an electronic warfare (ECM) environment; is Ground Control Intercept control still required; is training conducted in "stand-off" operations; in joint maritime operations; is a standardized, long range training regime in place?

38. PLA officers, interviews with author, 1994–2000. Kondapalli, "China's Naval Structure and Dynamics," assigns eight (vice nine) divisions and twenty-seven (vice twelve) regiments to the three fleets. The actual number assigned to each fleet may well vary in response to operational and administrative imperatives. In conversations some U.S. analysts questioned the existence of the "air groups," which may be formed for a particular tactical mission rather than exist as a permanent organizational structure.

39. Such as very small patrol craft and harbor service craft.

40. Kondapalli, "China's Naval Structure and Dynamics," 4.

41. Individual ship numbers are found in *Strategic Survey 2000*, Baker, *Naval Institute Guide to Combat Fleets*, and Sharpe, *Jane's Fighting Ships: 2000–2001*, and will be discussed in detail in chapter 5. The numbers accuracy is suspect for submarines and small combatants, since as many as half of these vessels may be held in reserve.

42. Chen Yeong-kang, paper on China's submarine force presented for the April 2000 CNA Conference on the PLAN, Washington, D.C. Sharpe, *Jane's Fighting Ships: 2000–2001*, 120, states that the *Ming*s are split between the North and South Sea Fleets. The uncertainty about the total number of submarine flotillas results from different estimates in Sharpe,

Jane's Fighting Ships: 2000–2001; Baker, *Naval Institute Guide to Combat Fleets;* Trevethan, "PLA Navy Air Force Order of Battle"; Taiwan sources; PLAN sources; and U.S. analysts.

43. Sharpe, *Jane's Fighting Ships: 2000–2001,* 126, reports that an expected second *Luhai* has not begun construction as of early 2000; Baker, *Naval Institute Guide to Combat Fleets,* 107, and Young, *Chinese Military Digest,* report a second ship is being built, but according to my interviews with PLAN and U.S. analysts, the next DDG, probably under construction in a Dalian shipyard, will be sufficiently different from *Shenzhen* (the first *Luhai*-class ship) to denote a new ship class.

44. "China to Receive Second Russian Destroyer in November 2000," *Agentstvo Voyennykh Novostey,* 10 July 2000, FBIS-CEP2000710000147.

45. *Strategic Survey 2000,* 178, lists a third *Luhu* under construction, but it seems more likely, given China's propensity to build small ship classes, that construction of the follow-on *Luhai*-class of DDG has superseded further *Luhu* construction. Taiwan Navy sources show different PLAN strength figures.

46. The key determinant to voyage length for almost all these amphibious ships is fresh water availability on board.

47. This is a "soft" number, subject to many factors, including the amount and type of cargo to be carried by embarked troops, the duration and distance of the embarkation, and other factors. The LSTs and LSMs are designed to land troops during an opposed assault; the troop transports are more likely designed to administratively offload troops, pier side. Also, during an amphibious assault, some of the LSTs and LSMs would carry predominantly cargo—such as supplies and vehicles—and almost no troops; others might be loaded only with troops. Furthermore, the condition of many of these vessels is unknown; many of them may not be seaworthy or marginally so.

48. In fact, many types of mines can be laid by aircraft, as well as by almost any fishing boat or merchant ship, but laying a truly useful, navigable minefield requires expertise and exact navigation not normally found on such miscellaneous vessels. The PLAN also has forty-two drone minesweeping boats in the reserve. Baker, *Naval Institute Guide to Combat Fleets,* 119–20, reports many of China's dedicated MIW ships are equipped to sweep only moored contact mines.

49. "Hotel" services include food and housing, but also denote maintenance and operation of all shore-side facilities for supporting operating units, to include such things as piers, dry docks, classrooms, and recreation facilities. The PLAN practice of housing ship crews ashore when their ships are in port increases the importance of these services.

50. One senior PLA officer told me that in time of war, the PLAN commander would be senior to the PLAAF commander as deputy MR commander; the same PLA officer told another U.S. interlocutor that the

two would be equal in status as MR deputy commanders. As pointed out by Blasko, "New PLA Force Structure," 284, "A true indicator of the PLA's commitment to joint operations would be for the commander of the Eastern or Southern Theaters to be a naval officer." In an August 2000 conversation with a senior PLA officer, I was told that the PLA is reconsidering this command arrangement, with an eye toward increasing the authority of the fleet commanders to conduct "maritime campaigns" without army participation.

51. Li, "Organizational Changes," 154ff.
52. Jencks, "China's 'Punitive' War on Vietnam," 805–6, describes the 1979 formation of the PLA's "Southern Front" by the Kunming and Guangzhou MRs and the "Northern Front" by the Xinjiang, Lanzhou, Beijing, and Shenyang MRs during the war with Vietnam. Paul H. B. Godwin further explained these command arrangements to the author.
53. Lists of bases for the three fleets, provided in Baker, *Naval Institute Guide to Combat Fleets*, 103, differ somewhat from those in Sharpe, *Jane's Fighting Ships: 2000–2001*, and Kondapalli, "China's Naval Structure and Dynamics." I learned of Liangiang's special status in conversation with senior PLA officers. The PLAN commander, as of mid-2000, had a VIP-equipped Yak-42 aircraft for his personal use. "China's Dalian New Shipyard Established," *Xinhua*, 18 August 2000, in FBIS-CPP20000818000083, reports the presence of a 300,000-ton dock and a 900-ton crane, both formidable assets.
54. U.S. analysts, conversation with author. Sharpe, *Jane's Fighting Ships: 2000–2001*, 119; Baker, *Naval Institute Guide to Combat Fleets*, 107–8, gives Ningbo as the *Kilos*' home port.
55. U.S. analysts, interview with author; *World Factbook 1999*. Woody Island may be capable of supporting four fighter aircraft in hangars plus approximately thirty on hard stands, in the open, but does not offer a significant maintenance or fresh-water wash down capability, although additional fresh water tanks have been constructed. It also does not appear to have the ground control radar capability usually required by Chinese tactical aviators.
56. *Jane's Fighting Ships* for the past decade show this amphibious concentration in the South Sea Fleet. Two of the *Qiongsha* class have been converted to hospital ships; only one of the troop transports may be operationally active.
57. *Xinhua*, 1 October 1999, in FBIS-CHI-99-0930; PLA personnel and U.S. analysts, interviews with author.
58. Finkelstein has highlighted the 1999 regulations that assigned the GSD responsibility for PLA-wide training and for issuing operational tasking to all rapid reaction forces. The current Marine Corps command structure was described to me by senior PLA officers.
59. Senior PLAN officers, conversations with author.

60. Kenneth Allen described this air defense arrangement to me.

61. Senior PLA officers and U.S. analysts, interviews with author.

62. Swanson, *Eighth Voyage of the Dragon,* 204, points out these forces' similarities to imperial predecessors.

63. Sharpe, *Jane's Fighting Ships: 2000–2001,* 145–47. See "State to Set Up 200,000-Strong Maritime Cruise Unit," *Xinhua,* 6 December 1996, in FBIS-CHI-96-236, for a report of a 200,000-man "maritime cruise unit" established in 1996, to be manned by reservists and to assume coastal defense duties. A more recent report is "Linhai City of Zhejiang Sets Up Sea-Borne Militia Unit to Ensure Boats for Civilian Use Will Be Able to Come at the First Call," *Zhongguo Tongxun She,* 6 May 2000, in FBIS-CPP20000506000062, reporting that the "province's first armed forces department of the aquatic product oceanic administration and a sea-borne militia unit was set up." The "aquatic product oceanic administration" is not further identified, but presumably is a translation of a Maritime Safety Administration office. Also see *Xinhua,* 18 June 1999, in FBIS-CHI-99-0618, for a report that Shanghai had established a "Maritime Safety Administration, the first of its kind in China's coastal areas, . . . to supervise the management of navigation marks, the surveying of sea-routes, and the inspection of ships and maritime facilities."

64. Tang Min, "PRC Marine Environmental Protection Law Praised," *China Daily,* 3 April 2000, in FBIS-CPP20000403000020, reports that the "amended Marine Environmental protection Law" came into effect on 1 April 2000. The complexity of coast guard-type responsibilities in China is obvious, and shown in "State Council Forms Marine Bureau in Shenzhen," *Xinhua,* 27 December 1999, in FBIS-FTS19991227000826, which reports that the "Shenzhen Marine Bureau was formed [to carry out] marine supervision." It combined the previous "separate port supervision departments under the Shenzhen Government and the Ministry of Communications." The new bureau is responsible for "managing overseas ships sailing and anchoring in Shenzhen water space, abiding by the related international marine treaty, maintaining order in sea navigation and transportation, supervising ships antipollution facility, handling water pollution, maintaining public navigation facilities and regulating the shipping economy." No reference is made to the other organizations that seem to have similar responsibilities.

65. Text of "Marine Environmental Protection Law of the PRC," in *Xinhua,* 26 December 2000, in FBIS-FTS20000207000268.

66. "PRC Establishes 12 State Maritime Safety Administrations," *Xinhua,* 28 December 1999, in FBIS-CPP19991228001478; *Xinhua,* 18 June 1999, in FBIS-CHI-99-0618, claimed that in 1999 the MSA dealt with 1,880 safety violations and "saved the lives of nearly 2,500 people" in marine waters and on the Yangtze River. The drive to improve maritime safety,

following the disastrous passenger ferry sinking in late 1999, was also indicated in "China Takes Steps to Ensure Navigation Safety," *Xinhua*, 21 February 2000, in FBIS-CPP20000221000132. Also see Guo Aibing, "Chinese Transportation Officials Urge Sea Safety Measures," *China Daily*, 28 January 2000, in FBIS-FTS20000128000198, for the report that in 1999 "769 passengers died in ship or boat accidents—a 26.9 percent increase over 1998," as the result of 249 boats sunk at a cost of more than $30 million. The MSA predecessor, the "Bureau of Harbor Superintendency," was responsible for antipollution and SAR efforts, including the SAR Coordination Centers. *Xinhua*, 26 March 1999, in FBIS-CHI-99-0327, reported that "a three-dimensional border and coastal defense communications network . . . has been completed and become operational"; *Xinhua*, 22 November 1999, in FBIS-CHI-99-0647, discusses the command and control structure for at least part of this coastal defense system.

67. *Xinhua*, 26 March 1999, in FBIS-CHI-99-0327, reported that "a three-dimensional border and coastal defense communications network . . . has been completed and become operational"; *Xinhua*, 22 November 1999, in FBIS-CHI-99-0647, discusses the command and control structure for at least part of this coastal defense system.

68. "PRC Will Enforce Rules on Coastal Vessels 1 May," *Xinhua*, 29 May 2000, in FBIS-CPP20000329000034.

69. Gerard Yoest, U.S. Coast Guard director of international relations, conversation with author, Washington, D.C., June 2000.

70. Ibid., "PRC Will Enforce Rules on Coastal Vessels 1 May."

71. See Blasko, "New PLA Force Structure," 286, for this thought. Western analysts have yet to explore the topic of PLAN fleet interoperability in detail.

Chapter 5. Ships and Aircraft of the PLAN

1. See J. T. Dreyer, *PLA and the Kosovo Conflict*, 11, for a discussion of PLA attraction to RMA terms such as "a system of systems."

2. *People's Navy*, 18.

3. Baker, *Naval Institute Guide to Combat Fleets*, 107. Three *Song*s have been launched, but the PLAN may be trying to decide between more of this class or investing in additional *Kilo*- or *Amur*-class boats.

4. The *Xia* may have been *covertly* going to sea on a regular basis, of course, but this is highly unlikely, given the unanimity of foreign observers that it has remained in port. U.S. analysts, conversations with author. Also see Sharpe, *Jane's Fighting Ships: 2000–2001*, 116, as well as previous editions.

5. One of these, the ex-USS *Wake,* served in the American, Japanese, and KMT navies before commissioning into the PLAN, perhaps the only warship ever to serve in four different navies and surrender from three of them.

6. Blackman, *Jane's Fighting Ships: 1955–1956,* 152–55, provides these numbers, but they should be treated as estimates. The "183 ships" figure is from *People's Navy,* 3, and apparently does not include over 200 "obsolete" small craft seized from various government organizations as PLA forces captured coastal areas.

7. This discussion draws on Kondapalli, "China's Naval Equipment Acquisition," 1510–11.

8. *People's Navy,* 6.

9. Ibid., 9, 17–18, 49.

10. Blackman, *Jane's Fighting Ships: 1955–1956,* 151–52. Of the 156 Soviet-assisted projects resulting from the 1950 Sino-Soviet treaty, forty-one dealt with defense, and of these only five concerned shipbuilding.

11. Swanson, *Eighth Voyage of the Dragon,* 196.

12. Zhan, "China Goes to the Blue Waters," 187.

13. Blackman, *Jane's Fighting Ships: 1960–1961,* 117–21.

14. Blackman, *Jane's Fighting Ships: 1960–1961,* 117–18; McDevitt 2000, 6.

15. Ibid., 61–66.

16. Moore, *Jane's Fighting Ships: 1978–1979,* 63.

17. Moore, *Jane's Fighting Ships: 1976–1977,* 100–109. The PLAN also included the first Chinese range instrument ships for tracking guided missile flights, and the first Chinese-built amphibious transports.

18. Moore, *Jane's Fighting Ships, 1980–1981,* 104–13.

19. Ibid., 118.

20. There have been many reports of these problems, including Kathy Chen, "China's Inability to Keep Subs Running Shows Broader Woes Plaguing Military," *Wall Street Journal,* 1 August 1997, p. 1; "New PLAN to Train, Purchase Vessel Mix," *Jane's Defence Weekly,* 16 December 1998, 25. See Sharpe, *Jane's Fighting Ships: 2000–2001,* 119, for reports of the battery (and other engineering) problems. Training problems are noted in Fisher 1999, 164. "Chinese Subs Experience Battery, Training Problems" 1997, 5, repeats these reports as well as noting that Iran and India have experienced similar engineering problems with their Kilos, as has Egypt. Marina Shatilova, "Zvezda Shipyards Receives order to Repair Chinese Submarine," *ITAR-TASS,* 16 June 2000, in FBIS-CEP20000616000016, reports that the shipyard in Bolshoi Kamen, near Vladivostok, "will repair a Chinese submarine this year." Also see "Russia to Repair Chinese Submarines," *Agentstvo Voyennykh Novostey* (Moscow), 26 March 2001, in FBIS-CEP20010326000109, reported that repair of one of the PLAN's Kilos would begin in 2001. Finally, Baker, *Naval Institute Guide to Com-*

bat Fleets, 107, reports that "up to ten Chinese submarines" are scheduled for refits in Russia.

21. See, for instance, Jacques Isnard, "Chinese Submarine Was 'Submarining' on a Freighter in Channel," *Le Monde* (Paris), 4 February 1999, p. 4, in FBIS-FTS19990204000699, which mentions ten additional *Kilo*-class subs for China; Umbach, "Financial Crisis Slows," 36, gives this number as "10–12 additional" *Kilo*s. My conversations with U.S. analysts and senior PLAN officers do not support these reports, but the *Song* may suffer from high acoustic noise problems.

22. U.S. analysts, conversation with author; Baker, *Naval Institute Guide to Combat Fleets,* 597, reports that construction has halted on construction of the *Amur* family of submarines. The NATO designation for the *Amur* is the "*St. Petersburg* class." However, Richard Scott, "Submarines Stay the Course," *Jane's Defence Weekly,* 18 October 2000, 4, reported that "work is progressing" on the first two *Amur*s. Several types of AIP engineering plants are under development in France, Germany, Sweden, and the United States, but none have been operationally proven. An excellent, brief explanation of AIP technology is contained in Scott 1999, 41–50. AIP-propelled submarines will also continue to be limited in speed: the faster they go underwater, the shorter the time they can remain submerged.

23. Adm Zhang Lianzhoung, quoted in Perry, "Hunting Beyond Red October," 1, 18.

24. *Jane's Defence Weekly,* 16 December 1998, 25, reports the *Han*'s engineering problems.

25. The PLAN uses "type" numbers for its submarines. For example, the *Romeo* is designated Type-033, the *Ming* is Type-035, the *Song* is Type-039, the *Han* is Type-091, and the *Xia* is Type-092.

26. "New Nuclear Submarines to Be Launched by Year 2002," *Ming Pao,* 8 December 1999, B17, in FBIS-FTS19991207002001, is surely too optimistic, given China's shipbuilding record; U.S. analysts, conversations with author. Several late-1999 press reports that China was going to purchase two *Akula*-class SSNs from Russia have not been substantiated. The *Akula* is a c. 1980 designed submarine, but very quiet and far superior to the *Han.*

27. Lampton and May, "Managing U.S.-China Relations," 15.

28. "Taiwan Intelligence Indicates Mainland Submarine to Test-Fire Anti-Submarine Missiles in a Month," *Ping Kuo Jih Pao,* 7 April 1997, p. A-16, in FBIS-CHI-97-097, reported that a *Song*-class submarine was going to test fire a new ASW missile, the Yingji-8, but this has not been confirmed. Also see Sharpe, *Jane's Fighting Ships: 2000–2001,* 119.

29. Karniol, "China Buys *Shkval* Torpedo," 6. Submarine-launched anti-surface-ship torpedoes may be "free-fired," but most modern weapons

are "wire-guided," which allow the submarine to update target information after the torpedo is launched. Torpedoes may use several methods of homing in on the target; most effective may be "wake-homing," where the torpedo finds the disturbed water created by a surface ship's propeller(s), and then simply follows this "wake" to the ship. The Shkval rocket-propelled torpedo is relatively inaccurate, but travels at such a high rate of speed—perhaps up to 200 knots, which is far faster than other torpedoes' 40–50 kits—that it is difficult to avoid.

30. Bai Chuan, "Chinese Navy's Development and Construction," *Ching Pao 258* (Hong Kong), 1 January 1999, 41–43, in FBIS-CHI-99-024.

31. Nikolay Novichkov, "Russian Shipyards Builds Destroyer for China," *Moscow ITAR-TASS*, 25 December 1999, in FBIS-FTS19991225000307; "Russia Delivers Second Destroyer to China," *Moscow Interfax*, 25 November 2000, in FBIS-CEP20001127000314.

32. U.S. analysts told me that China paid $880 million for the two ships, which is close to the Taiwan navy analysts' price of $800 million; $800 million *per ship* is quoted in "Russia Wraps Up Construction of Destroyer for PRC Navy," *Moscow Interfax*, 23 December 1999, in FBIS-FTS19991223000319, although Beijing probably convinced Moscow to accept goods instead of cash for a significant portion of the ships' price.

33. Russian designation for the version of this missile sold to China is "Moskit 3M-80E." This supersonic, sea-skimming missile receives targeting data from the launching ship and uses a seeker capable of employing three different sensing systems—radar, infrared, or "home on jam"—to find the target ship at the end of its flight; complex terminal flight maneuvers increase its effectiveness. An air-launched version has been developed by Russia, for arming the aircraft carrier version of the Su-27, but has not been sold to China. "US Cannot Prevent Russia Selling China Anti-Ship Missiles," *Moscow Interfax*, 14 April 2000, in FBIS-CEP20000414000094.

34. *Sovremenny* characteristics are provided in Sharpe, *Jane's Fighting Ships: 2000–2001*, 121; also see Liu Hsiao-chun, "Chinese Navy Strengthens Its Fighting Capabilities on Oceangoing Voyage," *Kuang Chiao Ching* (Hong Kong), 16 April 1997, in FBIS-CHI-97-088. Smith, "New Chinese Guided-Missile Ship," describes the Moskit as capable of carrying a nuclear warhead, but various annual issues of *Jane's Fighting Ships* have been inconsistent on this question.

35. Liu, "Chinese Navy Strengthens Its Fighting Capabilities."

36. Nikolay Novichkov, "First Lot of Russian Moskit Missiles Shipped to China," *ITAR-TASS*, 16 May 2000, in FBIS-CEP20000516000142. Roman Khrapachevskiy and Igor Ivanov, "Profits of War," *ITAR-TASS*, 16 May 2000, in FBIS-CEP200005170002000, report that the second batch of twenty-four missiles will arrive in China "at the end of the year." They

also report that Beijing is considering buying *Molnaya*-class patrol boats, which are armed with four Moskits.

37. Russian designation is Yakhont 3K55E; NATO designator is SS-NX-27, a member of the Novator family of new Russian cruise missiles being developed (the "X" means that NATO considers the missile to still be in the experimental stage). Baker, *Naval Institute Guide to Combat Fleets,* 576, describes this missile's range as varying with its flight profile—150 meters "low" and 300 meters "high."

38. Grazebrook, "New Generation," 18, reported that the Grizzly would be installed in the *Sovremennys* sold to China, but this has not been confirmed.

39. Nikolay Novichkov, "Russia Delivers Eight Anti-Sub Helicopters to China," *ITAR-TASS,* 10 December 1999, in FBIS-FTS19991210000351, describes this sale as including three Ka-27 and five Ka-28 aircraft. Colton, "Chinese Naval Aviation," 8, also notes that the PLAN has acquired four Ka-28 Helix D helos for logistics and search and rescue missions.

40. "Modern-class Destroyer to Patrol Off China," *Wen Wei Po* (Hong Kong), 13 February 2000, p. A-1, in FBIS-CPP20000214000053, and my discussion with U.S. analysts report that as a class, the *Sovremennys* suffer serious problems with their main propulsion plant. Several sources have reported that China will buy more of these ships, including: Morison, "Indian Navy," 4; Saradzhyan, "China to Double Its Order," 17; Ivan Ivanov, "China Seeks to Buy More Warships from Russia," *ITAR-TASS,* 7 March 2000, in FBIS-CEP20000307000247; Novichkov, "China to Purchase Two More Russian 956E Destroyers," *Moscow ITAR-TASS,* 23 December 9, in FBIS-FTS19991223001458; and "Warships' Sale to China," 6; Zhang, "Sino-Russian Arm Sale," adds that Russia will also sell China the Yakhont. Russia has reportedly offered to sell, at very low prices, its four Pacific Fleet ships of this class; buying these ships, built between 1982 and 1987 and infrequently operated during the past decade, would be a very risky proposition, and "Russia to Build Two More Destroyers for China," *Kyodo/ITAR-TASS,* 29 June 2000, in FBIS-JPP20000629000075, reported that Russia had agreed to build two new *Sovremennys* for China. More probable is the report by Yelena Konnova, "Chinese Ceremonies: Russian Destroyer Joins Chinese Army [*sic*]," *Kommersant* (Moscow), 28 November 2000, in FBIS-CEP20001129000060, that "talks" about additional sales are ongoing. The most comprehensive description of Russian naval (and other military) sales to China is in Kan, Bolkcom, and O'Rourke, *China's Foreign Conventional Arms Acquisitions.*

41. Some of the *Ludas* may be undergoing retrofit for the YJ-2 SSM, which has a different engine and increased range of 65 nautical miles.

42. Sharpe, *Jane's Fighting Ships: 2000–2001,* 125, describes this VDS as an active sonar, but a passive capability is almost certainly present, as well.

43. This system projects canisters of "chaff"—strips of metal foil cut to specific lengths—which burst at altitude above and away from the launching ship. These "blooms" serve as alternate targets for incoming missiles and draw them away from the ship. The United States sold SRBOC to China in the late 1980s.

44. Sharpe, *Jane's Fighting Ships: 2000–2001*, 125; author's discussion with McVadon. Interestingly, much of the combat direction center equipment use English-language displays and labels, as I observed during a visit to PLAN ships and a combat systems training facility in Dalian, and as reported in "China Gets to Grips with *Luhu* Technology Gap," 8. Also see Crawley, "Chinese Navy Changing," 1, report that "many [officers and sailors] know some English, which is required to operate the European-built weapons and electronics systems and U.S.-built gas turbines."

45. The LM-2500 is manufactured by General Electric and is widely used in U.S. Navy ships, including *Spruance*-class destroyers, *Perry*-class FFGs, *Arleigh Burke*–class DDGs, and Aegis-equipped cruisers.

46. Si Liang, "Special Article," *Zhongguo Tongxun She*, 15 February 2000, in FBIS-CPP20000215000069; pictures are contained in *Jianchuan Zhishi* [*Naval and Merchant Ships*] 7, no. 238 (1999), and in "*Luhai* Pictures 1999." The Taiwan Navy's *La Fayette*–class corvettes, for instance, are much sleeker in appearance and apparently much stealthier.

47. Sharpe, *Jane's Fighting Ships: 2000–2001*, 126.

48. Author's visit on board *Jiangwei* hull number 539 (hull numbers are occasionally changed), in May 1998. The CDC resembled that of an American missile ship, c. 1968.

49. Sharpe, *Jane's Fighting Ships: 2000–2001*, 131, suggests that this one *Jianghu* was converted to serve as a test ship for several features later installed in the *Luhu* and *Luhai* classes.

50. See McVadon, "Systems Integration," for a discussion of the PLAN's program for installing a CDC in the *Jianghu*s.

51. Sharpe, *Jane's Fighting Ships: 2000–2001*, 134–35.

52. The 100,000 figure is very "soft." Zhang, "China Enhances the Production." Most of these mines, over 90 percent, are old-fashioned "contact" mines, although China's inventory does include mines with various detonation devices, including pressure, magnetic, and acoustic.

53. Cheung, "Reforming the Dragon's Tail," 237; also see Wan Xiaoyun, "Problems and Solutions for War Zone–wide Mobilization Under High-Tech Conditions," *Zhanyi Houwin*, 705–6, cited in Bi, "Managing Taiwan Operations," 12. Also, "Fujian mobilizes Civilian Vessels in Drills," *Fuzhou Fujian Ribao*, 16 July 1999, 2, in FBIS-CHI-99-0802 for a report or an exercise in which "more than 100 civilian vessels" conducted "mobilization and drills." See Hugar, "Sea Dragon Network," for extensive

discussion of the rapidly growing and "capitalistic" Chinese merchant marine, which supports this conclusion.

Furthermore, the past several hundred years of warfare have demonstrated the difficulties of organizing and controlling a nation's merchant fleet: the Napoleonic Wars, the American Civil War, and last century's two world wars all evidenced this. Even U.S. efforts in Vietnam showed how difficult it is to organize a large, disparate merchant marine force to support an overseas wartime effort (John Prados, discussion with author about unpublished manuscript, 1992). Also see "PLA Refits Merchant Ships in Reserve," *Ming Pao,* 2 November 1999, B14, in FBIS-CHI-99-1102, for reports that these ships are also being outfitted to augment the PLAN in warfare missions.

54. Sharpe, *Jane's Fighting Ships: 2000–2001,* 138–39.
55. Su Kuoshan and Su Dianlong, "Fourth Space Survey Vessel Enters Service," *Xinhua,* 18 July 1999, in FBIS-CHI-99-0730, described this ship as "belonging to . . . the State Oceanography Bureau."
56. Sharpe, *Jane's Fighting Ships: 2000–2001,* 138.
57. "Mainland Tests Long-range Missile," *South China Morning Post,* 3 August 1999, reported the successful DF-31 test. The PLAN's lone *Golf*-class ballistic-missile submarine is being modified to serve as a test platform for the JL-2, as it did for the JL-1.
58. Stokes, *China's Strategic Modernization,* provides an excellent synopsis of China's current cruise-missile development programs.
59. Baker, *Naval Institute Guide to Combat Fleets,* 103, estimates 485 fixed-wing aircraft and 28 helicopters; Sharpe, *Jane's Fighting Ships: 2000–2001,* 115, estimates "over 800 aircraft" but notes some of these are "laid up unrepaired." Sidney Trevethan, "PLA Navy Air Force Order of Battle," gives a figure of 1,098 PLAN aircraft as of March 2000.
60. Hooten, "China: Surface to Surface Missiles," issues 15, 21, 22.
61. Sharpe, *Jane's Fighting Ships: 2000–2001,* 117.
62. Senior PLA officer, conversation with author, April 2000.
63. Shen Lijiang, "Aerospace News," *Hangkong Zhishi* [*Aerospace Knowledge*] (Beijing), 9 August 1998, in FBIS-CHI-98-028.
64. Farrer, "China's Air Force," 20–21.
65. Liu Wutian and Sha Zhiliang, "Air Unit of the Navy Succeeds in Air Refueling," *Zhongguo Qingnian Bao,* 29 April 2000, in FBIS-CPP20000501000044, reported the PLANAF's first successful air-to-air refueling evolution on 26 April 2000, at least a year after the PLAAF accomplished this feat.
66. Guo Yuanfa, "The Painstaking Development of an Ace Aircraft," *Liaowang,* 4 October 1999, 32–33, in FBIS-FTS19991209000604, reported that this aircraft had been in development since before 1984; it is only now entering the operating forces.

67. Colton, "Chinese Naval Aviation," provides an excellent description of Chinese naval helicopter production and employment.

68. A good summary of these reports is contained in Hirschfeld, "China's Aircraft Carrier Program," 148, who notes that "the public record on China's carrier plans is wildly inconsistent."

69. Moore, *Jane's Fighting Ships, 1990–1991*, describes these ships. *Kiev* and *Minsk*, commissioned in the 1970s, are members of the *Kiev*-class (forty thousand tons displacement), capable of embarking up to twelve YAK-36 VSTOL aircraft and about twenty Ka-25/27 helicopters; they are not really aircraft carriers, but cruisers with very large flight decks. *Varyag*, commissioned in 1982–83, is a member of the *Kuznetzov* class of 67,500 tons displacement; it has a ski-jump bow (instead of catapults), arresting cables, and can embark up to twenty-two Su-27/ Su-25 fixed-wing aircraft and seventeen Ka-27/31 helicopters. Yelena Konnova and Mikhail Kozyrev, "Beijing's Aircraft Carrier Collection," Moscow *Nezavisimaya Gazeta*, 12 May 2000, in FBIS-CEP20000516000183, reported that "not all armaments and control systems had been dismantled" on the ship.

70. Initial reports that *Varyag* would be refitted for PLAN operation—"Beijing Purchases Aircraft Carrier from Ukraine Through Macao Company and Then Puts It on Active Service After Re-Equipping It," *Kuo Jih Pao*, 17 April 1998, p. A-20, in FBIS-CHI-98-107, are not supported by the ship's poor material condition, as reported in the Chinese press: see "PRC Converts Old Aircraft Carrier into Military Theme Park," *Xinhua*, 8 May 2000, in FBIS-CPP20000508000073, for the report that the carrier "was poorly maintained by the Russian navy." Furthermore, *AFP* reported on 4 November 1999 that *Minsk* had suffered a fire that burned for fourteen hours (FBIS-FTS19991104000496). Pictures and eyewitness accounts of these ships indicate that they did not receive the careful preservation treatment required during long-term inactivation to enable a ship to be returned to duty.

71. Chanda, "China," 15, is one of several reports that the PLAN built a simulated aircraft carrier operating facility in northeastern China, where "Chinese pilots have since 1984 been practicing simulated carrier-deck landings using arresting wires." Chanda also cites a report that "in 1987, an F8 aircraft was shot off a catapult at the Lushun Naval Base."

72. Huang Tung, "Latest Development of Chinese Navy," *Kuang Chiao Ching* (Hong Kong), 16 May 1997, in FBIS-CHI-97-113, argues that "the Chinese Navy is now attaching growing importance to developing an aircraft carrier with each passing day." The article also notes that *De Gaulle* is nuclear-powered, without advocating that feature for a Chinese carrier. Also see *Sankei Shimbun* report of China's "construction of its own flattop . . . in 2010," cited in *AFP*, 8 April 1997, in FBIS-EAS-97-098. "China Commits to Carrier Construction with Daunting Aircraft,"

1999, 1, reports that Beijing has ordered three sixty-thousand-ton carriers built at Shanghai's Jiangnan Shipbuilding Company. (Coincidentally, Jiangnan built Yangtze River gunboats for the United States in the 1920s; see Cole, "Real Sand Pebbles," 16–23.) A forty-to-fifty-thousand-ton ship is estimated to cost from $600 million ("China Plans to Build Its First Conventionally Powered Aircraft Carrier at End of Year," *Guangzhou Ribao*, 13 January 2000, in FBIS-FTS20000113000410; Taiwan Navy analyst) to $800 million (*Navy News and Undersea Technology*, 23 August 1999).

73. Hirschfeld, "China's Aircraft Carrier Program," 150.

74. Senior PLAN officers and U.S. analysts, conversations with author; also see "Report on PRC Plan to Build Aircraft Carrier Dismissed," *Ta Kung Pao*, 15 January 2000, in FBIS-FTS20000117000045.

75. *Chakri Naruebet* is a twelve-thousand-ton ship with a ski-jump bow that usually embarks six "Harrier" short-takeoff-vertical-landing (STOVL) jets and six large helicopters. This ship cost $400–500 million, is a proven class (similar to Spain's *Principe de Asturias*), and would seem to represent a very suitable "first carrier" for the PLAN.

76. Lam, "PLA Weapons"; Si Yanwen and Chen Wanjun, "Navy to Develop More High-Tech Equipment," *Jiefangjun Bao*, 10 June 1999, in FBIS-CHI-1999-0611. Similar statements were attributed to Jiang Zemin in Pamela Pun, "PLA Told to Speed Weapons Research," *Hong Kong Standard*, 6 November 1999.

77. Sharpe, *Jane's Fighting Ships: 2000–2001*, 126.

78. Ibid., 123, has a good picture of *Qingdao*'s VDS unit.

79. McVadon, "Systems Integration," 225.

80. See ibid., 217–44, for a thorough discussion of this issue.

81. Author's visits to *Jiangwei*- and *Luhu*-class ships in 1998 and 2000.

82. Quoted in McVadon, "Systems Integration," 227.

83. Ibid., 234. Also see, "Unswervingly Take the Road of Strengthening Armaments with Science and Technology," *Jiefangjun Bao*, 3 July 1999, 1, in FBIS-CHI-99-0712, which admitted that "supply and maintenance can directly affect the generation and development of battle readiness," especially for high-technology weapons systems.

84. Chen Wanjun and Zhang Chunting, "Shouldering the Important Task of a Century-Straddling Voyage—Interviewing Newly Appointed Navy Commander Lieutenant-General Shi Yunsheng," *Liaowang* 8 (Beijing), 24 February 1997, 2, in FBIS-CHI-97.

Chapter 6. Personnel, Education, and Training

1. Quoted in "Opening Up New Prospects for Ideological, Political Building of China's Military Academies," *Jiefangjun Bao*, 23 May 2000, in FBIS-CPP20000523000043.

2. Women were observed apparently fully integrated into Marine units at Zhangjiang by Ronald Montaperto. Li Chang, "First Female Marine Corps of Chinese Navy," *Military Window* 2 (reprinted in *Ta Kung Pao*, 15 June 1998, p. E-1, in FBIS-CHI-98-19), reports an all-female Marine unit, using strangely zoological prose: the women Marines were described "as agile as monkeys . . . light as birds . . . bold and forceful as race horses . . . crafty as foxes . . . clever as rabbits . . . and fierce as tigers."

3. Of all the topics addressed in this work, manning and personnel may well be the least transparent. To an extent conclusions are drawn from incomplete data and some projection of generic naval manning concerns. Significant works that shed light on PLA personnel issues include Bullard, *China's Political-Military Evolution;* Caldwell, *China's Conventional Military Capability;* Cheng, *Party-Military Relations;* Jencks, *From Muskets to Missiles;* Joffe, *Chinese Army After Mao;* Mulvenon, *Professionalization;* and Swaine, *Military and Political Succession.*

4. Quoted in "Opening Up New Prospects," see note 1, above.

5. This assumes the following naval strengths, discussed by McDevitt, "PLA Navy," 8: U.S. Pacific Fleet, 132,000; India, 53,000; Japan, 44,000; Taiwan, 38,000; Australia, 14,000. McDevitt does not include the ROKN, which numbers 54,000 personnel.

6. Shichor, "Demobilization," 336–59, discusses PLA demobilization since 1950.

7. Senior PLA officers, conversations with author.

8. These numbers do not include patrol craft, minesweepers, and the smaller amphibious and logistical craft. China also deploys militia-type forces; Chang Hsiao-ming, "Mainland China to Set Up 200,000-Strong Maritime Cruise Unit to Defend 3 Million Square Km of Marine Territory," *Ping Kuo Jih Pao*, 6 December 1996, p. A-20, in FBIS-CHI-99-1028, probably referred to a retrenchment of the already existent maritime adjunct forces, rather than to a new organization.

9. Data from Sharpe, *Jane's Fighting Ships: 2000–2001.*

10. Three PLA divisions in the Nanjing MR are also trained in amphibious warfare.

11. "Regulations on Military Service of Active-Duty Soldiers of the Chinese PLA," chap. 1, art. 7, *Xinhua*, 11 July 1999, in FBIS-CHI-99-0728.

12. *Xinhua*, 1 October 1999, FBIS-CHI-99-0930; PLA officers and U.S. analysts, conversation with author.

13. "Troop Reduction by a Huge Million," *Zhongguo Xinwen She*, 14 September 1999, in FBIS-CHI-99-1017, discussed "nine rounds of fairly large-scaled simplification and reorganization" since the PRC was founded, with the ninth announced in September 1997, when Jiang Zemin "proposed" a 500,000-man reduction over the next three years.

14. The U.S. Navy trains an individual *both* to maintain *and* operate a system. Most other navies, however, train individuals *either* to maintain *or*

operate its equipment. In the Russian navy, for instance, extensive use is made of warrant and junior commissioned officers to maintain a piece of equipment, while other personnel are trained specifically to operate the gear. The PLAN follows the Russian model, according to PLAN officers, conversations with author.

15. Senior PLA officers and PLAN ship commanders, conversations with author, 1994–2000.

16. Tang Liehui, "Work Hard to Explore Optimal Solution to Man-Weapon Integration," *Jiefangjun Bao*, 15 June 1999, 6, in FBIS-CHI-99-0711.

17. Jia Xiaowei, "Pay Close Attention to Network Warfare Which Has Quietly Arrived," *Jiefangjun Bao*, 24 August 1999, 6, in FBIS-CHI-99-0925.

18. Quoted in Fu Quanyou, "Vigorously Conduct Military Training of Science and Technology to Strengthen Great Wall of Steel," *Qiushi* (Beijing), 1 August 1999, 12–17, in FBIS-CHI-99-0902, 4.

19. "China Reports High Employment for College Graduates," *Xinhua*, 13 April 2000, in FBIS-CPP20000413000172, states that "university graduates are in great demand" and that "postgraduates and students from well-known universities are being actively pursued by employers" according to the Ministry of Education in Beijing.

20. "Army Seeks Mobility in Force Cuts," 23.

21. "State Council, CMC Issue Winter Conscription Notice," *Xinhua*, 9 October 2000, in FBIS-CPP20001009000042. A campaign to "prevent illegal activities" in recruitment is discussed in "China's Annual Conscription Begins," *Xinhua*, 1 November 2000, in FBIS-CPP20001101000088.

22. Senior PLA officer, interview with author.

23. Su Ruozhou, "Major Reform in Our Army's Service System," *Jiefangjun Bao*, 13 July 1999, 2, in FBIS-CHI-99-0811, discusses the two-year requirement. I discussed longer PLAN enlistments with senior PLA officers. The length of various technical training schools vary, but a recruit may, after completing three months of "boot camp," spend an additional three to six months in school. By comparison, a technician in the U.S. Navy may spend as long as twenty-four months in schools before reporting to his/her first ship—after agreeing to extend his/her enlistment from four to six years. Also see Blasko, "New PLA Force Structure," 24.

24. Senior PLA officers, conversations with author.

25. I first discussed with PLA officers implementing an ROTC-like program in China in 1993; discussions since then between U.S. and PRC National Defense University (NDU) faculty—which typically occur at least twice a year—have frequently included ROTC as a discussion topic. The modern American Naval ROTC program (the Holloway Plan) was initiated in 1946 with the goal of organizing units at prominent U.S. universities to produce officers educated in technical and engineering curricula.

26. Senior PLA officer, interview with author. See Xhang Jiajun and Zhang Xuanjie, *Xinhua*, 28 May 1999, in FBIS-CHI-99-0601, for the report that

the "Second Artillery Corps signed an agreement with the Northwest Engineering University in Xian today to cultivate cadres for guided missile troops" and will "supply a certain number of outstanding university and graduate students for the Second Artillery Corps every year," with the Corps establishing a "national defense scholarship" at the school to "encourage and fund" likely students. A similar report is found in Liu Jianxin, "Wuhan University, Military Agree on Training Officers," *Xinhua,* 28 October 1999, in FBIS-CHI-99-1103: the "Guangzhou Military Region and Wuhan University have signed an agreement on jointly training mil-itary cadres. . . . This military region will . . . expand the selection of outstanding personnel from institutions of higher learning across the country. . . . All major military regions and armed services have separately designated one local university to be the designated school for training their own cadres."

27. Liu, "Wuhan University," reports that the Guangzhou MR has a five-year goal of gaining 40 percent of its new personnel annually from up to "76 institutions of higher learning in 17 provinces and municipalities." PLA National Defense University delegations made extensive inquiries about the U.S. ROTC system, during late 1990s visits to the United States. Henley, "Officer Education," 66, discusses a previous program that established links between the PLA and civilian universities.

28. Chen Wanjun and Li Chaogui, "Navy Makes Advances in Equipment Modernization," *Xinhua,* 13 May 1998, in FBIS-CHI-98-137.

29. "Navy to Recruit Officers from Non-Military Colleges," *Xinhua,* 17 August 1999, in FBIS-CHI-99-0817: Also see *Xinhua* (Hong Kong), 21 June 1999, in FBIS-CHI-99-0622, for the note that these civilian university programs will be linked to the military academy structure. This linkage is no doubt intended to maintain control of the ideological as well as the subject-matter content of the "civilian" program—the latter long a concern within the U.S. Naval ROTC program. Wang Dianbin, "Open Up New [Personnel Sources]," *Jiefangjun Bao,* 9 May 1999, 2, in FBIS-CHI-99-0523, discusses the U.S. ROTC system and similar systems in Great Britain and Russia.

30. "PRC Military Promotes Young Officers to Senior Posts," *Xinhua,* 25 April 2000, in FBIS-CPP20000425000154, reports that the Guangzhou MR has promoted younger officers than ever before, in part because of their educational level, both university and graduate-school graduates.

31. See, for instance, "Joining the Army with Knowledge and Achieving Merit in the Military," *Jiefangjun Bao,* 2 July 2000, 1, in FBIS-CPP20000703000077, which states that "the college-graduate cadres today will be the most crucial people for constructing our military's modernization tomorrow."

32. "Navy to Recruit Officers from Non-Military Colleges," *Xinhua,* 17 August 1999, in FBIS-CHI-99-0817.

33. Gen. Fu Quanyou, quoted in "Fu Quanyou Stresses Need to Do Good Job in Selecting, Managing, and Building Officers' Contingent," *Xinhua*, 4 September 1999, in FBIS-CHI-1999-1022.

34. Hu Wanzhang and Li Yuliang, "Military Academies to Recruit 5,000 Students from the Local Sectors This Year," *Renmin Ribao*, 5 May 1988, 3, in FBIS-CHI-88-090.

35. Officers at the PLAN First Surface Vessel Academy (in Dalian), the Dalian (PLA) Military Academy, and the Xi'an Air Force Engineering College, conversations with author, September 1998; senior PLAN officer, conversation with author, May 2000. My interviews with senior PLA officers indicate that candidates indicate their college preferences when they take the examination, but this is of secondary importance in the selection process. Besides military academies, other "special schools" include certain arts and literature institutions, as well as the Beijing Opera school. "Almost 800 Graduates of Chinese Civilian Universities Join Army," *Xinhua*, 6 November 2000, in FBIS-CPP20001106000124, reports the direct entry since 1991 of forty thousand "non-cadets," presumably personnel with particular skills.

36. My conversations with senior PLA officers; one PLA officer, a senior captain with more than thirty years service, said he had never met an enlisted man with more than eighteen years in the navy.

37. PLAN officers, conversations with author, afloat and ashore, 1994–2000.

38. Blasko, "New PLA Force Structure," 13. Adding U.S. DOD civilians would increase the size of the American "military" by a half.

39. "Regulations on Military Service of Active-Duty Soldiers of the PLA," chap. 1, art. 14.

40. Su, "Major Reform," 4.

41. Yang, "From a Navy in Blue," 4. *People's Navy*, 35–40, dates the establishment of the following navy schools: 1949 (Andong Naval School, East China MR Naval School in Nanjing, PLAN Academy in Dalian), 1952 (Support Services School and Political Cadre School in Qingdao), 1953 (Submarine School in Qingdao), 1954 (Naval Command School and the Naval School of Mechanics, both in Dalian), 1957 (Communications School and the Navy Advanced School, both in Qingdao; the Naval Academy in Nanjing).

42. Quoted in Mulvenon, *Professionalization*, 11. One could argue that this recent consolidation will facilitate CCP control of PLA education, but the motivation for the reorganization is far more likely due to the need to streamline the educational process to take advantage of educational technology and to standardize technical training.

43. "Unify Our Ideas and Actions with Central Commission's Policy Decisions," *Jiefangjun Bao*, 21 June 1999, 1, in FBIS-CHI-99-0628. This is the latest in a series of "overhauls" of the military education system. See Henley, "Officer Education," 56.

44. Quoted in "Put Military Academy Education in a Strategic Position of Priority Development," *Jiefangjun Bao*, 23 June 1999, 1, in FBIS-CHI-99-0629.
45. Fu, "Fu Quanyou Stresses Need to Do Good Job," 6.
46. "Basic Military Project for Development in the New Century," editorial, *Jiefangjun Bao*, 15 April 2000, 1, in FBIS-CPP20000417000056.
47. Cited in Luo Yuwen, "Zhang Wannian Stresses Efforts to Train High-quality New-style Military Talent," *Xinhua*, 19 April 2000, in FBIS-CPP20000419000099. A 23 August 2000 editorial in *Jiefangjun Bao*, "Reaching Common Understanding," in FBIS-CPP20000823000051, reemphasized the responsibility of academies to stress "winning wars" and "Eradicating corruption," while adhering "to the absolute leadership of the Party." Students were to be taught first to be "qualified in the political sense, and second in . . . professional skills."
48. Huang Huamin and Luo Yuwen, "Jiang Stresses Technology, Loyal Personnel in PLA," *Jiefangjun Bao*, 27 June 1999, in FBIS-CHI-99-0627. Senior defense officials Li Lanqing, Zhang Wannian, Chi Haotian, Fu Quanyou, Yu Yongbo, Wang Ke, Wang Ruilin, and Cao Gangchuan also attended this meeting.
49. Quoted in "Strengthen Education in Revolutionary Integrity," *Jiefangjun Bao*, 5 July 1999, 1, in FBIS-CHI-99-0712.
50. Shen Yaojin and Wang Huamin, "Central Military Commission issues Program for Education Reform and Development of Military Academies," *Jiefangjun Bao*, 15 April 2000, 1, in FBIS-CPP20000417000061.
51. Quoted in Mulvenon, *Professionalization*, 12.
52. Quoted in "An Important Measure for Strengthening the Training of High- and Medium-Ranking Cadres," *Jiefangjun Bao*, 21 June 1999, 1, in FBIS-CHI-99-0629.
53. See, for instance, *Xinhua* (Hong Kong), 21 June 1999, in FBIS-CHI-99-0622, for a *Jiefangjun Bao* report that the number of academies are being reduced in the interest of making individual schools larger and more efficient. "China Sets Up Defense Campus," *Straits Times*, 20 June 1999, reported that the PLA "has set up a new National Defense Science and Technology University" in Changsha, and "directly under the command of the CMC" will offer a wide range of courses at the general staff college (0-5/0-6) level.
54. "Put Military Academy Education in a Strategic Position of Priority Development," *Jiefangjun Bao*, 23 June 1999, in FBIS-CHI-99-0629. During the past year, there have been numerous reports of military academy reform; for another "ROTC" plan, see Zhang Jiajun and Zhang Xuanjie's article in *Xinhua*, 28 May 1999, in FBIS-CHI-99-0601: "The Second Artillery Corps signed an agreement with the Northwest Engineering University in Xian today to . . . supply a certain number of outstanding

university and graduate students for the Second Artillery Corps every year. The Second Artillery Corps will establish a national defense scholarship . . . to encourage and fund outstanding students."

55. "PRC Navy Official on Upgrading Equipment, Weapons," *Xinhua*, 22 April 1999, in FBIS-CHI-99-0422.
56. Commandant of the Guangzhou Naval Academy, discussion with author, May 1994, and commandants of the Dalian Naval Academy, discussions with author, April 1996 and May 1997.

   Yang, "From a Navy in Blue," gives 1991 as the founding of this academy, but that probably refers to a change in mission for the school, from one of training new cadets to one of conducting more advanced training for new officers who have already graduated from an academy.
57. Senior PLA officers, conversations with author, including 1994 and 1998 discussions at the PLA Command and Staff College in Nanjing.
58. "PRC's Navy Sets Up 'Practice Base' for Postgraduates," *Xinhua*, 13 December 1999, in FBIS-FTS19991212000948; senior PLA officers, conversations with author, 1998–99.
59. Senior PLA NDU personnel, conversations with author.
60. "PLA Officers Said 'Younger, Better Educated,'" *Xinhua*, 25 July 1997, in FBIS-CHI-97-206, reports that the average age of officers at the MR level has dropped to 57.3 from 59.3 in the last two years and that 78.4 percent of such officers are now college graduates, in contrast to 49.2 percent in 1992. Similar statistics for "combat commanders" are 51.4 years old and 90.2 percent college graduates.
61. Huang Caihong, Chen Wanjun, and Zhang Zhao, "The PLA Navy Has Enhanced Comprehensive Combat Effectiveness," *Xinhua*, 19 April 1999, in FBIS-CHI-99-0423.
62. Chen Wanjun, "Navy Improves Combat Capability," *Xinhua*, 26 July 1999, in FBIS-CHI-99-0729, discusses commanding officer "comprehensive examinations."
63. Kondapalli, "China's Naval Training Program," 1338, lists these as "microelectronics, PERT [Program Evaluation and Review Technique], CPM [Critical Path Method], navigation, dynamics, telemetering and remote control, and aviation and astro-navigation."
64. Chen Yeong-kang, Paper on the PLAN submarine force presented at the April 2000 CNA Conference on the PLAN.
65. Li and Liu 17 June 1999. The others are the National University of Defense Technology at Changsha, the Science and Engineering University in Nanjing, the Information Engineering University in Zhangzhou, and the Air Force Engineering University in Xi'an.
66. "Shao Zijun Says the Navy Engineering College is Aimed at Developing New Naval Military Talent," *Xinhua*, 7 August 1999, in FBIS-CHI-99-0826.

67. "PRC's Yu Yongbo Reviews Military Propaganda Network," *Xinhua*, 26 December 1999, in FBIS-FTS20000120000818; "PLA Information Network Begins Operations," *Xinhua*, 28 December 1999, in FBIS-FTS19991228000766.

68. Senior PLA officers, conversation with author; also Xu Sen, "Building a Modern Naval Battlefield—Overview of the Naval Vessel Training Center," *Jiefangjun Bao*, 15 September 1999, 6, in FBIS-CHI-99-0923.

69. Kondapalli, "China's Naval Training Program," 1334.

70. These numbers require more research, but they *are* based on my conversations with senior PLA and Taiwan Navy officers and with PLAN commanding officers aboard their ships (five instances, from 1989 to 2000), with the 24th Air Division chief of staff in 1997, the 9th Air Division commander in 2000, and from Allen, Krumel, and Pollock, *China's Air Force Enters the 21st Century*. One PLAN source told me that a submarine commander may serve in his billet for six years, but operate underway for only about three hundred days during that period.

71. Visits by author and other U.S. observers, 1990–2000, to PLAN training facilities in Dalian, Qingdao, Shanghai, and Guangzhou, and to PLA training facilities in Beijing (NDU, Armored Engineering College, and the Air Force Command College), Dalian (Shenyang MR Military Academy), Xi'an (PLAAF Engineering College), and Nanjing (PLA Staff and Command College) showed computerized training facilities that seemed analogous to U.S. Navy facilities sometime in the late 1960s.

72. Luo Jie and Wang Guangxin, "Vessel Formation Training Moves from Inshore Areas to Coastal Waters," *Jiefangjun Bao*, 13 April 2000, in FBIS-CPP20000413000069.

73. Tang, "Work Hard to Explore Optimal Solution," 2.

74. Ibid., 4.

75. Admiral Zhang Lianzhong, quoted on "Navy Chief on Technical, Tactical Upgrading," Beijing Domestic Service, 5 May 1988, in FBIS-CHI-88-090.

76. Quoted in Mao Xiaochun and Chen Hui, "Chief of Staff Fu Quanyou on High-Tech Military Training," *Xinhua*, 16 October 1999, in FBIS-CHI-99-1016.

77. Baker, *Naval Institute Guide to Combat Fleets*, 129; the older officer-training ship, *Zheng He*, is pictured on p. 130. It looks like a small passenger liner, but as inspected by the author in 1989, *Zheng He* is equipped with classrooms and various navigation, electronics, and gunnery systems for instructional purposes. Liu Yonglu and Cao Jinping, "The Vessel 'Shichang' Officially Enters Active Service," *Jiefangjun Bao*, 28 January 1997, 1, in FBIS-CHI-97-086. Chen Wanjun and Chen Guofang, "Birth of China's First Defense Mobilization Vessel," *Jianchuan Zhishi* [*Naval and Merchant Ships*] 2, 6 February 1997, 2, in FBIS-CHI-97-089, describes *Shichang* in detail, stating that it was originally con-

structed as a civilian roll-on/roll-off cargo vessel before conversion by the Qiuxin Shipyard in Shanghai, and that the ship is assigned to the Dalian Naval Vessels Institute. The November 2000 exercise is described in Yu Xiaomei, "To Defend the Republic's Territorial Waters, the Navy Conducts the First Comprehensive National Defense Mobilization Exercise at Sea," *Jiefangjun Bao,* 8 November 2000, in FBIS-CPP20001108000040. If *Shichang* did operate with both the East and North Sea Fleets, it would indicate that it is an asset controlled by PLAN headquarters.

78. Tao Ke and Cha Chunming, "Naval Reservists Complete Long Training Cruise," *Xinhua,* 31 July 1999, in FBIS-CHI-99-0801, reported that 250 enlisted and officer naval reservists embarked for a "national defense mobilization training" cruise; "China uses Commercial Ships to Carry Troops in Exercise" 31 July 2000.

79. Xu Sen, "Building a Modern Naval Battlefield," *Jiefangjun Bao,* 15 September 1999, 6, in FBIS-CHI-99-0923, describes the North Sea Fleet training center and compares it to similar centers built by the United States, France, Great Britain, and others. Crews are trained in navigation and ship handling, weapons systems, and electronic warfare.

80. Senior PLA officers, conversations with author.

81. Ren Yanjun, "Entire Army Bears in Mind Sacred Mission, Makes Ample Preparations for Military Struggle," *Jiefangjun Bao,* 12 April 2000, 1, in FBIS-CPP20000412000032, describes "the army as a whole . . . successively [sending] tens of divisions and brigades into training bases to conduct exercises under simulated and virtual battleground environments with real personnel, real vehicles, real bullets and real explosives to train for actual combat capabilities."

82. This paragraph draws heavily on Blasko, Klapakis, and Corbett, "Training Tomorrow's PLA," 490–91. "Increasing Capacity of 'Winning Wars' Is Fundamental," *Jiefangjun Bao,* 30 January 1999, 1, in FBIS-FTS19990205000303, argues that "to firmly grasp the direction of military training that relies on science and technology, we must . . . standardize it." Kondapalli, "China's Naval Training Program," 1344–48, provides a useful list of PLAN exercises from 1957.

83. Maj. Gen. Chen Youyan, quoted in You, "Revolution in Military Affairs," 350.

84. See, for instance, three *Jiefangjun Bao* articles: Zhang Guoyu and Wang Boming, "Carry Out Scientific and Technological Training and Create Brilliant Historic Achievements," 19 January 1999, 6, in FBIS-FTS19990208000125; Li Jianyin, "On Welcoming the Cross-Century Military Training Revolution," 26 January 1999, 6, in FBIS-FTS19990209000171; and Gao Jianguo, "Change the Pattern of Personnel Training," 26 January 1999, 6, in FBIS-FTS19990208000103.

85. Zhang Guoyu and Wang Boming, "Carry Out Scientific and Technological Training and Create Brilliant Historic Achievements" [one of a series], *Jiefangjun Bao*, 28 January 1999, 6, in FBIS-FTS19990205000009, 4, also observed that "simulation training has become a training form most close to 'actual combat.'"

86. Zhang Zhenzhong and Chang Jianguo, "Train Talented People at Different Levels for Information Warfare," *Jiefangjun Bao*, 2 February 1999, 6, in FBIS-FTS19990210001865; Pillsbury 1997, contains an extensive selection of PLA writings on the RMA and information warfare.

87. Zheng Shuyan and Gao Aisu, "Group Army Trains Hard to Learn Multidimensional Maneuver Combat Skills," *Jiefangjun Bao*, 20 June 1997, 1, in FBIS-CHI-97-199.

88. See, for instance, Chen Yuanming and Yan Jinjiu, "Chinese Navy Successfully Conducts First Wharf-Free Fuel Supply Operation under Combat Conditions," *Jiefangjun Bao*, 26 May 1997, 1, in FBIS-CHI-97-121; Zhang Peng and Wang Peihong, "PLA Navy Builds Modern Diving Facility in Qingdao," *Xinhua*, 12 May 1998, in FBIS-CHI-98-135.

89. Si Liang, "Chinese Navy Holds Exercises Again and Again Recently and Stands in Combat Readiness," *Zhongguo Tongxun She*, 5 August 1999, in FBIS-CHI-99-0805.

90. Ibid., 499–515. Some of these exercises involved both combined arms and amphibious training.

91. Shen Hairong and Chen Tangsheng, "Certain Group Army of Nanjing Military Region Makes Fresh Breakthrough in Its Capability of Fighting and Winning Battles at Sea," *Jiefangjun Bao*, 8 August 2000, in FBIS-CPP20000808000036, state that "the group army has built a simulated landing training site for each of its infantry regiments."

92. Blasko, Klapakis, and Corbett, "Training Tomorrow's PLA," 522.

93. See "Air Force Chief Says PRC Capable of Defending Airspace," *Xinhua*, 21 February 2000, in FBIS-CPP20000221000158, for PLAAF commander Lt. Gen. Liu Shunyao's claim that the air force is determined to "defend the country's territorial sovereignty in regard to land, airspace and sea and its maritime rights."

94. McVadon, "PRC Exercises," 250. Also see Garver, *Face Off*, 117.

95. I am indebted to Yoest for this information. Not connected with the annual sea and air rescue exercises (SAREX) is a 1987 sea and air rescue (SAR) agreement between China's Bureau of Harbor Superintendency (now called the Maritime Safety Administration) and the U.S. Coast Guard. Vietnam's Coast Guard operates as an agency of the Ministry of Defense, while those of China and the United States operate under nominally civilian ministries—the Ministry of Communications in the former case; the Department of Transportation in the latter. The December 2000 exercise is reported in "PLA, U.S. Military Join Hands in Rescue Exercise," *Xinhua*, 6 December 2000, Internet: www.insidechina.com/news.

96. "PRC, Macao, Hong Kong Hold Joint Marine Rescue Exercise Near Shenzhen," *Xinhua,* 5 June 2000, in FBIS-CPP20000605000152, reports that a five-hour exercise, involving "more than forty vessels and two helicopters," was "organized by the Ministry of Communications and China Marine Salvage Center." The center is a semiprivate organization that provides SAR services in China's coastal waters.

97. Tseng Shu-wan, "PLA's Field Forces Frequently go to Fujian to Take Part in Rotational Training Under Conditions More Similar to Actual Combat," *Wen Wei Po,* 8 April 2000, in FBIS-CPP20000408000014. Also see "East China Sea Fleet Recently Conducted Cross-Region Exercise," *Sing Tao Jih Pao,* 12 May 2000, in FBIS-CPP20000512000038. "Zhanjiang Military Sub District, Guangdong Military District, Conducts a Military-Civilian Exercise," Internet: www.taungpao.com.hk, 2 June 2000, in *Force Protection Report,* Camp Zama, Japan, U.S. Army Asian Studies Detachment of the 500th MI Group Report ASD-00-0100, 2.

98. "Chinese Navy Improves Anti-Submarine Tactics," *Xinhua* (Hong Kong), 2 July 1999, in FBIS-CHI-99-0805.

99. Jiang is quoted, and this exercise is described, in "On Anti-Submarine Air Operations Exercise," *Jianchuan Zhishi* (Beijing), 4 June 1999, 13–14, in FBIS-CHI-99-0702. Also see Fu Quanyou in "Fu Quanyou Stresses Need to Do Good Job," for citations of Jiang's "strategic thinking of 'strengthening the Army through science and technology'" as applicable to the PLAN.

100. "PLA Navy Completes Highly Difficult Drills," *Jiefangjun Bao* article, 10 January 2000, cited in *Zhongguo Tongxun She,* 10 January 2000, in FBIS-FTS20000112001752.

101. *People's Navy,* 41, reports an ideological extreme in a 1958 report that the East China Sea Fleet commander "respond[ed] to a call by the CPC Central Committee and the CMC to undergo training as a sailor on Ship 311 [and] wears a sailor uniform with a private's insignia." Bullard, *China's Political-Military Evolution,* 27, estimates that at the height of the Cultural Revolution, 70 percent of a soldier's time was devoted to nonmilitary activities; by 1984, 70 percent was devoted to military duties. See Heaton, "Professional Military Education," 125, for a description of the ideological character of the PLA as either "Maoist" or "Dengist:" Mao stressed the importance of men over machines and held up the PLA as the socialist model that embodied his thought. Deng's concept was described in 1979 by Defense Minister Xu Xiangqian as stressing the importance of expertise and "expert" taking precedence over "red."

102. See Joffe, "Military and China's New Politics," for discussion reinforcing this conclusion.

103. Shambaugh, "Commentary on Civil-Military Relations in China," discusses this question of the PLA-state-party relationship.

5. Ren Xiangdong, "PLA Ground, Naval, and Air Units Implement New-Generation Combat Regulations," *Liaowang*, 7 June 1999, 32–33, in FBIS-CHI-99-0629, 12, contains the statements quoted in this section.

6. Most notable are the *Kilo*-class submarines and *Sovremenny*-class destroyers armed with the potent Moskit cruise missiles, but also important is the non-equipment assistance, including the services of Russian engineers, that has been acquired by the Chinese.

7. Shi Yunsheng, cited in Huang, Chen, and Zhang 1999, 13–15. Also see Zhang Wei, *Jianchuan Zhishi*, January 1997, 8–9, in FBIS-CST-97-006.

8. Finkelstein, "China's New Security Concept," 3, makes this point; U.S. Navy Staff, *Undersea Warfare*, 13, notes that two salvos of two missiles each were launched simultaneously in this latest test; Holzer, "Study," 3, 36, discusses the post-Aegis program.

9. It appears that the defense budget allocation process is no friendlier to the "Gators" of the PLAN than it is in any other country's navy. Troop-carrying ships, no matter how vital to the power projection mission, simply have neither the glamour nor the profit margin of nuclear-powered submarines or guided-missile destroyers. Hence, the PLAN is only slowly strengthening its amphibious warfare capability.

10. Wan Xiaoyun, "Problems and Solutions for War Zone–wide Mobilization Under High-Tech Conditions," *Zhanyi Houwin*, 705–6, cited in Bi, "Managing Taiwan Operations," 12. Also, "Fujian mobilizes Civilian Vessels in Drills," *Fuzhou Fujian Ribao*, 16 July 1999, 2, in FBIS-CHI-99-0802 for a report or an exercise in which "more than 100 civilian vessels" conducted "mobilization and drills."

11. Bi, "Managing Taiwan Operations," 45–46.

12. Quoted in Ahrari, "China's Naval Forces," 34. UNCLOS 1982, describes the rights of innocent passage. Valencia and Van Dyke, "Vietnam's National Interests," 233, elaborate on China's interpretation of this article, which is shared by thirty-eight other nations, including the Scandinavian countries.

13. Logistics facilities have been built on some of the Spratlys. Sharpe, *Jane's Fighting Ships: 2000–2001*, 138ff., reports that the PLAN currently has three modern "unrep" ships, one in each geographic fleet, plus a dozen or more smaller cargo (dry or liquid carriers) in the South Sea Fleet that are not capable of underway replenishment.

14. *Jiefangjun Bao*, 24 October 1996, 1, in FBIS-CHI-96-210, reported that this exercise included joint operations among "the three armed services and the issues of coordination and supplies," and "involved sea-crossing, changing ships, and ship formations," with the troops fighting "an integrated war and [attacking] the enemy from the three dimensions." Also see Zhang Zenan's interview with Sr. Capt. Lin Shuangqiao, "Developing and Expanding Chinese Landing Ship Forces," *Jianchuan*

Zhishi [*Naval and Merchant Ships*], 6 January 1997, 10–11, in FBIS-CHI-97-051: Lin is identified as the "army's chief of staff for naval operation" and an amphibious warfare expert. He describes the "vertical assault" aspect of amphibious landings and claims that the PLA demonstrated this capability in October 1995 and March 1996 exercises near Taiwan.

15. Chen Wanjun and Zhang Chunting, "Shouldering the Important Task of a Century-Straddling Voyage—Interviewing Newly Appointed Navy Commander Lieutenant-General Shi Yunsheng," *Liaowang* 8 (Beijing), 24 February 1997, 2, in FBIS-CHI-97.

16. Wang Zudian (identified as a Space Technology Information Research Institute researcher), "The Offensive and Defensive of High-Technology Arms Equipment," in *Liaowang Weekly*, 21st ed., quoted in *Xinhua* (Hong Kong), 24 May 1999, in FBIS-CHI-99-0526.

17. Maj. Gen. Chen Mingduan, "On Several Principles Which Should Be Followed in Maritime Militia Guerrilla Warfare," *Beijing Guofang* 11 (15 November 1997), in FBIS-CHI-98-126.

18. Lennox, *Jane's Strategic Weapon Systems*, issue 22.

19. *Worldwide Submarine Challenges, 1996*, 27. Predicting the year in which the next PLAN FBM will actually go to sea on deterrent patrol is a risky proposition, given China's poor track record in this area. Furthermore, other U.S. analysts believe China is emphasizing the Type-093 SSN, with few resources being devoted to Type-094 development as of mid-2000.

20. Coordinated sea and shore-based air operations were theorized by the Royal Navy immediately following World War I, employed inefficiently by the United States during the Korean and Vietnam conflicts, but more effectively during the Persian Gulf war and the Kosovo campaign.

21. Two PLA lieutenant generals, conversations with author, May 1996; senior PLAN officers, conversations with author. An aircraft carrier routinely can fly just twelve hours a day, primarily because it carries just one crew of flight deck personnel, who must rest after twelve hours of operations. Two carriers on-station means that flight operations can be conducted twenty-four hours a day. Thailand's accession of a carrier must also be galling to PLAN carrier advocates, but see "Jet Deal Should not Just Fly Through," *Bangkok Post*, 2 July 1999, in FBIS-EAS-99-0702, for the report that due to its reduced budget resulting from Thailand's economic malaise, the navy has been unable to maintain *Chakri Naruebet*'s aircraft and cannot afford the fuel to send it to sea.

22. PLAAF Air Division commander, conversation with author, May 2000; Liu and Sha, "Air Unit of the Navy Succeeds in Air Refueling," *Zhongguo Qingnian Bao*, 29 April 2000, in FBIS-CPP20000501000044, reported the PLANAF's first successful air-to-air refueling evolution on 26 April 2000.

23. The Israeli decision is reported in a 12 July 2000 Associated Press report and in the *New York Times* and other newspapers. The A-50 negotiations are reported in "China to Get Russian [A-50s] in 2001," *ITAR-TASS*, 13 December 2000, in FBIS-CEP20001213000333.

24. Kenneth Allen, interview with author, Washington, D.C., July 2000. Also see Allen, Krumel, and Pollack, *China's Air Force Enters the 21st Century*, 120–33, for a discussion of PLAAF training shortfalls.

25. Antiaircraft carrier officers may well argue that maritime air power can be more efficiently provided by land-based forces. Klintworth, "Latest Soviet Carrier for Beijing Fleet?" 1992, 26–27, in an article about possible PLAN acquisition of the ex-Soviet carrier *Varyag*, a story that has been frequently repeated, most recently in July 2000 in *Jane's Navy International*, 9, surely a very long, unfulfilled story. Chanda, "China," 15, reports that "China's Foreign Ministry opposes the carrier as both financially and politically costly, since it would fuel fears about China's regional ambitions."

26. The allied experience defending SLOCs against German submarines in two world wars, especially the American efforts in *U.S. coastal waters* in 1942, demonstrates the difficulty of this task.

27. Some strategists have used the UNCLOS, ratified by China in 1996, as rationale for including "military control of the seas [as] legitimate maritime economic activities." Li Jie and Xu Shiming, "The UN Law of the Sea Treaty and the New Naval Mission," *Hsien-Tai Chun-Shih* (Beijing), February 1997, quoted in Hugar, "Sea Dragon Network," 73.

28. Baker, *Naval Institute Guide to Combat Fleets*, 584ff.; Sharpe, *Jane's Fighting Ships: 2000–2001*, 554ff.; *Strategic Survey 1999–2000*, agree on the declining state of Russia's Pacific fleet.

29. SIPRI, *Armaments, Disarmament and International Security*, 193, reports that while "military expenditure in the ASEAN countries increased by an aggregate of 52 per cent over the nine-year period 1988–96," Malaysia has cut its military expenditures by at least 5 per cent, Thailand by 30 per cent, and South Korea by 4.1 per cent.

30. Singapore Armed Forces DCOS, interview with author, May 1999.

31. Sengupta, "RMN Receives First FS-2000 Frigate," 23, reported Malaysia's commissioning of two new, British-built *Yarrow*-class guided-missile frigates in October and November 1999. RMN chief, Vice Adm. Dato Seri Abu Bakar stated (quoted, 54) that the submarine purchase is still planned but probably would not occur before 2010.

32. Gen. Chokedai Hongthong (Army chief of staff), quoted in "Thai-U.S. Military Exercises to Take Place More on Land," *Bangkok Post*, 10 April 1999, in FBIS-EAS-99-0412, stated that the nineteenth Cobra Gold exercise would include Thai-U.S. naval exercises in the Gulf of Thailand since "Thailand had received bigger U.S. financial assistance to organize this year's war games."

33. Nolt, *China-Taiwan Military Balance*, 13, notes that these ships were so poorly constructed that Thailand had to rebuild their propulsion plants, while Gardiner, *Conway's All the World's Fighting Ships*, 59, reported that the Chinese frigates sold to Thailand "lack[ed] truly watertight doors and damage control equipment, and their sensors and weapons are largely obsolete."

34. "Chuan to Discuss Military Cooperation with China," *Nation* (Bangkok), 23 April 1999, in FBIS-EAS-99-0422.

35. Wassana Nanaum, "Thai Navy Harriers Grounded Due to Spare Parts Problem," *Bangkok Post*, 1 June 1999, in FBIS-EAS-99-0601, reported that the carrier's aircraft were grounded until Thailand received twenty Harrier engines from the United States. "Country Report," 12, reported the value of these engines as $84.5 million.

36. "Anonymous Indian Embassy official in Washington," quoted in Barber, "Indian Navy Exercises."

37. "China Objects to Indian Navy's Presence in South China Sea," *New Delhi Indian Express*, 14 October 2000, in FBIS-SAP20001014000051; "India, China Reiterate Resolve to Maintain Border Peace," *New Delhi Hindustan Times*, 5 April 2000. The Indian External Affairs Minister, Singh, during a November 1999 visit to Beijing, agreed with his hosts that there were no serious security problems between their two countries: see Tan Hongwei, "China Strives to Build a Fine Peripheral Environment," *Zhengguo Xinwen She* (Beijing), 5 September 1999, in FBIS-CHI-99-1023, for Singh's statement that India "does not regard China as a threat," a statement that must be regarded with some skepticism.

38. "India's Military Spending: Prospects for Modernisation," 1–2. The Shanghai visit was reported in "Indian Navy Embarks on Naval Diplomacy," *Times of India* (Mumbai), 27 June 2000, in FBIS-SAP20000627000010. The Indian press frequently discusses the Chinese "threat"; see, for instance, "India Fearing Burma-PRK-China Axis," *Asian Age* (New Delhi), 16 November 2000, in FBIS-SAP20001116000030; "India, Myanmar to Forge Strategic Ties," *Hindu* (Chennai), 17 November 2000, in FBIS-SAP20001117000062; "Burmese Foreign Minister Allays India's Fears on Use of Coco Islands by China," *Times of India*, 21 November 2000, in FBIS-SAP20001121000005.

39. Scobell, "Show of Force," 129, presents the well-reasoned conclusion that "the seizure of Taiwan is now a central scenario for the PLA," with a missile assault the most likely mode of attack; one recent U.S. Naval Attache to Beijing described PLAN strategists and planners as "completely focused on the Taiwan mission." Also see Hu Fan (research fellow at PLA NDU's Institute of Strategic Studies), writing in *Zhongguo Pinglun* and quoted in "Mainland Steps up Preparations for Military Struggle Against Taiwan," *Zhongguo Tongxun She*, 1 June 2000, in FBIS-CPP20000601000126; and Shlapak, Orletsky, and Wilson, *Dire Strait?*

40. The U.S. Marine Corps arrives at this ratio by assuming that any successful offensive ground operation requires the attacker to possess a 3-to-1 advantage over the defender; an amphibious assault requires an additional "2" for the 5-to-1 ratio so enough troops are available to hold the beachhead while the main body attacks inland. Yuan Lin, "Sea-Crossing Offensive Capability of Chinese Armed Forces," *Kuang Chiao Ching* 29 (Hong Kong), 16 August 1997, in FBIS-CHI-97-272, argues unconvincingly that a 2-to-1 ratio will be sufficient.
41. See Coakley and Leighton, *Global Logistics and Strategy*, 406–15, for a detailed discussion of the difficulties associated with an amphibious assault on and capture of the island.
42. U.S. Navy Meteorological Service officers, interview with author, August 1999. Also see McVadon, "PRC Exercises," for a comprehensive discussion of this subject.
43. See, for instance, discussion of a "36 hour war" in Wen Jen, "PLA Deliberates Military Tactics Against Taiwan," *Tai Yang Pao* (Hong Kong) 5 June 2000, in FBIS-CPP20000605000009.
44. Baker, *Naval Institute Guide to Combat Fleets*, 771–72, notes that the German-built ships have been "difficult to maintain."
45. It would probably take at least five days for the Japan-based minesweepers to begin operations, ten days for the first minesweeping helos to begin operations, and thirty to forty-five days for the full force of the USN minesweeping effort to be felt.
46. Lennox, *Jane's Strategic Weapon Systems*, issue 22, Taiwan's antiballistic missile defenses might further decrease M-9 and M-11 effectiveness.
47. The will demonstrated by the people of the United Kingdom during World War II may be most instructive, but that observed in the populations of Germany, Japan, the Soviet Union, and ironically China during that war also demonstrate the ability of human will to withstand even horrific onslaughts.

Chapter 8. China's Maritime Strategy

1. Lt. Gen. Mi Zhenyu, "A Reflection on Geographic Strategy," *Zhongguo Junshi Kexue* [*China Military Science*] (Beijing) 1 (February 1998): 6–14, in FBIS-CHI-98-208.
2. Blasko, "New PLA Force Structure," 260.
3. Alfred Thayer Mahan is the most famous writer on maritime strategy; see Sumida 1999 for a recent, provocative analysis of his theories and impact. Although, as Hill, *Maritime Strategy*, 85, points out, if China were to employ this strategy, say in the case of Taiwan, "the penalties for getting it wrong may be quite severe." Hill also delineates five indicators of "sea dependence" (229) all of which apply to China: seagoing trade,

fish catches, size of merchant marine, ship building and repairing, and the offshore zone.

4. This list is a variation on the seventeen points delineated by Rosenberg, "Process," 150ff.
5. Gray, "Seapower and Landpower," 4.
6. Ibid., 13. Also, Gray, *Explorations in Strategy*, 27.
7. Beijing's unhappiness with the present international environment is discussed in Finkelstein's interesting 1999 paper, "China's New Security Concept."
8. Godwin, "Changing Concepts of Doctrine," 573–90.
9. Vladimir Lenin, cited in Watson, "Evolution of Soviet Naval Strategy," 115.
10. Muller, *China's Emergence as a Maritime Power*, 13; about two thousand former Republic of China naval personnel who defected to the communist regime in 1949 formed the core of the new PLAN.
11. Ibid., 15; Swanson, *Eighth Voyage of the Dragon*, 194, also notes that Xiao had attended the same school as Mao, in Changsha. Yang, "From a Navy in Blue," 4, states that more than a hundred PLA officers were sent to study at the Voroshilov Naval Institute in 1951, while 275 officers studied at the Soviet submarine squadron at Lushun, on the Liaotung Peninsula.
12. Muller, *China's Emergence as a Maritime Power*, 16.
13. Kondapalli, "China's Naval Strategy," 2038.
14. See Lewis and Xue, *China's Strategic Seapower*, for the most complete description of this process.
15. Vertzberber, *China's Southwestern Strategy*, 144; Sharpe, *Jane's Fighting Ships: 1995–1996*, 114: China built at least one *Xia*-class fleet ballistic missile submarine, patterned on the U.S. *George Washington* class/Soviet *Hotel* class.
16. Quoted in McGruther, *Evolving Soviet Navy*, 47–48, 66–67.
17. Huang, "Chinese Navy's Offshore Active Defense Strategy," 13.
18. Quoted in Hahn, "PRC Policy in Maritime Asia," 20.
19. Quoted in Hahn, "China: Third Ranking Maritime Power," 47.
20. See Jencks, "PRC's Military and Security Policy," 74, about a 1989 study ordered by Liu, *Balanced Development of the Navy in the Year 2000*, which called for a strategy of "active offshore defense."
21. See Huang, "Chinese Maritime Modernization and Its Security Implications," 225–32, for this discussion.
22. Yuan, "China's Defense Modernization," 70; Huang, "Chinese Navy's Offshore Active Defense Strategy," 119, use the two estimates, respectively.
23. Downing, "China's Evolving Maritime Strategy, Part 1," 130; Huang, "Chinese Maritime Modernization and Its Security Implications," 230.
24. Cited in Chen Yung-kang and Chai Wen-chung, "A Study of the Evolving PRC Naval Strategy," *Chung-Kuo Ta-Lu Yen-Chiu*, 1 September 1997,

7–10, in FBIS-CHI-97-329. Also see Huang, "Chinese Navy's Offshore Active Defense Strategy," 16ff., for a good discussion of the "First" and "Second Island Chains."

25. Wylie, *Military Strategy,* 49, is a classic work on modern naval strategy. Also see Winnefeld, *Joint Air Operations,* 66: "The soldier shapes and exploits his environment; the sailor must adjust to it."

26. Downing, "China's Evolving Maritime Strategy, Part 2," 186–91. Also see Kondapalli, "China's Naval Strategy," 2042.

27. See Godwin, "Technology, Strategy, and Operations," for the most complete discussion of ongoing Chinese efforts to improve warship system capabilities, and Godwin, "From Continent to Periphery," 464–87.

28. Downing, "China's Evolving Maritime Strategy, Part 2," 191.

29. Ibid., 188.

30. Three ships are normally required to maintain one on patrol at all times, although an SSBN armed with a missile capable of hitting its target without going very far to sea (e.g., the Russian *Typhoon*-class submarine) would not need this two ship "backup."

31. Quoted in Watson, "Evolution of Soviet Naval Strategy," 120.

32. Ping Kefu, "Development Strategy for Chinese Navy in 21st Century," *Jianchuan Zhishi* 8 (August 1994): 2–3, in FBIS-CST-96-014, 34–37.

33. Cited in Huang, "Chinese Maritime Modernization and Its Security Implications," 9.

34. Quoted in Ji, "Test Case," 379.

35. Quoted in Jun Zhan, "China Goes to the Blue Waters," 191.

36. Quoted in Huang Caihong, "Witnessing Maritime Exercise of the Chinese Navy," *Liaowang* 45 (6 November 1995), in FBIS-CHI-95-235.

37. Ping, "Development Strategy for Chinese Navy in 21st Century."

38. Cao Zhi and Yang Zhiwang, "Interview with Vadm Yang Yushu, East Sea Fleet Commander," Beijing *Xinhua,* 26 March 1997, in FBIS-CHI-97-085, quote Yang as stating that "the Navy serves as an important window of the Chinese military and is an important part of China's military diplomacy."

39. South China Sea incidents are discussed, and Liu is quoted, in Garver, "China's Push Through the South China Sea," 1022–23. Also see the comprehensive discussion of the South China Sea situation in Valencia, *China and the South China Sea Disputes.*

40. Barber, "Indian Navy Exercises," 1. "Intelligence," *Far Eastern Economic Review,* 20 April 2000, 4, reports that the Vietnamese Navy's deputy chief, Do Xuan Co, was exploring the possibility of repairing or even building ships in Indian shipyards.

41. Griswold and Parker, "Counter Narcotics," 6–8, discuss the flow of illegal drugs from Burma and on 15 discuss China's response.

42. Baker, *Naval Institute Guide to Combat Fleets,* 475. Also see Brooke, "Myanmar's Armed Forces and Their Ongoing Campaigns," 11, although he reports the forthcoming delivery of *Jianghu*-class frigates, Baker reports that the *Jianghu*s, ordered in 1994, probably have been canceled for financial reasons. "China's Ambitions in Myanmar," 2, reports $1–2 billion of Chinese arms deliveries to Burma in the 1990s. Also see Brooke, "Armed Forces of Myanmar," 14, and "Myanmar's Armed Forces and Their Ongoing Campaigns," 11. "Navy Relocating Donkyun Villagers for China-Burma Joint Military Exercises in July, August in Coastal Region," *Oslo Democratic Voice of Burma,* 1 July 2000, in FBIS-SEP20000703000062, and "Burma, China to Hold Joint Military Exercises in July, August in Coastal Region," in FBIS-SEP20000703000034, report the forcible removal of villagers to clear an exercise area for "joint military exercises" involving "planes, warships, naval vessels and Army officers from" the PLA.

43. See, for instance, Banerjee, "China," 71; Ray-Choudhury, "Trends in Naval Power"; Jencks, "PRC's Military and Security Policy," 89, discusses the contradictory reports that have been made about the military character of this construction. It must be noted that it is Indian authors who make the most extreme claims of Chinese intrusion into Burma. Senior PLA, Taiwan, and U.S. officers interviewed by me and others maintain that relatively minor technical assistance and training by a small number of PLAN personnel is the most that is occurring.

44. See Brooke, "Myanmar's Armed Forces and Their Ongoing Campaigns," 11, and Opal-Rome, "China Moves Roil Region," 1.

45. "China, Myanmar Issue Joint Statement," 6 June 2000, Internet: www.china.org.cn/English.News/Politics/0606/22.htm. Saritdet Marukatat and Bhanravee Tansugbhapol, "Mekong River Navigation Accord Singing Slated for March," *Bangkok Post,* 27 February 2000, in FBIS-SEP20000228000017, further explains one of these regional agreements, which aims to free up navigation on the Mekong River by China, Burma, Thailand, and Laos. "India, China Agree for a Forward Looking Relationship." Internet: www.insidechina.com/news.php3?id=155883, reports vice foreign ministerial talks that "discussed all aspects of bilateral relations including border trade

46. Yergin, Eklof, and Edwards, "Fueling Asia's Recovery," 42, estimate China will import "as much as 3 million" barrels of oil per day by 2010. This article also provides a useful survey of possible alternative Chinese energy sources, including new oil fields in the Tarim Basin and Kazakhstan, and investing in Venezuelan, Iraqi, Iranian, and Indonesian fields. Also see Hugar, "Sea Dragon Network," 22–24, for a discussion of Chinese oil imports.

47. See, for instance, Si Yanwne and Chen Wanjun, "Navy to Develop More High-Tech Equipment," *Jiefangjun Bao*, 9 June 1999 in FBIS-CHI-99-0611, citing Gen. Cao Gangchuan, director of the General Armaments Department, that "it is necessary to put [Navy] armament development in a prominent position of army building . . . increase armaments' scientific and technological contents; and improve the quality and speed of armament development" and *Xinhua*, 10 June 1999, in FBIS-CHI-99-0609 citing Cao that "the navy's rapid reaction capacity, emergency field repair ability and defense readiness must also be improved."

48. See Lewis and Xue, "China's Search for a Modern Air Force," 10, for Deng Xiaoping's statement that "the army and the navy both need air cover. . . . Without air cover, winning a naval battle is also out of the question."

49. A former U.S. defense attaché in Beijing has recently stated that the PLAN and PLAAF have been receiving most of the recent PLA modernization funding, and specifically mentioned the one-third figure going to the navy. Lewis and Xue, "China's Search for a Modern Air Force," 11, claim that the 1985 strategic shift to non-nuclear-war scenarios gave the air force and the navy "pride of place" within the PLA. Also see Huang, "Chinese Navy's Offshore Active Defense Strategy," 9 (table 1) for the estimate that 32.7 percent of the PLA's 1993 budget was allocated to the PLAN.

50. Quoted in *Xinhua*, 21 April 1999, in FBIS-CHI-99-0421.

51. Perhaps Shi is acknowledging the limits within which he has to operate: the United States was able to maintain a task force off the coast of West Africa for *seven months* in 1990–91, before finally evacuating civilians from strife-torn Liberia. (Pointed out in Till, "Maritime Strategy," 193.) A PLA view of "Internet Warfare" is provided in in Jia Xiaowei, "Pay Close Attention to Network Warfare Which Has Quietly Arrived," *Jiefangjun Bao*, 24 August 1999, 6, in FBIS-CHI-99-0925; and in Leng Binglin, Wang Yulin, and Zhao Weniang, "Bring Internet Warfare Into the Military System is of Equal Significance with Land, Sea, and Air Power," *Jiefangjun Bao*, 11 November 1999, 7, in FBIS-CHI-99-1227. See especially Pillsbury 1997.

52. Chen and Zhang, "Shouldering the Important Task," 3. Shi, 5, also calls for a "scientifically feasible . . . Navy development strategy" as part of the "defense development strategy . . . subject to the national "development strategy."

53. See Lu Ning, *Dynamics of Foreign-Policy Decisionmaking in China*, 126ff., for an interesting description of the 1988 naval conflict with Vietnam, when, according to the author, PLAN forces exceeded and drove national strategy.

54. Sr. Col. Huang Xing and Sr. Col. Zuo Quandian, "Holding the Initiative in Our Hands in Conducting Operations, Giving Full Play to Our Own Advantages to Defeat Our Enemy—A Study of the Core Idea of the Operational Doctrine of the PLA," *Zhaongquo Junshi Kexue* [*China Military Science*] 4 (20 November 1996): 49–56, in FBIS-CHI-97. The authors, who both serve at the Academy of Military Science, clearly identify the U.S. as "our enemy" (8), but display a very imperfect knowledge of American weapons systems.

55. "Bolt from the blue" was first used in modern maritime strategy in the early twentieth century to describe a possible surprise German naval attack on Great Britain. See Marder, *From the Dreadnought to Scapa Flow,* 144, and Roskill, *Strategy of Seapower,* 104, for discussion of this concept.

56. Sr. Capts. Yan Youqiang ("Director of a Naval Headquarters Research Institute") and Chen Rongxing, "On Maritime Strategy and the Marine Environment," *Zhongguo Jushi Kexue* 2 (Beijing) (20 May 1997): 81–92, in FBIS-CHI-97-197. This may be a good description of China's maritime strategic thought.

57. This is the view from Manila and Hanoi, while Singapore expresses its distrust of China by urging a continued, strong U.S. naval presence in Southeast Asia (senior Singapore Joint Staff officer and deputy director, conversations with author, Singapore Armed Forces Training Institute, May 1999); Indonesia and Thailand are at least more comfortable with that presence than otherwise. Only Malaysia continues to maintain, at least in public, that China is not a threat (and the U.S. naval presence unnecessary) (deputy commandant and staff officers, conversation with author, Royal Malaysian Defense College, May 1999).

58. Furthermore, Germany built the wrong navy; it was unable to serve as more than a coastal defense force and, in the final analysis served little more purpose than to absorb vast quantities of national resources while needlessly alienating Great Britain and other powers. See Marder, *From the Dreadnought to Scapa Flow;* Roskill, *Strategy of Seapower;* E. L. Woodward, *Great Britain and the German Navy;* and Steinberg, *Yesterday's Deterrent.*

59. Lambert, *Sir John Fisher's Naval Revolution,* 121–26, explains the concept of "flotilla defense." Jon Sumida brought this to my attention.

Conclusion

1. Mao Zedong's campaign in the 1960s to establish a "third wave" of industrial development well inland arose primarily from security rather than economic or social concerns.

2. "Reviving Russia's Navy," 2.

3. Johnston, "China's Militarized Interstate Dispute Behavior," 1–30.

4. Shen Zhongchang, "A Rudimentary Exploration of 21st Century Naval Warfare," *Zhongguo Renmin Kexue* 1 (20 February 1995), in FBIS-CHI-95-113, supplement, 28.

5. Yung, "People's War at Sea," provides a cogent analysis of these three options for China.

6. Swaine, "Chinese Military Modernization," 36.

7. This system, discussed with the author by senior PLAN officers, is not significantly different from that in the United States.

8. Yung, "People's War at Sea," 37–38. Yang, "From a Navy in Blue," also notes China's poor record reverse-engineering combatant ships.

9. See Lardy, *China's Unfinished Economic Revolution*, for a perceptive analysis of China's economy. He notes the high percentage of nonperforming loans, social and political costs of putative reforms, the weak financial position of state-owned enterprises, and a marked decline in government revenues as evidence of the economy's questionable health.

10. Yung suggested some of these numbers in remarks to me at the June 2000 CNA Conference on the PLAN.

11. Sharpe, *Jane's Fighting Ships: 2000–2001*, 117, states that four of the *Han*s are operational; Baker, *Naval Institute Guide to Combat Fleets*, 107, reports that only one boat was "fully active as of 1999."

12. Finkelstein, "China's New Security Concept," pointed out to the author that as a result of regulations issued in 1999, the GSD is responsible for both PLA modernization and operational tasking.

13. In discussion with the author's group, Chi noted that one of the benefits of mobilizing the PLA to assist in flood control work that summer had been to get the military back in among the people, to rekindle the feeling—damaged by the Tiananmen Square incident—that the PLA was the military of the Chinese people.

14. In terms, that is, of conventional naval power as currently understood. Technological developments—space-borne sensor and weapons systems, for instance—might allow China to achieve global power capabilities, albeit not in traditional naval forms.

15. Schuster, "Special Report," is the most complete description of Beijing's efforts to increase its influence in the South Pacific island nations.

16. Discussed in Huang Caihong, "Moving Toward the World and Peace—Roundup on Five Decades of PLA Foreign Military Interaction," *Xinhua*, 14 September 1999, in FBIS-CHI-99-1005, and "China's Military Diplomacy Unprecedentedly Dynamic," *Xinhua*, 15 September 1999, in FBIS-CHI-1999-1016. "Shanghai Five to Agree Line of Kyrgyz, PRC, Tajik Borders," *Almaty Interfax-Kazakhstan*, 7 April 2000, in FBIS-CEP20000407000134, is another indicator of Beijing's success in resolving its continental border disputes.

17. Yan Youqiang and Chen Rongxing, "The Developing Trends of Naval Battles and Their Impact on PLA Campaigns," *Zhongguo Junshi Kexue* 2 (Beijing), 20 May 1997, 81–92, in FBIS-CHI-97-197.

18. See Wilhelm, *China and Security in the Asian Pacific Region,* 44, for the contention that long range PLAN deployments would be a departure from Chinese military tradition and that PLAN arguments "have not convinced the CMC to allocate the resources" for a large blue-water navy.

19. Cited in Shambaugh, "China's Defense Industries," 51.

20. Wilhelm, *China and Security in the Asian Pacific Region,* 42.

BIBLIOGRAPHY

Agnote, Dario. "China to Continue Military Buildup in Spratly Islands." *Kyodo News,* in *Washington Times,* 22 October 1999, p. A-14.

Ahrari, Ehsan. "China's Naval Forces Look to Extend Their Blue-Water Reach." *Jane's Intelligence Review* 10, no. 4 (April 1998): 31–36.

Alexander's Gas and Oil Connections: News and Trends E and SE Asia (cited hereafter as *Alexander's*), vols. 3–7. Internet: www.gasandoil.com/goc/news/nts0835.htm.

Allen, Kenneth W., Glenn Krumel, and Jonathan D. Pollack. *China's Air Force Enters the 21st Century.* Santa Monica, Calif.: RAND, 1995.

Armed Forces Staff College. *Joint Staff Officers' Guide.* Publication No. 1. Washington, D.C.: National Defense University Press, 1996.

"Army Seeks Mobility in Force Cuts." *Jane's Defence Weekly* 30, no. 25 (16 December 1998): 23.

Association of Southeast Asian Nations (ASEAN). "ASEAN Chairman's Statement at the Sixth Meeting of the ARF." July 1998, 2. Internet: www.aseansec.org/politics/pol-arf6.htm.

———. Information web site: www.aseansec.org/politics/pol_arf6.htm.

Austin, Greg. *China's Ocean Frontier: International Law, Military Force and National Development.* Canberra: Allen & Unwin, 1998.

Baker, A. D., III, ed. *The Naval Institute Guide to Combat Fleets of the World, 2000–2001.* Annapolis: Naval Institute Press, 2000.

Ball, Desmond. "Military Acquisitions in the Asia-Pacific Region." *International Security* 18, no. 3 (Winter 1993–94): 78–112.

Banerjee, Ruben. "China: Worrying Approach." *India Today,* 30 April 1994, 71.

Barber, Ben. "Indian Navy Exercises Seen Apt to Irk Beijing." *Washington Times,* 8 May 2000, p. 1.

Bi, Jianxiang. "Managing Taiwan Operations in the Twenty-first Century: Issues and Options." *Naval War College Review* 52, no. 4 (Autumn 1999): 30–58.

Blackman, Raymond V. B., ed. *Jane's Fighting Ships: 1955–1956.* London: Jane's Fighting Ships Publishing, 1956.

———. *Jane's Fighting Ships: 1960–1961.* New York: McGraw-Hill, 1961.

———. *Jane's Fighting Ships: 1970–1971.* London: Jane's Yearbooks, 1971.

Blanche, Bruce, and Jean Blanche. "Oil and Regional Stability in the South China Sea." *Jane's Intelligence Review* 7, no. 11 (November 1995): 511–14.

Blasko, Dennis. "Evaluating Chinese Military Procurement from Russia." *Joint Force Quarterly* 17 (Autumn/Winter 1997–98): 91–96.

———. "A New PLA Force Structure." In *The People's Liberation Army in the Information Age,* ed. James C. Mulvenon and Richard H. Yang, 258–88. Santa Monica, Calif.: RAND, 1999.

Blasko, Philip T. Klapakis, and John F. Corbett Jr. "Training Tomorrow's PLA: A Mixed Bag of Tricks." *China Quarterly* 146 (June 1996): 488–524.

Bodeen, Christopher. "Concrete Claims." *Far Eastern Economic Review* 158, no. 51 (21 December 1995): 14.

———. "Taiwan Military Uses Pratas Islands." Associated Press, 20 October 1999.

Brooke, Micool. "The Armed Forces of Myanmar." *Asian Defence Journal,* January 1998, 14.

———. "Myanmar's Armed Forces and Their Ongoing Campaigns." *Asian Defence Journal,* March 1999, 11.

Bullard, Monte. *China's Political-Military Evolution: The Party and the Military in the PRC, 1960–1984.* Boulder, Colo.: Westview Press, 1985.

Caldwell, John. *China's Conventional Military Capability.* Washington, D.C.: CSIS, 1994.

The Case of Peng Teh-huai, 1959–1968. Hong Kong: Union Research Institute, 1968.

Catley, Bob, and Makmur Keliat. *Spratlys: The Dispute in the South China Sea.* Sydney: Ashgate, 1997.

Chanda, Nayan. "China: Aiming High." *Far Eastern Economic Review,* 20 October 1994, 15.

———. "The Right Stuff." *Far Eastern Economic Review,* 20 October 1994, 15.

Chang, Gordon H., and He Di. "The Absence of War in the U.S.-China Confrontation over Quemoy and Matsu in 1954–1955: Contingency, Luck, or Deterrence?" *American Historical Review* 98, no. 5 (December 1993): 1500–1524.

Chapman, Richard. "Senkaku-Diaoyutai Island Dispute." U.S. Pacific Command Virtual Information Center, 29 February 2000. Internet: www.vic.pacom.mil.

Chen, Hurng-yu. "A Comparison Between Taipei and Peking in Their Policies and Concepts Regarding the South China Sea." *Issues and Studies* 29, no. 9 (September 1993): 22–58.

Chen, Kathy. "China's Inability to Keep Subs Running Shows Broader Woes Plaguing Military." *Wall Street Journal,* 1 August 1997, pp. 1, 11.

Ch'en, Jerome, ed. *Mao.* Englewood Cliffs, N.J.: Prentice-Hall, 1969.

Cheng, Hsiao-shih. *Party-Military Relations in the PRC and Taiwan.* Boulder, Colo.: Westview Press, n.d.

Cheung, Tai Ming. *Growth of Chinese Naval Power: Priorities, Goals, Missions, and Regional Implications.* Singapore: Institute of Southeast Asian Studies, 1990.

————. "Reforming the Dragon's Tail: Chinese Military Logistics in the Era of High-Technology Warfare and Market Economics." In *China's Military Faces the Future,* ed. James R. Lilley and David Shambaugh, 228–46. Washington, D.C.: AEI and M. E. Sharpe, 1999.

"China and Malaysia Agree to Boost Defense Co-operation in the South China Sea." *Alexander's* 4 (19 July 1999).

"China Commits to Carrier Construction with Daunting Aircraft." *Navy News and Undersea Technology,* 23 August 1999, 1.

"China Gets to Grips with Luhu Technology Gap." *Jane's Navy International* 101 (November 1996): 8.

"China Launches a Powerful New Super Warship." *Jane's Defense Weekly,* 1 February 1999. Internet: www.taiwansecurity.org/News/Janes-990201.htm.

"China, Myanmar Issue Joint Statement." 6 June 2000. Internet: www.china.org.cn/English.News/Politics/0606/22.htm.

"China's Ambitions in Myanmar." *Strategic Comments* 6 (July 2000): 1–2. London: International Institute of Strategic Studies.

"China's Offshore Oil Sector Profitable in 1998." *Asia Pulse,* 18 January 1999, 21.

"China's Sea Change." *Far Eastern Economic Review* 163 (10 February 2000): 6.

"China Uses Commercial Ships to Carry Troops in Exercise." *Dow-Jones Newsletter,* 31 July 2000.

"Chinese Naval Presence Rising off Japan." *Japan Times,* 22 March 2000, p. 1.

"The Chinese Navy." In *Shanghai Defense Force and Volunteers.* Shanghai: *North China Daily Herald,* c. 1929.

"Chinese Subs Experience Battery, Training Problems." *Navy News and Undersea Technology,* 1 September 1997, 5.

Ching, Frank. "Manila Foiled in Spratly Row." *Far Eastern Economic Review,* 8 April 1999, 33.

Chung, Chien-pung. "The Spratlys and Other South China Sea Islands Disputes." *Journal of Social, Political, and Economic Studies* (Spring 1999): 17–36.

"Clashes over Fish in Pacific Asia, 1994–1997." 1999. Internet: www.middlebury.edu/SouthChinaSea/maps/dupont3.

Coakley, Robert W., and Richard M. Leighton. *Global Logistics and Strategy: 1943–1945. The United States Army in World War II,* ed. Stetson Conn. Washington, D.C.: Center of Military History of the U.S. Army, 1989.

Cole, Bernard D. *Gunboats and Marines: The United States Navy in China.* Newark: University of Delaware Press, 1982.

————. "The Real Sand Pebbles." *Naval History* 14, no. 1 (February 2000): 16–23.

Cole, Bernard D., and Paul H. B. Godwin. "Advanced Military Technology and the PLA: Priorities and Capabilities for the Twenty-First Century." In *The Chinese Armed Forces in the 21st Century*, ed. Larry Wortzel. Carlisle, Pa.: Strategic Studies Institute of the U.S. Army War College, 1999.

Colton, Luke. "Chinese Naval Aviation: An Overview of PLAN Helicopters." Draft paper prepared for the Henry L. Stimson Center, Washington, D.C., 24 March 2000.

"Concrete Claims." *Far Eastern Economic Review*, 21 December 1995, 14.

Cordner, Lee G. "The Spratly Islands Dispute and the Law of the Sea." *Ocean Development and International Law* 25, no. 1 (January–March 1994): 62–74.

"Country Report." *Asian Defence Journal*, November 1999, 12.

Crawley, James W. "Chinese Navy Changing from Lean to Mean." *San Diego Union-Tribune*, 26 March 1997, p. 1.

Daugherty, Leo G. "Commentary on 'PLAN Marines.'" Paper presented at the Center for Naval Analysis (CNA) Conference on the PLAN, Washington, D.C., April 2000.

Deng, Gang. *Chinese Maritime Activities and Socioeconomic Development, c. 2100 B.C.–1900 A.D.* Westport, Conn.: Greenwood Press, 1997.

Deng, Xiaoping. "Speech at an Enlarged Meeting of the Military Commission of the Party Central Committee" (14 July 1975). In *China Reports* 468 (31 October 1983): 14–22.

Directory of PRC Military Personalities. Honolulu: Serold Hawaii, October 1999.

Donovan, Robert J. *Tumultuous Years: The Presidency of Harry S Truman, 1949–1953.* New York: W. W. Norton, 1982.

Down, Erica Strecker, and Phillip C. Saunders. "Legitimacy and the Limits of Nationalism: China and the Diaoyu Islands." *International Security* 23, no. 3 (Winter 1998–99): 127–33.

Downing, John W. "China's Evolving Maritime Strategy, Part 1." *Jane's Intelligence Review* 8 (March 1996): 129–33.

————. "China's Evolving Maritime Strategy, Part 2." *Jane's Intelligence Review* 8 (April 1996): 186–91.

Dreyer, Edward L. "The Poyang Campaign, 1363: Inland Naval Warfare in the Founding of the Ming Dynasty." In *Chinese Ways of Warfare*, ed. Frank A. Kierman Jr. and John K. Fairbank. Cambridge: Harvard University Press, 1974.

Dreyer, June Teufel. *The PLA and the Kosovo Conflict.* The Letort Papers. Carlisle, Pa.: U.S. Army War College Strategic Studies Institute, May 2000.

"East Asia: Spratlys Initiative." *Oxford Analytica Brief.* U.S. Pacific Command Virtual Information Center, 6 December 1999. Internet: www.vic.pacom.mil.

"East Asia: Straits Challenge." *Oxford Analytica Brief.* U.S. Pacific Command Virtual Information Center, 10 February 2000. Internet: www.vic. pacom.mil.

Eckholm, Erik. "Despite Tensions, China and Japan Reaffirm Ties." *New York Times,* 30 August 2000.

Energy Information Administration. *The Petroleum Resources of China.* DOE/EI-0501. Washington, D.C.: Department of Energy, 1987.

———. *South China Sea Region.* Washington, D.C.: Department of Energy, 1998.

"Exploration Sags Off Viet Nam." *Oil and Gas Journal* 95 (3 November 1997): 32.

Fairbank, John K. *China: A New History.* Cambridge: Belknap Press, Harvard University Press, 1992.

———. "Maritime and Continental in China's History." In *The Cambridge History of China.* Vol. 12, *Republican China: 1912–1949,* pt. 1, ed. John K. Fairbank and Dennis Twitchett. Cambridge: Cambridge University Press, 1983.

Farrer, Mark. "China's Air Force—Kosovo Spurs a Race to Change." *Asia-Pacific Defense Reporter* 25, no. 6 (October/November 1999): 20–21.

Fesharaki, Fereidun. "Review of China's Petroleum Demand, Supply, Organizational Reforms, and Overseas Investment." Honolulu: East-West Center, January 1998.

"Fighters Trail Philippine Plane Over Spratlys." Reuters report. Yahoo! Headlines, 1 November 1999. Internet: www.newsindex.com/cgi-bin/result.cgi?

Finkelstein, David M. "China's New Security Concept: Reading Between the Lines." Center for Naval Analysis Issue Paper. Washington, D.C.: CNA, April 1999.

Fisher, Richard. "Appendix to Chapter 5: Foreign Arms Acquisition and PLA Modernization." In *China's Military Faces the Future,* ed. James R. Lilley and David Shambaugh. Washington, D.C.: AEI and M. E. Sharpe, 1999.

Forage, Paul C. "The Foundations of Chinese Naval Supremacy in the Twelfth Century." In *New Interpretations in Naval History: Selected Papers from the Tenth Naval History Symposium Held at the United States Naval Academy, 11–13 September 1991,* ed. Jack Sweetman. Annapolis: Naval Institute Press, 1992.

Foreign Broadcast Information Service, China. Referred to as FBIS. (FBIS-CHI-99-0421, for example, indicates the 421st item referring to China published in 1999.)

Freeman, Charles W., Jr. "China, Taiwan, and the United States." In *Asia After the "Miracle": Redefining U.S. Economic and Security Priorities,* ed. Selig S. Harrison and Clyde V. Prestowitz Jr., 169–84. Washington, D.C.: Economic Strategy Institute, 1999.

Gardiner, Robert, ed. *Conway's All the World's Fighting Ships, 1947–1995.* Annapolis: Naval Institute Press, 1995.

Garver, John W. "China's Push Through the South China Sea: The Interaction of Bureaucratic and National Interest." *China Quarterly* 132 (December 1992): 999–1028.

———. *Face Off: China, the United States, and Taiwan's Democratization.* Seattle: University of Washington Press, 1997.

"Gas Tussle in South China Sea." *China Weekly Fax Bulletin,* 24 March 1997. Orbis Publications, Washington, D.C.

Godwin, Paul H. B. "Change and Continuity in Chinese Military Doctrine: 1949–1999." Paper presented at the CAPS-RAND Conference on the PLA, Washington, D.C., July 1999.

———. "Changing Concepts of Doctrine, Strategy, and Operations in the People's Liberation Army 1978–87." *China Quarterly* 112 (December 1987): 573–90.

———. "Force Projection and National Military Strategy." In *Chinese Military Modernization,* ed. C. Dennison Lane, 69–99. Washington, D.C.: AEI Press, 1996.

———. "From Continent to Periphery: PLA Doctrine, Strategy and Capabilities Towards 2000." *China Quarterly* 146 (June 1996): 464–87.

———. "Technology, Strategy, and Operations: The PLA's Continuing Dilemma." Draft article, 1998.

———, ed. *The Chinese Defense Establishment: Continuity and Change in the 1980s.* Boulder, Colo.: Westview Press, 1983.

Gray, Colin S. *Explorations in Strategy.* Westport, Conn.: Greenwood Press, 1996.

———. "Seapower and Landpower." In *Seapower and Landpower,* ed. Colin S. Gray and Roger W. Barnett, 3–26. Annapolis: Naval Institute Press, 1989.

Grazebrook, A. W. "New Generation Naval AAW Missiles." *Asia-Pacific Defense Reporter* 23, no. 5 (August–September 1997): 18.

Griswold, James, and Rick Parker. "Counter Narcotics: Burma, China, and Laos." U.S. Pacific Command Virtual Information Center, 22 August 2000. Internet: www.vic.pacom.mil.

Hahn, Bradley. "China: Third Ranking Maritime Power—and Growing." *Pacific Defense Reporter* 15, no. 4 (October 1988): 46–51.

———. "PRC Policy in Maritime Asia." *Journal of Defense and Diplomacy* 4, no. 6 (June 1986): 19–21.

Hanrahan, Gene Z. "Report on Red China's New Navy." U.S. Naval Institute *Proceedings* 79, no. 8 (August 1953): 84–85.

Harrison, Selig S. *China, Oil, and Asia: Conflict Ahead?* New York: Columbia University Press, 1977.

He, Di. "'The Last Campaign to Unify China': The CCP's Unmaterialized Plan to Liberate Taiwan, 1949–1950." *Chinese Historians* 5 (Spring 1992): 222–45.

Heaton, William R. "Professional Military Education in the People's Republic of China." In *The Chinese Defense Establishment: Continuity and*

Change in the 1980s, ed. Paul H. B. Godwin, 121–38. Boulder, Colo.: Westview Press, 1983.

Henley, Lonnie D. "Officer Education in the Chinese PLA." *Problems of Communism* 36, no. 3 (May–June 1987): 55–71.

Hiatt, Fred. "Marine General: U.S. Troops Must Stay in Japan." *Washington Post,* 27 March 1990, p. A-14.

Hill, Rear Adm. J. R., USN (Ret.). *Maritime Strategy for Medium Powers.* Annapolis: Naval Institute Press, 1986.

Hiramatsu, Shigeo. "China's Naval Advance: Objectives and Capabilities." *Japan Review of International Affairs* 8, no. 2 (Spring 1994): 120–36.

Hirschfeld, Thomas J. "China's Aircraft Carrier Program: A Virtual Dragonfly?" *Korean Journal of Defense Analysis* 10, no. 1 (Summer 1998): 141–54.

Hobkirk, Michael D. *Land, Sea, or Air? Military Priorities, Historical Choices.* New York: St. Martin's Press, 1992.

Hoffman, Fred S. "Red Chinese Reportedly Building New Naval Base." *Seattle Times,* September 1971, p. 1.

Holzer, Robert. "Study: U.S. Navy Must Go Beyond *Aegis* Radar Era." *Defense News,* 7 June 1999, 3, 36.

Hooten, E. R., ed. "China: Surface-to-Surface Missiles." *Jane's Naval Weapons Systems, 1996.* Coulsdon, Surrey: Jane's Information Group, 1998.

Huang, Alexander. "Chinese Maritime Modernization and Its Security Implications: The Deng Xiaoping Era and Beyond." Ph.D. diss., George Washington University, 1994.

———. "The Chinese Navy's Offshore Active Defense Strategy: Conceptualization and Implications." *Naval War College Review* 47, no. 3 (Summer 1994): 7–32.

———. "The Evolution of the PLA Navy and Its Early Combat Experiences." Paper presented at the Center for Naval Analysis Conference on the People's Liberation Army Navy, Washington, D.C., April 2000.

———. "The PLA Navy at War, 1949–1999: From Coastal Defense to Distant Operations." Paper presented at the CNA Conference on the PLA's Operational History, Alexandria, Va., June 1999.

———. "Transformation and Refinement of Chinese Military Doctrine: Reflection and Critique on the PLA's View." Paper presented at the CAPS-RAND Conference on the PLA, Washington, D.C., July 1999.

Hugar, Wayne R. "How Far Will the Dragon Swim?" U.S. Naval Institute *Proceedings,* no. 125 (March 1999): 48–51.

———. "The Sea Dragon Network: Implications of the International Expansion of China's Maritime Shipping Industry." Masters thesis, Naval Postgraduate School, 1998.

"India, China Agree for a Forward Looking Relationship." Internet: www.insidechina.com/news.php3?id=155883.

"India's Military Spending: Prospects for Modernisation." *Strategic Comments* 6, no. 6 (July 2000): 1, 2. London: International Institute of Strategic Studies.

"Intelligence." *Far Eastern Economic Review* 163 (20 April 2000): 4.

International Institute of Strategic Studies. *The Military Balance, 1999–2000.* London: Oxford University Press, 2000.

———. *Strategic Survey 1999–2000.* London: Oxford University Press, 2000.

Isnard, Jacques. "Chinese Submarine Was 'Submarining' on a Freighter in Channel." *Le Monde* (Paris), 4 February 1999, p. 4.

Israel, Fred L., ed. "Dwight D. Eisenhower, First Annual Message." *The State of the Union Messages of the Presidents, 1790–1966.* Vol. 3, *1905–1966.* New York: Chelsea House Publishers, 1967.

"Japan Concerned by PRC Ships' Increasing Activities." *Sankei Shimbun* (Tokyo), 18 April 2000, in FBIS-JPP20000418000045.

Jencks, Harlan. "China's 'Punitive' War on Vietnam: A Military Assessment." *Asian Survey* 19, no. 8 (August 1979): 801–15.

———. *From Muskets to Missiles: Politics and Professionalism in the Chinese Army, 1945–1981.* Boulder, Colo.: Westview Press, 1982.

———. "The PRC's Military and Security Policy in the Post–Cold War Era." *Issues and Studies* 30, no. 11 (November 1994): 65–103.

———. "A Test Case for China's Defense and Foreign Policies." *Contemporary Southeast Asia* 16, no. 4 (March 1995): 375–403.

Jian, Sanqiang. "Multinational Oil Companies and the Spratly Dispute." *Journal of Contemporary China* 6, no. 16 (November 1997): 591–602. Internet: www.proquest.umi.com/pqdweb?TS-9375917.

Joffe, Ellis. *The Chinese Army After Mao.* Cambridge: Harvard University Press, 1987.

———. "The Military and China's New Politics: Trends and Counter-Trends." In *The People's Liberation Army in the Information Age,* ed. James C. Mulvenon and Richard Yang, 22–47. Santa Monica, Calif.: RAND, 1999.

———. "Taiwan and the Chinese Military." Draft article, August 2000.

Johnson, Douglas. "Drawn into the Fray: Indonesia's Natuna Islands Meet China's Long Gaze South." *Asian Affairs* 24 (Fall 1997): 153–61.

Johnston, Alastair Iain. "China's Militarized Interstate Dispute Behavior, 1949–1992: A First Cut at the Data." *China Quarterly* 153 (March 1998): 1–30.

Juo, Ting-yee. "Self-Strengthening: The Pursuit of Western Technology." In *The Cambridge History of China.* Vol. 10, *Late Ch'ing, 1800–1911,* pt. 1, ed. John K. Fairbank, 491–590. Cambridge: Cambridge University Press, 1978.

Kan, Shirley A., Christopher Bolkcom, and Ronald O'Rourke. *China's Foreign Conventional Arms Acquisitions: Background and Analysis.* Washington, D.C.: Congressional Record Service, 10 October 2000.

Karniol, Robert. "China Buys *Shkval* Torpedo from Kazakhstan." *Jane's Defence Weekly* 30, no. 14 (26 August 1998): 6.

Kearsley, Harold K. *Maritime Power and the Twenty-First Century.* Aldershot, U.K.: Dartmouth Press, 1997.

Khalizad, Zalmay M., Abram N. Shulsky, Daniel L. Byman, Roger Cliff, David T. Orletsky, David Shlapak, and Ashley J. Tellis. *The United States and a Rising China: Strategic and Military Implications.* Santa Monica, Calif.: RAND, 1999.

Klintworth, Gary. "China's Naval Ambitions Stir Up Fears in Region." *Singapore Straits Times,* 1 August 1992, p. 13.

———. "Latest Soviet Carrier for Beijing Fleet?" *Asia-Pacific Defence Reporter* 25, no. 4 (August–September 1992): 26–27.

Kondapalli, Srikanth. "China's Naval Equipment Acquisition." *Strategic Analysis* 23, no. 9 (December 1999): 1509–29.

———. *China's Naval Power.* New Delhi: Knowledge World, 2001

———. "China's Naval Strategy." *Strategic Analysis* 23, no. 12 (March 2000): 2037–51.

———. "China's Naval Structure and Dynamics." *Strategic Analysis* 23, no. 7 (October 1999): 1095–1115.

———. "China's Naval Training Program." *Strategic Analysis* 23, no. 8 (November 1999): 1333–53.

———. "Military Academies in China." *Strategic Analysis* 23, no. 1 (April 1999): 27–43.

Krepon, Michael, ed. *Chinese Perspectives on Confidence-Building Measures.* Washington, D.C.: Henry L. Stimson Center, 1997.

Lam, Willy Wo-Lap. "PLA Weapons to Be Upgraded by 2010." *South China Morning Post,* 15 December 1999, p. 12.

Lambert, Nicholas A. *Sir John Fisher's Naval Revolution.* Columbia: University of South Carolina Press, 1999.

Lampton, David M., and Gregory C. May. "Managing U.S.-China Relations in the Twenty-First Century." Unpublished paper. Washington, D.C., 1999.

Lardy, Nicholas R. *China's Unfinished Economic Revolution.* Washington, D.C.: Brookings Institution, 1998.

LeGrand, Rear Adm. C. M., Judge Advocate General Corp, USN. "Memorandum for Undersecretary of Defense (Policy) and Director for Strategic Plans and Policy, 'Chinese Straight Baseline Declaration.'" Washington, D.C.: Department of Defense Representative for Ocean Policy Affairs, 21 May 1996.

Leifer, Michael. *China in Southeast Asia: Interdependence and Accommodation.* CAPS Paper No. 14. Taipei: Chinese Academy of Policy Studies, 1997.

———. "Chinese Economic Reform and Defense Policy: The South China Sea Connection." Paper presented at the International Institute of Strategic Studies–CAPS Conference, Hong Kong, July 1994.

———. "Chinese Economic Reform and Security Policy: The South China Sea Connection." *Survival* 37, no. 2 (Summer 1995): 44–59.

Lelyveld, Michael. "Iran: Oil Deal With China May Have Hit a Snag." Radio Free Europe/Radio Liberty, 22 June 2000. In *Asia Times*. Internet: www.atimes.com/c-asia/c-asis.htm.

Lennox, Duncan, ed. *Jane's Strategic Weapon Systems*. JSWS-Issue 22. Coulsdon, Surrey: Jane's Information Group, 1999.

Levathes, Louise. *When China Ruled the Seas: The Treasure Fleet of the Dragon Throne, 1405–1413*. New York: Oxford University Press, 1994.

Lewis, John W., Hua Di, and Xue Litai. "Beijing's Defense Establishment." *International Security* 15, no. 4 (Spring 1991): 87–109.

Lewis, John W., and Xue Litai. *China Builds the Bomb*. Stanford, Calif.: Stanford University Press, 1988.

———. "China's Search for a Modern Air Force." *International Security* 24, no. 1 (Summer 1999): 64–94.

———. *China's Strategic Seapower: The Politics of Force Modernization in the Nuclear Age*. Stanford, Calif.: Stanford University Press, 1994.

Li, Jun-ting, and Yang Jin-he, eds. *Overview of the Chinese Armed Forces*. Beijing: People's Publishing Agency, 1989.

Li, Nan. "Organizational Changes in the PLA, 1985–1997." *China Quarterly* 158 (June 1999): 314–49.

———. "The PLA's Evolving Warfighting Doctrine, Strategy and Tactics, 1985–95: A Chinese Perspective." *China Quarterly* 146 (June 1997): 443–63.

Li, Xiaobing. "PLA Attacks and Amphibious Operations during the Taiwan Straits Crises of 1954–1958." Paper presented at the CNA Conference on the PLA's Operational History, Alexandria, Va., June 1999.

Lin, Cheng-yi. "Taiwan's South China Sea Policy." *Asian Survey* 37 (April 1997): 323–39.

Lo, Jung-pang. "The Emergence of China as a Sea Power During the Late Sung and Early Yuan Periods." *Far Eastern Quarterly* 14, no. 4 (August 1955): 489–503.

Lu, Ning. *The Dynamics of Foreign-Policy Decisionmaking in China*. Boulder, Colo.: Westview Press, 1997.

"Lufeng 22-1." BP Amoco announcement, 18 October 1999. Internet: www.offshore-technology.com/projects/lufeng/index.

"Luhai Pictures." *Jane's Defence Weekly* 31, no. 5 (1 February 1999): 16. Internet: www.taiwansecurity.org/News/Janes-990201.htm.

MacFarquhar, Roderick. *Origins of the Cultural Revolution*, vol. 2. New York: Columbia University Press, 1983.

Marder, Arthur M. *From the Dreadnought to Scapa Flow: The Royal Navy in the Fisher Era*. Vol. 1, *The Road to War, 1904–1914*. London: Oxford University Press, 1961.

Marolda, Edward J. "The U.S. Navy and the Chinese Civil War, 1945–1952." Ph.D. diss., George Washington University, 1990.

McDevitt, Michael A. "The PLA Navy: Past, Present, and Future Prospects." *Comments on the Conference on the PLA Navy.* Alexandria, Va.: CNA, May 2000.

McGruther, Kenneth R. *The Evolving Soviet Navy.* Newport, R.I.: Naval War College Press, 1978.

McLean, John. "Philippines Protests at Vietnam Spratly 'Attack.'" BBC Online Network, 28 October 1999. Internet: http://news.bbc.co.uk/hi/english/world/asia-pacific/newsic_491000/491603.stm.

McVadon, Eric. "PRC Exercises, Doctrine and Tactics Toward Taiwan: The Naval Dimension." In *Crisis in the Taiwan Strait,* ed. James R. Lilley and Chuck Downes, 249–78. Washington, D.C.: National Defense University Press, AEI, 1997.

———. "Systems Integration in China's People's Liberation Army." In *China's Military Faces the Future,* ed. James R. Lilley and David Shambaugh. Washington, D.C.: AEI and M. E. Sharpe, 1999.

Moore, John E., ed. *Jane's Fighting Ships: 1976–1977.* New York: Franklin Watts, 1977.

———. *Jane's Fighting Ships: 1978–1979.* New York: Franklin Watts, 1978.

———. *Jane's Fighting Ships: 1980–1981.* London: Jane's Publishing, 1980.

———. *Jane's Fighting Ships, 1990–1991.* Coulsdon, Surrey: Jane's Information Group, 1991.

Morison, Samuel Loring. "Indian Navy Blue Water Capability Grows as Russia's Diminishes." *Navy News and Undersea Technology,* 8 May 2000, 4.

Muller, David G., Jr. *China's Emergence as a Maritime Power.* Boulder, Colo.: Westview Press, 1983.

Mulvenon, James C. *Professionalization of the Senior Chinese Officer Corps: Trends and Implications.* Santa Monica, Calif.: RAND, 1997.

Mulvenon, James C., and Richard H. Yang. *The People's Liberation Army in the Information Age.* Santa Monica, Calif.: RAND, 1999.

Needham, Joseph. *Science and Civilization in China,* vols. 1–6. Cambridge: University Press, 1954–86.

"New Oil Well Producing in South China Sea." *Asia Pulse,* 15 January 1999.

"New PLAN to Train, Purchase Vessel Mix." *Jane's Defence Weekly* 30, no. 25 (16 December 1998): 25–26.

Noer, John H., with David Gregory. *Chokepoints: Maritime Economic Concerns in Southeast Asia.* Washington, D.C.: National Defense University Press in cooperation with the Center for Naval Analysis, 1996.

Nolt, James H. *The China-Taiwan Military Balance.* New York: Project on Defense Alternatives, 2000.

O'Donnell, John R. "An Analysis of Major Developmental Influences on the People's Liberation Army-Navy and Their Implication for the Future." Master's thesis, U.S. Army Command and General Staff College, Ft. Leavenworth, Kans., 1995.

"Oil Exploration in the South China Sea: What Is the International Business Interest in the Region?" U.S. Pacific Command Virtual Information Center, 24 June 1999. Internet: www.vic.pacom.mil.

Opal-Rome, Barbara. "China Moves Roil Region." *Defense News,* 8 February 1999, 1.

Paltiel, Jeremy T. "PLA Allegiance on Parade: Civil-Military Relations in Transition." *China Quarterly* 143 (September 1995): 784–800.

Parker, Richard. "China's Overseas Bases." U.S. Pacific Command Virtual Information Center, 2 February 2000. Internet: www.vic.pacom.mil.

———. "Conflicting Territorial Claims in the South China Sea: The Spratly Islands Dispute." U.S. Pacific Command Virtual Information Center, 21 January 2000. Internet: www.vic.pacom.mil.

———. "Scarborough Shoal: The Next Mischief Reef?" U.S. Pacific Command Virtual Information Center, 28 March 2000. Internet: www.vic.pacom.mil.

Perlez, Jane. "Israel Drops Plan to Sell Air Radar to China Military." *New York Times,* 13 July 2000.

Perry, Tony. "Hunting Beyond Red October." *Los Angeles Times,* 21 October 1997, pp. 1, 18.

"Philippine Navy Fires Warning Shots." Associated Press News, 4 February 2000. Internet: www.asia.dailynews.yahoo.com/headlines/regional/philippines.htm.

Pillsbury, Michael, ed. *Chinese Views of Future Warfare.* Washington, D.C.: National Defense University Press, 1997.

"Profile-China's Oil Industry: August 1999." *Asia Pulse,* 12 August 1999. Internet: www.first search.oclc.org/FETCH.

Raudzens, George. "Military Revolution or Maritime Evolution? Military Superiorities or Transportation Advantages as Main Causes of European Colonial Conquests to 1788." *Journal of Military History* 63, no. 3 (July 1999): 631–42.

Ray-Choudhury, Rahul. "Trends in Naval Power in South Asia and the Indian Ocean During the Past Year." *SAPRA India Monthly Bulletin,* January 1996. Internet: www.subcontinent.com/sapra/96jan/si019603.

"Reviving Russia's Navy." *Strategic Comments* 6 (July 2000): 1, 2. London: International Institute of Strategic Studies.

Rosenberg, David Alan. "Process: The Realities of Formulating Modern Naval Strategy." In *Mahan Is Not Enough: The Proceedings of a Conference on the Works of Sir Julian Corbett and Admiral Sir Herbert Richmond,* ed. James Goldrick and John B. Hattendorf. Newport, R.I.: Naval War College Press, 1993.

Roskill, S. W. *The Strategy of Seapower: Its Development and Application.* Westport, Conn.: Greenwood Press, 1962.

Sae-Liu, Robert. "Chinese Expand Aerial Refueling Capability to Navy." *Jane's Defence Weekly* 33, no. 25 (21 June 2000): 14.

Saradzhyan, Simon. "China to Double Its Order of Russian-Made Destroyers." *Defense News* 15 (27 March 2000): 17.

Schmetzer, Uli. "Shadow of China Has Philippines Looking to U.S. Military." *San Diego Union-Tribune,* 11 November 1998, p. A-15.

Schram, Stuart. *The Political Thought of Mao Tse-tung.* Rev. ed. New York: Praeger, 1969.

Schuster, Carl O. "Special Report: The PRC's Growing Influence in the South Pacific." U.S. Pacific Command Virtual Information Center, 21 June 2000. Internet: www.vic.pacom.mil.

Scobell, Andrew. "Show of Force: Chinese Soldiers, Statesmen, and the 1995–1996 Taiwan Strait Crisis." *Political Science Quarterly* 115, no. 2 (Summer 2000): 227–46.

Scott, Richard. "Boosting the Staying Power of the Non-Nuclear Submarine." *Jane's International Defence Review* 32, no. 11 (November 1999): 41–50.

Scully, R. Tucker. (Deputy Assistant Secretary of State for Oceans, Fisheries, and Space.) "International Perspectives Upon Fisheries Policy." Remarks at the Fifth North Pacific Rim Fisheries Conference, Anchorage, Alaska, 1 December 1999.

Sengupta, Prasun K. "RMN Receives First FS-2000 Frigate." *Asian Defence Journal,* November 1999, 23.

Shambaugh, David. "China's Commander-in-Chief: Jiang Zemin and the PLA." In *Chinese Military Modernization,* ed. C. Dennison Lane, 209–45. New York: Kegan Paul International, Washington, D.C.: AEI Press, 1996.

———. "China's Defense Industries: Indigenous and Foreign Procurement." In *The Chinese Defense Establishment: Continuity and Change in the 1980s,* ed. Paul H. B. Godwin, 43–88. Boulder, Colo.: Westview Press, 1983.

———. "China's Military Views the World: Ambivalent Security." *International Security* 24, no. 3 (Winter 1999): 52–79.

———. "China's Post-Deng Military Leadership." In *China's Military Faces the Future,* ed. James R. Lilley and David Shambaugh, 11–38. Washington, D.C.: AEI/M. E. Sharpe, 1999.

———. "Commentary on Civil-Military Relations in China: The Search for New Paradigms." Paper presented at the CAPS/RAND Conference on the PLA, Washington, D.C., July 1999.

Sharpe, Richard, ed. *Jane's Warships of the World: 1976–77.* London: Jane's Publishing Group, 1977.

———. *Jane's Warships of the World: 1989–90.* London: Jane's Publishing Group, 1990.

———. *Jane's Fighting Ships: 1995–1996.* London: Butler and Tanner, 1996.

———. *Jane's Fighting Ships: 1999–2000.* Coulsdon, Surrey: Jane's Information Group, 1999.

———. *Jane's Fighting Ships: 2000–2001.* Coulsdon, Surrey: Jane's Information Group, 2000.

Shichor, Yitzhak. "Demobilization: The Dialectics of PLA Troop Reduction." *China Quarterly* 146 (June 1996): 336–59.

Shlapak, David A., David T. Orletsky, and Barry A. Wilson, *Dire Strait? Aspects of the China-Taiwan Confrontation and Options for U.S. Policy.* Santa Monica, Calif.: RAND, 2000.

Simpson, B. Mitchell, III. *Essays on Maritime Strategy.* Newport, R.I.: U.S. Naval War College Press, 1972.

Singh, Swaran. "Continuity and Change in China's Maritime Strategy." Institute for Defence Strategy and Analysis (Delhi), n.d.

Smil, Vaclez. "China's Energy and Resource Uses: Continuity and Change." *China Quarterly* 156 (December 1998): 935–51.

Smith, Craig S. "New Chinese Guided-Missile Ship Heightens Tension." *New York Times,* 9 February 2000, sec. A.

"South China Sea Region." Energy Information Administration of the U.S. Department of Energy, August 1998. Internet: www.eia.doe.gov/emeu/cabs/schina.htm.

Spence, Jonathan D. *The Search for Modern China.* New York: W. W. Norton, 1990.

State Department. *Public Papers of the Presidents of the United States: Harry S Truman, 1950.* Washington, D.C.: Government Printing Office, 1965.

Steinberg, Jonathan. *Yesterday's Deterrent: Tirpitz and the Birth of the German Battle Fleet.* London: Macmillan, 1965.

Stockholm International Peace Research Institute (SIPRI). *Armaments, Disarmament and International Security.* Oxford: Oxford University Press, 1998.

Stokes, Mark A. *China's Strategic Modernization: Implications for the United States.* Carlisle, Pa.: U.S. Army War College, Strategic Studies Institute, 1999.

Storey, Ian James. "Creeping Assertiveness: China, the Philippines and the South China Sea Dispute." *Contemporary Southeast Asia* 21, no. 1 (April 1999): 95–118.

"Stratfor's Global Intelligence Update." 14 April 1999, 2.

Studeman, Michael. "Calculating China's Advances in the South China Sea: Identifying the Triggers of 'Expansionism.'" *Naval War College Review* 51, no. 2 (Spring 1998): 68–90. Internet: www.usnwc.edu/nwc/art5-sp8.htm.

Sumida, Jon Tetsuro. *Inventing Grand Strategy and Teaching Command: The Classic Works of Alfred Thayer Mahan Reconsidered.* Baltimore: Johns Hopkins Press, 1997.

Swaine, Michael D. "Chinese Military Modernization and Asia-Pacific Security." Paper presented at the Aspen Institute's Second Conference on U.S.-China Relations, Washington, D.C., March 1999.

———. *Military and Political Succession in China.* Santa Monica, Calif.: RAND, 1992.

————. *The Role of the Chinese Military in National Security Policymaking.* Rev. ed. Santa Monica, Calif.: RAND, 1998.

Swanson, Bruce. *The Eighth Voyage of the Dragon: A History of China's Quest for Seapower.* Annapolis: Naval Institute Press, 1982.

Till, Geoffrey. "Maritime Strategy in the Twenty-First Century." In *Seapower: Theory and Practice*, ed. Geoffrey Till, 176–99. Portland, Oreg.: Frank Cass, 1994.

Torda, Thomas J. "Struggle for the Taiwan Strait: A 50th-Anniversary Perspective on the First Communist-Nationalist Battles for China's Offshore Islands and Their Significance for the Taiwan Strait Crises." Unpublished manuscript, 1999.

Trevethan, Sidney. "PLA Navy Air Force Order of Battle." Federation of American Scientists web site, 1999. Internet: www.fas.org/nuke/huide/china/agency/plan-af-orbat-st.htm.

Troush, Sergei. "China's Changing Oil Strategy and its Foreign Policy Implications." Washington, D.C.: Brookings Institution, Center for Northeast Asian Policy Studies Working Paper, Fall 1999.

Twitchett, Denis, and John K. Fairbank, eds. *The Cambridge History of China.* Vol. 14, *The People's Republic, Part K: The Emergence of Revolutionary China, 1949–1965.* Cambridge: Cambridge University Press, 1987.

Tyler, William Ferdinand. *Pulling Strings in China.* London: Constable, 1929.

Umbach, Frank. "Financial Crisis Slows but Fails to Halt East Asian Arms Race-Part Two." *Jane's Intelligence Review* 10, no. 9 (September 1998): 34–37.

United Nations. United Nations Convention on the Law of the Sea (UNCLOS). 1982. Internet: www.un.org/Depts/los/stat2los.txt.

U.S. Geodetic Survey. Report. USCINCPAC memo, 15 September 1999.

U.S. Navy Staff. *Undersea Warfare.* Washington, D.C.: U.S. Navy, 1999.

Valencia, Mark J. *China and the South China Sea Disputes.* Adelphi Paper 228. London: Institute for International Strategic Studies, 1995.

————. "Energy and Insecurity in Asia." *Survival* 39, no. 3 (Autumn 1997): 85–106.

————. *A Maritime Regime for North-East Asia.* New York: Oxford University Press, 1996.

Valencia, Mark J., and Jon M. Van Dyke. "Vietnam's National Interests and the Law of the Sea." *Ocean Development and International Law* 25, no. 2 (June 1994): 217–50.

Valencia, Mark J., Jon M. Van Dyke, and Noel A. Ludwig. *Sharing the Resources of the South China Sea.* Boston: Martinus Nijhoff Publishers, 1997.

Vertzberber, Yaacov Y. I. *China's Southwestern Strategy: Encirclement and Counterencirclement.* New York: Praeger, 1987.

Wain, Barry. "China, ASEAN Meeting Demonstrates Deep Divisions." *Asian Wall Street Journal,* 10 March 2000.

————. "Hanoi and Beijing Take a Step Closer." *Asian Wall Street Journal,* 12 May 2000.

"Warships' Sale to China." *Far Eastern Economic Review* 163 (30 December 1999): 6.

Watson, Bruce W. "The Evolution of Soviet Naval Strategy." In *The Future of the Soviet Navy: An Assessment to the Year 2000,* ed. Bruce W. Watson and Peter M. Dunn, 113–29. Boulder, Colo.: Westview Press, 1986.

Whiting, Allen S. "ASEAN Eyes China: The Security Dimension." *Asian Survey* 37, no. 4 (April 1997): 299–322.

Whitson, William H., with Huang Chen-hsia. *The Chinese High Command: A History of Communist Military Politics, 1927–71.* New York: Praeger, 1973.

Wilhelm, Alfred D., Jr. *China and Security in the Asian Pacific Region Through 2010.* CNA Research Memorandum 95-226. Alexandria, Va.: Center for Naval Analysis, 1996.

Winnefeld, James A., with Dana A. Johnson. *Joint Air Operations: Pursuit of Unity in Command and Control, 1941–1991.* Santa Monica, Calif.: RAND, 1993.

Woodward, E. L. *Great Britain and the German Navy.* Oxford: Clarendon Press, 1935.

The World Factbook, 1999. Washington, D.C.: Central Intelligence Agency. Internet: www.odci.gov/cia/publications/factbook/pag.htm.

Worldwide Submarine Challenges, 1996. Washington, D.C.: Office of the Chief of Naval Operations, 1996.

Wortzel, Larry M. "The Beiping-Tianjin Campaign of 1948–49: The Strategic and Operational Thinking of the People's Liberation Army." Paper prepared for the U.S. Army War College's Strategic Studies Institute, Carlisle, Pa., n.d.

Wright, Mary Clabaugh. *The Last Stand of Chinese Conservatism: The T'ung-chih Restoration, 1862–1874.* Stanford, Calif.: Stanford University Press, 1957.

Wright, Richard N. J. *The Chinese Steam Navy, 1862–1945.* Annapolis: Naval Institute Press. Forthcoming.

Wylie, Rear Adm. J. C., USN (Ret.). *Military Strategy.* 1967. Reprint, Westport, Conn.: Greenwood Press, 1980.

Yang, Andrew Nien-Dzu. "From a Navy in Blue Towards a Blue Water Navy: Shaping PLA Navy Officer Corps (1950–1999)." Paper prepared for the Center for Naval Analysis Conference on "The PLA Navy: Past, Present and Future Prospects," Washington, D.C., April 2000.

Yergin, Daniel, Dennis Eklof, and Jefferson Edwards. "Fueling Asia's Recovery." *Foreign Affairs* 77, no. 2 (March–April 1998): 34–50.

You, Ji. "The Revolution in Military Affairs and the Evolution of China's Strategic Thinking." *Contemporary Southeast Asia* 21, no. 3 (December 1999): 344–64.

Young, Philip. *Chinese Military Digest,* 1999. Internet: www.gsprint.com/cmd/cmd.htm.

Yu, Hui. "Remarks on China's Ratification of the 1982 UN Convention on the Law of the Sea." In *Asian Yearbook of International Law,* vol. 5, ed. Ko Swan Sik, 211–30. Amsterdam: Kluwer Law International, 1997.

Yuan, Jing-dong. "China's Defense Modernization: Implications for Asia-Pacific Security." *Contemporary Southeast Asia* 17, no. 1 (June 1995): 67–84.

Yung, Christopher D. "People's War at Sea: Chinese Naval Power in the Twenty-First Century." CNA Research Memorandum 95-214. Alexandria, Va.: Center for Naval Analysis, March 1996.

Zaloga, Steven J. "Russia's *Moskit* Anti-Ship Missile." *Jane's Intelligence Review* 8, no. 4 (April 1996): 155–58.

Zhan, Jun. "China Goes to the Blue Waters: The Navy, Seapower Mentality and the South China Sea." *Journal of Strategic Studies* 17, no. 3 (September 1994): 180–208.

Zhang, Shu Guang. *Mao's Military Romanticism: China and the Korean War, 1950–1953.* Lawrence: University Press of Kansas, 1995.

Zhang, Yihong [Andrei Pinkov]. "China Enhances the Production of the Rocket Propelled Mines." *Kanwa News No. 520,* 20 May 1999. Internet: www.kanwa.com.

———. "Sino-Russian Arm Sale Is Reaching the Second Stage in 2000." *Kanwa News No. 112,* 12 January 1999. Internet: www.kanwa.com.

"Zhanjiang Military Sub District, Guangdong Military District, Conducts a Military-Civilian Exercise." Declassified military intelligence report. In "Force Protection Report (Camp Zama, Japan: U.S. Army Asian Studies Detachment of the 500th MI Group Report #ASD-00-0100)," 2 June 2000, 2. Internet: www.taungpao.com.hk.

Other Sources

Note: Information obtained from officers in the U.S., Chinese, and Taiwan armed forces is cited without attribution.

Foreign Broadcast Information Service (FBIS).

Prados, John. Discussion with author about unpublished manuscript on the U.S. logistics effort in South Vietnam. 1992.

U.S. Navy Meteorological Service officers. Interview with author. August 1999.

U.S., PLA, and Taiwan military officers. Interviews with author. 1994–2000.

U.S. scholars studying the PLA. Interviews with author.

Visits to PLA army and air force bases and schools; naval schools, bases, shipyards, and ships; and garrisons by author. 1994–2000.

Yoest, Gerard P. Director of International Affairs for the U.S. Coast Guard. Interview with author. June 2000.

INDEX

academies, military, 117–18, 121, 122
Academy of Sciences, 104
Aegis system, 143
Agenzia Generale Italina Petroli, 42
aircraft carriers, 108–9, 146–49, 152
air force, 99, 101–2, 106–9, 146–49, 181.
    See also People's Liberation Army–Air
    Force (PLAAF); People's Liberation
    Army–Navy Air Force (PLANAF)
air independent propulsion system (AIP),
    97
Alatas, Ali, 45
All-Army Propaganda and Cultural
    Information Network, 124
American Kirkland Oil Company, 43
Amoco, 42
amphibious force (PLAN), 80, 84, 103,
    129–30, 186
Amur-class submarines, 97
Antarctic, first Chinese expedition to, 34
antiair warfare defense systems, 99,
    101–2, 109
antisubmarine warfare systems, 99–102,
    110–12
Aquino, Corazon, 43
Arctic, Chinese expeditions to, 34
Ardasier Bank, 44
area-defense systems, 109
arms systems, 73; acquisitions, 17–18,
    69–70, 93–104, 183–87; air force,
    106–9; Chinese-built, 25, 27, 94–95,
    183–84; deficiencies, 23, 109–12;
    geographic distribution, 79–80, 90.
    See also missiles
Art of War (Sun), 140

Association of Southeast Asian Nations
    (ASEAN), 38, 44, 47–50. *See also* Code
    of Conduct, ASEAN
Australian navy, 153, 154
auxiliary forces, Chinese maritime, 86
Aviation Engineering College, 122

Baja, Lauro, 44
"Balikitan 2000," 43–44
ballistic missiles, 104–6, 146, 157, 163
Beibu Bay, 41
Beiyang Fleet, 5, 6
blue water (open sea), 10, 63, 143,
    172–73, 177, 188–89. *See also* offshore
    defense
Bohai's (Bo Sea) Takang field, 55, 56, 58
boot camp (PLAN), 116
brown water (littoral areas to 100 mile
    offshore), 10, 63, 149, 163. *See also*
    coastal defense
Brunei, 39, 45
B-6 aircraft, 84, 107
Burma, 171, 188

Camago field, 42
Cao Guangchuan, 109
captains (PLAN), 74–75, 122
Central Military Commission (CMC), 69,
    120–21, 122–23
Chakri Naruebet (aircraft carrier), 152
Chen Bingde, 134
Chen Geng, 57–58
Cheng Mingshang, 169
Chiang Kai-shek, 21
Chi Haotian, 134, 187

China National Offshore Oil Corporation (CNOOC), 56, 58
China National Petrochemical Corporation (Sinopec), 55
China National Petroleum Corporation (CNPC), 55, 61
China Salvage Company, 87
China Shipbuilding Corporation (CSC), 183–84
Chinese Communist Party (CCP), 7, 10, 72, 74–75, 86, 134–36. *See also* political ideology
Chinese Naval Officer's Manual, 138–39
civilian employees of PLAN, 118
coal, 54, 62
coastal defense, 87, 161, 163–64, 166, 178, 188–89. *See also* brown water
Coastal Regional Defense Forces, 87
coast guard, 86–87
Cockchafer (HMS), 7
Code of Conduct, ASEAN, 48–50
combat readiness, 142
combined arms exercises, 129–30
"Combined Campaigns" Program, 141–42
commanders (PLAN), 68–73
"Command of the Sea," 159, 161
Compagnie Generale de Geophysique, 42
Conoco, 42
contiguous zone (CZ), 31, 32, 33
continental shelf (CS), 31–32, 45, 57
Crestone, 41–42
Crotale system, 100, 101, 109
cruise missiles, 105, 145

Dachen Islands, 21
Dajiang-class ships, 107
Dalian, naval academy at, 122
Dalian Naval Base, 82
Dauphin (Z-9A) helicopters, 100, 101, 102, 108
Dayun-class replenishment ships, 107
Democratic Progressive Party (DDP), 155
Deng Xiaoping, 10, 24, 26–29, 46, 95, 119–20, 164
Desert Storm, 72, 142, 143–44, 145
Diaoyu (Senkaku) Islands, 28, 30, 34, 51–53, 88
doctrinal development, 87–91, 112, 130, 138–58, 182–83
Dong Feng-31 (DF-31) missiles, 106
Dongsha, 34

Dongshan Island, 129
Dulles, John Foster, 21
Duncan Reef, 40, 84

East China Military Command, 16
East China People's Navy, 17
East China Sea, 7–8, 51–53, 55–56, 58–59, 63–65, 149, 166, 172
East Sea Fleet, 21, 71, 76, 80, 88–90, 122, 129, 170
economy, Chinese, 24–26, 37–40, 54–66, 169, 172, 180–89
education of personnel, 70–71, 117, 119–28, 133–37. *See also* training
"863 Program," 66
Eisenhower, Dwight, 19
energy sources. *See* petroleum
engineers, naval, 122
engines, 97, 100, 101, 180
enlisted personnel, 116, 118, 124
Equipment Department (PLAN), 73, 77–79
"Essentials for Reform and Development of Military Universities and Schools" (CMC), 120–21
Estrada, José, 44
exclusive economic zone (EEZ), 31, 32, 33
Exocet missiles, 106, 150, 152

FBC-1 (strike aircraft), 107
Fiery Cross Reef, 40, 84
First Island Chain, 166, 175–76, 189
Fisher, Sir John, 177
fisheries, 27, 38, 51, 64–65
fixed-wing aircraft, 108
"floating schools," 116
flotillas, 79–80, 177–78
foreign relations, 27, 59, 69, 72, 95, 111, 167, 181–82, 188
France, 5, 39, 40, 107–8
frigates, 95
Frontier Guard Department, 87
Fuqing-class ships, 93, 104
Fu Quanyou, 120, 126

"Gang of Four," 23, 24
gas, natural, 54–60
General Office of Headquarters Department (PLAN), 75

General Staff Department (GSD), 75–76, 81, 127

geographic maritime strategies, 9–10, 79–80, 165–72

Gorshkov, Sergei, 164, 168, 169

Gray, Colin, 160–61

Great Britain, 7

Great Leap Forward, 21, 179

Great Proletarian Cultural Revolution (GPCR), 23–24, 119, 164–65

green water (from 100 miles offshore to next land formation), 10, 63, 149

Guangdong Fleet, 5

Guangdong Province, 39

Guangzhou military region, 83, 84, 117, 122, 127

guerrilla warfare, 146

Gulf of Tonkin, 37, 41

Gulf War. *See* Desert Storm

Hainan, 19

Hainan-class gunboats, 102, 171

Hai Ying-2 (HY-2) (surface-to-surface missile), 99–100, 102

Han-class submarines, 79, 98, 106

Hang Qi-61 (HQ-61) (antiair warfare system), 101

Hangzhou (guided-missile destroyer), 80

Harbin (guided-missile destroyer), 100

Harpoon missiles, 150, 151, 152

Headquarters Department (PLAN), 73, 75–76

helicopters, 99, 100, 101, 107–8

Hong Kong, 56, 130

Houjian-class missile patrol boats, 25, 93, 102, 106

Houxin-class missile patrol boats, 93, 102, 106, 171

HQ-7 point-defense system, 109

Hua Guofeng, 24

Huangyan Island, 43, 44

Huludao, naval academy at, 122

Hungnam port, 20

Hydrographic Department, 104

Imperial Commissioner's Office for the Control and Organization of the Coastal Areas, 2

Inchon, amphibious landing at, 20

India, 22, 153, 171

Indian Ocean Rim Association for Regional Cooperation (IORARC), 35

Indian Ocean sea lines of communication (SLOCs), 63–64, 171–72

Indonesia, 37–38, 39, 45, 151, 154

Indonesian Straits, 64

information warfare (IW), 92, 128, 174

Intelligence Department, 75

island, definition of, 32, 36

island chains, 165–66

Israeli air control platforms, 148

Itu Aba, 36

Japan: defeat of Beiyang Fleet, 6; fisheries treaty with China, 65; influence on Chinese revolution, 7; modernization of navy, 90; occupation of Paracel Islands, 39; territorial disputes, 51–53; threat to China, 8, 11–12, 24, 149–50, 170, 175–76

Japan Maritime Self-Defense Force (JMSDF), 52, 149, 154, 174

Jianghu-class guided-missile frigates, 25, 80, 93, 101–2, 106, 108

Jiang Qing, 23

Jiangwei-class guided-missile frigates, 80, 93, 101, 106, 108, 109

Jiang Zemin: downsizing of PLAN, 67; on maritime rights, 169–70; on naval development, 9–11; on personnel training, 113–15, 120, 121, 130; and PLAN commander, 72; on political ideology, 134; and South China Sea disputes, 44

joint combat operations, 141

joint hat (joint warfare coordinator), 72

joint training exercises of PLAN fleets, 129–30

Ju Lang-1 (JL-1) missiles, 27, 104, 106

Ju Lang-2 (JL-2) missiles, 106, 146

Ka-28 helicopters, 99, 101

Khrushchev, Nikita, 22

Kiev (aircraft carrier), 108

Kilo-class submarines, 27, 69, 79–80, 97

Komar-class patrol boats, 102

Korea, 6, 51, 150, 154, 174. *See also* South Korea

Korean War, 17, 20, 119, 179
Kosovo, campaign in, 142, 145
Kuomintang (KMT), 10, 16–17, 21, 162, 163

Lada-class submarines, 97
landing-ships-mechanized (LSMs), 80, 103
landing-ships-tanks (LSTs), 80, 103
La Perouse (Soya) Strait, 8
"Law on the Territorial Sea and the Contiguous Zone" (1992), 34, 39, 144–45, 170–71
Lee Teng-hui, 47
Liangxiang airfield, 82
Li Hongzhang, 5
Lile Tan, 43
Lin Biao, 22
Lincoln Reef, 40, 84
Liugondao Naval Base, 82
Liu Huaqing, 17, 26, 46, 72, 165–72, 175–76
Liyu Tan, 43
LM-2500 engines, 100, 101, 180
Logistics Academy, 122
Logistics Department (PLAN), 73, 77
logistics force, 71–72, 186
Lombok Strait, 8, 64
Louisa Reef, 39, 45
Luda-class guided-missile destroyers, 25, 80, 93, 95, 99–100, 106, 108, 109
Lufeng 22-1 oil field, 60
Luhai-class guided-missile destroyers, 80, 84, 93, 100–101, 106, 109, 143
Luhu-class guided-missile destroyers, 80, 93, 100, 106, 108, 109, 110
Lushun Naval Base, 82
Luzon Strait, 8

Makassar Strait, 64
Macclesfield Bank, 84
Malacca Strait, 8, 64, 177, 188
Malampaya field, 42
Malaysia, 36–39, 45, 151, 154
Mao Zedong, 10, 17–24, 162–63, 179
Marine Corps, Chinese, 25, 26, 84, 113, 114–15, 139, 140, 186
Marine Environmental Protection Law of the PRC, 86–87
Maritime Safety Administration (MSA), 65, 86, 87

Mariveles Reef, 44
Matsu, capture of, 21
Meiji Jiao. *See* Mischief Reef
Melbourne (aircraft carrier), 108
M-11 missiles, 157
merchant ships, 103, 104
midair refueling, 78–79, 147
Middle Eastern countries, 61–62
Military Affairs Department, 76
Military Assistants Department, 75
Military Environmental Protection Department, 87
military-industrial complex, 24–25, 26, 182, 183, 186
military regions (MRs), 81
Military Strategic Studies Department, 75
mine warfare (MIW), 80, 102–3, 156–57
Ming-class submarines, 80, 97
Ming Dynasty (1368–1644), 3
Ministry of Communications, 104
Minsk (aircraft carrier), 108
Mischief Reef, 40, 43, 44, 50–51
missiles, 23, 95, 98–101, 104–6, 145–46, 157, 163
Mi Zhenyu, 159
M-9 missiles, 157
Moskit missiles, 98–99
multiship task group deployment, 167

Nanchang (replenishment-at-sea ship), 84
Nanjing military region, 83, 127
Nansha. *See* Spratly (Nansha) Islands
Nanyang Fleet, 5
Nanyun-class ships, 104, 107
National Defense Law of 1997, 134
National Defense University, 120, 122, 135
national policy on energy resources, 57–58
national security, 3–4, 8–11, 25, 28, 30, 172–75, 178, 186–89
Natuna Islands, 37, 38, 39, 45
Naval Coastal Defense System, 87
Naval Command School, 122
Naval Engineering University, 70, 122, 123
Naval Political School, 122
Naval Research College, 166
Naval Technical Aviation School, 122

Navigation Engineering College, 122
navy, history of, 2–15. *See also* People's
    Liberation Army–Navy (PLAN)
Navy Electronics Engineering Academy,
    70, 123
Navy Engineering Academy, 70, 123
Navy Equipment Verification Center, 94
Navy Medical Academy, 122
Navy Military Academy, 122
Navy Military Training Working
    Conference, 132
Navy's First Aviation School, 21
Navy Weapons Assessment Research
    Center, 93, 94
network-centric approach to naval
    operations, 92, 128, 174
"New Technology Agreement" (1959), 94
New Zealand Navy, 153
"998 Plan," 108
Ningbo Naval Base, 83
noncommissioned officers (NCOs), 118,
    119
North Sea Fleet, 21, 80–82, 85–86,
    88–90, 129, 130, 132, 170
nuclear deterrent force, 25, 104–6, 165
nuclear energy sources, 62
nuclear weapons, 20–21, 23, 27

officers (PLAN), 70–71, 74, 117–18, 119,
    121–23
offshore defense, 161, 166, 173. *See also*
    blue water
oil. *See* petroleum
Okean exercises, 24, 147
operations, doctrinal, 112, 130, 138–58,
    182–83
Operations Department of The General
    Office, 75
Ople, Blas, 43–44
Osa-class patrol boats, 102
Osumi Passage, 8

Paracel (Xisha) Islands: air base on,
    45–46; Chinese claim under 1992 law,
    34; description, 36–37; energy sources
    near, 59, 60; history of territorial
    claims, 25, 28, 39–41; and South Sea
    Fleet, 84
Pearl River Mouth Basin, 59–60
Peng Dehuai, 20
Penghu, Chinese claim of, 34

People's Armed Police (PAP), 67
People's Liberation Army (PLA): budget,
    95, 148; capture of Dachen Islands,
    21; "Combined Campaigns" program,
    141–42; downsizing, 67–68, 115;
    impediments to modernization,
    24–25; occupation of Hainan, 19; and
    political ideology, 133–34
People's Liberation Army–Air Force
    (PLAAF), 78, 81, 85–86, 103, 106–7,
    114, 148, 186
People's Liberation Army–Navy (PLAN):
    command relationships, 81–85;
    downsizing, 67–68, 114;
    establishment, 2, 10–11, 17; future,
    173–78, 183–89; geographic areas of
    responsibility, 78; history and
    development, 16–29; impediments to
    modernization of, 24–25, 109–12, 182,
    183–85; missions, 138–39; structure
    and organization, 67–91, 118–19. *See
    also* navy, history of;
    professionalization of PLAN;
    recruiting for PLAN
People's Liberation Army–Navy Air Force
    (PLANAF), 21, 73, 77–79, 82–86,
    106–7, 146–48, 186
People's Republic of China (PRC), 10–11
People's War, 20, 22–23, 141, 159, 163–64.
    See also political ideology
personnel, 113–37; education, 119–24;
    future, 187; and modern operational
    doctrine, 145–46; structure and
    organization, 67–91; training, 124–33
petroleum: in East China Sea, 51–52;
    imports and exports, 60–65, 172, 181;
    offshore supply, 27, 37–39, 41–43,
    54–60, 180
petty officers (PLAN), 118–19
Philippine Oil Development Company, 42
Philippines, 36, 39, 42–44, 151, 152–53
Phu Lam. *See* Woody Island
Plan of Action for the 21st Century, 152
point defense systems, 109
political commissars (PLAN), 73–74, 76,
    122, 135–36
Political Department (PLAN), 73, 76–77
political ideology, 121–22, 133–37. *See
    also* People's War
Political-Military Affairs Department, 75
Pratas Reef group, 36

professionalization of PLAN, 133–37
Project-094 boat, 146
"purple" hat (joint warfare coordinator), 72
Putin, Vladimir, 182
Qian Qichen, 47, 49–50
Qingdao, naval academy at, 122
Qingdao (guided-missile destroyer), 100
Qingdao Naval Base, 82
Qing (Manchu) Dynasty (1644–1912), 4–5, 28
Qiongsha-class ships, 80, 84, 104
Quemoy, capture of, 21

Ramos, Fidel, 43
rear admirals (PLAN), 74, 122
recruiting for PLAN, 115–18
Reed Bank, 43
reefs occupied by PLAN, 40
refueling, midair, 78–79, 147
replenishment-at-sea ships, 84, 103–4
Republic of Korea Navy (ROKN), 150, 154, 174
research and development, PLAN, 70, 104, 143
reserve officer training corps (ROTC), 70, 117, 120
revolution in military affairs (RMA), 70, 127, 141, 145, 146, 154
RIMPAC 98 training exercises, 136–37
Romeo-class submarines, 96–97
Russia. *See* Soviet Union

Salen Energy, 42
Scarborough Shoals, 43, 44
sea and air rescue exercises (SAREX), 130
sea and air rescue (SAR), 24
"Sea Control," 160, 161, 167, 174
"Sea Denial," 160, 161, 167, 177
sea lines of communication (SLOCs):
    defense of, 63–66, 144, 149, 180–81;
    importance to China, 9, 38; Indian
    Ocean, 171–72; map, 35; Soviet threat
    to, 24
Sea of Japan, 7–8
Second Island Chain, 166–67
Senkaku Islands. *See* Diaoyu (Senkaku) Islands
Shang-You-1A (SY-1A) missiles, 106
Shenzhen (guided-missile destroyer), 80,

100–101
Shichang (training ship), 108, 126
Shihab, Alwi, 45
shipbuilding, 25, 27, 83, 94–95, 97, 183–84
Ship Construction, Department of, 94
shipping, 63–64. *See also* sea lines of communication (SLOCs)
Shi Yunsheng, 68–73, 89, 112, 118, 123, 145, 173
Singapore Navy, 151, 154
Sino-Korean Sea Safety Cooperation Meeting, 65
Sino-Vietnamese Working Group, 41
Siping (guided-missile frigate), 102
sonar systems, 110
Song-class submarines, 69, 79–80, 93, 97
Song Dynasty (A.D. 960–1279), 2
South China Sea, 8; economic interests
    in, 37–40, 172; energy resources in,
    37–39, 41–43, 55, 56, 58–60; fishing
    bans, 64; and future of PLAN, 189;
    map, 33; patrolling of, 88, 144–45;
    SLOCs, 63, 149; territorial disputes
    in, 30, 34–51, 152–54; territorial
    significance to China, 25, 28, 166,
    170–71, 172, 177
South China Sea Informal Working Group, 45
Southeast Asia, revolutionary movements in, 22
Southeast Asia Treaty Organization (SEATO), 21
South Korea, 65, 150. *See also* Korea
South Korean Ministry of Maritime and Fishery, 65
South Sea Fleet, 21, 25, 78, 80, 83–85, 88–90, 104, 129
sovereignty. *See* territorial interests, Chinese maritime
Soviet Union, 7, 8; deterioration of
    relations with China, 22–23, 163; and
    development of Chinese Navy, 17–18,
    28, 181–82; and equipment, 92–95, 97,
    98, 102, 108, 146–48; influence on
    PLAN strategy, 161–62, 164, 167,
    168–69; and military education
    system, 119; and nuclear power,
    20–21, 62; threat to China, 24, 25,
    170; training model, 124
Sovremenny-class guided-missile

destroyers, 27, 69–70, 80, 93, 98–99, 143
space-surveillance ships, 27, 34, 104
Spratly (Nansha) Islands: Chinese claim under 1992 law, 34; description, 36–37; energy sources near, 59–60; and future maritime conflicts, 189; history of territorial claims, 28, 39–45, 47; Qian Qichen on, 49–50; and South Sea Fleet, 84
State Environmental Protection Administration, 86
State Fishery Administration, 87
State Marine Administration, 86–87
State Maritime Affairs Administration, 87
Stirling engines, 97
strategy, 9–10, 159–78. *See also* operations, doctrinal
submarines, 79–80; acquisition and construction, 27, 83, 93, 95, 146; modern fleet, 96–98, 185; operational missions, 139; in potential China/Taiwan conflict, 156; South Sea Fleet, 25. *See also individual classes of submarines*
Sunda Strait, 8, 64
Sun Zi, 140
Super Frelons helicopters, 107
super rapid blooming offboard chaff (SRBOC), 100
surface ships: acquisition and construction, 17–18, 25, 27, 69–70, 83, 93–104, 183–87; deficiencies, 23, 109–12; geographic distribution, 79–80, 90; operational missions, 138. *See also individual classes of ships*
surface-to-surface missile systems, 99–100, 101, 106
survey and research ships, 27, 104, 107
Su-27 fighters, 27
Swallow Reef, 44
systems integration, 111–12

Taiping Dao, 36
Taiwan: and aircraft carriers, 146–47; Chinese actions against, 4, 18–19, 21, 28, 163; Chinese claim under 1992 law, 34; distance from mainland China, *18;* and East Sea Fleet, 88, 90; influence on PLAN training exercises,

129–30; modernization of Navy, 150–51; Navy, 103, 174; and occupation of Spratly Islands, 36, 39, 40; potential PLAN action against, 154–58, 177, 189; strategic importance of, 11, 166, 170
Taiwan Strait, 8, 142
Technical Working Groups (TWG), 48
technology: in military education, 121, 122; and operational doctrine, 140–46; and People's War, 22–23, 163–64; and personnel needs, 115; reliance on foreign, 66–68, 92, 111; in training, 125–28, 130, 132–33, 136–37, 142
territorial interests, Chinese maritime, 9, 28, 30–54, 173, 189
Territorial Sea and Contiguous Zone Law (1993), 40
territorial seas, 31–34, 39–45
Thailand, 37, 152, 154
theater missile defense (TMD), 11–12
Tiananmen Square incident, 180
trade. *See* shipping
training, 123–33, 136–37, 142, 145. *See also* education of personnel
Training Department, 75–76
Treaty of Shimonoseki, 52
troop transports, 104, 144
Truman, Harry, 19
Tsugaru Strait, 8
Tsushima (Korea) Strait, 8
Type-093 and -094 submarines, 98, 185

Unified College Entrance Examination, 117
United Nations, 44, 64
United Nations Convention on the Law of the Sea (UNCLOS), 31–34, 41, 47–49
United States: Chinese reliance on, 25, 180; cooperation with Philippines, 43–44, 153; and equipment, 27, 93; "hands off" policy in South China Sea, 51; influence on Chinese revolution, 7; and Japan, 39, 149–50; on offshore energy resources, 59; participation in sea and air rescue exercises, 130; presence in Asian waters, 188; and SLOC protection, 181; technical superiority, 140,

United States (*continued*)
143–44; threat to China, 8, 11–12, 19, 147, 154, 157, 174, 175–76; training model, 124
universities, 117

Varyag (aircraft carrier), 108
vice admirals (PLAN), 74–75, 122
Vietnam, 5, 22, 26, 36, 37, 39–42, 130, 153
Visiting Forces Agreement (VFA), 43–44, 153

Wan Bei-21 field, 42
Wanhsien, battle in, 7
warlords, 6–7
warships. *See* submarines; surface ships
Weihai Naval Base, 82
Wei Liucheng, 58, 59
Wolei (minelayer), 80
women, 113–14, 119
Woody Island, 40, 45–46, 84
World Trade Organization, 56, 61–62
Wuhan Naval Base, 83
Wuhan University, 117
Wuhu-class surveillance ships, 104

Xia-class submarines, 27, 79, 93, 98, 104, 165
Xianyang Hong-class surveillance ship, 107
Xiao Jingguang, 17, 162
Xisha. *See* Paracel (Xisha) Islands
Xu Xiangqian, 188

Yakhont missiles, 99

Yang Sen, 7
Yellow Sea, 7–8, 58, 63, 64–65, 149, 166
Ying Ji surface-to-surface missiles, 100, 101, 102, 106
Yongxing Tai. *See* Woody Island
The Young School, 161–62
Yuan (Mongol) Dynasty (1280–1368), 3
Yudao-class landing-ships-mechanized, 84
Yudeng-class landing-ships-mechanized, 103
Yu Guoquan, 183
Yuhai-class landing-ships-mechanized, 103
Yukan-class landing-ships-tank, 80, 84, 103
Yuliang-class landing-ships-mechanized, 103
Yulin Naval Base, 84
Yuting-class landing-ships-tank, 80, 84, 103

Z-8 helicopters, 107
Zhang Aiping, 17
Zhang Chunqiao, 23
Zhang Lianzhong, 167–68
Zhang Wannian, 12, 121, 134
Zhang Xusan, 46
Zhanjiang Naval Base, 83, 84
Zheng He, 3
Zheng He (officer-training ship), 27
Zhi-9A helicopters, 100
Zhou Enlai, 19
Zhu Bangzao, 35
Z-9A (Dauphin) helicopters, 100, 101, 102, 108

ABOUT THE AUTHOR

Bernard D. Cole is the associate dean of faculty and academic programs and professor of international history at the National War College in Washington, D.C., where he teaches courses in strategy and Sino-American relations. Prior to teaching, Dr. Cole served as a surface warfare officer in the U.S. Navy for thirty years, retiring as a captain in 1995. He spent all of his extensive sea duty in the Pacific, including service in Vietnam with the 3rd Marine Division and command of a frigate and a destroyer squadron.

Born and raised in New Jersey, Dr. Cole holds an undergraduate degree from the University of North Carolina at Chapel Hill, an M.P.A. in national security affairs from the University of Washington, and a Ph.D. in history from Auburn University. He is also the author of a prizewinning essay on Asia at sea, and *Gunboats and Marines: The U.S. Navy in China, 1925–1928,* which won the North American Society for Oceanic History's John Lyman Book Award. He lives in Burke, Virginia.